JACK

GEOFFREY PERRET

JACK

A Life Like No Other

RANDOM HOUSE / NEW YORK

Library of Congress Cataloging-in-Publication Data
Perret, Geoffrey.
Jack : a life like no other / Geoffrey Perret.
p.   cm.
Includes bibliographical references and index.
ISBN 0-375-50363-3 (acid-free paper)
1. Kennedy, John F. (John Fitzgerald), 1917–1963.   2. Presidents—United States—Biography.
3. United States—Politics and government—1961–1963.   I. Title.
E842.P47 2001   973.922′092—dc21   [B]   2001019392

Printed in the United States of America on acid-free paper
Random House website address: www.atrandom.com
2 4 6 8 9 7 5 3
First Edition

Book design by J. K. Lambert

This book is dedicated to

THOM BRESNAHAN

JOSEPH COPPOLA

CARLO AND SHIRLEY D'ESTE

Whenever I think of Boston now,
I think of them.

Acknowledgments

I have been fortunate while researching this work because of the wealth of new sources that became available only in the 1990s. This is especially true of thousands of official documents, the White House tapes made during John Kennedy's presidency, the diaries that Kennedy maintained during his foreign travels as a congressman, and the correspondence of Joseph P. Kennedy.

These documentary sources make it possible to corroborate or refute, comprehend or amplify, the many thousands of interviews that have been the principal source for the vast majority of books about JFK. They have enabled me to produce what is, in fact, the first one-volume cradle-to-grave biography of one of the most written about and most intensely discussed figures of the twentieth century. I have been phenomenally lucky.

I am indebted to the dedicated staff of the John F. Kennedy Library in Boston, notably to Megan Floyd Desnoyers, Ron Whealan, Jim Hill and June Parry. It was my good fortune, too, to have had the help of Dr. Sheldon Stern, for many years the historian at the library. Sheldon read the entire manuscript for factual accuracy, but whatever errors remain are entirely my responsibility.

My researches in Boston were also helped greatly by William Fowler and Peter Drummey at the Massachusetts Historical Society. What I owe them is impossible to describe here, but I cannot esteem them too highly.

I was fortunate as well in having the help of Dr. Howard Gotlieb at Boston University. A legendary figure in his field, Dr. Gotlieb is the creator of one of the great modern manuscript collections.

My friend in the Manuscript Division at the Library of Congress, Jeffrey M. Flannery, proved as tenacious, as knowledgeable and as helpful as ever.

The staffs at other archives where I have worked on this book—Columbia University, Princeton and Stanford—were unfailingly models of courtesy and professionalism. I am grateful to them all.

I am grateful, too, to Paul B. Fay, Jr., of San Francisco, for talking to me and allowing me to read his long and extensive oral history.

Other writers envy me my editor, Robert D. Loomis, as well they might.

Contents

JACK

Question Mark

I t is close to noon on May 29, 1917, and uncomfortably cold for the time of year as Dr. Frederick Good drives through Boston to attend Mrs. Joseph P. Kennedy. The streets still glisten from yesterday's thunderstorms and the thermometer shows 48 degrees. Those children born here today will be the first citizens of a new America, for this city, part Anglican and Brahmin, part Irish and Catholic, eternally proud of being the cradle of the American Revolution, is once again at war.

Every one of the big downtown stores has a window display promoting the Liberty Loan, and in Filene's main window stands a full-size replica of the Liberty Bell. A few blocks farther along Washington Street, Gordon's Olympia is showing *The British War.* Posters outside promise "Thrilling scenes of warfare. Men steeled for battle and death, leaping into action with daring abandon . . ."

On Boston Common, red, white and blue bunting shivers at the lampposts, and the Ninth Infantry Regiment has set up a tent for enrolling recruits. Not far from the tent stands the Shepherd store on Tremont Street, with a large sign out front that reads: YOUR OLD GLOVES — FOR THE WHITE GLOVE SOCIETY. EVERY PARTICLE OF THE GLOVE IS USED TO ADVANTAGE; THE LARGER PIECES ARE SEWN TOGETHER TO MAKE WIND-PROOF WAISTCOATS FOR *SOLDIERS* AND *SAILORS* . . .

These days, live performances in the theaters along Boylston Street feature a fifteen-minute harangue by pitchmen rousing theatergoers to do their patriotic duty and buy the first issue of the Liberty Loan. A good pitchman can make buying a $50 war bond seem the moral equivalent of going over the top at the front. "Hang the Kaiser . . . Down with the Hun . . . Hail Columbia!"[1]

Normal life still goes on, of course. At city hall a long-running investigation by the Finance Commission into corruption by Mayor James M. Curley and his political allies is wending its sinuous and ultimately futile way to irresolution. Curley's defense against the accusations of corruption in awarding city contracts is "We all have friends, and if we didn't take care of them we wouldn't be worthy of them," which goes straight to the tribal roots of Boston's politics. There has been speculation lately that a weakened Curley might face an election challenge from the former mayor, John F. "Honey Fitz" Fitzgerald. But today's *Boston Herald* states firmly that Honey Fitz has no such plans.[2]

The newspaper story is correct, for the truth is that what Honey Fitz has his eye on these days is running for the Senate in 1918, and on this day he is preparing to go to Washington for a meeting with President Woodrow Wilson. Fitzgerald will urge him to conscript able-bodied male alien residents who have lived in the United States at least five years; long enough, that is, to become American citizens. And if they are not conscripted, they at least should pay a special tax. One way or another, they must bear part of the burden of this war. He knows that Wilson probably won't accept his proposals, but Honey Fitz can count on winning a few headlines for them back in Boston even if they are rejected. A genuine opportunist? Yes, but also a genuine patriot.[3]

Meanwhile, his eldest daughter, Rose, is expecting her second child. A mile south of Boston Common—within sight, in fact, of anyone who mounts the steeple of Park Street Congregational Church, and looks beyond the Common—there stands a two-and-a-half-story gray clapboard house at 83 Beals Street, in Brookline. And on the second floor of that house, in the main bedroom, Rose Fitzgerald Kennedy is going into labor. The housemaid is boiling pans and kettles of water in the kitchen and carrying them upstairs.

The felicitously named Dr. Good arrives at the house to join his assistant, Dr. Edward O'Brien, and Good's nurse. O'Brien and the nurse have been at the house for most of the past twenty-four hours, and now Good will take charge in person.[4]

The baby's father, Joseph P. Kennedy, is not at Beals Street and won't return until after the child is born. Kennedy is the president of the Columbia Trust Company, a local bank. Rose wants him to stay away, and he prefers it, too. He is a domineering, controlling man. When a woman gives birth these days, there is nothing for the husband to do except sit around and fret.

For Joe Kennedy, brimming with nervous energy and unbridled ambition, his time is far better spent on business, on making that first million, than clinging to the fringes of an event he can do nothing to shape. True, he had been present at the birth of their first child, Joseph Jr., a little less than two years before, but he and his wife had been vacationing together then.

For Rose, a devout woman, this second birth couldn't have been timed more propitiously. May is the month of the Blessed Virgin. "Hail Mary, full of grace, the Lord is with thee, blessed art thou amongst women, and blessed is the fruit of thy womb . . ."

Her bed has been placed next to the south-facing window, to give the two doctors as much daylight as possible, and today the sky is cloudy but bright. The fashionable approach to childbirth among upper-middle-class women in 1917 is "Twilight Sleep," which involves injecting the mother-to-be with morphine and scopolamine. The traditional anesthetic is foul-smelling, foul-tasting, potentially deadly ether.[5]

Good doesn't believe in Twilight Sleep. O'Brien applies the ether. Rose's water breaks, but by two o'clock it is evident that the baby is turned the wrong way in the womb. Gripping the Good forceps, on which he holds the patent, Frederick Good reaches in and turns the baby around. A little after three P.M., it emerges. Once the cord has been cut, the nurse wraps it gently in an embroidered blanket and places it in the bassinet beside the bed. Rose is still unconscious, but she has prepared for this moment—she has tied a rosary to the bassinet. And there he lies, John Fitzgerald Kennedy, curled up like a small pink question mark in a sunny upstairs room that smells of blood, hot kettles and ether.

=

Joe Kennedy's father, Patrick J. Kennedy, was, as photographs of him in late middle age show, a large, square-built man with rimless spectacles, a huge walrus mustache and a mild gaze. He was prosperous and he looked it and all that he possessed was his own creation.

Born in Boston in 1858 to a pair of impoverished Irish immigrants, P.J.

had begun with nothing but the riches of a mother's love. His father had died before he could even walk or talk. His mother, Bridget, worked as a clerk, then as a hairdresser, and eventually became co-owner of a small notions shop. While she eked out a living for her family, her three daughters stayed at home and looked after P.J. At fourteen, he was deemed old enough to go to work and found employment as a packer at the docks.

Living thriftily and saving diligently, after a time he had enough money to open a saloon. He proved to have a flair for the business, because within a few years he had opened two more saloons and become a wholesale liquor dealer.[6]

Bars were as integral to the political scene of post–Civil War Boston as personation, and almost any man who voted right deserved a free beer, or maybe several free beers, come polling day. Alcohol and politics—each seemed almost an extension of the other. The saloon was the working-man's club, where politics were debated and ward bosses held court.

For P.J. it was but a short, lateral step from alehouse to statehouse. In 1885 he was elected to the state assembly, and three years later he and his wife had a son, Joseph Patrick Kennedy, born in September 1888 at the family's large and comfortable town house on Meridian Street in East Boston.

After six years as an Assemblyman, P.J. was elected to the state senate. Meanwhile, his liquor interests were paying off so handsomely that in 1895 he and a friend founded a bank, the Columbia Trust Company, with capital of $130,000, and as befitted a banker he bought a mansion, one that overlooked the inner harbor and provided handsome views across the water of Boston's financial district. It was here that Joe Kennedy grew up, in a rich man's house with a coterie of servants, and among the privileges he enjoyed was an insider's awareness of how the city's political and business life was run.

Naturally enough, P.J. brought up his son according to the light of his own experience. Life, he taught him, was struggle. "Always come first. Second place is failure."[7]

In those early years, Joe Kennedy's competitiveness was expressed as a ferocious work ethic. As an adolescent, he sold newspapers, candy and peanuts down at the docks. He lighted coal fires on Saturdays for Orthodox Jews and ran errands at Columbia Trust on his vacations.[8]

To broaden his horizons and improve his life prospects, his parents took him out of the Catholic school system and enrolled him, at age thirteen, at the Boston Latin School, one of the most prestigious public schools in the country. BLS had long been the secondary school that enjoyed the closest relationship with Harvard.

Academic standards at his new school were dauntingly high, and here was one competition that Joe Kennedy could never win. He was quick-witted rather than intellectual, often astute but never profound. His best subject was math, yet he was hopeless at geometry, which calls for imaginative powers he did not possess. Any subject that required a capacity for abstract thought seemed beyond him. He failed physics, French and Latin and had to repeat his junior year.

When he graduated from Boston Latin in 1908, Joe Kennedy stood five feet ten inches tall, a good-looking youngster with blue eyes, pale freckled skin and red hair. He didn't smoke, drink, tell blue jokes, gamble or drink coffee. His preferred beverage was milk, and he had but two goals in life: to be a college athlete and to make a lot of money.

He applied for Harvard not because he possessed either scholarly ability or inclination but because his parents insisted he go to college, and there was nowhere better. Although his Boston Latin grades—which averaged out at a C—might seem hopelessly inadequate for Harvard, he was accepted. Harvard is a great university for many reasons, one of which is that it has never accepted applicants solely on grades or test scores. Family connections count, as does a family's prestige, but most of all it looks for evidence of promise. An interesting applicant who appears likely to become a figure of national importance twenty or thirty years down the road stands an excellent chance of getting in, even with mediocre grades. And Joseph P. Kennedy *was* different. One of the few Catholics at overwhelmingly Anglican Boston Latin, he had nonetheless been elected president of his graduating class. He had also been the leading batter in the city's high school baseball league.

Although his father was rich, Joe Kennedy always had a job. While his grades counted against him, there was a lot to be said for Harvard's decision to accept him. He seemed to be a young man on his way to somewhere.[9]

At Harvard he struggled academically, as before, and had to major in Music Appreciation to be certain of graduating. For the rest of his life, Joe Kennedy retained a love of music, being particularly partial to Beethoven. But his was a purely sentimental appreciation of music, the easy rapture of the overwhelming and obvious. He was not a man for works such as

Beethoven's late string quartets, brooding meditations on the inexorability of age and decay.

While edging towards his degree, he prospered as few students ever did. With a friend, Joe Donovan, he bought a secondhand bus for $600. They spent their summer vacations running bus tours to Concord and Lexington from Boston's South Station. There was a tour operator already doing the same, and selling bus tickets at the city's main railroad terminal required a permit. P.J. ensured that Joe and his friend got one, in effect forcing the existing operator to share the business with them.

On summer days Donovan drove while Joe, wearing a nifty white cap with a black patent-leather visor, gave his busloads of tourists history through a megaphone—"We're driving up to the Bunker Hill monument, but it was built on the wrong hill . . ." It paid beyond his expectations. By the time he graduated from Harvard in 1912, Kennedy and Donovan had each cleared $5,000, at a time when the average family income was less than $2,000 a year.[10]

Joe's dreams of athletic glory had also been fulfilled, if only symbolically. Besides, it was the glory that mattered to him, not the search for self via fair competition. Joe Kennedy had discovered that while he had been a big hitter in high school baseball, at Harvard he was too mediocre to make the team. Yet he still intended to win his Harvard letter, and only those chosen to play in the Big Game—against Yale—could be lettermen. It seemed hopeless.

Joe began looking for a shortcut and found one. The team captain, Charles B. McLaughlin, turned out to be interested in operating a movie theater after graduation. For that he would need a city license. If P.J. wanted to block it, no doubt he had enough clout at city hall to do it. On the other hand, if he wanted to help young McLaughlin out . . .

Joe Kennedy materialized on the Harvard bench at the start of the Big Game in his senior year and sat there patiently through eight and a half innings as Harvard clawed its way to a 4–1 lead on the strength of McLaughlin's pitching arm. At the top of the ninth, McLaughlin disposed of the first two Yale batters, called a time-out, and Joe Kennedy trotted from the bench to take over at first base. Another Yalie stood at home plate, swung at a pitch from McLaughlin and hit a ground ball towards first. Kennedy scooped it up, tagged the runner out and walked away, shoving the ball in his pocket. McLaughlin trotted up to him and said he'd like the winning ball, please. Joe shook his head. "I made the putout, didn't I?"[11]

Then as now, roughly half of Harvard undergraduates had attended public schools, and the rest were preppies. It was the preppies who established the ethos of undergraduate life, and only they were eligible for membership of the final clubs such as Porcellian, AD and Spee. The clubs stood at the summit of social life at Harvard and bestowed a cachet that members carried for the rest of their lives. Yet even a prep school background and a Social Register family provided no guarantee of a final club invitation.

Here, then, was another competition, one for acceptance and social éclat, but it was a competition that Joe Kennedy knew he could never win, and that rankled. Although he could now and forever call himself a "Harvard man," there were in truth two kinds at Harvard College—those who were at it, and those who were of it.[12]

≡

John Francis Fitzgerald was a short man, with a stocky build and a ready smile. Born in 1863, he stood about five feet three inches tall and was never shy about his ambitions. Nicknamed "the Little Napoleon," he had the sweetest of sweet teeth, and this love of the sugary over the savory gave rise to a much happier nickname—"Honey Fitz."[13]

Although his beginnings were humble, they were not as straitened as those of P. J. Kennedy. Bright and ambitious, he had won a scholarship to Boston Latin School and graduated from Boston College, doing well enough there to be accepted at Harvard Medical School. Blood and pills, however, did not interest him much, and he quit.[14]

Honey Fitz began his working life as a clerk in the Customs House and spent his free time as a ward heeler. Boston at this time was divided into more than a dozen wards, each the fiefdom of some ward boss. The wards amounted to urban principalities, and politics within and among them consisted of tribal squabbles over the spoils of office.

The ward boss that Honey Fitz toiled for in Boston's North End was Matthew Keany, a man at odds with most of his fellow bosses. No matter. In September 1889 Honey Fitz married a farmer's daughter, Mary Hannon, and moved into a rented apartment in a part of the North End so densely crowded and unsanitary it was known as "Calcutta." That was where Rose was born, in July 1890. Growing up in one of Boston's worst slums was something that Rose, in later life, was at pains to disguise.[15]

The North End, once solidly Irish, was becoming increasingly Italian, but Honey Fitz was just the man to turn this neighborhood into his political base. For one thing, he could talk a blue streak across an exhaustive range of subjects, whether he knew anything about them or not, and do it with a twinkle in his eye. That would deliver the Irish, who loved a good talker, especially one of their own. In appealing to the Italians, he had the inestimable gift of musical ability. Honey Fitz boasted a decent tenor voice and played the piano well. He charmed the Italians by singing to them and made them feel important. They were prepared to do something for him they had never done for anyone—go to the polls and vote.

Honey Fitz also was venturing into territory Irish ward bosses shunned —he sought the support of blacks and Jews. And he continued to live in Calcutta. Honey Fitz's courage paid off. In 1893 he was elected to the state senate, where he got to know P. J. Kennedy, who chaired the Board of Strategy, the four-man oligarchy that selected all Democratic party candidates for local, state and national office.

Honey Fitz and P.J. didn't get along, partly because Keany was a thorn in the board's side, but mostly because P.J. could not stand Honey Fitz— "He's insufferable!" P.J. told his pals. As if to prove it, Honey Fitz dared to challenge the incumbent Congressman for Boston, Joseph O'Neil, a man with the Board of Strategy's imprimatur.[16]

In June 1894 he wrested the Democratic nomination from O'Neil in the party primary and won the congressional seat handily in November. Honey Fitz then moved himself, but not his family, to a boardinghouse in Washington. In March 1897, having just been reelected, he took his wife and two eldest daughters—Rose, who was nearly seven, and Agnes, age five—to Washington for the inauguration of President William McKinley. A few days later, he took the girls to meet the new President. The kindly, avuncular McKinley was charmed by them and gave Rose a carnation from his desk. Then, handing a carnation to Agnes, he said, "This is for the prettiest little girl I have ever seen in the White House."[17]

Honey Fitz loved being a Congressman, but after three terms, it came to an end. P. J. Kennedy and the Board of Strategy were preparing to do to him what he had done to O'Neil, and Honey Fitz was vulnerable. He had moved out to leafy and prosperous Concord following his reelection in 1896, in clear defiance of state law, which required a Congressman to live in his district. He wisely chose not to seek a fourth term on Capitol Hill.[18]

Honey Fitz moved back to the North End in 1903, to run for mayor. To generate some favorable publicity for his candidacy, he bought up a small and struggling newspaper, *The Republic,* for $500, and stumbled into a gold mine. It occurred to Honey Fitz one day that newspapers were oriented almost entirely towards men. But what about women? Why was there so little in a newspaper for them? He began running gossipy stories about what the social elite, both Brahmin and Irish, were doing, buying, saying.

The Republic's circulation soared, and as circulation rose, the paper filled up with large, expensive advertisements placed by the owners of that late-nineteenth-century revolution in retail, the department store. Honey Fitz became rich, earning $25,000 a year, the equivalent of $500,000 a century later, and there were no federal income taxes at the time.[19]

What people noticed about him, though, wasn't the money; it was the charm. "As I came up old Hanover Street this morning, up the dear old North End," he might tell his wife and daughters after a day of campaigning for mayor, "every man and child had a smile for me. It seemed as if the very paving stones rose up and greeted me." He referred to the dear old North End so often that a local journalist starting calling its residents "the Dearos." To Rose, her adored father was thus monarch of all he surveyed—"King of the Dearos."[20]

Honey Fitz had a simple campaign slogan and pushed a populist theme: "Down with the bosses! The people, not the politicians, must rule!" The bosses he had in mind were the ward bosses and the Board of Strategy that controlled the regular party organization. In January 1906 he was sworn in as mayor.

Honey Fitz enjoyed a delightful two years, but this was an unhappy time for Rose. She showed an early love of reading and finished high school at sixteen. Better still, she was accepted to Wellesley. The recently installed cardinal of Boston, William H. O'Connell, was appalled that the daughter of the mayor, one of the most prominent Catholics in the state, would be enrolled at a secular and socially progressive college that was a bastion of the Anglican upper class. O'Connell advised Honey Fitz that this was not a wise thing to do, and Honey Fitz accordingly informed Rose that she was too young for college. She would attend, instead, the Convent of the Sacred Heart in downtown Boston. Missing out on Wellesley disappointed Rose profoundly, then and forever.[21]

Honey Fitz ran for reelection in the fall of 1907 and was defeated. His administration had been no more corrupt than most of its predecessors or many of its successors. Nevertheless, corruption was making one of its fitful appearances as an issue that could swing a campaign, and Honey Fitz lost to a reformer. Unabashed for the rest of his life he assured people, "I was the last honest mayor of Boston," and doubtless believed it.[22]

In the summer of 1908, nursing his disappointment, he sailed for Europe with his family for an extended visit. By this time, he had four daughters and two sons. The two oldest girls, Rose and Agnes, were installed in a gray, cold and depressing convent on the German-Dutch border. There the two girls would improve their French, German and piety. While they coughed and sneezed through a grim, quasi-military regimen, their father was learning about life on the grand boulevards of European capitals.

He turned out to be a natural *flâneur*. Boston, caught between its Puritan past and its Irish present, rarely produced the real article, but Honey Fitz had what it took—the overflowing geniality, the dandyish cut of his clothes, the fresh rose in his lapel, the constant tipping of his black derby to respectable women, the ready smile that lit up his rubicund features.

After nearly a year away, the Fitzgeralds returned to Boston to launch Honey Fitz's second mayoral campaign. He sang and glad-handed his way remorselessly back into office. His first language was blarney, and he warbled his favorite song, "Sweet Adeline," more than thirty times a day, to gatherings of whatever size or composition. Yet when reelected in November 1909, he found himself mayor of a city that suddenly seemed too dull to hold a true cosmopolitan.

Honey Fitz resourcefully discovered good reasons for travel in each day's newspapers. The Panama Canal was about to be opened. What implications would it have for the port of Boston? Best go take an all-expenses-paid visit. There was a report that Hamburg was booming, handling more ships than ever. Best go find out why. Newspapers said Brussels was profiting from Belgium's new system of inland waterways. Were there lessons there for Boston? The mayor felt a trip coming on. Rose, his translator and aide, went along with him on most of his foreign travels, which gave her an awareness of the wider world rare for a young woman of her time.

Even so, her many days at sea did not prevent her from making a debut into society in January 1911, a ritual that amounted to advertising a young woman as being of marriageable age and, quite possibly, of marriageable mind. Rose soon found herself with two suitors—Hugh Nawn, a Brahmin sprig of whom her father approved, and Joseph P. Kennedy, of whom he didn't.

Rose had first met Joe at the age of eight or nine, during a summer vacation at Old Orchard Beach in Maine. As things began getting serious, however, Honey Fitz tried to discourage Rose from allowing Joe Kennedy to court her.

Hugh Nawn, a Harvard man, was the son of Honey Fitz's good friend Harry Nawn, a millionaire. Honey Fitz tried to pressure Rose into forgetting Joe and marrying Hugh. He even told the press that Rose and Hugh were about to announce their engagement, but Rose balked. Rose had a picture of Joe that she took everywhere she went, and she held on to it.[23]

Honey Fitz did not think she would ever be happy with go-getting, self-absorbed Joe. But he relented slightly when Joe graduated from Harvard, and he more or less caved in following Joe's success in 1913—only a year after graduating from college—in blocking an attempted takeover of Columbia Trust by a big, well-established Boston bank. Joe had been working since graduation as a state bank examiner, a job arranged for him by P.J. This gave young Joe an insight into Boston's financial community that was a valuable education in itself, one that he demonstrated by saving Columbia Trust from a powerful predator.

The result was that Joe, at the age of twenty-five, was made president of the bank, to be hailed then and ever after as the youngest bank president in the United States, although there were tens of thousands of banks at that time—most of them small and shaky, like Columbia Trust—and there was probably at least one other boy president somewhere. What mattered was that Joe's sudden eminence overcame Honey Fitz's objections. Joe and Rose announced their engagement—in *The Republic*—in June 1914.[24]

By then, Joe was straightening out the Collateral Loan Company—a glorified pawnshop—run by Honey Fitz and some of his pals. Its accounts were chaotic and its reputation for probity low even by pawnbroking standards. State officials and city police were already committed to an investigation, and Joe shrewdly did all he could to help them root out evidence of fraud.[25]

That was not the end of Honey Fitz's troubles, though. In 1914 an upstart Democrat named James M. Curley was challenging him for reelection as mayor. The mayor might have weathered the challenge had it not been for a cigarette girl named Elizabeth Ryan, better known as "Toodles." Like many another cigarette girl, Toodles attracted the attention of numerous men and some of them, like Honey Fitz, could not keep their hands to themselves. Just how close they became is pure guesswork. Toodles admitted only to being groped, and Honey Fitz admitted to nothing.[26]

Curley announced a series of public lectures with the title "Great Courtesans in History—From Cleopatra to Toodles." It hardly helped matters that Honey Fitz was currently leading a "morals campaign" to stamp out vice in Boston. Curley called off the lecture series after Honey Fitz announced he would not be running for reelection after all.

Rose and Joe were married on October 7, 1914, by Cardinal O'Connell in the private chapel at his residence. With Honey Fitz currently in disgrace, he was not about to attend a grand public ceremony and give away his daughter knowing there was a good chance of an embarrassing or untoward incident being sprung on him by some rabid Curleyite. A private wedding, but one conducted by the cardinal himself, seemed the wisest course.

Joseph P. Kennedy, Jr., was born in Hull, Massachusetts, on July 28, 1915, almost exactly nine months after his parents' wedding. "Well," pronounced a delighted Honey Fitz, now freed from the cares of office, "of course he is going to be President of these United States!"[27]

After the birth of their son, Joe and Rose began looking for a suitable house. They settled for 83 Beals Street, an unprepossessing dwelling built to a standard plan in solidly middle-class Brookline, home to Boston University and just across the Charles River from Cambridge.

On the top floor were two tiny rooms for live-in servants. On the second floor were two bedrooms and the only bathroom in the house, plus a small room Rose used for her sewing. The dining room, kitchen and parlor took up the ground floor. Much of the parlor was given over to a grand piano where Honey Fitz liked to play and sing when he came visiting. The furniture throughout was dark and ugly, solid and expensive, in the approved bourgeois taste of the time. Rose wasn't capable of imagining anything better or different. Instead, she sought to relieve the gloomy atmosphere with prints of well-known paintings that she had seen and liked when traveling in Europe, works by Rembrandt, J.W.M. Turner and Frans Hals.[28]

This, then, was the house where Joe and Rose's second child, named John Fitzgerald Kennedy—in honor of Honey Fitz—was born. As he grew into manhood and his father became stupendously, famously rich, JFK would come to love this cramped, gloomy house. To him, its very ordinariness, its crushing dullness, was the appeal. In time, his birthplace became to him as iconically humble in its way as the crudest log cabin on an imagined frontier.

CHAPTER 2

Childish Things

I n November 1916 Joseph P. Kennedy cast the most heartfelt ballot of his life to date. Like most of his countrymen, he had opposed American involvement in the Great War from the moment the guns of August began to roar in 1914. Wars made no sense to him, least of all this one.

Unlike many of his Harvard classmates, he remained unmoved by accounts of Allied heroics on the battlefields of France. Nor did he put any faith in the exalted war aims that the Allies proclaimed to justify the slaughter in the trenches. One night in 1916, he and Rose stepped into the small nursery at 83 Beals Street and gazed on Joe Jr. sleeping in his crib. "This is the only happiness that lasts," he said.[1]

When Woodrow Wilson ran for reelection that fall of 1916, his campaign slogan was both boast and promise—"He kept us out of war!" By voting for Wilson, Joe Kennedy was voting for more of the same noninvolvement.

In January 1917, however, the Germans opened a campaign of unrestricted submarine warfare; that is, they would sink any ship, of whatever nationality, that their U-boats encountered. Admiral Henning von Holtzendorf assured an apprehensive Kaiser, "England will lie flat on the ground before a single American soldier sets foot on the Continent."[2]

On April 2 Wilson finally asked Congress for a declaration of war, returned to the White House and burst into tears. Two months later, shortly after John F. Kennedy was born, Joe Kennedy, along with other males aged twenty-one to thirty, registered for the draft.

The only previous American attempt at conscription had been during the Civil War, and the main purpose then had been to pressure men into volunteering. Comparatively few men had actually been drafted. This time, the Army was going to need millions of men, and most would be conscripts.

The War Department wrote the legislation and, to make it generally acceptable, called for local boards to implement the law. It also tried to make conscription more palatable by writing the legislation so that most married men—especially those with dependent children—stood virtually no chance of being called up. Joe Kennedy's Harvard classmates, meanwhile, were volunteering in droves. Roughly 60 percent of the class of 1912 wound up in uniform. He, along with the remaining 40 percent, did not.

Woodrow Wilson had done almost nothing to create an American defense industry in the two and a half years before he declared war on Germany. American troops fighting in France had to be armed by the British and French with everything from revolvers to tanks. There was also the challenge of defeating the U-boats before they could starve Britain out of the war. The answer was convoys, but convoys needed destroyers to protect them, and there was a desperate shortage of destroyers, as there was of everything else.

One of the principal shipyards turning out "tin cans" was owned and operated by Bethlehem Steel on the Fore River, south of Boston. In September 1917 Joe Kennedy was offered the post of assistant general manager of the Fore River Shipyard. He knew nothing about ship construction, but that did not matter. Economic mobilization relied on getting men who understood management, finance and organization into defense industries, and the same thing happened all over again in World War II. Kennedy took the job, at a generous salary of $15,000 a year.

The shipyard workforce ballooned from six thousand workers to nearly twenty-two thousand, with no increase in the size of the canteen. Showing, as always, a keen eye for an opportunity, Kennedy built his own cafeteria, the "Victory Lunchroom," and may have made more from coffee and rolls than he did from his salary.[3]

In February 1918, to Kennedy's astonishment, he was informed by his draft board that he had been placed in Class 1, making him eligible to be called for the physical examination and IQ test at any time. Selective Service would later turn the system around and, more sensibly, issue classifications only after the exam and the IQ test. For now he was in no immediate danger of being drafted, and as a husband and father of two dependent children, he almost certainly would not be, even without an occupational deferment. Kennedy nevertheless lodged an appeal.

Men employed in shipyards, like those employed in airplane factories or munitions plants, were automatically exempted. The district board upheld the local board anyway, not realizing that the exemption applying to riveters and steamfitters, welders and platers, also covered managers and executives in war industries. This error was typical. The widespread practice of boards ignoring or misinterpreting the guidelines on occupational deferments persisted from war to war until, in 1967, such decisions were taken away from them. For now, a Bethlehem executive informed the Emergency Fleet Corporation that putting Joseph P. Kennedy into Class 1 was "inexcusable from any point of view," and the classification was duly revoked by Selective Service in Washington. Then and later he was excoriated as a draft dodger, something that, whatever his other faults, he was not.[4]

By the time war production ground to a halt in the spring of 1919, Fore River had become the most productive shipyard in the United States, Kennedy had a duodenal ulcer and Rose had hardly seen her husband for more than a year. He left the shipyard, returned to his family and went back to his bank.[5]

≡

In September 1918 Rose gave birth to a daughter, Rosemary, who proved to be such a slow learner that she seemed mentally handicapped. For Joe Jr. and baby Jack this hardly mattered. Their mother took all three of them along whenever she went shopping, pulling Rosemary in a kiddy car and holding Jack by the hand, while Joe Jr. walked unaided, blessed with all the assurance and attention of the firstborn. Rose also went to Mass each morning, taking the children with her, hoping this would make them pious.[6]

Apart from the strong religious element that she brought ineluctably to the task, Rose's ideas of child rearing came out of *The Care and Feeding of Children,* by L. Emmett Holt. The child-rearing bible of the next generation, Dr. Benjamin Spock's *Baby and Child Care,* was a reaction mostly against the strictures of Dr. Holt, who disapproved of open displays of love and affection.

What Holt prescribed was both authoritative and easy to grasp. He was, after all, one of the world's greatest researchers in pediatric medicine. Even so, he warned mothers against kissing their babies—"Tuberculosis, diphtheria, syphilis and many other grave diseases may be communicated in this way. . . . Infants should be kissed, if at all, upon the cheek or forehead, but the less even of this the better." On the other hand, they were to be smacked if they misbehaved.[7]

Jack Kennedy grew up recognizing from an early age the crucial role that his mother played even within a household dominated by his imperious father. "She was the glue that held our family together," he told people in later life. Yet there was a legacy, too, of lasting disappointment. He had never enjoyed the enveloping warmth and unconditional acceptance that is a mother's love. Thanks mainly to Holtism—and in sharp contrast to much Catholic tradition—the woman who should have lavished that love on him seemed to be holding back, a wound not just in childhood but for decades beyond. "My mother never hugged me!" he told a friend. "Never . . . never!"[8]

Shortly after Joe left the Fore River shipyard, Rose found she was pregnant again. The child was due in February 1920. At first overjoyed, she made a devastating discovery only weeks before the birth: Joe was having an affair with an English actress named Betty Compson. Heavily pregnant, Rose moved out of the house on Beals Street and back in with her parents, leaving Joe Jr., Jack and Rosemary in the care of a nursemaid.[9]

Honey Fitz didn't want her back. These were trying times for him. He had been reelected to Congress in November 1918 only to be ousted on charges of corruption a year later.[10] More than that, though, he lived by the code of the Victorian paterfamilias: a man's responsibility was to provide as well as he could for his family, and a wife should repay him by being loyal and, if necessary, forgiving.

One frosty night shortly after Rose went back to her parents, he came into her room, the stern father. "You've made your commitment, Rosie, and you must honor it now. . . . Your children need you and your husband needs you. . . . You can make things work out. I know you can. . . . So go now, Rosie, back where you belong."[11]

Forced to leave her parents' home, Rose was too hurt and resentful to head straight back to Beals Street. She took refuge in a religious retreat run by Cardinal O'Connell, but the priests and nuns agreed with Honey Fitz—her place was on Beals Street.[12]

This time she obeyed, only to find herself plunged into another crisis: Jack had scarlet fever, his temperature was rising remorselessly and he could not stop vomiting. Rose couldn't do much for her child—she was about to give birth to a fourth child, Kathleen. Dr. Good shuttled between her bedroom and Jack's sickroom.

Jack, not yet three, seemed about to die. Joe used his political connections to get him admitted to the overcrowded Boston City Hospital, which was already swamped by a scarlet fever epidemic that had closed the schools. Jack's skin peeled off, and as he hovered between life and death, Joe Kennedy prayed with a rare intensity, promising to give half his fortune to the Church if the child survived. After a month in the hospital, Jack began to rally. He would live after all.[13]

Rose took a close interest in her children's health thereafter, developing a file-card system that provided a reliable medical history for all of them. She also lined them up once a week and made them swallow, suitably grimacing, a dessertspoon of cod-liver oil and malt extract, as prescribed by Dr. Holt.

Even before he went to school, young Jack traveled all over eastern Massachusetts in his father's Rolls-Royce, so that Rose—who was something of a frustrated schoolteacher—could educate him, Joe Jr. and his sisters. "The Puritans landed here, at Plymouth Rock, in 1620. . . . This place, children, is where the tea was dumped in Boston Harbor. . . . They called this ship 'Old Ironsides' because . . . And Paul Revere said, 'One if by land, two if by sea. . . .'" Boston is almost a history classroom, and Rose inculcated a love of history that Jack responded to more than the others.[14]

She also knelt with the children when they prayed, listened to them repeat their catechism, told them about the Christian martyrs and sought in the religion she spoke about so often a solace against the disappointments of the epiphenomenal world. "There is a Divine Plan," she told herself. Even unhappiness and loneliness and a disloyal husband made sense—it had to—if you only believed strongly enough.[15]

On Sunday afternoons when the weather was good, Joe and Rose and the children—all of them, boys and girls alike, dressed in their mother's favorite color, pink—climbed aboard the Rolls-Royce. They headed for a farm near Acton owned by Rose's cousins the Hannons. Honey Fitz, with his wife and children, was usually there, too. The adults gathered indoors, and the strains of Honey Fitz playing the piano and singing, in his wavering tenor voice—"Annie Laurie," perhaps, or "Shine On Harvest Moon"—wafted through the open windows as Jack and the other children played in the yard.[16]

Having managed to bungle economic mobilization for war, the Wilson administration demonstrated how much it had learned from this experience by bungling economic demobilization for peace. Within months of the Armistice, the economy was spiraling down, and the recession promised to be both long and deep.[17]

It didn't make much sense, then, for Joseph P. Kennedy to return to running Columbia Trust Company. The postwar economic crisis was likely to push thousands of small banks like his into the embrace of bigger banks or into insolvency. He left in the spring of 1919, after talking himself into a job with Hayden, Stone and Company, one of the country's most successful stockbroking firms, with offices in Boston and New York.[18]

Although not yet a millionaire, Joe Kennedy was getting there fast. He was earning considerably less than he had during the war, yet he now had the chance to develop contacts in the financial community that he had never enjoyed before.

A year after leaving the Fore River Shipyard, he bought a large house, on two acres of land, in one of the most fashionable parts of Brookline. The family began spending their summer vacations on Cape Cod, and Joe Kennedy applied to join the exclusive—and distinctly WASPish—Cohasset country club in 1922. He was blackballed. "When will the nice people of Boston accept Catholics?" Rose wondered despairingly.[19]

By 1925 Joe Kennedy was a millionaire and well on his way to becoming a multimillionaire. The economy had recovered and the stock market was beginning to boom. For someone like him, with inside information, getting rich was easy. Finding a new challenge, one that would engage his entire interest, was what he needed now.

He found it partly in the liquor business; his father, after all, had prospered as a liquor dealer, so there was a certain inherent logic to his choice, except for one thing—this was the era of Prohibition, of speakeasies, Al Capone, near beer and bathtub gin. His detractors claim that Joe Kennedy became a bootlegger in partnership with major crime figures, but there is no evidence for this beyond the uncorroborated and untested assertions of known perjurers and murderers such as Frankie Costello.[20]

There was no need for him to do that, anyway. Restaurants, bars, liquor dealers, distilleries, breweries and vineyards had huge stocks of pre-Prohibition wine, beer and liquor on hand when the law went into effect in 1920. Those stocks were not destroyed. Joe Kennedy bought up entire warehouses filled with pre-Prohibition alcohol.[21]

Stocks like his were consumed in the early 1920s, but at considerably more than pre-Prohibition prices. Large profits could be made by anyone who obtained withdrawal permits—granted by the Prohibition Bureau for "medicinal" or "religious" purposes—for liquor already accumulated. Joe Kennedy knew a lot of doctors and a lot of priests, and the Prohibition Bureau was both incompetent and corrupt.

Huge quantities of wine and brandy were also being produced for medicinal and religious purposes. No major distillery, brewery or wine producer went out of business during Prohibition. Production continued much as before. Whiskey was also being imported legally in large quantities, to be kept in storage for the time Prohibition was repealed, something that seemed inevitable from the mid-twenties on. Joe Kennedy used his father's contacts in the liquor trade and his own contacts with government officials to secure permits for importing Scotch legally and holding on to it as a speculative investment.[22]

Meanwhile, his keen interest in showgirls was giving rise to an interest in show business. In 1926 he bought Film Booking Office, a movie distributor with offices in London, Los Angeles and New York. Boston now became the wrong place to live. The next year he moved the family to a large rented house in Riverdale-on-Hudson, with a view of the river.

He had also been renting a summer cottage—in truth, a rambling fifteen-room house—at Hyannis on Cape Cod. He and the family liked it so much that he bought the place within a few months of leasing the Riverdale property. During these years, however, Joe Kennedy spent comparatively little time at either of his two homes. He was in Hollywood much of the time, where he improved the production and distribution of movies and attempted to save the career and finances of Gloria Swanson, sex goddess of the silent screen.

Joe Kennedy not only bedded Swanson but wanted to marry her, something she rejected. Even so, when she and her then husband had a son, Swanson named the child Joseph.[23]

While he was in Hollywood, Joe Kennedy helped create RKO (Radio-Keith-Orpheum) and made millions from movie production and distribution, acquiring a wide range of glamorous friends and acquaintances. But talkies were about to change the business forever, so he got out. He returned to the East Coast in 1929 and bought a twenty-room Georgian mansion with extensive grounds in Bronxville, a suburb of New York City. This was a statement house in a way that the large but banal residence in Riverdale was not.

He astutely pulled out of the stock market shortly before the October 1929 crash. So did dozens of other Wall Street operators. The crash had been foreseen by—among others—Alexander Dana Noyes, financial editor of *The New York Times*. The history of financial bubbles has a clearly defined pattern: one key element is that just before a collapse, the inside operators cash in their equities and move their money into bonds, leaving the ever-expanding army of optimists to take the hit.[24]

As America entered the 1930s getting remorselessly poorer, Joe Kennedy, now rolling in tax-free bonds and building up huge stocks of Scotch whiskey in anticipation of the end of Prohibition, was getting remorselessly richer.

=

At five, Jack Kennedy began his formal education at the Edward Devotion School, a public school a few blocks from the large Brookline house. Two years later, he and Joe Jr. were enrolled at the Dexter School, which consisted of the lower forms of Noble and Greenough, one of Boston's elite private schools, a Brahmin bastion where Catholics were rare and Jews or blacks unknown.[25]

Boys pick on anyone who is different, and being a Catholic was more than enough. So, too, was the fact that many of the parents whose children attended Noble and Greenough simply despised the Kennedys and the Fitzgeralds as boorish arrivistes trying to buy their way into society. Inevitably, some of that attitude rubbed off on their children, so Jack Kennedy was taunted and provoked and forced into fights. On the other hand, he was a wizard with marbles, a skill that was bound to create a degree, however reluctant, of playground respect.[26]

And then there was the Joe problem. Joe Jr. was quick with his fists and eager to assert his little-man's rights as firstborn. "When Dad's not here, I'm the boss!" he'd crow, and thump Jack just to make sure he got the point. That rankled, but it has always been tough being the smaller, younger brother.[27]

The relationship with his mother was the one that seriously troubled little Jack. As Joe spent more and more time away from home, so did Rose. Jack resented her frequent absences, and told her so. "Gee, *you're* a great mother to go away and leave your children all alone," he said to her one day in 1923. She thought that was cute, choosing to ignore the hurt expressed.[28]

That summer, when the family returned home after spending their vacation on Cape Cod, Jack came to Joe in an agitated state and made a confession. "Well, here I have been home only a few hours and the cops are chasing me already." He had teased a little girl who had gone to tell a policeman what a naughty boy he was. Jack had run home and hidden in the cellar until nightfall. Not that it seemed to deter him too much. A month or so later he and Joe went shoplifting.[29]

Jack was wounded, too, by the obvious fact that his mother thought far more highly of Joe Jr. That was something he never would accept. Rose had blinded herself by deciding that it simply wasn't possible to have two intellectually gifted boys within the same family, and since she had already given the crown for brains to Joe Jr., that issue was settled despite good evidence to the contrary. One day when Jack was seven, for example, she overheard him earnestly arguing with the Canadian governess who worked for the family that the only logical political course for Canada was merger with the United States.[30]

Rose was a voracious reader all her life. Jack became an omnivorous reader, too. This was probably a manifestation of his innate curiosity, but it may have owed something as well to a desire to win his mother's attention, if not her affection, for part of the intense competitiveness within the family was for parental attention.

The one person Jack could always turn to for unquestioning love, freely displayed, was Honey Fitz. Whenever the old man's car pulled up outside, Jack shouted, "It's Grampa!" and rushed to the door to throw his arms around him.[31]

Grandfather and grandson were intensely, lastingly devoted to each other. While the other children soon tired of the old man's well-worn anecdotes, Jack listened to him reminisce and, still enthralled, begged for more. "Tell that one again, Grampa."[32]

Through Honey Fitz he came to know Clement Norton, a lawyer turned journalist. One day when he was about ten, Jack encountered Norton emerging from the Athenaeum, the famous private library near the statehouse in Boston. Norton was carrying an armload of books. "What are those?" Jack asked.

"I'm going to read these books," said Norton. "Then I'm going to put down the whole story in a few pages."

"I want a copy," said Jack. For years thereafter he received summaries of serious books from a highly paid Harvard-educated lawyer and writer.[33]

In 1927 the Kennedys moved to Riverdale, and Jack found his forty-cent-a-week allowance was no longer enough. He asked his father to increase it and was told to put his request in writing. "A Plea for a Raise, by Jack Kennedy. Dedicated to my father, Mr. J. P. Kennedy" proved a persuasive document. Forty cents had been enough, he acknowledged, "for aeroplanes and other playthings of childhood, but now I am a scout and put away my childish things." Being a scout brought responsibilities—"I have to buy canteens, haversacks [and] things that will last for years. . . ." The raise he sought—and won—was an extra thirty cents.[34]

One thing Joe would no longer allow either of his sons was a bicycle. When the boys were still small, he had bought a bicycle for each. In a competitive fury, they had raced each other around the block, setting off in opposite directions, and collided when they arrived back where they'd started.[35]

The local schools were excellent, and the boys were enrolled at Riverdale Country School, where Jack's love of reading—especially history—was encouraged. One book in particular fascinated him, *England's Story,* by Eva March Tappan. All the same, his grades at Riverdale were mediocre, averaging a C+.[36]

Miss Frazer, the children's governess, had taught the girls how to make wicker baskets. Jack got hooked on it, too, sitting on the huge porch of the Riverdale house for hours, wetting reeds, weaving them together, competing with his sisters.[37]

Joe and Rose had agreed that he would direct their sons' education, while she would decide on schooling for the girls. The Kennedy daughters inevitably went to convent schools. In 1930 Joe decided to send Joe Jr. and Jack to Choate, a highly regarded prep school, but Jack was not ready yet for Choate's entrance examination. He was sent instead to Canterbury, a small Catholic boarding school in New Milford, Connecticut.[38]

Jack was desperately homesick, writing his parents frequently, hoping they would visit him. They never did. He remembered his boarding school loneliness for the rest of his life.[39]

He learned to play bridge, but the only thing about Canterbury that he liked was football. Jack reported to his father on every game, and when they beat Bronxville School 7–2, he was ecstatic. Bronxville had out-weighed Canterbury "by twelve pounds per man." Jack had been an end on defense and a fullback on offense "and played the whole game."[40]

Even so, his health was poor and he complained of feeling tired much of the time. Jack came down with hives that winter at the same time that he was in bed with a cold. He also suffered from blurred vision and was in and out of the school infirmary. Then in May 1931 he fell seriously ill with appendicitis and was rushed to Massachusetts General Hospital for an emergency appendectomy. Jack emerged from this second brush with premature death to a future that to him looked bleak: his parents had decided it was time for him to take the Choate entrance exam.

At Choate, Joe Jr. was making friends with the offspring of the Brahmins. This was the way into their world for him, possibly for the family, almost certainly for Jack. Jack, though, seemed destined to continue plodding in his brother's footsteps through life, tasting what Joe Jr. had already tasted, which robs experience of its sweetness for any younger brother.

CHAPTER 3

Growing Pains

P icture him now, at age fourteen, as the black Rolls-Royce purrs through the gates of Choate School at noon on Friday, October 2, 1931, and sitting high up, he looks out from the backseat through the large windows of the gleaming automobile—a freckle-faced, gangling youth, so thin he seems emaciated, yet already taller than most adult males and still growing. His red hair is turning brown and the prominent front teeth look almost comical against the narrowness of his face. Although his voice has broken, Jack Kennedy still sounds much like his mother and continues to resemble her, while Joe Jr.—who has been at Choate for a year now—looks and sounds more and more like their father.

Following a slow recovery from his emergency appendectomy, young Jack has spent the summer being tutored for Choate's entrance exam. In August he managed to pass the English, French and math sections but failed Latin. That is why he is arriving two weeks into the new term, to retake the Latin part of the exam after more tutoring and much maternal praying. This time he passes, and at one-thirty, after Jack completes his registration, Joe Jr. helps him carry his suitcases up the steps and into Choate House, a rambling three-story structure where the third formers (or freshmen) live.[1]

Jack shakes hands with his new housemaster, Earl G. "Cap" Leinbach, and pretty blond Mrs. Leinbach. Cap—a nickname derived from his service as an Army captain in France during the Great War—shows Jack to his room and introduces him to his roommate, Godfrey Kauffmann, an intense young man whose parents own the Washington *Star.* Kauffmann has stamped himself on his own half of the room—and, in setting the tone, on almost all of it—by installing an antique desk and expensive rugs. The Kennedys have been oblivious to elegance or charm in any home they have occupied, and now Jack takes an immediate dislike to Kauffmann. It is a dislike that his roommate reciprocates in full.[2]

Choate covers a large expanse of well-tended lawns shaded by handsome trees. Its stone buildings are meant to project an air of timelessness and tradition, but that is an illusion. This is, in fact, a small business catering to the offspring of the rich. Its faculty, students and their parents like to think of it as being the American equivalent of Eton. However, the school dates from only 1894, and its most famous graduate at the time Jack Kennedy enters is Paul Mellon, the son of a Gilded Age robber baron, who is now a major benefactor to Choate.

Following the English schools it imitates, Choate has its students begin each school day by singing a dismal and void "school hymn" that unconvincingly intones:

> Thy name we will sing, thy praise ever telling
> Thou who in youth keepest watch o'er us all.
> In life's gladsome morning, thy spirit compelling,
> Thy sons, ever faithful, respond to thy call.

Instead of a principal there is a headmaster, stout, balding, pipe-smoking George St. John, the seeming model of the avuncular dominie Mr. Chips. The assistant headmaster is his younger brother, Clarence Wardell St. John. The St. John family, whose business this is, pronounce their name in the English style—"Sinjin"—and have reinforced the English tone by putting half a dozen Englishmen or English-educated Americans on the faculty. The English influence includes a yearly production of a Gilbert and Sullivan operetta. The fact that half the parts are for women means, for example, that in the year when *Patience* is produced, a dozen or so sons of Choate get to play the "Rapturous Maidens."[3]

Although ostensibly nondenominational, the school's tenor is distinctly religious, and the religion is resolutely Anglican. The two founders of Choate were both high-church Anglicans, and the St. Johns are devout Episcopalians. There is St. Xavier's Catholic Church in Wallingford, where the few Catholics such as Jack Kennedy can go to Mass on Sunday and make confession on other days. Even so, all students are required to attend the Episcopalian services held weekly in the chapel; they are central to the Choate experience.[4]

The education that Choate provides is doubtless excellent, especially as a preparation for an Ivy League college, and Richard Pinkham, the senior proctor assigned to guide Jack Kennedy on a tour of the school, is clearly proud of its high standards. Yet young Jack shows no interest whatever in Choate's academic riches. Unimpressive, thinks Pinkham. Below standard.[5]

Jack has no ambition to prove himself as a student. His aim is simply to survive more institutional living and make a life for himself somewhere beyond the sky-blotting shadow of Joe. Room to breathe, to be himself, matters far more than mastering the ablative, calculating pi or memorizing some Shakespearean sonnet.[6]

=

For several summers in the mid-twenties, Joseph P. Kennedy rented the fifteen-room Malcolm Place at Hyannis Port. A large, not particularly attractive house, it boasted a superb view of Nantucket Sound and an expansive lawn that sloped down to the water. The children loved it, and in 1928 Joe bought Malcolm Place for $25,000. JFK called it the "Big House," their nearest thing to a home.

The Kennedys enlarged it to accommodate both their steadily expanding brood and the stream of guests, mainly friends of the children, who came to stay. When the whole family was at Hyannis Port for a weekend, with their friends installed in the spare bedrooms, Rose had so many things to keep track of that she pinned notes to her clothes. Some weekends she ran out of space. The overflow was sported, reluctantly, by the black-clad female servants.[7]

Friday night was movie night down in the basement, with its twenty-seven-seat cinema, including large wicker chairs at the back for Joe and Rose. Saturdays were devoted to golf, swimming, sailing and another movie after dinner. Each evening Rose went onto the large porch and posted a schedule of activities and meals for the following day. She also maintained a bulletin board next to the dining room, where she pinned newspaper and magazine pieces that she thought the children ought to read. Every article was a potential topic for discussion.[8]

Despite the hyperactive days, there was not much light relief when dinnertime rolled around. Joseph Kennedy did not simply dominate the conversation; he controlled the flow. Acting as a kind of debate chairman, he held aloft each subject that was presented for the light of Kennedy brains and wit to play upon, listened to what the others had to say and insisted on involvement: "What do you think, Jack?" he'd ask. "Give us your opinion."[9]

The talk was lively and freewheeling, but while the range of subjects and the intensity of some exchanges surpassed almost anything likely to enliven a typical suburban dinner table, everything turned on what interested Joe Kennedy, which was mainly current affairs.

He was not fascinated by the interaction of ideas; he knew and cared little about poetry, serious music or literature, history, dance, painting or architecture. His sole artistic interest was the movies—admittedly the great art form of the twentieth century—but there, too, his interest was limited, mainly to the money and production side. Joe Kennedy seemed not to notice cinema's mesmerizing potential for advancing humanity's understanding of itself.

The competition the children were pushed into was rigged. It had only a passing acquaintance with fairness. Joe Kennedy was never going to be anything but the Big Number One; Jack would never be allowed to supplant Joe Jr. in his parents' esteem; the girls were never going to supplant the boys. And Rose? She refused to take it seriously. She was likely to head for the beach, fully exercising her right not to get involved.

Everything about the Big House—competitive, busy, with never a wasted minute—reflected Joe Kennedy, and there were also numerous reminders that this was an Irish-Catholic home. A framed poem was placed prominently on one of its dull walls, along with Rose's garish prints of the Immaculate Conception and the Sacred Heart of Christ. Patrick Pearse, one of the leaders of the Easter Rising in Dublin 1916, wrote it shortly before he died. Pearse was executed by a British Army firing squad while strapped to a kitchen chair, wounded and already close to death, on the rain-swept cobbles in the courtyard of Dublin Castle:

> Lord, I do not grudge my two sons that I have seen go out
> And break their strength and die,

They and a few, in bloody protest for a glorious thing.
They shall be spoken of among their people.
The generations shall remember them,
And call them blessed.
But I will speak their names to my own heart
In the long nights.
The little names that were familiar once
Around my dead heart.
Though I grudge them not
I weary, weary of the long sorrow.
And yet I have my joy—
They were faithful and they fought.[10]

Rose kept as busy in her own way as everyone else. She took a long walk every day and played golf enthusiastically. All her life, she remained a prodigious reader, in three languages. But the strongest force, the one that sustained her through grief and disappointment, was religion.

By the time Joe bought the Hyannis Port house, Rose Kennedy probably knew more than she ever needed or wanted to know about his New York chorus girls, Hollywood starlets, aspiring models and biddable secretaries. Not that she was beyond criticism herself. Rose was good-looking, lively and energetic; her growing children were proud of how attractive their mother was. But while a convent education has turned more than a few young women into sexual adventurers, the effect of that gloomy, guilt-ridden part of Rose's upbringing was to turn her into an unyielding icicle. Sex was permissible only for procreation. That's what the nuns said. Otherwise it was a mortal sin. So she submitted, rigidly, possibly reciting the rosary but without actually counting the beads, or maybe she yawned into the forgiving darkness while Joe, her brusque, no-nonsense, no-time-wasted husband asserted his will, briefly.

He became angry and frustrated at her sexual revulsion, blamed her for it and cruelly upbraided her one day in front of some friends. "Now, listen, Rosie! This idea of yours—that there is no romance outside of procreation—is simply wrong. It was not part of our contract at the altar, and the priest never said that and the books don't argue it. And if you don't open your mind on this, I'm going to tell the priest on you." Many a man might sympathize. But has there ever been a woman who was bullied out of frigidity into sexual pleasure?[11]

Unable to give herself entirely to him, reflecting back at him his own inability to give himself uniquely to her, Rose drew her faith ever more closely around herself. It resembled tightening a tourniquet on a wound until the blood flow is cut off. The damaged limb first goes numb, then stops bleeding.

"God will not give us a cross heavier than we can bear. Either you survive or you succumb," she told herself. She believed implicitly in this self-contradictory consolation. Rose also may have felt there was something ennobling in it, that through Joe's sordid affairs a forgiving, loving God had chosen—for mysterious purposes all his own—to test her strength, her commitment. And she was not going to fail. When, towards the end of her life, she weighed one thing against another, she decided that the most important thing had been faith, not family.[12]

Nevertheless, she would not and could not yield indefinitely to Joe's ambiguous embrace; not even for the blessed purpose of procreation. In December 1930 Pope Pius XI published an encyclical on marriage, *Casti Connubii*. Its message for Rose and all Catholic wives still of childbearing age was that they must continue to bear children. Yet in the summer of 1931, when she realized she was pregnant again—for the ninth time—she told Joe there would be no more sex between them. This child would be the last. From now on, she said, they would have separate bedrooms.[13]

Such was the private world that Jack Kennedy emerged from when he entered Choate—a home that was large yet lacked privacy; a family that was almost claustrophobically close-knit yet riven at the top; a life that was free from the kind of cares that dragged down many ordinary families in the 1930s yet one not truly free within itself, given the boundaries staked out and patrolled by a domineering father.

=

Jack's half of the room in Choate House, the one that he shared with young Godfrey Kauffmann, was a clue that no teacher could miss. Yet nearly every faculty member who had to deal with him, from the headmaster down, was convinced that young Jack Kennedy was not using the brains God gave him. It was their responsibility to cram enough self-discipline into the boy to get him into an Ivy League college, but it seemed a thankless uphill struggle.

The clue they slighted was that Jack had turned his half of the room into a shrine to the word. There were piles of books (just as there were piles of clothing) everywhere—on the floor, on the chairs, on the bed, on the dresser. And whether at school or at home, he invariably seemed to have a book in his hands. He also may have been the only student at Choate with a subscription to *The New York Times,* a newspaper that he did not so much read as devour. Reading is ever the high road to learning, but the Choate faculty chose not to notice Jack's, clucking instead over the difficulty of holding his attention in class, over his losing battles with Latin and French, deploring what to their stuffy and conventional dress sense looked like a slovenly appearance, and being predictably irritated by his evident refusal to take seriously Choate's ways, Choate's beliefs, Choate's self-regard.[14]

His classmates, however, noticed something else. Jack Kennedy and his friends liked to listen—as did millions more—to the popular radio show *Information Please.* His friends such as Ralph "Rip" Horton found they could answer some of the questions, but Jack could answer up to half of them. "How do you know all this stuff?" they'd ask.

"I guess I read a lot," Jack replied, neither boasting nor being unduly modest. And as he explained to Horton, he did not simply read widely. He tried to memorize what he read, argued with it, summarized the writer's argument and filed the summaries away in his mind.[15]

Joseph Kennedy told all his sons they had to do something important with their lives. They were not to consider going into business or to worry about money. He'd see to that. That may have been one reason why Jack as a student seemed so unfocused compared to many of his classmates, whose potential careers had already been mapped, by themselves or their parents. And then there was Joe Jr. To tag along behind Joe and emulate him was simply unthinkable, for various reasons, including the fact that Joe intended, one day, to be President.

Deeper, though, than any pother about possible careers was his common humanity, without a cure or escape. Like nearly everyone else in the world, Jack needed and wanted to feel loved, to feel he was special, beginning with his parents, the star around which other lives revolved. He had never felt that at home; still less could he hope to find it in a boarding school. But if he could not win other people's affection, he could make sure he got their attention.

Dressing differently was one way, being better-read was another. But what Jack sought as the sure way to get people to like and admire him was athletic glory, something almost certain to create friendships and respect. Joe Jr. was on the basketball team, so Jack tried out for basketball but failed. He was too thin, too light, to excel in anything but golf, in which his height and superb coordination gave him an advantage. Yet the dream of gridiron success was stubborn. Flattened many times before he finally abandoned it, he still yearned to play football.[16]

In November 1933, just back from installing Joe Jr. at the London School of Economics, Joseph Kennedy visited Choate to watch Jack play on the junior varsity football team. To Jack's chagrin, his father was not impressed with his performance on the field. But what hurt even more was the way his father talked to the teachers about how well Joe Jr. was doing over in England, where he was studying under one of the most famous thinkers of the age, Harold J. Laski. In talking about Joe Jr., the father exuded a paternal pride that he never evinced for Jack.

Joe Jr. had been no more the sporting hero than his younger brother, and his grades at Choate were virtually identical to Jack's. The difference was that he was not only far more willing to obey the rules, but putative politician that he was, he identified with the rule makers and enforcers. He had smilingly ingratiated himself with the faculty, much as he had done with his father. Joe Jr. respected older people, provided they were figures of authority. Jack could not resist challenging such people, ready to reject them before they got a chance to reject him.

Although his father paid Jack a few calls, Rose did not visit him at Choate, not once. He begged her to write to him, something she rarely did, and in his letters, he did not try to hide his anguish. "The trouble with Thanksgiving," he wrote to her, "is that you get home just long enough to see how much you are missing."[17]

Instead of writing to Jack, Rose wrote regularly to Clara St. John, the headmaster's wife. She fretted from afar over Jack's colds, his weight, his fallen arches, pinkeye, swollen glands, sports injuries, knees and mysterious stomach ailments. To build up his strength and put some flesh on his bones, Rose insisted that he be given malt extract and cod-liver oil every day, plus a glass of milk with a raw egg stirred into it. The cod-liver oil was disgusting, but the egg-and-milk concoction was worse. Young Kennedy pinched his nose, then rolled his eyes heavenward like an involuntary martyr before shutting them tightly and gulping down the viscous mixture.[18]

Almost from the time he enrolled, he was in and out of the school infirmary with a succession of mysterious ailments and never seemed to go long without a cold. He showed, that is, the typical signs of someone with an immune system weakened by depression, prey to whatever is going around, and in every school there is always something. Even so, the infirmary offered an escape from the demands of the classroom and teachers, a refuge from the petty rules about neatness and tidiness. Best of all, Jack could read there, and think and think.

In the spring of 1933, towards the end of his sophomore—or fourth form—year, he got himself chosen business manager for Choate's yearbook, *The Brief.* It was not an assignment for which there was much competition, because it meant being responsible for getting advertising. For Jack, it was hardly a challenge: Joe Kennedy had his friends place ads for their businesses in *The Brief* despite its exiguous circulation. Joe Jr. was already on *The Brief,* of course.[19]

While rapidly filling the yearbook with advertising, Jack got to know another toiler on the yearbook, one of Choate's best athletes, K. LeMoyne "Lem" Billings. Claiming descent on his mother's side from the Elder Brewster who had arrived in America in 1620 aboard the *Mayflower,* Billings was also remotely related to George Washington. He was more directly descended, on his father's side, from a French artist at the court of Louis XVI called LeMoigne. His father, a Pittsburgh doctor, had died prematurely, leaving almost nothing to support a grief-stricken family. Billings had been enrolled at Choate before his father died, and the family managed to keep him there with a little help from the school. Billings felt he was Choate's token poor boy, a way of making it look good, but he had to endure being patronized by other students and pitied by the faculty.

Shortly after Jack got to know Billings, the school year ended and he went home for the summer. For a week or so, the whole family was there at the same time. It was a chance for all eleven Kennedys—Joe and Rose, plus the nine children—to pose under a tree for a conventional happy (rich) family photograph. In it, Joe Jr. and Jack stand side by side, striking identical poses—hands in pockets—and identically dressed. But Jack is the one you notice, because he occupies the middle of the picture, and the handkerchief in his breast pocket has been pulled out so far it seems about to fall to the ground—or rise skyward and take flight.

Reunited at school that fall, Jack and Billings forged a lasting friendship, as misfits will. Both felt themselves—and really were—outsiders at Choate. The loyalty they could not give to the school they now granted each other. Besides, despite being shortsighted, Billings was the avatar of some of Jack's own frustrated hopes. At six feet two and 175 pounds he was an athletic star: the strongest member of crew and a football stalwart on muddy fall afternoons. Jack, with his easy charm, quick wit, popularity and rich family, possessed what Billings, with a foot planted on Plymouth Rock, clearly lacked.

And at last Jack Kennedy found a teacher, Harold Lauren Tinker, who appreciated him for the unique individual he knew himself to be. Tinker was not annoyed for a moment that young Kennedy spent much of each class staring out the window. When he turned his attention to a poem or a novel, Jack grasped its insights faster and more accurately than almost any of his classmates. There was the morning, for example, when Tinker quoted "The length of things is vanity; only their height is joy," from George Santayana's *Soliloquies in England*. Jack turned away from the window, pink face radiant, green eyes bright. He'd instantly grasped—and thrilled to—Santayana's poetical insight.[20]

His feeling for literature was remarkable. That—and the sensitivity it implied—set him apart from the aspirant lawyers and future bond salesmen of America who, oozing self-importance, dominated student life at Choate. An inchoate responsiveness to the wider world, with which Jack had only had a fleeting contact to date, illuminated an essay he wrote for his English class, taking justice as his theme at a time when the Depression was at its deepest.

"Justice is pictured as a lady holding scales in her hands on which is weighed right and wrong. Always is the word linked with God. . . . But does God render to everyone his just due?" Jack doubted it. "A boy is born in a rich family, brought up in a clean environment with an excellent education and good companions, inherits a fool-proof business from his father [and] eventually dies a just and honest man.

"Take the other extreme. A boy is born in the slums, of a poor family, has evil companions, no education . . . turns into a drunken bum and dies. Was it because of the rich boy's ability that he landed in the lap of luxery [*sic*]. . . . Was it the poor boy's fault that he was born in squalor? . . . How much better chance has the boy born with a silver spoon in his mouth of being good than the boy who from birth is surrounded by rottenness and filth. . . . Justice is not always received even from The Most Just, so how can we poor mortals hope to attain it?"[21]

That Christmas of 1933 Jack invited Billings to Palm Beach, where his father had recently bought a Spanish-style mansion, all red tiles and whitewashed stucco, on North Ocean Boulevard. While Choate was gripped in ice and snow, they were catching sea turtles in the warm waters off the South Florida coast, then posing for the camera, hands on hips. The photograph still exists; the inane grins of young warriors triumphant envelop their boyish faces as they plant their feet on the dead turtles' unyielding backs.

They played tennis, too, and just before they returned to Choate, Jack fell and skinned a knee. It did not seem more than an unguent and Band-Aid case, but back at school in January 1934 it developed into blood poisoning. He was moved to Peter Bent Brigham Hospital in Boston.[22]

While Jack recuperated, he had plenty of time to read. Propped up in bed, he plunged into the dense, multivolume account of the politics and strategy of the Great War, *The World Crisis,* by Winston Churchill. Struggling to make sense of a violent past, Jack Kennedy sought an understanding well beyond his years. He seems to have sensed even at age sixteen that with the world now roiled by another economic and political crisis, his generation confronted a violent, desperate future.[23]

Health steadily failing, he became delirious. Choate's faculty and students were urged to pray for him. Blood poisoning was a major killer in the dark days before antibiotics. In 1924 Calvin Coolidge, Jr., had suffered a similar injury at the same age, on the White House tennis courts, and died. Dwight Eisenhower, too, had come close to death from a skinned knee. Jack Kennedy was suspended for several days in that tenebrous zone where death chooses, yet he survived.

He returned to school a few weeks later, and sometime that spring he and Billings decided to lose their virginity. In evening dress and bowler hats they visited a brothel in Harlem one night. Jack went first, with a white girl, while Lem, clutching his hat, waited for him to finish. Lem went next. With the warmth of the whore still upon him, Jack became terrified he had caught syphilis or gonorrhea and, in a humiliating ritual undergone by other young men of his time, hastily bought a small, supposedly antivenereal kit that consisted of a dubious-looking cream that had to be forced into the penis via a tiny tube. Billings followed suit in the rearguard action, much as he had done in the sexual advance.[24]

This venture had scarcely passed before Jack fell ill once more, this time with blocked bowels. His father had him moved to the Mayo Clinic in Rochester, Minnesota, which was in the forefront of diagnosis and treatment for many diseases. But it would be years before the medicos there figured out what was wrong with Jack's bowels.

He was suffering from spastic colon, better known nowadays as irritable bowel syndrome, an illness that afflicts more than ten million Americans and gave rise to a classic of psychological literature, Erik Erikson's *Childhood and Society.* Jack's was an almost paradigmatic case—he was lonely, feeling unloved and unfairly locked into a competition with his big brother that he could only lose—and the illness ended the day Joe Jr. died.[25]

Over a three-day period at the Mayo Clinic, he had eighteen enemas. To his skin-creeping revulsion, he had to endure a doctor's finger up his rectum, then a tube an inch in diameter and, finally, a small flashlight. He wrote regularly to Billings, telling him how much he hated Rochester—"God-damndest hole I've seen." His letters were filled with the foul-mouthed preening and strutting common to adolescent boys who feel they are being daring and grown-up when they say "fuck" or "pussy," "shit" or "cunt."

Worrying that the cause of his illness would turn out to be VD, he nevertheless was obsessed with sex. As his red blood cell count fell, along with his weight, his teenage testosterone output seemed to be increasing, as it does for most seventeen-year-old males. He boasted about the beautiful nurses who cared for him, and he talked about propositioning one of them. Billings, however, was not much interested in girls; he was only trying to pretend he was.

What Billings wanted was a sexual relationship—with Jack Kennedy. That was not something he was going to announce openly. As for trying to seduce Jack . . . well, Billings was so gauche, so insecure and so ugly he would not have known where to begin. Openly admitting that his burgeoning sexual emotions were directed entirely at Jack was to risk destroying their friendship and losing the great love of his life.

Instead, Billings took advantage of distance to drop a hint. The homosexuals at Choate exchanged billets-doux written on toilet paper: easy to fold up small and pass in class or the corridor. Jack Kennedy was aghast when he opened Billings's flimsy, fragile letter and wrote back sternly, "Please don't write to me on toilet paper any more. I'm not that kind of boy."[26]

After a month of being probed and flushed out, he returned to Hyannis Port for what remained of the summer vacation. His irritable bowel syndrome recurred from time to time and invariably left the Mayo Clinic's finest scratching their heads and admitting bewilderment.

During his third year at Choate, Jack had moved into the west wing of Hill House. He did not have a roommate that year, but on returning to Choate in the fall of 1934 for their final year, Jack and Billings said they wanted to room together. The teacher responsible for the west wing, J. J. Maher, resisted this idea, but the head overruled him. Maher put them in a room next to his own. Known as a strict disciplinarian, the teacher was by now something of an expert on Jack Kennedy's untidiness, his contempt for school rules and his penchant for juvenile pranks that mocked Choate's starchy image.

Maher was soon lamenting what he called Jack and Lem's "silly, giggling inseparable companionship," but the proximate cause of the crisis that was about to break was the Victrola that Jack brought back with him from Hyannis Port that fall. "Jack's room is a club for his friends," Maher protested to the headmaster. Indeed it was. They gathered there, a biblical number in all—twelve, that is, not counting Jack—to listen to his record collection. Jack, meanwhile, was restive at his proximity to Maher. "We are up on Mr. Maher's corridor right next to him, and everything we say, he lobs in and adds his comments. We are practically rooming with him," Jack informed his father.[27]

Maher told the headmaster that Jack was not only careless in taking care of his room but struggling academically, too. When the report was forwarded to Joe Kennedy, he delivered the ultimate threat: withdrawal of a father's love. "Don't let me lose confidence in you again," he wrote to Jack, "because it will be nearly impossible to restore it."[28]

Feeling equally exasperated, Maher took to entering the room when Jack and Billings were in class and piling all of Jack's possessions— books, football boots, clothing, bedding—into a huge mound on the floor. When Jack returned, he had to put everything away. Maher seemed pleased with his tactic, but it was in truth a provocation, ratcheting emotion—on both sides—dangerously upwards.[29]

As Maher's overwrought missives landed on his desk, George St. John denounced Jack and his friends before the entire school in the strongest language he permitted himself: they were "muckers," an expression typically defined as "a vulgar or ill-bred person." This kindly headmaster, with a lot of experience teaching young men, ought to have known better. As fractious youth will, they loved it. Call a rebel a rebel and he'll wear it like a medal. They took the head's insulting name and turned it inside out. The secondary meaning of mucker was someone who shoveled horse shit off the streets. A virtual army of muckers had to tackle the huge piles of dung and large pools of urine that characterized urban street life in the days before automobiles.

So now Jack Kennedy and his twelve friends went into Wallingford and got a jeweler to craft what appeared, at a casual glance, to be a Phi Beta Kappa key, and not by coincidence. Close inspection revealed a small shovel fashioned from 22-carat gold, with "CMC"—for Choate Muckers Club—engraved on on one side and the name of the wearer on the reverse, a close parody of the Phi Bete model. So adorned, they wore their golden shovels on their vests, much as the head and other faculty members paraded their membership in Phi Beta Kappa.[30]

St. John was outraged. Contumacy is so direct a challenge that it must be crushed or submitted to. As he prepared to strike back, however, Harold Tinker gave him some advice: it was obvious, said Tinker, that the root cause of the crisis was the personality clash between Maher and Kennedy. If the head had to choose between them, "It would be better for the school to fire Maher and hold onto Kennedy than to keep Maher and throw Jack Kennedy out."[31]

One February morning in 1935 St. John summoned all thirteen Muckers to his study and told them they were being expelled. Several gasped in disbelief. They were to pack their bags, said St. John, and leave on an afternoon train. Back in their rooms, they started packing, but how would they explain their expulsion to their parents? After lunch, they were summoned back to the head's study. He had decided, he announced, that they did not have to leave after all. But the Muckers Club must be abandoned and better behavior shown.[32]

The head's expulsion edict had been the prep school equivalent of the mock execution, a dumb show performed for the good of the school rather than the benefit of wayward youth. To throw out twelve rich boys—plus Billings—would generate reams of publicity, all of it bad. The first prep school that becomes famous for ruining the college prospects of its privileged seniors might as well start selling its buildings and grounds to Wal-Mart.

Nevertheless, St. John was not satisfied with the mock execution alone. He asked the ringleader's father, Joseph P. Kennedy, to come and see him about Jack. Father and son played their parts with due solemnity. Jack appeared to be contrite while his father pretended to be appalled when, in truth, he thought the Muckers Club was a pretty good stunt. Himself an eternal outsider in the world of the Sinjins, he chortled and said under his breath to Jack as they left the head's study, "If that crazy Muckers Club had been mine, you can be sure it wouldn't have started with an *M*!"[33]

Choate was about to become a thing of the past. Jack Kennedy was applying to college. He had a photograph taken about this time that would accompany his application to Harvard. It shows a seventeen-year-old with a sensual mouth, large ears and a mass of light brown hair larded with brilliantine and carefully sculpted until it resembled a high, curling wave slamming into a sea wall. The gaze is fresh—and blank; a face yet to be written upon. There is not a hint of a problematical medical history. He appears to be an enviable example of a good-looking, healthy youth on the verge of a virile manhood, but a sensitive lad all the same.

The hair is not the only singular feature—so is the way he dresses. The knot of his tie, crammed up against the large, soft collar, is so tiny it almost disappears. No other Choate graduate of 1935 sports a tie knotted like this, as the yearbook shows. The tie itself is of no interest at all; the way he wears it says *he* is.

As he prepares to depart, Jack Kennedy names his penis "J.J.," after John J. Maher. Here is an essential part of his style, already half formed— don't get angry, don't be indignant. Take your revenge by mocking the foe.[34]

CHAPTER 4

Life Forces

No one did death better. Irish Catholics of Joseph P. Kennedy's time were brought up to look it squarely in the face; no blenching. A good wake was a celebration of the life, not a time for weeping. These were people who walked with death every day, in a way that Protestants rarely do. Catholic prayer reminds the faithful of their fleeting mortality. Countless millions, rosary in hand, ask the Virgin Mary daily, "Pray for us sinners now and at the hour of our death."

Like most Catholics, Joe Kennedy carried a nagging awareness of life's fragility and brevity, and he intended to do something about it in this world, not the next. Behind his lust for power, money and fame was a steady gaze fixed from behind owlish glasses on that summit of bourgeois ambitions—a dynasty; a legacy that spanned generations. Something of Joe Kennedy was going to survive whatever death might do to him.[1]

Every day of his life was squeezed until it yielded a net gain: more money, progress towards power, an advance in his ambitions for his children, a measure of fame. Something, anyway. But the first order of business was riches.

Like his friend Barney Baruch, he was essentially a stock-market lone wolf, especially after he left Boston. Kennedy kept his own counsel, went his own way. He sometimes joined stock pools, which were organized to drive the value of a mediocre stock sky-high, then sell before it plunged. Sometimes pools were formed to drive a good stock down, buy it up while it was depressed and cash in handsomely on the inevitable rebound. There were countless opportunities for any quick-witted operator with inside information in the unregulated markets of the 1920s.[2]

In 1927 a Harvard economics professor, William Z. Ripley, published a hand-wringing tome titled *Main Street and Wall Street* that described this anarchic state. President Calvin Coolidge read it and was horrified. So much speculation and so little regulation was certain to produce a financial panic. The only question was when.[3]

As the Depression bit deep in the early 1930s, big stock-market speculators of the 1920s were blamed for it. For every million a well-known speculator had accumulated, there were a million of his fellow citizens who cursed him. Even though he almost certainly did nothing that was against the law, Joe Kennedy, with his enormous pelf, was an easy man to despise.

Even so, he was indifferent to what others thought of him, shrugging off criticism as nothing but jealousy. What interested him instead was what the Depression meant in American life. Before 1917 government did not have much impact on most people's lives unless they happened to be federal employees or former military personnel. World War I had enlarged the scope of government, but it was the Depression that brought the biggest changes, by making government the guardian of prosperity and the ultimate social provider.

As the Depression began dragging down the economy and fracturing American society, Joe Kennedy could see the future, and he told his friend Morton Downey, a nightclub crooner, "The people who run the government will be the biggest people in America."[4]

Kennedy was one of the few truly rich men in the Democratic party, and he had known Franklin D. Roosevelt ever since 1917, when Roosevelt was assistant secretary of the Navy and Kennedy was running the Fore River Shipyard. Both strong-willed, highly opinionated and egotistical, they had inevitably irritated each other while simultaneously developing a wary mutual respect.[5]

In 1932 Kennedy backed Roosevelt's bid for the White House and played a key role in securing his nomination at the Democratic convention in Chicago. Joe Kennedy took over two floors of the Waldorf on election night, November 8, for his family and friends to celebrate Roosevelt's victory. When the early returns showed Roosevelt already heading for a landslide, he told the leader of the orchestra he'd hired, "Play 'Happy Days Are Here Again!'"[6]

The reward Kennedy wanted was to be appointed secretary of the Treasury, but he assured Roosevelt he would settle for something less. "I'll take any job you want me to, and I'll even work for nothing, so long as it's interesting. I never want to be bored."[7]

After making him wait more than a year, Roosevelt finally offered him a challenge suited to his talents and experience. He appointed Joe Kennedy to the newly created five-man Securities and Exchange Commission. Roosevelt leaned heavily on the other four members of the SEC to elect Kennedy their chairman. "Joe is able, loyal and will make good. What more can one ask?"[8]

Kennedy found the SEC interesting and worthwhile. If capitalism was saved, his family would get the benefit of his riches. If it wasn't, they wouldn't. The SEC had two choices, he told his fellow commissioners: it could try to use the power of the federal government to compel the exchanges into behaving better by imposing huge fines and long jail sentences; or it could try to persuade the people who ran them that they could still thrive, without fear of Congress or the courts, if the exchanges reformed themselves. The first option would probably fail, but there was a good chance of making the second one work.[9]

Reelected chairman of the SEC on July 1, 1935, Kennedy was already becoming restless. Two days later he reminded Roosevelt that he had told him, even before he took the job, he did not want to do it for much more than a year.[10]

Despite his acknowledged success in establishing the SEC, Joe Kennedy never shook off a reputation for having come by his riches dishonestly. Worse, he had a growing reputation as an anti-Semite. That was something he found irritating and his family found embarrassing.

Joe Kennedy had a number of Jewish friends, including his Harvard classmate Arthur Goldsmith, Bernard Baruch, David Sarnoff, Arthur Krock and Herbert Bayard Swope. Those Jews he knew and respected had, in a way, overcome their Jewishness; they weren't really Jews to him. In the company of his rich Jewish friends, he referred without any embarrassment to other Jews—the mediocre ones or those he simply disliked—as "kikes" and "yids."[11]

His philandering, too, damaged his reputation. Over the years, the skirt chasing became increasingly zealous, ever more obvious. When he moved to New York, Joe Kennedy was famous for telling people, "If money is what you're after, go where the money is." Ditto sex. The best place to find beautiful, sexy and willing young women was in Broadway shows, night-clubs and the movies.

While his infidelities did irrecoverable and inexcusable damage to the relationship with Rose, Joe Kennedy's version of marriage—the limited partnership that was paraded as an ideal union, absent the content—wasn't unusual for rich and powerful men, then or now. Bernard Baruch was much the same—lifelong marriage, photogenic children, press discretion and numerous women.[12]

≡

The summer of 1935, when he graduated from Choate, Jack spent many days sailing, usually with Joe Jr. He was now six feet tall and looked the picture of health, but he wasn't all charm; not yet, anyway. Released from the constraints of Choate, he could be boisterous and obnoxious, and during the Edgartown Regatta that summer, Jack and Joe Jr. threw a party that turned into a mini-riot. The police were called and the brothers shared a jail cell that night.[13]

Shortly after this, there was a costume party at the Wianno Yacht Club. Jack decided to go as Mahatma Gandhi, and four girls dressed up as his wives. Lem Billings showed up at the party wrapped in a sheet he hoped might pass for a sari. Oh, me? he'd say when people asked who he was. I'm wife number five.[14]

Jack had applied to Harvard and Princeton and was accepted by both. But his father decided he should have a year at the London School of Economics, to study under Harold J. Laski as Joe Jr. had done. Laski is almost forgotten now but in his time was a highly respected socialist thinker who had taught at Harvard for a while just after World War I. A superb classroom performer in the 1920s, the Depression of the 1930s had turned him into a Stalinist dupe, not only admiring Stalin but applauding his crimes. Laski hailed Stalin's chief executioner, Andrei Vishinsky, for "doing what an ideal Minister of Justice would do if we had such a person in Great Britain."[15]

Supreme Court Justice Felix Frankfurter, spellbound by his recollections of Laski at Harvard a decade earlier and unaware of what Laski had really become, told Joe Kennedy to send his sons to study under Laski.

Jack, however, wanted to go to Princeton, where Billings had been given a scholarship. His father would not be moved: Jack must spend a year studying under the mighty Laski, as Joe Jr. had done. It seems likely, too, that his father would force him to attend Harvard once the year in London was up and tell him to forget about Princeton.

As that summer drew to a close, Jack Kennedy reluctantly packed for England and crossed the Atlantic with his parents. Joe Jr. was by now back home and a big man in Harvard Yard. Anything Jack did under Laski's tutelage was bound to be compared to Joe's achievements and found wanting. That was what had happened at Choate.

Hardly settled in at Claridges, Jack was struck once again by a flare-up of his irritable bowel syndrome. There was not much that could frighten Joe Kennedy, but Jack's thin young body could. When Jack fell seriously ill in London, his father had no choice but to give way for once and admit defeat. There was to be no wisdom gathered by a reluctant Jack from the deluded Laski. His father brought him home as soon as he was strong enough to travel.

Jack, still looking weak, his flesh tones those of a badly bruised, over-ripe mango, mustered enough strength to go to Princeton and enroll. Besides Lem Billings, another former Mucker, Rip Horton, was also there . . . and Joe wasn't. Jack moved into Lem's dingy rooms on the fourth floor of South Union Hall. For someone in poor health, it was a dismal choice. The bathroom was in the cellar. After taking a bath or a shower, or using the toilet, Jack had to climb seventy-five steps to return to his room.[16]

Some months earlier, Jack Kennedy had met a very pretty girl named Olive Cawley at the Choate spring dance, but he had warned her, "Don't fall in love with me!" By the time he left Choate, Olive had become his regular girlfriend, yet he felt frustrated. She thwarted all attempts on her virginity. Heavy petting was as far as she would go.[17]

Jack fell ill once again; he had not completely recovered from his illness in London. He checked in to a hospital in Boston when the semester ended, spent Christmas in Palm Beach, then returned to Boston for more dreary hours in a hospital bed, being tested, probed and irrigated.

Getting out of bed after yet another solemn medical confab at his bedside during which he was told nothing, he peered at his chart. One word seemed to jump out—leukemia. That explained why the medicos had seemed so grim. "They were mentally measuring me for a coffin," he informed Billings. During previous hospitalizations, his white blood cell count had been dangerously low, the mark of a failing immune system. Now, though, it had risen alarmingly, a common symptom of leukemia.[18]

At eighteen, youth takes as its right a sense of being eternal, even when surrounded by the solicitous in white coats. Dying is what old people do. Jack laughed off the diagnosis. Whatever the tests said, his body was telling him something more believable—he was too young to die.

He diverted himself by writing to Lem. Jack's letters overflowed with normal erotic desires, but he expressed them with all the self-conscious, attention-seeking profanity of an adolescent demonstrating his manliness by waving it like a flag. Sex drives a lot of young men slightly crazy anyway, and Jack, like them, had to pretend he was in control before it took him over completely.

What frightened him was the thought that he might have picked up a venereal disease, and he was shocked to find crabs breeding in his pubic hair. But whatever Jack had, he was passing it on. When one of his girlfriends, "Bunny" Day, came to see him, he gleefully informed Billings, "I laid B.D. in the bathtub."[19]

In his letters, he regularly insulted Billings as "You shit . . . you prick . . . bastard . . . LeMoan . . ." It is inconceivable that Billings the moonstruck ever risked addressing Jack in such terms. Both knew their parts: Jack was the hero, Lem his comic sidekick.

Towards the end of February, Jack checked out of the hospital to recuperate again in Palm Beach, where he could get laid for $3 at the Gypsy Tea Room and work on getting his tan back. From North Ocean Boulevard, he berated Billings with airmail missives for losing his scholarship. "You have been a damn fool . . . you have made a flop out of everything in the last two years. . . ." Billings was welcome to come to Palm Beach for Easter as they had planned, but it would be better for him to stay at Princeton and study hard until he got that scholarship back.[20]

Since leaving the SEC, Joe Kennedy had gone on to the Maritime Commission, which was trying to rebuild the Merchant Marine. Roosevelt, along with others such as Dwight D. Eisenhower, knew there was another war coming. The collapse in world trade since 1930 had wiped out a third of the U.S. Merchant Marine. Just as he had persuaded Congress to provide money for rebuilding the Army and Navy as a way of fighting the Depression, Roosevelt was going to put government money into the construction of new merchant ships, under the direction of the Maritime Commission, for the war that was coming.

Meanwhile, Arthur Krock of *The New York Times* was writing a book that would be published in Joe Kennedy's name in time for the 1936 election. Titled *I'm for Roosevelt,* it offered a rich man's endorsement of the New Deal. Joe Kennedy was eager to look like a writer, just as he wanted to appear a devoted husband, without having any idea in either case of where to begin.

As he labored over the draft of *I'm for Roosevelt* in Palm Beach that winter, Krock told Joe that Jack needed fresh air, sunshine, physical labor, and he knew just the place. A friend of his happened to own a forty-three-thousand-acre ranch near Benson, Arizona, close to the Mexican border. Towards the end of April, Jack and a similarly scrawny and sickly friend from Choate, James D. "Smokey Joe" Wilde, found themselves out in the desert, living in a bunkhouse and earning a dollar a day as ranch hands.

Jack made adobe bricks, repaired fences and rounded up cattle. One Saturday night he and Wilde hitched a ride on a ranch truck that was heading for Nogales, just across the border. "Got a fuck and a suck in a Mexican hoar-house [*sic*] for 65 cents," he informed Billings, then began worrying frantically about whether he was incubating gonorrhea . . . or worse.[21]

After a month of rugged living, he felt stronger and fitter than he had for several years. Before returning to the East Coast, he headed for Hollywood, where he met and bedded a gorgeous movie extra. "The best looking thing that I have seen," he boasted to Billings. "I will show you her picture when I get in."[22]

Back on the Cape at the end of June, he was a different, much older young man than the adolescent who had graduated a year earlier from Choate. He had done, in a roundabout and slightly haphazard way, what young men with vague ambitions are often advised to do—take a year off between high school and college. In Europe the year off was part of a well-rounded person's education: the *Wanderjahr,* when young people left home, got a job, traveled, saw something beyond the cocoon of family life, along the way acquiring a better sense of the world and the place they intended to carve out for themselves within it. What has worked for millions of other adolescents worked perfectly for him.

He did a lot of sailing that summer, skippering *Flash II,* the twenty-two-foot Star boat that he and Joe Jr. owned jointly. With its narrow hull and towering mast it was a difficult boat to navigate, but at the end of August he won one of the big races of the season in the 1936 Atlantic Coast Championships. His margin of victory was four minutes, a feat other sailors found astounding. On land or on water, he traveled fast.[23]

Two weeks later Jack enrolled at Harvard, his father's choice. At nine-teen, he was a year older than most of his fellow freshmen, and more than two years older than some, at a time in life when a year or two counts for a lot.

=

"What a thing of beauty my body has become with the open air, riding horses and Mexicans," he'd told Billings.[24] Now he put it to the test—he tried out for the Harvard freshman football team and made it; tried out, too, for swimming and succeeded there as well; and was chosen for the freshman golf team. Athletic glory finally seemed at hand.

Yet hardly had he made the three teams when he fell ill again and spent a week or so in New England Baptist Hospital. When he emerged, he put himself on a weight-gaining ice-cream diet and bought his own ice-cream machine to assure supplies.[25]

Like other Harvard freshmen, he spent that first year living in a student dorm on the edge of the Yard, where he soon became easy to pick out even from a distance, walking briskly, gesturing emphatically, talking rapidly. Jack's homage to the power of lactic products to put some avoirdupois on that skeletal frame achieved nothing. Too much nervous energy.

He scraped along in class. What mattered were the gridiron, the pool and the tee. The freshman football team played five games that fall, and he got onto the field in three of them, playing right end. The team lost four games, tied one, racked up thirty-three points, and yielded eighty-six. The team Harvard tied was not even from another college, but a prep school, Wor-cester Academy. Two other prep schools—Phillips Exeter and Andover—thrashed them.[26]

For Jack Kennedy, there was no glory to be had out on the field, no matter how hard he chased after it. Even on a team as mediocre as this one, he couldn't really make the grade. He tried to make pass receiving his specialty at a time when there were far fewer passes thrown than now. Every time he caught the ball, he got flattened. His consolation was that the outstanding player on this cream-puff team was his roommate, Torbert Macdonald, who was the best kicker and broken-field runner it had.

The swimming team was a different story. The 1936 squad proved to be the best in a generation, winning all eleven meets that fall. Six of its opponents, however, were secondary schools, and one was from a nearby YMCA. Kennedy's specialty was the backstroke, and his efforts were good enough for him to be awarded "minor numerals." He also got minor numerals in golf, but that was a bittersweet success: the team only played three matches and was trounced every time.

He had long since learned the most important lesson of institutional living, whether it's in a large family, a hospital, a school, college or the military. You have to get along with other people, all kinds of people, and take them for what they are. Over the years, he learned to do that better than most people can or ever will. Gifted with a rare talent for friendship and capable of effortlessly drawing people to him, Jack Kennedy surrounded himself with an astonishingly varied circle of friends.

His father's riches and disdainful attitude towards most of Jack's friends would have worked against him had he himself not used all of his charm plus his privileged circumstances to win people over. Jack was nothing much on the football team, for example, but one October weekend during his freshman year he took five of his teammates down to the Cape. His father's secretary, Edward Moore, arranged for four girls to be there.

Among the Kennedy children, the benign-looking Moore was known as "Doc." Unmarried and childless, Doc Moore had a habit whenever the young Kennedys injured themselves of rushing towards them with Band-Aids, patching them up and making sure nothing was broken.[27]

Jack and his friends and the four girls turned the weekend into an orgy. "One guy got fucked 3 times, another guy three times (the girl a virgin!) and myself twice . . . I think the coaches heard as they gave us a hell of a bawling out."[28]

This was probably his first sex party, but it would not be the last. He organized them from time to time, weaving yet another garish strand into a life that had no room for grayness. The immediate consequence of this first experience was that the girl he'd had sex with became pregnant.

The most likely outcome was that she had an abortion, arranged by the ever-helpful Eddie Moore, and was paid to keep quiet. In those days, it was easy to arrange an abortion in a good hospital, conducted by a reputable surgeon, if you had enough money. It would appear on the doctor's schedule as a routine dilation and curettage. So while Jack Kennedy was briefly abashed at getting the girl pregnant, and frightened he'd gotten the clap, what would have been a crisis for other young men was no more than a minor irritant for him.[29]

Jack was popular on the swimming team, too, but not for arranging sex weekends. When sports reporters came around the locker room to do pieces on the surprisingly successful Harvard team, he hid in the showers. He knew that if he appeared, he was likely—as the son of a famous, not to say notorious, father—to get most of the press attention, instead of those who deserved it, the best swimmers on the team.[30]

In February 1937 Jack Kennedy suffered his first electoral defeat. He was a candidate for student office in the class of 1940 election and finished nowhere. Undeterred, he ran for the Smoker Committee. He got himself elected chairman, something Joe Jr. had been before him.

The committee's mission was one Jack could give himself to completely: organizing a party, the Freshman Smoker. The event was scheduled for May 5 in Memorial Hall. Joe Jr. had managed to get Rudy Vallee, a legendary crooner, plus his band.[31]

Jack, striving to do as well, booked not one jazz band but two, brought Ramona and Her Piano from New York, hired a toastmaster and a torch singer, a comedy duo, a tumbling act and a guest appearance by a legendary baseball player, Dizzy Dean. Tobacco was provided free, and freshmen paraded around the Yard that night dressed in tuxedos, puffing on enormous cigars. Ginger ale fizzed in champagne glasses, but it seems a safe bet that hip flasks put in a discreet appearance, too.

The smoker was a huge success and the committee had their photograph taken. All five members sat stiffly, hands on thighs, knuckles bunched as per the photographer's directions. The four young men seated with Jack Kennedy looked and dressed like management trainees working for a bank. He looked so different—in white bucks, with that odd, prominently sculpted mass of rufous hair—that he seemed to have wandered into the picture by mistake. They are but wallpaper; he is the statue.

During the winter of 1936, following Roosevelt's reelection, Joe Kennedy became more convinced than ever that the rise of Nazi Germany made another war inevitable. He told Jack at the Palm Beach mansion that winter, "You ought to plan on seeing Europe before the shooting starts." As the end of his freshman year approached, Jack did what his father had suggested—he made plans. He would take his car, and Billings, to see Europe for himself, drive around and decide whether Dad was right.[32]

CHAPTER 5

On the Road

Picture him now, on the morning of June 30, 1937, as Jack Kennedy stands dockside in New York. His first automobile, a Ford that he bought the week he enrolled at Harvard, rises and sways, lifted by chains and hooks onto the forward deck of the luxury liner *Washington*. He has been to Europe before, of course, but that was with his parents. For the next few weeks, he will be in control—not his family, not his teachers—as he drives across Europe. This is no ordinary Ford but a sedan-convertible. It has a fold-down top, including a small isinglass rear window, fitted to the body of a standard four-door sedan.

On the tiny desk in the inside cabin that he shares with Lem Billings is an essential item, a way of extending this trip long after it ends. Jack's sister Kathleen has given him a small Moroccan leather notebook embossed "My Trip Abroad" to record the events of his miniature but high-octane version of the young aristocrat's Grand Tour.

Once the liner is under way and at sea, he mingles with the other first-class passengers, is invited to cocktails with the captain and plays bingo with Lem. There are plenty of "Johnny Harvards" aboard, and too few good-looking young women. But he meets up with one named Ann Reed, who is attractive and friendly.

The night of July 5 Jack stays up until the early hours and even then doesn't go to bed. Instead, he stands at the rail, staring towards the southeast. He waits and waits, and as the sun rises, he can just make out a dark line emerging from the murk obscuring the distant horizon—Ireland! Back in his cabin he sleeps through most of the day.

The morning of July 7 the *Washington* docks at Le Havre. The Ford is clumsily unloaded, again with chains and hooks, and by the time it is back on terra firma, all four fenders are dented and scratched. Jack roars away at the wheel, heading for Rouen at high speed. All his life, he will be a demon driver, relying on superb reflexes to slam on the brakes just in time or swerve out of danger and miss collisions by inches. Rouen Cathedral is much bigger than he expects, and there is a fair to wander around, savoring the atmosphere, that night.

Next day he accelerates down the fast, straight roads that cross northeastern France to Rheims, where there is an even bigger and more famous cathedral. Billings is a keen student of art and architecture and is thrilled to be here. What fascinates Jack is the cathedral's Gothic façade—all thin, solemn saints and exquisite stone tracery, it still bears the scars of German artillery from twenty years earlier.

Driving south from Rheims, they reach the famous Chemin des Dames, a line of hills that rise suddenly from the northern plain, a terrain feature that looks almost impregnable to attack from below. Yet in March 1918 the Germany Army had silently, swiftly scaled the hills in the middle of a foggy night and from these heights launched one of the most dramatic offensives of the war.

What interests Jack even more than the Chemin, however, is the huge American war memorial at Château-Thierry, thirty miles farther south. Arriving at dusk, after the monument's cemetery has been locked, he and Billings climb over the gate, but barking and snarling rudely interrupt their reverent tribute to seven thousand young Americans dead for their country. They are chased around the headstones and out of the cemetery by a ferocious guard dog.

At nearly every town where he and Billings stop during this vacation, and refusing to be deterred by his shaky grasp on French, Jack Kennedy asks the people he encounters what they think of Roosevelt, and do they expect another war? He recoils at the mustard and garlic flavor of their replies; their body odor has weakened his esteem for the entire Gallic race by the time he reaches Paris on July 10.

Three days later there is a Mass scheduled at Notre Dame. The great cathedral is sure to be crowded because this Mass will be officiated by Eugenio Pacelli, the cardinal whom the entire Catholic world is nearly certain has been earmarked by God and the Vatican to become the next Pope. The faithful can almost catch a whiff of smoke borne backward from the future.

Carmel Offie, assistant to the American ambassador to France, arranges for Jack to sit near the altar. He finds himself in the same row as the President of France. Billings has to sit far back, seeing nothing except rows of heads immediately in front of him and catching fleeting glimpses of tiny figures in colorful robes moving about in the distance. An unexpected and powerful appreciation of the quasi-magical force of ancient rituals transfixes Jack Kennedy. He finds himself responding emotionally to the majesty of the ceremony, in a setting magnified by History and made imperishable, even if every stone were to vanish, by Hugo.

The next day he and Billings visit the Paris Exposition. Kennedy finds it uninteresting except for the display of modern aircraft. They fascinate him, for in them is an immanent power—they carry the future of war, the future of the world, his future, too, on their polished aluminum wings. Before leaving the Paris Expo, he and Billings have their silhouettes drawn on cards in black ink by an artist who signs himself "H. Nolden. Silhouettist."

Most evenings in Paris he and Ann Reed go to see a movie, but this night he and Billings join the enormous crowd that is singing and dancing in the streets under lights strung from the trees. It is Bastille Day. While around him in the happy night all Paris is *en fête,* Jack meets up with some American friends at Harry's Bar and does the artistically correct thing—gets slightly drunk on champagne. "Pretty interesting evening," he scrawls in his diary back at his hotel. The laconic entry of the tired reveler, crawling into bed as dawn breaks.

Over the next few days, he visits the Louvre, Les Invalides and Napoleon's Tomb and ascends the Eiffel Tower with a protesting, reluctant Billings—"Think of it as a kind of hill," says Jack. To Billings's relief, the tower has an elevator. Having hit the main tourist sites, Jack returns to the Expo to stare at the airplanes some more.

On July 17 he and Billings drive to Chartres, stopping at Versailles along the way. He scoffs at the fourteen-room Petit Trianon as "Marie Antoinette's idea of roughing it," heedless in his self-satisfaction to the fact that the place he calls home is a fifteen-room house roughly the same size and not remotely as pretty. But perhaps his reaction isn't surprising. He is too young and too male to know how to react to exquisite taste in anything but a coarse way. That will change, but not for years.

The next day he and Billings drive from Chartres to Orléans. Following Mass, he walks around the town, a place imperishably linked to Joan of Arc. He feels cheated—big name, dull place. That afternoon, however, arriving at Chambord, he is thrilled: "Quite a sight."

This "hunting lodge" built for François I four hundred years earlier could accommodate two thousand people, but the roof is its most striking feature. He ascends the broad staircase and is intrigued to find the structures that cover the roof are a representation of a typical village circa 1500, carved entirely from dark gray slate.

Driving on to Amboise that evening, he and Billings find a fair in town —more lights in the trees, more dancing in the streets, more late-night revelry. Back in his cheap hotel room, he records this day's events in his diary, and as he draws to a close, he remembers something else. He writes, "Mother's birthday." Then he gets down on his knees, says his prayers and climbs into bed.

In the morning he and Billings visit the château of Amboise and stare into the Well of the Conspirators ("Where 1500 died," the impressed but disapproving Jack Kennedy informs his diary).

Afterwards they drive on to Chenonceaux. It seems to Jack, as to countless others, the most beautiful and interesting of all the châteaux of the Loire.

Stopping that night in Angoulême, their great discovery is a decent hotel costing a mere ten francs a night. "Very impressed by the little farms we have been driving through," he notes. There was a tidiness and neatness about them, even though the people in this area were poor. "Americans do not realize how fortunate they are. These people are satisfied with very little. . . ."

From Angoulême he and Lem drive rapidly to St. Jean de Luz, a Basque town close to the Spanish frontier. Here they will spend several days at a villa owned by a Harvard classmate's family. Jack goes to the beach in the morning, plays tennis or boules in the afternoon, watches movies in the evening. To see and hear Gary Cooper speaking (dubbed) French leaves him in stitches.

The civil war has been ravaging Spain for more than a year, and the town is filling up with Falangist refugees. Since leaving Paris, Jack has been reading P. G. Wodehouse in search of amusement and John Gunther's *Inside Europe* in search of understanding. Gunther's book is strongly anti-Fascist, anti-Nazi and anti-Franco. Kennedy finds he has little sympathy with the Francoists, who are trying to overthrow a democratically elected government by force. Yet the legitimate government is so torn by infighting, he knows Franco will win the war.

During their stay in St. Jean de Luz, Kennedy and Billings make the short trip to Biarritz to see a bullfight. "Very interesting," he decides, "but very cruel, specially when the bull gored a horse." The crowd had responded with raucous hilarity at seeing the poor creature run out of the ring with its entrails dragging in the dust. Jack was disgusted. The people in this part of the world—French and Spanish alike—are capable of any atrocity, he tells himself. His angry judgment is not tempered by the fact that in French bullrings, the bull is tormented but not killed, unlike in Spain.

Nor does his disdain for cruelty prevent him from buying a pair of *garrochas* as souvenirs. (*Garrochas* are the lances that the mounted picadors drive deep into the large hump of muscle around the bull's neck to goad it into aggressive charges.) A tourist has a tourist's needs, and by this time, he and Billings are already shod in the local footwear, handmade Basque sandals called espadrilles, which they will wear every day for the rest of their trip.

On July 27 he and Billings drive on to Toulouse, stopping at Lourdes along the way. The town is crowded with the sick seeking good health, "but things seemed to become reversed [for] Billings," who appeared in good health before arriving in Lourdes only to fall ill as they departed.

Jack passes much of the two days they spend in Toulouse reading *Inside Europe.* His thinking on the Spanish civil war has moved on: maybe I was too influenced by the Francoists we met in St. Jean de Luz, he tells himself. They talk about it as though the civil war was a fight between Spaniards, but they are wrong. The outcome depends on Germany, Italy and the U.S.S.R., all of whom have intervened, while Britain and France have not only stood back but put an embargo on arms for the legitimate government. Spain, Jack now realizes, is only a pawn—bleeding, tragic, suffering the usual humiliations of the pawn—in a much bigger and bloodier game.

From Toulouse, they head for the walled city of Carcassone, one of the most memorable man-made sights in the Western world. They pause for a couple of hours to look at the walls, and Jack can't help showing off. He climbs hand over hand down the ancient, crumbling brick face of a wall fronting a moat. Billings takes a photograph that shows Jack hanging precariously by fingers and toes with a drop of about fifty feet into the waterless moat yawning below. Billings labels this picture, once developed, "Human Fly."

After covering 350 miles in a single day, they reach Cannes at nightfall on July 30. This is Jack Kennedy's first glimpse of the Riviera, and he is entranced. It is a place he will return to many times. "A much different France here than the poverty stricken France through which we drove," he notes warmly.

Two days later he and Billings reach the Italian border and have to endure a two-hour opera-buffo performance of form-filling, stamping, questioning and intense peering by seedy-looking officials trying to make it clear that it is a great privilege to be allowed to enter Fascist Italy. As they drive into Milan, they see pictures of Benito Mussolini everywhere. But, Kennedy wonders, "How long can he last without money? And is he liable to fight when he goes broke?"

He and Billings visit Milan's vast, imposing cathedral, and at a small church on the edge of town, they gaze at da Vinci's dank and crumbling *Last Supper.* After driving on to Piacenza, he finally finishes *Inside Europe.* "Gunther seems to be more than partial to Socialism and Communism and a bitter enemy of Fascism," he notes. But one crucial question hadn't been addressed: "What are the evils of Fascism as opposed to Communism?"

The morning of August 4, as they check out of their hotel in Piacenza, the woman who runs it accuses Billings of tearing up a towel and stuffing part of it into the toilet. At least fifty hotel clients and staff rush into the tiny reception area to witness the proprietress denounce, in vehement, musical Italian, Billings the vandal, the uncultured American, the towel ripper. Kennedy pushes 50 cents in lire into her hand for a new towel and they leave, hurriedly, for Pisa.

Along the way they pick up a German named Krause, a young man who loathes Hitler. He tells them there *will* be a war, because nothing can stop Germany from attacking Russia. Driving on towards Rome, Kennedy picks up another German to sit in the backseat alongside Krause, this one called Martin. In Pisa they climb the steps to the top of the Leaning Tower and cast oblique glances over at the red-tiled roofs of the picturesque town.

During the afternoon of this day, August 5, something happens that will change Jack's life profoundly. Thirty miles north of Rome, the road runs close to an attractive beach. Jack has swum in the Loire during the drive across France. Now he wants to swim in the Mediterranean, sea of history, poetry and legend. He drives off the road and across the beach, almost to the water's edge, changes into a pair of shorts and plunges in.

He has suffered numerous ailments before, but never any problems with his back. There is an underlying weakness, though. His entire left side is smaller than the right. The left shoulder, for example, is lower than the right; his left leg is half an inch shorter than the right, giving him an uneven gait. The result of all this asymmetry is a spine that is slightly twisted and therefore unstable. Yet so long as he doesn't do anything foolish, he could be well into middle age before it becomes a serious problem.

Following the swim, he climbs back into the Ford and tries to drive off the beach, but the tires spin in the sand. He, Billings and the two Germans deflate the tires and start to push the car across the beach. It takes two hours of unremitting effort before the Ford is on the asphalt again. Over the next few days, Jack Kennedy's back will become increasingly stiff and painful.

In Rome they say goodbye to Krause and Martin. The next morning, Jack heads straight for the office of the *New York Times* correspondent, Arnaldo Cortesi, but Cortesi is too busy to see him.

Kennedy and Billings take in the tourist sights of the Eternal City—the Colosseum, St. Peter's Square, Trevi Fountain. At the round, domed Pantheon they confront a pair of huge doors standing twenty feet high. These doors are so heavy, the guide tells them, three men could not move them. Curious, Jack reaches out and pushes them—and they swing shut. "He must have meant three Italian men," Jack says to Billings as they leave, and they burst into laughter.

At the Vatican, Kennedy has a private audience with Cardinal Pacelli, who knows Joe and Rose and asks, in almost impenetrable English, how they are. Kennedy feels moved by what he feels is Pacelli's deep spirituality. "He really is a great man," he tells his diary.

It is wild misjudgment. The future Pius XII will one day be known as "Hitler's Pope." Although the man was no saint, this characterization is unfair. As he rose in the Church's hierarchy, Pacelli agonized over the powerful threats emerging to the Vatican's independence. First Communism, then Fascism, then National Socialism—all of them militant revolutionary philosophies. He was resolute against atheistic Soviet Communism but sought to appease Hitler and Mussolini, much like other political leaders of the time. He compromised too readily and too often with evil; a little man who so devoted himself to the short-term interests of the Church that he failed to fulfill his spiritual duty to the moral demands of an era. One day Jack Kennedy would despise appeasement and appeasers, but not yet.

On August 8, following Mass at St. Peter's—which strikes him as by far the most wondrous sight he's seen in Europe—Jack and Billings drive to Naples, picking up two German soldiers en route, Georg and Heinz.

The temptation to go up Mount Vesuvius at night proves irresistible. Even with its powerful V-8 engine, the Ford strains and groans against the vertiginous slope. Eventually, the four young men stand around the car, enthralled as the slashing fires of minor eruptions break theatrically through the volcano's thin crust; so close they reel from the sudden rush of heat, choke and blink as green mantles of sulfur swirl around them, taste untamed nature in its bitterness and flames and feel that they are somehow bearing up to the challenge—physical and aesthetic—of the forces that buried Pompeii.

It is late when Jack and Billings finally begin looking for a hotel; the two Germans will sleep in the car. After being turned away from several establishments, they finally find themselves in a situation where the Kennedy charm might help. A chambermaid, some years older than they and decidedly on the homely side, comes to the door to tell them the place is full.

In a few words of halting Italian while grasping the chambermaid's rough hands, Kennedy presents their dilemma and gazes into her eyes. She thinks there is a room after all. Billings spends the night in it. Kennedy sleeps with the chambermaid. His diary entry for this day runs, "Went to bed tired but happy!" This is a code that he and Billings have agreed on for the diaries that both are keeping. It means, "Got laid!"

In the morning he and Billings visit Capri and look at the Blue Grotto. "Not blue enough," Kennedy decides. Then they return to Rome with the *soldaten,* in shorts and hiking boots, still occupying the backseat.

Back in Rome, Jack finally gets to talk to the *New York Times* correspondent. Cortesi tells him that a major war is possible, but only because the democratic countries, and the Russians, won't risk a showdown with Hitler by calling his bluff. But the European powers are by now so well prepared for war—unlike the situation in 1914—that no one wants to fight.

Later that day Jack and Billings meet two attractive Italian girls and in the evening take them to the only nightclub in Rome, the Villa de la Rosa. Surmounting the barriers of language, both are able to record, "Went to bed tired but happy!"

Next day, at lunch, they are surprised to see the two girls again. Billings's date of the previous evening demands "carfare." Their dates are not streetwalking prostitutes but two young women who operate in that more complex area where presents are expected in the morning without a discussion in advance. They are offered courteously as, say, money for a taxi, or a dress, or some earrings, minimizing the role of the cash nexus. True to form, Billings either didn't understand or simply failed to show his appreciation.

That matter resolved, they visit the church of St. John Lateran and ascend the steps in traditional style, on their knees. In the morning they set off for Florence, but not without a ferocious argument over their hotel bill. "Left amidst the usual cursing porters," Kennedy tells his diary. Florence proves a big disappointment. The only thing he thinks worth seeing in the whole place is Michelangelo's *David*.

The next day they head for Venice, but by now Jack's back is hurting and Billings has to do more and more of the driving. In Venice, Jack is astonished to discover that there is more than the Grand Canal. There are dozens of canals. In fact, the whole place seems to have been built on water.

On August 16 they drive north to Austria, heading for Innsbruck, and along the road, they stop and pick up a female hitchhiker. When they reach Innsbruck that evening, instead of looking for a hotel, he and Billings decide to stay in the youth hostel where the hitchhiker is bedding down.

This is their first and only experience of a youth hostel, and both are taken aback by the grim, impoverished crudeness that young Europeans—especially males—accept without murmur as they ramble without money around the Old World. The hostel in Innsbruck is jammed with sweating, unwashed international youth, and new arrivals in muddy boots, toting heavy, lumpy rucksacks, bang on the door late into the night.

Leaving their hitchhiker behind, they drive on the next day to Munich. The city is festooned with pictures of Hitler, and Nazi insignia are everywhere. To Kennedy it seems obvious that Hitler has no answer to Germany's fundamental problems—too many people, too few resources, and too many countries arming against German ambitions. Even so, he takes a liking to the Germans, who seem cleaner and more honest than the Italians he is glad to have left behind.

Between Munich and Nuremberg, he buys a dachshund puppy for $8. He calls it "Offie" (for Carmel Offie) and plans to give it to Olive Cawley, his regular girlfriend. Kennedy falls harder for the dog, though, than he has for any girl. He praises Offie's great beauty to his diary and has himself photographed sitting on the front fender of the Ford, tenderly and proudly holding up Offie for emulsion's posterity, then he sneezes.

As he and Billings drive across southern Germany, Jack starts looking for another dachshund of equal prettiness, but although he looks at many, none compares. Offie isn't an ideal traveling companion, however. As puppies will, Offie defecates and urinates as the urge strikes him, which is often. The Ford's seats and carpets accumulate small brown stains and reek of urine.

Jack is feeling wretched. He is in such agony from his back that he has bought a supportive belt, but he can no longer drive. Billings does all the driving now. And as he shifts uncomfortably in the car, Jack cannot stop sneezing. His eyes are rheumy, his sinuses pouring. It feels almost like drowning.

In Amsterdam he visits a doctor who administers a few tests and tells him he's allergic to dog dander. Offie will have to go. Driving to the Hague—which he finds dreary beyond words—Jack manages to sell Offie for five guilders.

Crossing into France, he and Billings catch a ferry to England. Joe Jr. and Kick are in London, and Rose is expected to show up soon aboard a liner that will stop at Southampton. On August 27 Jack, Joe Jr. and Kick meet their mother, she sails on to France and Jack returns to London with his brother and sister. The next day he falls seriously ill. He lies in bed for most of that week, back still hurting, body covered with hives, doctors and nurses coming and going.

The dream of escape at the wheel of his Ford, with the road as freedom, with movement as life, has ended in anticlimax. Jack is now back in the world of the Kennedys, where Joe Jr. is the morning and the evening star.[1]

CHAPTER 6

When Worlds Collide

L ooking back, it seems obvious they were going to part in bitterness, yet for several years in the middle of the Depression, they seemed so close they might have been brothers. Joe Kennedy and Franklin Roosevelt had a lot in common, or so it appeared, and many of the New Dealers around the President grew jealous of Kennedy and fumed to see a man like him going in and out of the Oval Office as if he were the most trusted of presidential advisers. Kennedy also had the best press of any New Dealer except Roosevelt. He got on well with journalists, whom he flattered and cajoled, unlike most politicians, who treated them with suspicion. Kennedy found himself praised for his dedication to public service in the ultraliberal *New Republic,* while also appearing on the cover of *Time,* owned by his Republican friend Henry Luce.[1]

In the summer of 1937 Robert Worth Bingham, then American ambassador to the Court of St. James, fell seriously ill. Joe and Rose set their sights on his replacing Bingham.[2]

Kennedy got his friends, such as Arthur Krock and the President's son James—formerly one of Joe's business partners—to press his case. Roosevelt, although at first incredulous, eventually found the idea of forcing the English to accept a toothy, bowlegged, redheaded Irishman as the American ambassador too amusing to resist. "A great joke," he told the doubters. "The greatest joke in the world."[3]

Arriving in England in March 1938, Joe and Rose Kennedy found, to their surprise, that King George VI and Queen Elizabeth were easygoing and friendly. Joe Kennedy discovered in the British prime minister, Neville Chamberlain, a man he both liked and respected. Chamberlain was a successful businessman who had gone broke twice on his way to becoming a millionaire. He was dogged, high-minded and not overly bright.

The fearsome loss of life in World War I had made many British politicians exceptionally cautious. There was also a desire to make amends for the punitive and impossible terms imposed on Germany by the Treaty of Versailles. After Germany quit the League of Nations in October 1934, however, Britain began preparing for another war, which wasn't expected until 1939 at the earliest.[4]

Joe Kennedy did not grasp what the British government was actually doing and made no effort to find out. Instead, he chose to throw what influence he had behind the upper-class dolts, right-wing newspapers and shortsighted plutocrats who continued to promote appeasement because they couldn't resist a sneaking admiration of Hitler.

Joe and Rose returned to the United States at the end of May 1938 for Joe Jr.'s graduation from Harvard. The Harvard faculty, asked by the university president to consider giving the ambassador an honorary degree, pointedly declined. Joe pretended not to care, but he'd felt the edge slide, the point stick.

Kennedy soon shifted his gaze to a prize greater than anything that Harvard's professors could grant him. He began sounding out various old friends about making a run for the White House in 1940. No President had ever sought a third term, and Roosevelt talked as though he was planning to go back to Hyde Park; however, he didn't mean a word of it.[5]

When Joe Kennedy returned to London at the end of July, Europe was on the brink of war. Hitler was threatening to move into Czechoslovakia. Kennedy informed the State Department: "I can't for the life of me see any reason why anyone would want to go to war to save the Czechs." He had missed the point completely, which wasn't saving the Czechs but stopping the Nazis.

One of his visitors during this crisis was Charles A. Lindbergh, whom Kennedy admired. "The English are in no shape for war," Lindbergh assured him. They were hopelessly wedded to the past "and can't realize the change aviation has made."[6]

Lindbergh later wrote a report for Kennedy that asserted, "Germany now has the means of destroying London, Paris and Prague if she wished to do so. England and France together have not enough modern war planes for effective defense or counter-attack." Kennedy promptly transmitted the report to Washington.[7]

Lindbergh's ignorance reinforced Kennedy's. The German Air Force was two thirds the size that it claimed to be, and aircraft production was barely 60 percent of the published figure. Few of the GAF's pilots were fully trained, and there were critical shortages of spare parts. The Luftwaffe itself concluded that the most ambitious military operation it might be able to mount that fall was close air support for the German Army in a short war against Czechoslovakia.[8]

Britain was much stronger militarily than Joe Kennedy and Charles Lindbergh wanted to believe. The Cabinet was confident that if they provoked a war with Germany now, Germany would lose. The British ambassador in Berlin, Sir Neville Henderson, concurred: "Germany would not last more than a number of months."[9]

Even so, Britain could only mount an offensive on the Continent in partnership with France, and the recently installed, unpopular Socialist government in Paris would not risk a confrontation with Germany under any circumstances. Nor were the Czechs willing to fight, even though they had a well-equipped, well-trained army. It is impossible to defend a country that will not defend itself.[10]

In the end, Chamberlain felt he had no choice as a responsible, democratic politician but to meet with Hitler in Munich that October. Supported by the French, he agreed not to contest a German takeover of western Czechoslovakia.[11]

Six months later Hitler tore up the guarantees he'd given at Munich and seized what remained of Czechoslovakia. His next objective was obviously Poland, and Chamberlain pledged that Britain would go to war to defend Poland's continued existence. The Poles would fight.

As these events unfolded, the once close friendship between Kennedy and Roosevelt collapsed. Kennedy believed strongly in appeasing Hitler, while Roosevelt wanted to see Hitler crushed.

Both were amoral men, but Roosevelt's amorality was limited, not a way of life. He was cunning, manipulative, devious, hypocritical and profoundly cynical, but to him these traits were part of the political arts and one of the reasons he found politics interesting.

Even so, politics were also about the kind of country America was, the kind of people Americans were, the kind of President a man could be if he was big enough. At times like this, the roots of democratic government and democratic life reveal themselves as a people's morality, not individual expediency. Roosevelt hadn't spent much time gazing at his moral compass on the way to the White House, but now he was consulting it daily.

Joe Kennedy's world was a different order of creation, a place where hardly anything came down to questions of right or wrong. The ambassador recognized almost nothing beyond self-interest in nations and individuals alike. His world resembled the ocean floor—cold, dark and littered with debris that had at some time represented other people's hopes and desires. All that mattered to him was his family, Joe Jr. most of all.

Roosevelt marveled at just how different he and Joe Kennedy were once fundamental moral issues entered into their relationship. The President told his son-in-law, John Boettiger, that Kennedy was "spoiled at an early age by huge financial success; thoroughly patriotic, thoroughly selfish and thoroughly obsessed with the idea that he must leave each of his nine children with a million dollars apiece when he dies (he has told me that often). . . . To him, the future of a small capitalistic class is safer under a Hitler than under a Churchill. . . . Sometimes I think I am 200 years older than he is!"[12]

Back in London, Joe Kennedy continued to urge Chamberlain to stick with appeasement at almost any price. Roosevelt had not originally intended to keep Kennedy in London long, but now it seemed a good place for him, too far from Washington to make any serious challenge for the presidency in 1940.

Roosevelt began a secret correspondence with Chamberlain's most likely successor, Winston S. Churchill, long a voice in the back-bench wilderness damning appeasement at every turn. The President thereafter ignored Kennedy's reports.[13]

CHAPTER 7

The End of Everything

One day early in September 1937 Jack Kennedy crossed Massachusetts Avenue carrying some of his possessions in his arms. He was moving out of Weld, the freshman dorm on Harvard Yard, and into Winthrop House, down near the river, where the jocks congregated and where Joe Jr., now a senior, was installed.

Jack continued warming the bench at junior varsity football games and was confident of keeping his place on the swimming team, but he knew he would never be a letterman in either sport. Unable to compete on that level, he was doing the next best thing—rooming with a jock.

In Winthrop he lived with Torbert Macdonald, a brawny, good-looking fellow and one of the best football players Harvard possessed. On fall Saturdays, when Torby was out there tearing through opposing teams, Jack was there with him, if only vicariously. Besides, Winthrop House had a touch-football team, run by Joe Jr.[1]

Jack's distinctive, high-pitched laugh sounded regularly across the Yard and could be heard along Winthrop's corridors, yet he rarely cracked a joke. His gift for amusing other students came from his ability to see the absurdities in everyday situations. He poked fun at the incongruities of human behavior or made droll comments on the gap between other people's high-flown rhetoric and their bad behavior. Torby's sense of humor was much the same as his, and when the two of them were on form, other students gathered around, lapping up their repartee.

The driving trip through Europe had brought yet another great leap forward in Jack Kennedy's maturation. He was still a wild driver, well known to the Cambridge and Boston traffic police. That was never going to change. Nor had the spoiled-brat syndrome been banished. The night of the 1937 Harvard-Yale game, he got into a furious altercation with a woman whose automobile he had backed into on a Cambridge street. She later reported him to the Cambridge police, and instead of taking the heat, Kennedy got Billings to claim he had been at the wheel at the time of the accident.[2]

Even so, in his letters to Billings, who managed to hang on at Princeton after losing his scholarship, there was an abrupt decline in juvenile smuttiness, sexual obsession and insulting put-downs of his friend. Those elements were still there, but less frequent now.

When he moved into Winthrop, Jack received a visit from a smiling young black man, George Thomas, who carried a calling card that read "George—Gentleman's Gentleman." He was already looking after the wardrobes of several Harvard students, including Joe Jr.'s. George smoked large, foul-smelling cigars, but despite complaints from his young gentlemen, he refused to give them up. "Good for my asthma," he wheezed. He was a character, and Jack Kennedy and Torby Macdonald hired George as their valet.[3]

Shortly after moving into Winthrop, Jack was invited to join Spee, one of the final clubs. Several of his friends were being rushed by Spee, and they said they would join only if Jack could join with them. The most prestigious of the final clubs—Porcellian and AD—were out of Jack Kennedy's reach. Franklin D. Roosevelt had been rejected by Porcellian, and that still rankled even after he became President. And Joe Kennedy had never been accepted by any of them: another humiliation at the hands of the Brahmins.

For Jack, membership of Spee was enough. It placed him in the university's social elite, a triumph in itself for a Boston Irish boy with a father of dubious reputation. But his chances of getting into Spee were always good, because Joe Jr. was a member. It was Joe Jr., not Jack, who broke through the final club barrier. However glad Jack was to join, he was probably not too happy to be following in his brother's footsteps once again.[4]

The night of December 2, 1937, Jack and seven other young men endured some infantile hazing, swore the requisite quasi-masonic oath that they would guard closely all of Spee's secrets (most of which related to the initiation ceremony itself) and would come to the aid of other club members in time of need, now and forever.

Jack was entitled to wear the dark blue and canary yellow English-style regimental striped tie, which informed the universe that revolves around Harvard Square that here was a Spee man. He abandoned his personalized stationery and began writing home on Spee notepaper, which sported the club's absurd insignia. It was inspired by the coat of arms of Warwick the King-Maker, but instead of a bear rampant boldly clutching a ragged staff, Spee's bear loomed, seeming bemused, over a tree stump.

The Spee Club had only about three dozen undergraduate members at a time, and they took most of their meals together in the club's large, ivy-covered Georgian premises at the corner of Auburn Street and Mount Holyoke. The atmosphere aped that of an English gentlemen's club—dark wood, leather chairs, Hogarth prints, grim wallpaper.

From time to time Jack escaped the socially impeccable stuffiness of Spee and headed for a venue that in the long run was better suited to his interests and temperament—the Stork Club in New York.

Every night saw show-business and sporting celebrities and heavyweight writers such as Ernest Hemingway waved past the solid gold chain that guarded the club's entrance. The owner, a country slicker from Montana, Sherman Billingsley, managed to fill his premises nightly with aspiring models and the best-looking debutantes. They were the magnets that drew Broadway producers, movie stars, gossip columnists and rich college boys out for some free-spending fun. The models, flashing their teeth and their legs, gave the place an air of glamour. The debs gave it class.

Sexually charged pheromones wafted as plentifully through the air as the cigarette smoke circulating around the heavy drapes. Billingsley could not get enough of the debs and the models. Neither could Jack.[5]

Towards the end of the football season, when both the first team and the JV were playing at Princeton, Joe Kennedy came up from the Cape one weekend to watch the games; both sons were playing. There may have been some friendly roughhousing between Jack and the Kennedy chauffeur, but it was asserted more than fifty years later that the chauffeur tackled him and threw him to the ground, producing a serious back injury. Nowhere in Jack Kennedy's extensive—not to say exhaustive—discussions with doctors about his back did he even hint that he had suffered a back injury in the fall of 1937. Nor is it credible that Joe Kennedy would have continued to retain the services of someone who seriously injured any of his children.[6]

Jack's football ambitions ended for a less dramatic reason—not strong enough or heavy enough to stand the gaff. For Joe Jr., too, the 1937 season brought only disappointment. He had never missed a practice session and made the first team, but still did not receive his coveted H.

After sunning himself at Palm Beach that Christmas, Jack returned to Harvard in January, looking as tanned and healthy as ever, and almost immediately was bedridden with influenza. Hardly did he shake off the flu before his irritable bowel syndrome flared up. Jack found himself back in New England Baptist Hospital.

Having failed to diagnose the illness correctly, his doctor, Sara Jordan of the famed Lahey Clinic, proceeded to put him on a diet of hard-to-digest lactic products. From then on, Jack Kennedy ate all his vegetables pureed or creamed. He consumed soup or chowder nearly every day, and if he ate a meat dish, chances were that it, too, was swimming in cream. Dessert was usually vanilla ice cream with chocolate sauce. Dr. Jordan was a gastroenterologist and famous for her hostility to fried foods. But she hardly could have given him worse advice: Jack Kennedy was allergic to milk.[7]

In these years, and for the rest of his life, whenever he felt depressed, Jack Kennedy ate almost nothing. His behavior at such times verged on anorexic and was another reason why he remained thin even into middle age. There were countless lunches and dinners where the only course he ate was dessert.

The new diet did not augur well. As the academic year drew to a close, Jack had to return to the hospital, with his bowels blocked again. He got out in time to sail for Harvard in the competition for the MacMillan Trophy. The Harvard Yacht Club defeated nineteen other college crews to win the Intercollegiate Sailing Championship in the waters off Cape Cod, with Joe Jr. as team leader and JFK as skipper, in June 1938.

Make him skipper of a boat in a sailing competition, and the easygoing, readily laughing Jack vanished. Sailing was the one thing he seemed to lose himself in, when he became unsmiling, demanding and completely indifferent to being cold and wet.[8]

Days after the sailing championship, Joe Jr. graduated, without having distinguished himself either academically or athletically. Nevertheless, his father's greatest hopes still rode on Joe Jr.'s broad shoulders. Jack's big brother had overshadowed him during his first two years at Harvard, but he tried not to show it, tried not to feel it and no longer talked about it to his friends. His illnesses, on the other hand, told their own story of the emotional costs of sibling rivalry, a distant mother and an overpowering dad.

=

When Joe Kennedy returned to London in late July, he took his two eldest sons with him. Joe Jr. was going to work in the embassy for a while before enrolling at Harvard Law School. The Kennedys arrived in England as the Munich Crisis came to a head and the whole of Western Europe seemed to hang in the balance between war and peace. The atmosphere in London was febrile with anticipation.

Sandbags were piled around the doorways of the ministries that line Whitehall. Office windows were crisscrossed with white tape. Helmeted soldiers with bayonets fixed appeared on the streets. Camouflage netting sprouted under the mighty oaks in the major parks, concealing what appeared to be antiaircraft guns.

As he walked through Hyde Park those sunny August days, Jack Kennedy took a close interest in these gun emplacements and was shocked —logs for barrels, plywood for wheels, yet guarded by stern-faced soldiers. Why, he wondered, would a modern country have to resort to such a pathetic pretense of readiness? Where were the real guns? *Were* there any real guns? And, if there were, why weren't they being deployed?[9]

When he returned to Harvard a few weeks later, the Munich Crisis had been resolved with the Germans moving into Czechoslovakia, but those troubling questions remained. He was a junior now, free at last to concentrate on his major field, government. For him, as for millions of college students before and since, this was the great divide. Fulfilling degree requirements in the first two years of college is like paying taxes: doing what the authorities demand of you. Working on the major, however, is where a student gets to pursue his or her own interests and has a chance to show true ability. So it was with Jack Kennedy. The latent seriousness hidden until now behind a grinning jauntiness began to stir.

With the world moving towards war, Joe Kennedy thought his son would get a better, closer look at government in action in London than he could hope for within the peaceful confines of the Yard. Jack applied to spend the second half of his junior year abroad. Permission was granted— provided he increased his academic load and took extra courses during the fall semester. For a true C student, such a burden would have proved crushing and resulted in a downward spiral into D+ territory. In Jack's case, the extra workload merely provided additional fuel for an intellect suddenly sparked into life. He even found the time to sign up at the Stacey College of the Spoken Word for a course in public speaking.[10]

His living arrangements became more interesting and satisfying that fall. He and Macdonald were assigned a suite of rooms in Winthrop House that housed four students. Their new roommates were Benjamin Smith and Charles Houghton, both, like Macdonald, members of the football team. Testosterone heaven.

By this time, Jack's long and ultimately failed pursuit of Olive Cawley's virginity had ended. Back in Cambridge he soon met another beautiful heiress, Frances Ann Cannon, who was much brighter than Olive, witty, outgoing and confident. Every American housewife or hotel manager who bought a Cannon towel was making a small contribution towards this young woman's inheritance. Jack Kennedy's girlfriends were organized along a watershed as old as the hills: there was the kind you could marry, and the kind you screwed then forgot about, and it hardly mattered that his father's millions probably attracted them to him in the first place.

Olive and Frances Ann came from families so rich he never had to question the sincerity of their interest in him. And although he seemed not to have contemplated marrying Olive, Jack was so smitten with Frances Ann that the idea proved irresistible.

Even so, there was a problem—the Cannons of North Carolina were rock-solid Presbyterians. Joe and Rose did not like his taking a serious interest in her; the Cannons were equally unenthusiastic about their beautiful daughter getting involved with a Catholic. But Romeo took Juliet to Harvard football games, paraded her in front of his friends and eventually proposed marriage. She turned him down.[11]

In January 1939 Jack sat his midyear exams and made the dean's list this time with a solid B average. Having done that, and about to head for London, where Joe Jr. was already a big man around the embassy, Jack fell ill. Blocked bowels again; back to the Mayo Clinic. The doctors there changed his diet to something more sensible than the current 100 percent

cholesterol regime the Lahey Clinic prescribed. "Shit is about all I'm getting . . . they have put me on a diet of rice and potatoes," he lamented
plaintively to Billings.[12]

When he checked out of the clinic in February, he headed for New
Orleans, where Frances Ann had gone for Mardi Gras. But this pursuit,
too, ended in failure. She had decided to marry John Hersey, one of the
most promising young writers of his generation, a man only a couple of
years older than Jack but far ahead intellectually and creatively. Invited to
the wedding, Jack declined. "I would like to go," he admitted to Billings,
"but I don't want to look like the tall, slim figure who goes out and shoots
himself in the greenhouse half-way through the ceremony." In the end,
though, he attended the wedding.[13]

Shortly after his arrival in London, English newspapers reported that
young Jack Kennedy had been assigned a job at the embassy as "a glorified office boy," to discover whether he would like a diplomatic career.
The most popular newspaper in Britain, the *Daily Mirror,* ran a photograph of him on his first day at work, March 2, seated at a huge desk,
holding a telephone, immaculately and expensively dressed in a blue pinstripe suit he had just had made. His hero Churchill had a trademark blue
pinstripe suit, but Jack looked better in his. It was superbly tailored, and in
the *Mirror*'s photograph, he looks like he is bridging the worlds of the
diplomat and the lounge lizard.[14]

Dressed in white tie and tails, Jack was presented at court and met King
George VI, who was as affable as shyness and a nerve-racking stutter
allowed. The Queen was charming and gracious. Afterwards he took tea
with Princess Elizabeth (the future Elizabeth II) and flirted lightly with
her. She flirted back. He returned that evening in silk knee breeches that
clung tightly around the crotch and buttocks. He boasted to Billings—"I
looked mighty attractive."[15]

Joe Kennedy's friend in the Vatican, Eugenio Cardinal Pacelli, had
been elected Pope, and Kennedy asked Roosevelt to allow him to represent the United States at the coronation, on March 12, 1939. When Joe
arrived in Rome with Rose and eight of their children, Pacelli offered to
make Joe a papal duke. With his burgeoning ambition to succeed Roosevelt in the White House, he had little choice but to turn it down. He settled, instead, for the Order of Pius IX, an honor usually reserved for heads
of state. This went far beyond the rewards bestowed on an ordinary BCL
—or "Big Catholic Layman," in the private language of American priests.

Still, there were hardly any BCLs as important as Joe Kennedy. He had long been a fruitful source of large donations and was carefully cultivated over many years.[16]

One of the new Pope's first acts was to hold a private Mass for the Kennedy family. Jack felt moved by the splendor of the coronation and was thrilled to receive communion at the hands of a Pope, yet his mind was really elsewhere. Throughout the Kennedys' time in Rome, rumors flowed like the muddy Tiber, saying that Hitler was poised to make yet another dramatic move.

It came on March 15 when his troops took what remained of Czechoslovakia, making a mockery of the Munich agreement. Britain and France reacted with a pledge to defend Poland's borders. "Everyone thinks war is inevitable before the year is out. I personally don't, though Dad does," Jack reported to Billings.[17]

Convinced the war was coming, Joe told Jack to make a tour of the Continent and report his impressions of Europe at this critical time. He flew to France in May and in Paris met a girl—the kind you could meet almost any time at the bar of Georges V—who said she had been the mistress of the Duke of Kent. Like other rich men's tarts of that era, she dripped precious stones—a *poule de luxe* advertising the price of her favors—and carried some cute erotica to amuse and arouse a man. She showed Jack her cigarette case; on the inside was an engraving of Snow White, skirt hiked up around her wasp waist, legs spread wide and all seven dwarves, huge pricks out, stiff and straining, lined up to roger the maiden. If he hadn't been thinking about copulation before, that would get him started.[18]

Traveling through France, he found an atmosphere that was electric with tension. People were asking each other, Why hasn't Hitler attacked Poland? What is he waiting for? "The whole thing is damn interesting," he told Billings.[19]

He traveled across Germany to Danzig, which seemed to have joined the Reich already. There were Nazi symbols everywhere and people clicking their heels, jerking their right arms upwards, barking "Heil Hitler!" Here, too, people talked excitedly about the imminence of war.

Traveling south to Warsaw, he met Polish aristocrats who invited him to spend a night or two at their homes. These turned out to be enormous estates where the boundaries couldn't be seen even from the upstairs windows and white-wigged flunkies appeared and disappeared throughout the house. Dotted around these estates were hamlets where the estate workers lived in what amounted to feudal conditions. These were medieval peasants who, on meeting the well-dressed young foreigner, tipped their hats deferentially with one hand while prodding forward a fresh-faced, apple-cheeked daughter with the other. At night, however, Jack had no need of peasant girls. His bedmate was a Romanian princess he had picked up along the way.[20]

Traveling on to Lithuania, Jack spent several days in Riga, where Irena Wiley, the wife of an American diplomat, persuaded him to pose as an angel for a wooden panel she was carving. His was the youthful face, his the outstretched arms, of a divine being embracing a mournful-looking St. Thérèse of Lisieux. The panel eventually found its way to the Vatican, where it was incorporated into an altar.[21]

He caught the train to Moscow, which he found grim, sinister and depressing. From there he traveled on to Romania, Turkey and the Middle East. He rode a camel in Egypt and visited the Pyramids, went to Palestine and checked into Jerusalem's grandest hotel, the King David. His first night there, Jack was awoken by a bomb exploding on the hotel grounds.

European Jews, fleeing Nazi persecution and desperate to create their own state, were flowing into Palestine, to the fury of the indigenous Arabs. The British had administered Palestine since the breakup of the Ottoman Empire in 1918 and now found themselves caught between two irreconcilable populations.[22]

Always eager to visit tourist sites, Jack visited the rock from which Christ is claimed to have ascended into heaven and the Dome of the Rock mosque where Mohammed supposedly did the same, only better—the prophet was mounted on a white horse. What interested Jack most, though, was the politics of Palestine. He spent hours talking to British Army officers and senior civil servants. On his last night in Jerusalem, the ancient city was rocked by thirteen bomb explosions in Jewish neighborhoods.[23]

Jack Kennedy was struck by the competence and intelligence of the British officers and civil servants he met, but was convinced the policy they were implementing was doomed to fail. The British tried to treat both sides impartially, he informed his father. But "the necessary thing is not a solution just and fair but a solution that will work." To him, that meant partition.

The Arabs were never going to agree to partition. Had he spoken to Arab leaders, he soon would have found that was so. Here was what appeared to be a well-reasoned report, one that Joe Kennedy probably considered an excellent piece of work, and it was—for a college junior. It was, nonetheless, a true reflection of the young man who wrote it—impressive surface, nothing much yet underneath.[24]

When he arrived back in England in June, Jack found Torbert Macdonald already there, fresh off the boat, his junior year at Harvard completed and preparing to compete in a track meet. Torby finished third in the two-hundred-yard dash. By now, Jack knew many titled and wellborn people his own age. With Torby in tow, he visited country houses, attended parties and diplomatic receptions and pursued debutantes. "It's all darn good fun," he wrote Billings. "Never had a better time."[25]

And yet his mind remained stubbornly fixed on the only question that mattered now. Wherever he went in England, people said the war would begin between August 20 and September 8. He told them he did not think there was going to be a war, but with how much conviction?

At the end of July he returned to the Continent, taking Torby with him. They headed for Paris, picked up a rental car and set off for the Riviera, where Joe and Rose were vacationing at the Hôtel du Cap d'Antibes, owned by Joe's friend Andre Sula. Joe told Sula, "When I am called back, you will know that war is imminent."[26]

Driving across central France with his usual abandon, Jack lost control of the car, flipping it over. It skidded along on its roof before coming to a halt, surrounded by its occupants' scattered belongings. Upside down in the inverted small automobile, Jack remarked calmly, "Well, pal, we didn't make it, did we?"[27]

He had injured his back once again and wore a back support for the rest of the trip. Nevertheless, pain and discomfort did not deter Jack Kennedy from buttonholing people wherever he went and more or less grilling them. "Jack could never get enough of third-class trains and small hotels, throwing an endless stream of questions at everyone we met. He wasn't satisfied with official answers. He tackled peasants, soldiers, business-men; anyone who'd talk to him," Macdonald told their Harvard classmate Lawrence Lader.[28]

From the Riviera they went into Italy, traveled north to Austria and then east to Prague. In Munich they met up with a Rhodes scholar and football all-American whom Jack had met a few months earlier in London, Byron "Whizzer" White. The reception the three young Americans received from ordinary Germans was ominous—their car was stoned because it bore English license plates.

On August 21 they reached Berlin and two days later drove back into

France. That night Hitler and Stalin agreed to a pact between Germany and the Soviet Union to carve up Eastern Europe between them. Nothing now stood in the way of a German invasion of Poland.

On August 29 Joe Kennedy hurriedly left the Hôtel du Cap d'Antibes. Jack meanwhile had arrived back in London. On September 1 the Germans invaded Poland. Chamberlain sent an ultimatum to Hitler to pull back or face war with the British Empire. No one believed the Germans would cave in. Joe Kennedy called the White House. "The party is on," he told Roosevelt.[29]

Shortly before midday on Sunday, September 3, as church bells rang across London to mark the start of religious services, Joe and Rose, Joe Jr., Jack and Kick filed into the small, narrow Strangers' Gallery overlooking the green leather benches of the House of Commons.

Shortly after noon Chamberlain declared that Britain was now at war with Germany. While his father reflected somberly that this war justified his belief in appeasement, Jack was riveted not by the mournful, obviously depressed Chamberlain but by the spirited, stocky figure of Winston Churchill, breathing defiance.

"The storms of war may blow and the lands may be lashed with the fury of its gales, but in our own hearts this Sunday morning there is peace," growled Churchill, to shouts of "Hear! Hear!" and the waving of order papers. "This is not a question of fighting for Danzig or fighting to save Poland. We are fighting to save the whole world from the pestilence of Nazi tyranny. . . . It is a war, viewed in its inherent quality, to establish, on impregnable rocks, the rights of the individual, and it is a war to establish and revive the stature of Man. . . ."[30]

Here was a language that meant nothing to Joe Kennedy. To Jack, however, it was speech that combined poetry with politics, a language so exalted it reached the level of the great, historic drama of the moment. He wanted to be able to speak like that himself one day.

Back at the embassy, Joe Kennedy called Washington, and when Roosevelt came on the line, he repetitiously lamented, "It's the end of the world. The end of everything. The end of the world . . . everything. . . ."[31]

Some hours later, shortly before midnight on September 3, a German U-boat sank the British liner *Athenia,* carrying twelve hundred passengers from Liverpool to New York. One hundred and twelve people perished, twenty-eight of them Americans. The bedraggled and terrified survivors were taken to Glasgow. In this emergency, Joe Kennedy sent Jack and

Eddie Moore to reassure the Americans among them that their government would get them home safely.

Jack, in his pinstriped blue suit, visited the injured in hospitals and met with the rest in a large hotel, telling them, "The government has plenty of money for you all." But it wasn't replacement clothing or new luggage that was on their minds—they demanded a naval convoy to get them home. Amid the clamor, a young woman called out, "We defiantly refuse to go until we have a convoy. You have seen what they will do to us." There were shouts of approval.

Taken aback, Jack Kennedy tried to reassure the survivors on that point, too. There was an American liner due to sail the next week, with room for more passengers. "You will be safe in a ship flying the American flag. Under international law, a neutral ship is safe."

They shouted him down. He seemed to have forgotten that U-boat attacks on neutral shipping had pushed the United States into World War I. He had forgotten, too, that the U-boats were eventually defeated by the convoy system. A single ship on the open sea was irresistible to U-boats, because any neutral flag it was flying would be assumed to be false. Jack left Glasgow for London that night. None of the people he sought to reassure seemed reassured. His first venture into personal diplomacy had failed.[32]

The school of government at Harvard was new. Established in 1936, it was going to count Jack Kennedy among its first graduating class. The faculty consisted largely of young professors with careers to be forged. Eager to prove the intellectual value of their discipline, they were exactly the kind of open-minded, enthusiastic teachers that Jack Kennedy needed. More than half of that first class in the Department of Government wrote an honors thesis, something that in long-established departments such as English or History was limited to young men who were Phi Beta Kappa material, not those cruising the shallow waters of C+.

Jack arrived back at Harvard towards the end of September, slightly delayed but cloaked in the glamour of youth fresh from a war zone. He completed four of the standard courses in government that fall, while around him Harvard rang with furious debates over American intervention.

Joe Jr. was back at the law school and wasted no time organizing a branch of the fiercely isolationist America First movement. Many Harvard students, like Joe Jr., reflected the national consensus that American involvement in World War I had been a terrible mistake, one that their generation had a responsibility to avoid repeating.

For Jack Kennedy, it was not so simple. His love of things English, especially the English language and English history, had only been deepened by his travels there. His political and literary hero was, and would remain, Winston Churchill, a man who had led the most adventurous life imaginable and been at the heart of great events for nearly fifty years.

At the same time, Jack was still his father's son, and it showed. He wrote an editorial for the Harvard newspaper, *The Crimson*. Titled "Peace in Our Time," his ideas amounted to little more than a variation on the siren song of capitulation he had heard countless times from his father: Britain was finished. "There is every possibility—almost a probability— of English defeat," he wrote. Germany was the rising power in the world. Hitler was a gangster, but given a free hand in Eastern Europe, he would be willing to make a deal. Jack thought Roosevelt was the person to mediate an end to the current war. Britain and France would have to give up some of their colonies, "But if Hitler can be made to disarm, the victory would likewise be great for the democracies." His program amounted, in effect, to surrender in our time and would produce a Europe completely controlled by Nazis, with Britain and France as puppet states of the Third Reich. After this piece appeared in the newspaper, he was elected to the *Crimson*'s board, an accolade almost on a par with being chosen for Spee.[33]

Meanwhile, he was discussing with his tutor, Assistant Professor Bruce Hopper, a potential senior honors thesis. Once a week he got the benefits of an hour-long tutorial in Hopper's study, an elegant oak-paneled setting with leather armchairs, a large fireplace and a Latin inscription draped across one wall. To those who could read it, the inscription said, "It will give you pleasure to look back on this scene of suffering."[34]

Like most Harvard faculty members, Hopper believed in aiding Britain and France, and doing so at the risk of being dragged into the war. An Army veteran of World War I, Hopper had an éclat that Jack Kennedy could never resist, that of the combat veteran.

Another professor might have encouraged this average student to choose a small topic, something not too demanding. Most of Jack's twenty-two classmates who were submitting honors theses in government had selected topics that were not only intellectually exiguous but depressingly safe—"The McNary-Haugen Farm Relief Bill" . . . "The Massachusetts Emergency Finance Board" . . . "The Boston Registry of Motor Vehicles" and so on. Hopper readily accepted Jack Kennedy's proposal to take a big, hard-to-document topic and produce a thesis called "Appeasement at Munich."

In February 1940, at the start of the next semester, Jack began work on his thesis. Here, finally, was his chance to try to figure out why the British had been so unprepared for a showdown with Hitler that they placed fake guns in Hyde Park in August 1938. As he worked, he received dozens of books on world affairs shipped to him from London by diplomatic pouch, books that had been recommended by leading British academics, such as *Pacifism and the Left Wing* and *The Twenty Years' Crisis*.

The dominant forces in his thinking, however, were not the books he read, nor his Harvard professors, but Churchill and Lindbergh. Churchill had repeatedly demanded a bigger, more powerful Royal Air Force every year from 1932 to 1939. He had criticized every program for new aircraft production as being too little and too late and regularly warned that the Luftwaffe either was, or was on the verge of becoming, powerful enough to blast the RAF out of the sky.[35]

In April 1939 Jack Kennedy had met Lindbergh and his petite writer wife, Anne Morrow Lindbergh, when they came for lunch at the embassy in London. They were, a thrilled Jack thought, "The most attractive couple I've ever seen." Lindbergh pontificated as usual on the pathetic military weakness of the British, especially in the air, and he was so dazzling and persuasive a personality that it never would have occurred to Jack Kennedy to doubt a word he uttered. The arguments and outlook of Churchill and Lindbergh informed virtually every page of Jack Kennedy's senior honors thesis.[36]

He labored on it diligently nearly every day, either in the Winthrop House library or over at the Spee Club; enthralled for once by something that was entirely his own, something that engaged both his quicksilver mind and exuberant spirit. It was also something he had to do, if only because Joe Jr. had written an honors thesis.

Jack's ran to nearly thirty thousand words, twice the usual length. There were 350 footnotes and an annotated bibliography. As undergraduate efforts go, it was both competent and callow. Competent in the energy and seriousness invested in the research; callow in its failure to get beyond the surface and reach the roots of a challenging subject. Working from newspaper accounts and *Hansard,* the official record of proceedings in Parliament, he really hadn't a clue as to the pace, scope or nature of the modernization of the RAF in the 1930s. But then neither had Churchill or Lindbergh.[37]

His thesis depended, too, on ignoring the fact there would have been appeasement over Czechoslovakia however many aircraft Britain possessed. It was France, not Britain, that had provided security guarantees to the Czechs, but French governments lacked stability throughout the 1930s. In 1938 an unpopular Socialist and quasi-pacifist government led by Léon Blum had come to power in Paris. Blum was prepared to tear up those guarantees rather than risk war with Germany. On its own Britain could not have deterred Germany even had it rearmed as Churchill and Jack Kennedy proposed. All the same, undergraduates are not expected to be right about complex questions; it is an educational success when they are willing to work as hard as he did on trying to unravel an important and controversial issue.

As he wrote his thesis, Jack was also being treated for "mild, nonspecific urethritis." Urethritis in a man has symptoms that resemble those of gonorrhea: yellow-green discharge and an intense burning sensation in the head of the penis during urination.[38]

Most urinary tract infections are transmitted sexually, yet many are due to *E. coli* bacteria. These bacteria thrive in the bowels, but it is not unusual for them to appear in the urethra. *E. coli* bacteria are normally flushed out of the urinary tract during urination, but a slightly enlarged prostate provides sufficient obstruction to allow them to form colonies. The result is an infection.

As Jack Kennedy's medical records later showed, he had an enlarged prostate even as a young man. His urethritis fits a well-established pattern, and despite an exceptionally busy sex life, no record shows him being diagnosed as having gonorrhea. His naval medical record repeatedly states "No history or evidence" of venereal disease.[39]

His urethritis cleared up with the help of sulfa drugs, but for him, as for many patients with urinary tract infections, both the painful burning on urination and prostatitis remained, a common legacy of the condition in men.

In typical fashion, he finished his thesis with a furious burst of energy, dictating to five stenographers and handing it in at the very last minute.

Much of his life was like this—a frantic rush from one project to another, one place to another, always hurrying, often late.

The grade he received for "Appeasement at Munich" was magna cum laude. This, combined with much improved grades in his coursework, pulled his grade average on graduation up to a respectable B. Best of all, perhaps, Joe Jr. had only received a cum laude for his honors thesis on the decision of the Western democracies not to intervene in the Spanish civil war. "It seems to represent a lot of work," Joe Jr. told his father after reading Jack's thesis, "but it does not prove anything."[40]

Shortly before he graduated, Jack had his photograph taken with the rest of the *Crimson* staff. In the published photograph, three rows of Harvard men are standing; one row is seated. Forty-nine faces turn eagerly towards the camera. One, JFK's, stares fixedly *away*. He won't be just another face in the crowd.[41]

At commencement in June 1940, Jack Kennedy received his Bachelor of Science in Economics wearing his Spee Club tie, a black graduation gown and a pair of stained, disreputable-looking saddle shoes. He had finally achieved what he had once stated was his greatest educational ambition, to enjoy "the distinction of being a Harvard man." Even so, he remained what he always had been—different and, as is true of all those who really *are* different, slightly apart.

CHAPTER 8

Jack Intermezzo

Only one career had ever appealed—to be a writer—and his honors thesis just might be a first step towards the writer's life. There was a freedom in being a writer that nothing else offered, a chance to pursue his own ideas wherever they might take him, to be truly himself. Almost as soon as he had finished "Appeasement at Munich," Jack showed it to his father's friend Arthur Krock of *The New York Times,* by then the winner of two Pulitzer Prizes (and eventually the winner of four).

Krock assured Jack his thesis was solid enough to be turned into a book. "Appeasement at Munich" was out, though. Why not call it *Why England Slept*? said Krock. It would stand then as a kind of American counterpart to Winston's Churchill's famous criticism of British appeasement, called "While England Slept."[1]

Beyond getting his thesis published as a book, Jack had no idea what he wanted to do. In the 1940 *Crimson* yearbook, where he was asked to state what he would do after graduation, Jack had put down "Law School." But Harvard Law School, where Joe Jr. was studying, was simply unthinkable. If he did go to law school, he might apply to Yale, but he really had no desire to study law.

Stuck in this quandary, barely a month after graduating from Harvard, he fell ill once more—almost predictably so—with blocked bowels. His abdomen swelled and he endured once again the stabbing pains in his intestines. Dropping all thought of applying to Yale, he headed instead for Rochester, Minnesota.[2]

Jack checked in to a hotel while he submitted as before to enemas and rectal probing, puzzled doctors and the pretty, attentive nurses in starched white linen at the famed Mayo Clinic. The Mayo's doctors put him back on a diet of rice and potatoes; an improvement over the ice cream and milk shake regimen Sara Jordan had prescribed, but he didn't care for the change—"It ain't too appetizing," he complained to his father.[3]

He didn't like Rochester, either, but he could divert himself by working on his book, which was being revised by Krock in New York and by Harvey Klemmer, one of Joe Kennedy's aides in London. As soon as a publisher agreed to take it, Joe persuaded Henry Luce to write an introduction for *Why England Slept.*[4]

The manuscript was being rushed into print while it was still topical, and Jack was invited to talk about his book on a Rochester radio station. He wrote out parts of what he wanted to say in advance, preparing himself almost as if this were an exam.

The interviewer wanted to know where the idea for the book had come from, and Jack recalled walking through London's parks during the Munich Crisis and seeing the dummy guns. Criticism of Munich, he said, was aimed at the pact. But it was not the government that was to blame—it was the British people. They were still too psychologically scarred by the trauma of World War I to respond effectively to the dangers of another war.

The Germans had taken advantage of this situation not by producing a mountain of armaments, he told his listeners, but by shaping their entire economy around war production. For example, there was a new automobile plant to build a "People's Car," or Volkswagen. But it could as easily turn out engines for airplanes as for automobiles.

Jack had anticipated most of the questions he'd be asked, and as he read out his prepared answers on modern aviation—"Tools are the bottleneck of aircraft production"—he sounded knowledgeable and confident. When he didn't have a reply ready, however, he groped. "The . . . uh . . . we . . . er . . . must realize that . . . uh . . . we must always keep our armaments equal to . . . um . . . our commitments. Munich should . . . er . . . should teach us that" was one of his less polished replies.[5]

When it was published in August 1940, *Why England Slept* drew enthusiastic reviews, partly because it seemed so precocious, but mainly because it seemed so timely. The fall of France in June 1940 had shocked countless Americans into recognizing that this was not just another dispute between the eternally squabbling Europeans but a struggle for the soul of Western civilization.

With public opinion galvanized by that new awareness, Roosevelt and the military were already mobilizing the economy for war. The President was also pushing public opinion to support aid to Britain even at the risk of being drawn into the conflict. As he did so, he received a gift of *Why England Slept,* suitably inscribed by the author.[6]

In London, Joe Kennedy was doing all he could to make Jack's book a success, persuading author and diplomat Harold Nicolson to write the introduction to the British edition. Yet Joe's ambassadorship was putting a strain on the relationship between the two countries. American diplomats and military attachés posted to London were told by the State Department to provide the British with moral support; that was the least one democratic country could offer another in such a desperate hour. Throughout the summer of 1940 Joe Kennedy chose, instead, to tell almost every British politician and diplomat he knew that their country was doomed, the struggle hopeless. They had better quit now and accept whatever terms Hitler was offering.[7]

As Americans debated national defense and the British looked eagerly at American books for indications that the United States might soon enter the war, *Why England Slept* had a topicality on both sides of the ocean that guaranteed sales. Joe Kennedy was suspected of buying up thousands of copies to get it onto the best-seller list. The book would have been successful even without that.

At this distance, the most striking feature of *Why England Slept* is how wrong—and wrongheaded—it is. If Jack Kennedy can be faulted here, so can his professors. They approved his work without knowing any more about the relationship among British public opinion, rearmament and appeasement than he did.

Chamberlain's appeasement policy—which Jack deplored and Joe Kennedy admired—was only half the story. The other half was that although Chamberlain had sought to avoid war with Germany in 1938, as chancellor of the exchequer from 1932 to 1937, he had unfailingly supported a rearmament program designed to defend Britain's skies and repel any German invasion. If that strategy succeeded, the coming war would last for years and probably end in a German defeat, which was what had happened in 1918.

Little of this thinking appeared in the newspapers or the parliamentary debates of the time. The government did what it believed was right and wisely said as little as possible about military planning, despite repeated attacks from its fiercest critic, Winston Churchill.

British rearmament can be said to have begun in earnest in May 1933, when detailed design work began on the Rolls-Royce Merlin engine. Powered by this engine, the Spitfire prototype flew in March 1936. It was a pure air-superiority machine, faster and more maneuverable than the best German fighter under development, the Me-109. The Royal Air Force's other frontline fighter, the Hurricane, was a rugged, inexpensive aircraft capable of taking on the German bombers and twin-engine escort fighters. Delivery of Hurricanes began in 1937, Spitfires in 1938.

Meanwhile, Fighter Command was established in July 1936 under Air Marshal Sir Hugh Dowding, who began pushing the development of the world's first radar sites. Early-warning radar was integrated with Dowding's forward airfields. The Royal Air Force was striving to achieve technological superiority in the air by 1940, but even as early as the fall of 1938, the time of the Munich Crisis, Britain had the means to defend itself against any German air offensive and could defeat an attempted invasion.[8]

Yet according to *Why England Slept,* the British moved so slowly they failed to take full advantage of the year of grace that the Munich Pact provided. In truth, during the year following Munich, Spitfires, Hurricanes and fully trained pilots flowed into Fighter Command's forward squadrons, and the network of radar sites began operating.[9]

The rearmament strategy that Britain pursued in the 1930s was aptly and accurately characterized by Churchill in June 1940—"Hitler must break us in this island or lose the war." Forever identified with appeasement, Chamberlain nevertheless was one of the architects of Britain's ability to stand up to Hitler when appeasement failed. The British had done a better job of rearming their Air Force than the Germans. The Battle of Britain, which came to a climax in September 1940, just as *Why England Slept* hit the best-seller lists, vindicated Britain's preparations for war and denied Hitler the only kind of conflict he was prepared for—a short one.[10]

Jack Kennedy never acknowledged that British rearmament policy had been realistic and successful. Instead, like Lindbergh, most of his professors and, indeed, an entire generation of scholars and commentators, he believed unquestioningly that a Germany armed with overwhelming air power had forced a militarily weak and politically spineless Britain into appeasing Hitler in 1938. The Munich myth (weak leadership + air-power gap = appeasement of dictators) shaped Jack Kennedy's thinking about defense policy and international relations for the rest of his life.[11]

The second reason *Why England Slept* was important is this: like most first books, it was, in effect, autobiographical. The tale it told was of weakness and irresolution leading inevitably to a crisis. By refusing to make the necessary sacrifices in time, the British had brought themselves to the brink of annihilation. Only heroic exertion, a rallying of the spirit and the intellect, could stave off complete disaster. No one else could save them now. They had to find in themselves the courage and willpower to overcome both the external threat and their past mistakes.

His book concludes, "With this new spirit alive in England, my story ends. England was now awake; it had taken a great shock to bring home a realization of the enormity of the task it was facing. All the latent energy stored up in England during the last seven years is being expended on a drive for victory. . . ."[12]

He had spent much of the 1930s in and out of the hospital, where he found refuge from the punishing pressures of a domineering father and an overbearing big brother. But now Jack Kennedy had arrived at manhood, he stood at the edge of an existence where he would either carve out an identity for himself and do something worthwhile with his life or become resigned to being a footnote to the glory that was Joe Jr. and an appendix to his father's fame. Jack Kennedy, as one recent scholar remarks, "drew on his research for the facts [of *Why England Slept*] but on his own psychology for its analysis."[13]

Seeking answers to this personal challenge, he continued his voracious reading, especially in history. But he had also developed an abiding love of poetry and surely would have come across "The Gift Outright," by his favorite poet, Robert Frost. Imagine what these two lines would have meant to Jack Kennedy at this point in his life, how they would have seemed almost to be written for him:

> Something we were withholding made us weak
> Until we found out that it was ourselves . . .

It is a day in mid-September 1940 as he drives under the huge eucalyptus trees, past the low brown walls of Stanford University and between its faux Romanesque but charmless buildings. Jack is at the wheel of a 1940 cactus-green Buick convertible with eye-catching red leather seats. He is buying this automobile with the proceeds from his book, and already there is something wrong with it: the clock on the dashboard won't work.[14]

Still, the top is down, the sun is shining, the breeze tousles his mop of light brown hair, and sliding around on the backseat are half a dozen copies of *Why England Slept.* Looming over the campus is a three-hundred-foot tower with a gleaming red-tiled roof. Workmen are disassembling the scaffolding that cloaks this penile construction. As an example of architecture as sculpture, it might pass for an institution dedicated to sex research. It is, in fact, the Hoover Institution on War, Revolution and Peace.[15]

Why is he here? Because he doesn't want to go to law school and can't think of anything better to do. These days, almost the entire country seems unsure and anxious about its future. Jack Kennedy feels much the same regarding his own.

Joe Jr.'s current roommate at Harvard Law is Tom Killefer, a Stanford graduate, and Tom has extolled the beauty of Stanford. During visits to Palm Beach, he also claimed the Florida climate was nothing compared to California's. Jack has used Killefer's boasts as an excuse to come to Stanford and audit some courses in political science and business. He still talks vaguely of heading for Yale Law School a year from now, but there is no hint of enthusiasm.

During the summer, while playing tennis at Hyannis, Jack was serving when he felt as if he'd been knifed from behind. He was in agony from his back and, shortly after this, had to spend ten days in bed at the Lahey Clinic, seeking respite from the pain. Even now, if he drives for long, he becomes stiff and sore. He pulls up in front of a small one-bedroom cottage that he has rented for the fall semester. Here he will live alone, in bachelor squalor, and for the sake of his back he sleeps on a wooden board instead of climbing into bed.[16]

The handsome son of a rich and famous father and author of a recently published, highly praised book, Jack inevitably attracts the attention of *The Stanford Daily* and many of his fellow students. They take to him at once. He has been to so many places and has met so many famous people and has read so much, he is more like a professor in some ways than any student. Yet he is also young, amusing, sociable and fun-loving. And generous, too, freely giving away copies of his book, which he inscribes with an old-fashioned tortoiseshell fountain pen.[17]

Jack Kennedy becomes a big story on campus and gets almost as much coverage in the student newspaper as the university president, Ray Lyman Wilbur, noted educator and close friend of Woodrow Wilson. Wilbur ardently denounces Nazi Germany and criticizes Americans for being too "amusement-mad and provincial" to recognize Hitler for what he is—the source of unmitigated evil. His speeches mean nothing to most Stanford students. They are far more concerned with their undefeated football team than with Hitler. Jack, however, promptly signs up with the Stanford National Emergency Committee, which is promoting American mobilization. Meanwhile, Congress is debating the country's first peacetime draft, something that Stanford students support by a margin of three to one.[18]

Jack begins dating a bright and beautiful redhead from a rich family, Harriet Price, whose vivacious and outgoing nature is captured in her nickname, "Flip." He becomes a familiar sight over at the Pi Beta Phi sorority house, walking through the front door, standing at the foot of the stairs and yelling, "Flip!" From somewhere above her voice floats down—"Just a minute!" Then he goes into the living room, where he sits and chats with the other young men who are waiting for their girls to finish brushing their hair and applying lipstick.[19]

The draft is enacted, and by mid-October local draft boards are ready to start registration. Stanford students are allowed to register on campus, and on October 18, registration day, Jack stands in line with other male students and is registered for the draft by Leland T. Chapin, associate professor of music and drama, and the two of them stand, looking self-conscious, next to a small table as they are snapped for *The Stanford Daily.*

On October 29 the secretary of war, Henry Stimson, puts on a blindfold and draws the first batch of draft numbers, and the event is broadcast over the radio. Millions of young men, including Jack Kennedy, listen intently to the proceedings. The eighteenth number drawn is 2748, and the holder of number 2748 in the Palo Alto area is John F. Kennedy. This gives *The Stanford Daily* an excuse to plaster his picture across its front page for the third time in two weeks.[20]

The photograph shows Jack smiling, when in truth he is deeply upset.

College students whose numbers have been drawn won't be called for their draft physicals before July 1, 1941. They will be allowed to concentrate on their studies and finish the academic year without interruption. Jack's fear isn't that he will be drafted—it's that he won't. "They will never take me in the Army," he despondently tells Billings. "And yet if I don't go, it will look quite bad."[21]

He is, after all, a young man whose book is being touted as a clarion call to America to rearm now. There is also the Dad Problem—for years Joe Kennedy has been dogged by rumors and whispers that he was a cowardly draft dodger during World War I.

Jack continues to pursue a playboy existence, dating not only Flip Price but a brunette stunner named Nancy Burkett. He still drives so fast that he narrowly avoids spectacular accidents on California roads in the shiny new Buick convertible. He becomes well known at local roadhouses and at some of the better restaurants in San Francisco. Yet behind the bravura style that dazzles his fellow students is a turning inner world.

During that fall, as he eases his back in the tub or stretches out on the wooden board in his little cottage, he reads *My Son, My Son!* by the English novelist Howard Spring. This is the story of a rich and powerful man who builds a life around his hopes for his only child. The young man, however, is made arrogant and reckless by his father's wealth and the unscrupulous way his father uses it. In the end, the young man wrecks his own life and dies. Death proves the only escape from the crushing burden of his father's ambitions.[22]

For Jack, reading *My Son, My Son!* is a way of contemplating both his life and Joe Jr.'s. But it is two other books he reads this fall that will change the world, by changing him. The first is Lord David Cecil's *The Young Melbourne*. Ostensibly a biography of William Lamb, Lord Melbourne, before he became prime minister, the book turns out to be about Byron and his tumultuous affair with Melbourne's wife, Lady Caroline Lamb.

The long-dead Byron seems to jump off the page to show Jack Kennedy—as Byron still does for countless people every year—how life might be lived, given talent enough and courage to burn. Out of that brief, hectic, dramatic existence, spurred to mad heights by a lack of love in childhood, had come the Romantic movement. Byron, elected to nothing, had shaken by example the nineteenth century from end to end and inspired great struggles for artistic liberty and individual autonomy. Reckless, incestuous, libidinous, he could make life itself seem to offer little meaning beyond what a Byron knew and a Byron experienced in thirty-seven years.

Byron, with his physical disability—a clubfoot—dragging along in the starry dust of his coruscating passage through an amazed world, was a being that a Jack Kennedy, in pain nearly every day of his life, could embrace as an alter ego; another man—another writer—whose penis was as eager as his pen, yet willing, too, to die for a cause truly noble, the liberation of Greece.

The second book to become a map of Jack Kennedy's hinterland is *Pilgrim's Way,* the autobiography of John Buchan, a man he found easy to admire. Buchan was a polymath, or Renaissance man. Born into a lower-middle-class home in Scotland, he had won a scholarship to Oxford and gone on to be a soldier, historian, diplomat, governor general of Canada, a peer of the realm and the author of a classic thriller, *The Thirty-Nine Steps.*

Buchan's autobiography was less an account of his life than his recollections of some of the highly talented young men of his generation who served, and in many instances died, in World War I. Buchan extolled above all his close friend Raymond Asquith, son of the British prime minister from 1912 to 1916, Herbert Henry Asquith.

Buchan described Raymond Asquith in telling strokes: he had "a fine, straight figure, and bore himself with an easy stateliness. His manner was curiously self-possessed and urbane, but there was always something of a pleasant aloofness, as of one who was happy in society, but did not give it more than a fraction of himself. . . . Not greatly respecting many people, he had a profound respect for his father. . . ."

Asquith was a talented writer, but he wasn't sure what to do with his life and drifted into law, where he was successful without ever feeling fulfilled. "He loved the things of the mind—good books, good talk—for their own sake; he loved, above all, youth and the company of his friends. . . . He disliked emotion, not because he felt lightly but because he felt deeply. . . . Austerely self-respecting, he had been used to hide his emotions under a mask of indifference, and would never reveal them except in deeds."

When World War I began, Asquith got himself commissioned in the Grenadier Guards in order to serve on the Western Front. He was killed in action in September 1915 at the age of thirty-five. "Our roll of honour is long," wrote Buchan, "but it holds no nobler figure. . . . He loved his youth, and his youth has become eternal. Debonair, brilliant and brave, he is now part of that immortal England that knows not age or weariness or defeat."[23]

As he reads these words, Jack Kennedy feels thrilled and excited in a way that is new to him. Until now, he has known only that he cannot live in his brother's shadow. But that can never tell him what kind of man he must be; only what kind he won't be. Here, at last, is a vision he can embrace as a true expression of himself—"Debonair, brilliant and brave." He marks this passage, but it has already gone deep. For the rest of his life, Jack will urge anyone he wants to understand him to read *Pilgrim's Way*, for the light from the star that he begins moving towards shines out from that book.[24]

=

Joe Kennedy's usefulness as an ambassador had ended long before the fall of 1940. He had come to loathe the British, and they in turn despised him. He was not only a defeatist; he also sought safety in the English country-side when the German Air Force that he so admired began bombing London.

The German failure to destroy the Royal Air Force in the Battle of Britain, and the refusal of the British to be bombed into submission by the Germans, confounded his expectations. Rather than admit he had been wrong, he told Jack the Germans weren't really trying. "The boys"—Luftwaffe aircrews flying from bases near the Channel coast—"can make a good many trips" in a single night. The hapless British, on the other hand, "have to go all the way to Berlin and then drop only a few bombs."[25]

While Kennedy slid into irrelevance, the incomparable Edward R. Murrow, the greatest radio journalist in history, was becoming the real American ambassador. His moving accounts of ordinary people standing up to Hitler's war machine—cheerful in defiance, resilient in grief, right without being self-righteous—undermined the arguments of the isolationist America First movement and defeatists such as Joe Kennedy, Joe Jr. and Charles Lindbergh.[26]

The dramatic transformation in American public opinion between the fall of France in June and the November 1940 presidential election seemed to assure Roosevelt of victory. But the President was too experienced a campaigner to take anything for granted. He wanted Kennedy out of London and out of politics but in his corner, if not in his pocket. Even as Jack registered for the draft, Joe Kennedy was on his way home. After a stormy three-hour interview in the White House, he reluctantly endorsed Roosevelt for an unprecedented third term.[27]

Following the election, Kennedy met with three reporters. He thought they were there for an off-the-record backgrounder, but only one of the three had been told that. The other two felt free to report what Kennedy said, which included ridiculing Eleanor Roosevelt and her Jewish friends. He mocked George VI for having a stammer, said "I'd give all I've got to keep us out of the war," announced "Democracy is finished in England" and lavishly praised Charles Lindbergh. As published, the story created a storm of resentment and criticism. His friends, such as Arthur Krock, did what they could to soft-pedal it, but although Kennedy claimed he had been misrepresented, he had to admit the words were his.[28]

Shortly after, Roosevelt announced that Kennedy had resigned as America's ambassador to the Court of St. James. But for the rest of his life, Joe Kennedy insisted that people call him "Ambassador," as if it were a title of nobility, a life peerage, and liked to portray himself as the survivor of 136 air raids.[29]

As 1940 drew to a close, the British were fast running out of money to pay the United States for arms, food and fuel. On November 22, when Joe Kennedy met with the staunchly isolationist Herbert Hoover in the former President's Waldorf Towers suite, he told Hoover there was no point in helping Britain. Every dollar spent was "a bet on a losing horse."[30]

While privately disparaging aid to Britain, Joe continued trying to shake off newspaper attacks on him as an appeaser, a defeatist and an unyielding isolationist. Jack was eager to help, producing in a single day, December 5, a three-thousand-word defense that his father might use. He followed it up with an even more forcefully argued letter the next day.

These are remarkable documents. Anyone reading them without knowing they were from a son to his father would assume they were from father to son. A different Jack had suddenly emerged. He was now the one who held the upper hand, intellectually and morally. It was his father who needed and sought his advice. The confidence that flowed from having published a highly regarded book made it possible; so, too, had the transformation in Jack's idea of himself.

There could be no question of letting Britain go down to defeat for want of American help, he told his father. "If England is defeated, America is going to be alone in a strained and hostile world. In a few years . . .

she even may be on the verge of defeat or defeated—by a combination of totalitarian powers. Then there will be a turning of the people's opinions. They will say, 'Why were we so stupid not to have given Britain all possible aid. Why did we worry about money. . . .' "[31]

At the New Year, the administration submitted legislation to provide military and other kinds of assistance to Britain for two years. This new form of aid was known as Lend Lease, and Joe Kennedy was expected to lead the isolationists' attack on it. Instead, when he made a national radio broadcast on January 18, 1941, he disappointed the America Firsters by pointedly saying nothing against Lend Lease. He did not support it, either, and privately remained an angry man. "I hate all those goddamned Englishmen, from Churchill down," he raged to a fellow passenger on a flight to Palm Beach.[32]

Even so, he had moved—by his standards, a long way—towards accepting his son's arguments that the world, and the war, had moved on from appeasement, isolationism and defeatism.[33]

Jack, relaxing these days at the Palm Beach mansion, was still unsure of what to do with his life. He hadn't found Stanford interesting enough to go back. He continued to toy with the idea of enrolling at Yale Law School, but instead decided to join his mother and Kathleen, who were traveling in South America during the spring of 1941. Jack spent twelve pleasant days aboard a liner, the *Argentina,* heading for Rio. He was one of only three Americans aboard; the rest of the passengers were South Americans returning home. He learned to play a dice game called bidou, passed hours at poolside courting Latina lovelies and submitted cheerfully to the ritual of being dunked in the pool to mark his first transit of the equator.[34]

He returned to the United States towards the end of June, only to find that Joe Jr., having just finished law school, had done the last thing the isolationist parents of an isolationist son ever expected—he had enlisted in the Naval Reserve. He was now a Seaman Second Class. Rose was distraught. Jack, too, was upset . . . for a different reason.[35]

Joe Jr. had become something of a national figure this past year—a delegate to the July 1940 Democratic convention; author of an article in *The Atlantic Monthly* in January 1941; regularly interviewed on national radio shows and featured in the press as the leader of isolationism on American campuses. Now this. The budding hero.

Jack was suddenly almost frantic to get into uniform. The fast-growing

Army had a new way to a commission, Officers Candidate Schools, but he failed the physical. He tried the Navy; flunked its physical, too.[36]

The spoiled-brat syndrome flared up once again: no problem that cannot be fixed, no jam that cannot be gotten out of. There's always a way if you know the right people. In this case, Rear Admiral Alan G. Kirk, formerly naval attaché at the U.S. embassy in London and currently chief of naval intelligence. Kirk was one of the most influential officers in the Navy, a protégé of the chief of naval operations, Admiral Ernest J. King.

Joe Kennedy wrote to Kirk, and on August 5 Jack submitted to yet another physical by the medical board at Boston Navy Yard. Looking less closely at the young man before them than at their own promotion prospects and pensions, the members of the board waved Jack Kennedy into the Naval Reserve with a commission. The only physical defect the board noted was three missing teeth.[37]

The newly minted ensign outranked Joe Jr., who was still only a Seaman Second Class. What a short while before had seemed impossible was now a gold-braided reality—Joe Jr. had to address him as "Sir."[38]

CHAPTER 9

Love and War

That fall of 1941, with the Navy attacking and being attacked by German U-boats in the Atlantic, and Japan becoming increasingly bellicose in the Pacific as American oil and metal exports were cut off, Jack Kennedy found himself closer to the action than his brother, yet still without a piece of it. Working in a dingy room crowded with four drab government-issue tables, he helped compile intelligence digests based on the reports that flowed into the Office of Naval Intelligence situation room, right next door.

Japan was moving towards an attack on the United States before its fleet was beached for want of oil. Naval code breakers were reading sizable chunks of Japan's diplomatic and military cables. The intelligence digests, based on intercepted messages and the reports of foreign correspondents, went to senior naval officers and the captains of major warships at sea.[1]

The work Jack was doing obliquely reflected history in the making, yet it lacked interest. He was not cleared to read the important material, which was classified top-secret. His assignment proved to be about as exciting as writing for a company newspaper. But at least he was in Washington, where the atmosphere these days almost crackled with tension, and at weekends he got together with Lem Billings, who was living in Baltimore and working for Coca-Cola, in advertising and sales.

His sister Kick was in Washington, too, employed by the unshakably isolationist *Times-Herald*. The only major American newspaper more reckless with the truth and more laughably provincial in its outlook was the *Chicago Tribune*. This was no coincidence: the owners of these papers, Cissy Patterson in Washington and Robert R. McCormick in Chicago, were cousins.

Sometime around the beginning of November, Kick introduced Jack to the *Times-Herald*'s blond bombshell, Inga Arvad. There are many women who are beautiful without being sexy, and even more women who are sexy without being beautiful. Inga was irresistible—as sexy as she was beautiful; maybe more so. She was twenty-eight years old and five feet seven inches tall; in her high heels, five feet nine. That made her taller than most men, and she carried herself with a confident air that capitalized on her stunning appearance.

Born in Copenhagen in June 1913, she had married an Egyptian diplomat at the age of seventeen and moved to France. When his posting to Paris came to a close and he was recalled to Egypt, she filed for divorce rather than go to live in dusty, squalid Cairo. During a Riviera vacation in 1935 she had won a beauty contest, and her pushy mother had brought her to the notice of Paul Fejos, a Hungarian-born film director who had become an American citizen. Fejos cast her in one of his films. After her divorce came through, she promptly married Fejos, hoping a film career would follow.

Meanwhile, she traveled to Berlin, and by claiming to be a journalist working on Denmark's most respected newspaper, she was able to meet Hermann Goering's fiancée, Emmy Sonneman. Through Sonneman, she met Goering. As shrewd and determined as she was gorgeous, Inga parlayed her introduction to the Deputy Führer into interviews with Joseph Goebbels and two meetings with Adolf Hitler.

Thanks to Fejos, she also met—and, rumor had it, bedded—Axel Wenner-Gren, the richest man in Scandinavia. Wenner-Gren had founded Electrolux and held a one-third interest in Bofors, a Swedish arms manufacturer that specialized in flak guns and light artillery. Wenner-Gren also owned five million acres of prime timberland.

The Swedes' neutrality in World War II was underpinned by their selling raw materials—especially wood pulp and iron ore—in large quantities and at low prices to Nazi Germany, making it unnecessary for Hitler to reach out and take them. No Swedish industrialist cooperated more eagerly with Nazism than Axel Wenner-Gren.

By 1940 Inga's marriage to Fejos was foundering, and the Old World had become an uncertain and dangerous place as war raged across the continent. Fejos headed for South America to find and film lost cities of the Incas. Inga made her way to New York, arriving in February, and took courses in English and journalism at Columbia while she looked for a newspaper job. Inga had no luck in job hunting and was alienating her Jewish classmates with her outspoken admiration of Hitler and her denunciation of "the goddamn Chews." A fellow student at Columbia informed the FBI that Inga Arvad was probably a Nazi agent, if not a Nazi spy. The Bureau opened a file on her and began collecting information.[2]

Early in the fall semester, Inga was introduced to Arthur Krock, who was visiting Columbia for the day. She asked him to help her get a job, and Krock, almost dumbstruck by her overwhelming sex appeal, recommended her to the *Times-Herald*. She not only got onto the payroll but easily defeated another reporter, Page Huidekoper, who was trying to excite the interest of Ensign Jack Kennedy.[3]

Inga interviewed Jack for a column she was writing, "Did You Happen to See . . . ?" It was a slightly offbeat look at the kind of people who were showing up in Washington to help mobilize the economy for war; people such as dollar-a-year men from the Midwest, big back where they came from but disoriented and struggling to be noticed now. The *Times-Herald* didn't pay much, but that was neither here nor there, because shortly after she moved to Washington, Axel Wenner-Gren sent her $5,000, twice the average income in 1941.[4]

Her piece on Jack Kennedy began, "An old Scandinavian proverb says the apple doesn't fall far from the tree. No better proof can be found than John F. Kennedy. If former Ambassador Joe Kennedy has a brilliant mind . . . charm galore and a way of walking into the hearts of people . . . then son No. 2 has inherited more than his due. The 24 years of Jack's existence on our planet have proved that here is really a boy with a future. . . ." And so on in the same vein.[5]

The morning of Sunday, December 7, Jack and Billings cruised the Mall looking for a touch-football game they could get into. They found one near the Washington Monument. As they drove back to Jack's apartment afterwards, the news came over the car radio of the Japanese attack on Pearl Harbor.[6]

Shortly after, Jack and Inga began sleeping together. At roughly the same time, Kick informed Inga that Page Huidekoper, bitter at losing out in the competition to seduce Jack, had denounced her to the FBI as a Nazi spy. The *Times-Herald* was already in serious trouble for having printed top-secret war plans shortly before Pearl Harbor. So now the paper's editor, Frank Waldrop, walked both young women over to the FBI building and one of J. Edgar Hoover's underlings, to whom he said, "This young lady says this young lady is a spy. Good afternoon," and left them there.[7]

Inga demanded a letter from Hoover saying that she was not a subversive, something she was never going to get. Confronting the FBI was as sensible as pushing a stick into a wasp's nest. Hoover's reaction was to order "technical surveillance," which meant bugging her apartment, tapping her telephone, opening her mail and rifling her desk.

They found nothing that showed she was a security risk, but there was no doubt that she was a Nazi sympathizer. Inga regularly extolled Hitler and praised Germany. When Inga unburdened herself in postcoital rants to Jack about Churchill, the English and the Jews who were the cause of Germany's problems, he said very little. It is easy to imagine him staring at the ceiling, wondering how long this was going to take.[8]

Once the FBI realized who Inga's lover was, Hoover informed the chief of naval operations, Admiral Ernie King, that an officer in Naval Intelligence, "Ensign Joseph F. Kennedy [*sic*]," was having an affair with a woman suspected of Nazi affiliations. Meanwhile, Fejos had arrived in the United States from Peru only to find out that his wife was being unfaithful. He got in touch with the real Joseph Kennedy, then cast his net a little wider.

From the vantage of his syndicated gossip column, Walter Winchell soon informed his millions of readers, "One of ex-ambassador Kennedy's eligible sons is the target of a Washington gal columnist's affections. So much so she has consulted a barrister about divorcing her exploring groom. Pa Kennedy no like." On January 13, 1942, the day after Winchell's column appeared in the newspapers, Jack Kennedy learned that he was being transferred to Charleston, South Carolina. Describing it more than a decade later and still fuming, he told the author Robert Donovan, "They shagged my ass down to South Carolina because I was going around with a Scandinavian blonde, and they thought she was a spy!"[9]

Inga visited him in Charleston three times and for several months bom-barded him with letters and phone calls that pledged her devotion. At the same time, she was sleeping with a Danish writer, Nils Blok, ignoring the fact that he was a Jew. The fact that Nils Blok's father was rich probably helped. She also may have been sleeping with Bernard Baruch, whom she affectionately called "the Old Goat." Many of Baruch's mistresses were vivacious blondes, such as Clare Luce, and Inga in turn was attracted to rich and powerful older men. Although she knew by now that the FBI was tapping her telephone, she told Frank Waldrop there was nothing to fear so long as she retained Baruch's friendship.[10]

How cruelly ironic but poetically just that for about three months Jack Kennedy stopped playing the field in favor of a woman who did not even attempt to be faithful in return. Inga Binga, as Jack called her, had excited, amused and flattered him as no one else had ever done. She was brighter than the coeds, models, showgirls and starlets he had gone to bed with. Inga had seen as much of the world as he, had a personality that was as vibrant and charming as his own, was more sophisticated sexually and knew how to use her sex appeal without seeming cheap.

All the same, her tirades were more than a politically aware woman's attempts to influence his attitude to the war; they also betrayed a deep dis-appointment. Inga's attempts to teach Jack how to satisfy a woman had failed.

There was no foreplay or wooing, and he took swift release as the whole purpose of sex. There was never any desire to express affection physically. Jack Kennedy, when horny, wanted only thing—a quickie. "He was awkward and groping," Inga complained bitterly to Arthur Krock. "A boy, not a man. Intent upon ejaculation and not a woman's pleasure." As a lover, he could only get better, and he did so over time, but nearly all the scores of women he had sex with in the future were going to find themselves stranded on that same journey to nowhere that Inga Binga had already traveled.[11]

=

The physical exam that got Jack Kennedy into the Navy was so perfunc-tory it might have been based on a Marx Brothers film, with Groucho wielding a stethoscope in one hand, a double corona in the other, and for-getting which was which. But once in uniform, Jack Kennedy applied for sea duty.

Striving to appear a model of manly good health, he worked on developing a tan with the aid of a Mazda GE-2 sunlamp. Unfortunately, he overdid it, "bringing on peeling and that pearl gray luster that spells social disaster," he ruefully informed his friend William "Zeke" Coleman.[12]

He also signed up for the famous Charles Atlas course, a ninety-day program of isometrics. Jack began diligently pursuing the Atlas regimen before he met Inga and completed it after being banished to South Carolina.[13]

Charleston's antebellum prettiness was wasted on him. He was depressed over the anticlimactic ending to the affair with Inga, worried that she might be pregnant and as outraged as almost anyone would be at being spied on. Charleston was virtually owned and controlled by the Navy. He couldn't do anything without it being reported to the FBI or the Office of Naval Intelligence, as he well knew. Inga's visits consisted of brief sexual interludes followed by days of incandescent rage at being watched and bugged.

His job in Charleston turned out to be even more boring than the work he had done in Washington. With the United States finally at war, even routine naval correspondence classified as "confidential" was being put into code. His assignment was deciphering these codes, turning five-letter groups into words. The messages dealt with nothing important or even interesting. He applied once more for sea duty.[14]

Not surprisingly, his irritable bowel syndrome flared up once more and his back began hurting, too. Just as he'd overdone the sunlamp, he may have overdone the Charles Atlas exercises.

He was also dispirited by the way the war was going. The Japanese had invaded the Philippines, and it was only a matter of time before they seized the islands from General Douglas MacArthur. They had taken Singapore and most of Southeast Asia. An atavistic white man's fear now began to trouble Jack—the Yellow Peril. The future probably didn't belong to Germany after all, he decided, but to China and Japan.[15]

Jack applied for sick leave, and while his request was being processed, he received a letter from Kick. She wanted him to know that she was hoping to go to England and decide whether or not to marry a young man she had gone out with before the war, William "Billy" Hartington, heir to the Duke of Devonshire. The fact that he was a Protestant was an obstacle, but one that Kick seemed determined to overcome.[16]

Jack wrote back, "I would advise strongly against any voyage to

England to marry any Englishman." The British Empire was finished and England was as good as dead. "When a nation reaches the point where its primary aim is to preserve the status quo, it's approaching old age. When it reaches the point where it is willing to sacrifice part of that status quo to keep the rest, it's gone beyond old age, it's dying." England now was a relic of the past, with nothing to commend it and no future at all.[17]

There was a fierce undercurrent to this letter. It sounded as if the English had somehow betrayed his trust. But there was something else, too— a slighting, even if indirect, reference to his father, who had famously asserted in his 1936 book, *I'm for Roosevelt,* that he would gladly give up half his fortune if he could be assured of holding on to the other half. Was Dad washed up, too, along with Olde England?

Once his request for sick leave came through, Jack headed first to Rochester to reprise the all-too-familiar regimen of enemas and puzzled looks. After ten days there, he traveled to Boston and checked in to the Lahey Clinic for a prognosis on his back. It wasn't good. He was told he had suffered a ruptured disc and needed a spinal fusion operation.

Yet it would be the Navy's doctors, not civilians, who had the final say on the health needs of an active-duty officer. After repeated examinations, they decided his back problems were muscular: there was no ruptured disk. He was prescribed an exercise program to strengthen his back and advised to keep sleeping with a thick plywood board under his mattress.[18]

Returning to duty in Charleston, Jack broke more dull code, taught air-raid precautions at local defense plants and, to his disgust, was ordered to teach a Bible class on alternate Sundays. Some unknown superior officer may well have been reading too much into Jack Kennedy's habit of going to Mass each week, because in 1942 he was deeply troubled by religious doubts. He never lost faith in God, but throughout his adult life, he struggled to retain his belief in organized religion.[19]

He amused himself as best he could, but Charleston was a dull southern town; no Stork Club, no chorines, no fun. He missed Inga and called her several times to tell her so. Jack also visited Bernard Baruch's enormous estate, Hobcaw Barony, where Clare Luce was staying until the weather in New York warmed up. She had once persuaded him to date her daughter, Ann, but Jack found the mother a more interesting prospect. Clare Luce was equally drawn to him, but it would be some years before anything came of this mutual May-December attraction.[20]

If he was ever going to get sea duty, he would first have to go through one of the Navy's "get rich quick" programs for training reserve officers. In July he was finally assigned to the midshipmen's course at Northwestern University, run by the Great Lakes Naval Training Station. This provided no assurance of a seagoing assignment, since more than half of nonflying naval officers held down shore jobs, even in wartime.

Several weeks into the course, Captain John D. Bulkeley arrived to make a recruiting pitch for PT boats. That summer of 1942, Bulkeley was one of the most famous sailors in the world. His PT-boat squadron had plucked General MacArthur, Mrs. MacArthur and the general's son, plus thirteen members of his staff, from the besieged fortress of Corregidor, then taken them on a thirty-six-hour dash through the Japanese naval blockade. Bulkeley had won the Navy's first Medal of Honor of the war, and the rescue was already being immortalized in a film—*They Were Expendable*—directed by John Ford.

Bulkeley now needed officers for what he hoped would eventually grow into a huge force of boats. His pitch was emotional, direct and effective. The PT boat was a powerful weapon of war, hitting hard, hitting often, sinking Japanese cruisers and speeding away before the enemy knew what had hit him. Or so he claimed.

Until now Jack Kennedy had probably set his sea-duty ambitions no higher than serving on a small warship, such as a destroyer or a submarine, where action was almost guaranteed. But Bulkeley offered an exciting possibility—Jack's own command. He also had exactly the kind of background Bulkeley was looking for, experience handling small boats. Jack was among nearly a hundred young men who volunteered that day.

His medical record was nevertheless likely to count against him. On the other hand, there was always Dad. When Bulkeley returned to New York, he received a telegram from Joe Kennedy, inviting him to lunch the next day at the Plaza Hotel.

Lunch turned out to be an eight-hour marathon of arm twisting. "Jack has the potential to be President," Joe told him. "Do you have the clout to get him into PT boats? The publicity would do him a lot of good with veterans' groups." Joe wouldn't let Bulkeley go until he'd virtually promised to do it, and then there was one more request—"See that he's sent someplace that isn't too deadly."[21]

After graduating from midshipmen's school, Jack was entitled to leave before having to report to the PT training course at Melville, Rhode Island. His father was at Hyannis and handed him a gift from Clare Luce, a small gold coin, a lucky piece she wanted Jack to wear. He wrote to tell her he had been intending to buy a St. Christopher's medal, but the coin was now fastened to the identification tag hanging around his neck. "I'll string along with my St. Claire [*sic*]."[22]

Melville turned out to be a congeries of Quonset huts clustered among leafless trees trembling in the winter winds. The PT-boat course was mainly theory, with little boat handling and an abundance of navigation. Not a single torpedo was fired.[23]

Jack diverted himself by organizing touch-football games after each day's classes, still pursuing that dream of himself in which he was a star quarterback. It was a pursuit he never gave up, however much his back protested.[24]

He had to rope in enlisted personnel to flesh out the teams, and here was a heaven-sent opportunity for humble gobs to indulge their own fantasies . . . of revenge. Jack got closely acquainted with the elbows of a Seaman Second Class who spent as much of each game as he could sticking them in Kennedy's face while applying his knee to Kennedy's crotch, yelling in high excitement, "I'll cover *this* son of a bitch!"[25]

Jack was the only officer at Melville who had a car. After most games, he and his new pals crammed themselves into the Buick and went into Newport, nine miles away. At the weekend, they took the train to New York, where Jack was dating a showgirl, Angela Greene.

When the course ended, most of his classmates were assigned to PT-boat squadrons, but Jack had shown such skill in boat handling that he was ordered to stay on as an instructor. He protested his new assignment to the senior Senator from Massachusetts, David I. Walsh, who sat on the Naval Affairs Committee, and in the course of doing so, he greatly impressed Walsh with his grasp of military strategy.[26]

Like his father, Jack was never slow to spot an opportunity. He used his new position to get Torby Macdonald posted to Melville, even though Ensign Macdonald had not taken the midshipmen's course. "I'll tutor him," Jack assured the commander at Melville. After all, he was considered a qualified instructor, wasn't he?

Resigned to his new assignment, he hoped it wouldn't last more than a few months, after which he would get a boat to command and he'd have Torby assigned as his executive officer. A story, then, with a Hollywood ending—two best pals off to war together. But Jack's meeting with Senator Walsh suddenly paid off. In January 1943, just days after Macdonald arrived, Jack Kennedy was ordered to take four PT boats to Florida, after which he was going to find himself heading to the South Pacific.[27]

"... and Brave"

The scuttlebutt that there was somebody famous aboard spread
quickly among the able seamen manning *Landing Ship, Tank–449.*
He was a sissy, though; that was what they decided, an Ivy League
rich kid whose dad had been ambassador to England; somebody soft and
spoiled, better cut out for teacups at ten paces than fighting it out with the
slant-eyed Japs. Some might admit he was tall and good-looking, as well
as rich, the kind of gink that dames back home called "a solid sender" and
made eyes at. Lieutenant Kennedy had probably bagged more than a few
actresses, models and college girls, the kind who didn't even know working guys existed. But that was just one more reason to hate the bastard.[1]

Jack was too bright and observant to be completely unaware of what
the able seamen of *LST-449* thought about him as it carried him from the
naval base at Espíritu Santo across the Coral Sea to Guadalcanal in April
1943. Envy mixed with contempt was inevitable. He couldn't change that,
and he paid it virtually no attention; not now, not ever.

A Landing Ship, Tank wasn't really a warship but a four-thousand-ton,
flat-bottomed vessel designed to decant twenty tanks and their crews onto
a hostile shore. In the South Pacific, though, LSTs were used mainly to

move men and equipment, fuel and ammo, up to the fighting units. Lumbering and boxlike, with poor antiaircraft defenses, an LST was just about the worst kind of vessel to find yourself aboard in an air attack.

On April 7, as *LST-449*'s convoy approached the southeastern tip of Guadalcanal, destroyers and destroyer escorts came racing towards it, flashing signals to reverse course. *LST-449* was turning around just as the sky filled with death. Radar on Guadalcanal had picked up an aerial armada of 177 Japanese planes flying south from their huge base at Rabaul.[2]

The Japanese force split into three groups: one attacked airfields in the central Solomons, a second worked over shipping moored in the harbor at Tulagi—a small island adjacent to Guadalcanal—and the third group went straight for the convoy.[3]

Every operable fighter on Guadalcanal—seventy-six fighters in all—was scrambled. A huge dogfight swirled over the convoy, with more than a dozen planes shot down and crashing into the sea. Japanese planes swooped on *LST-449* to strafe it, while screaming high above, a "Val" dive-bomber released a five-hundred-pound bomb. Exploding just off the port bow, the bomb threw a towering column of water high in the air and the LST's stern was lifted up violently. It slammed down with even greater force, breaking the captain's neck. Buckled but not breached, *LST-449* continued to plow a course that would take her back to Espíritu Santo, three hundred miles to the southeast, but slowed now by a 22-degree list to starboard.[4]

Both of the 40-millimeter antiaircraft positions—or "gun tubs"—that protruded bulbously from the bow section were knee-deep in water as their shaken crews opened fire once more on the aircraft swirling overhead. Jack Kennedy, rushing up from below, saw the destroyer *Aaron Ward*, a few hundred yards away, take a direct hit from a Val. The explosion ripped apart its engine room and the destroyer began to sink.

In the cacophony and confusion, Jack joined a party of seamen feeding long, heavy belts of 40-millimeter ammunition to the gunners manning one of the gun tubs. Hot, expended cannon shells flew around him before falling, sizzling, into the water below, or clattered onto the deck where, leaning heavily to compensate for the severe listing of the ship, Jack maintained a precarious footing.

One of the Japanese planes strafing the LST was shot down and its pilot parachuted into the sea nearby. From his vantage point, Jack saw the man slip out of his life jacket and begin to swim away, using only his right hand and arm.[5]

Once the surviving airplanes flew off towards the north, *LST-449* drew close to the downed pilot. Crewmen prepared to throw him a line from the deck. With the LST barely twenty yards away, the pilot released his life jacket and brought his left hand into sight at last . . . holding a revolver. He fired two shots at his would-be rescuers, but his bullets flew harmlessly overhead. A machine gun opened up on him from the LST and missed. Moments later, a single shot, fired by a veteran soldier standing next to Jack, struck the downed pilot. "Took the top of his head off and he leapt forward and sank out of sight," Jack informed his parents.[6]

LST-449 limped back to Espíritu Santo to be pumped out, patched up and put on an even keel once more. The word among the ABs—the able-bodieds—now was that Kennedy was okay. He'd been cool and daring under fire, sharing the risks, getting into the fight.[7]

On April 13, *LST-449* finally reached Guadalcanal with its load of replacements, ammunition and fuel. Next day Jack reported to the PT base on nearby Florida Island, where his squadron was based. The setup on Florida Island consisted of a few Quonset huts, some native hovels, a crude dock. He was attached to *PT-47* while the squadron commander decided what to do with him.

Jack and the rest of the squadron officers lived on Tulagi Island, barely a mile across the water from Florida. He had steeled himself for the danger at the sharp end of war, but not for the squalor in the rear. The primitiveness he found himself in on Tulagi—shabby tents, fetid latrines adding their odors to the putrescent smell of the jungle—shocked him. Untidiness was one thing; uncleanliness was something he never grew used to.

On April 25 he got his own command, *PT-109,* a modern eighty-footer powered by three Packard engines. She was weather-beaten and filthy. Her engines were balky from a mistake some months earlier when seawater had gotten into the hundred-octane aviation fuel they ran on. It took a dozen men to man her, and there were only two assigned when he took command. His first task was to get her seaworthy again. His second was to assemble a crew from the replacement pool and form a reliable team.

Once he had a seaworthy boat and a crew, he took them out on training patrols that lasted from just before sunset until just after dawn. It was a thrilling experience to carve a path through the tropical night, trailing a stunning phosphorescent wake teeming with flying fish while porpoises cavorted at the bow, keeping pace with the boat.[8]

Other than that, there was plenty of boredom. Nothing much seemed to be happening. No one seemed sure just what to do with the PT boats. And Jack was becoming increasingly envious of John Hersey, who had a best-seller as well as "My Girl," Frances Ann.[9]

At the same time, Jack was discovering—not that he had ever doubted it—his talent for leadership. Enlisted men do not, as a rule, like officers much, but they seemed to like him. He was popular, too, with his brother officers. There were two kinds of officers in PT boats—Ivy Leaguers and Weed Leaguers. But as a Roman Catholic, Jack wasn't Yankee enough to be considered a truly representative Ivy Leaguer. He became, in effect, an honorary Weed Leaguer, and they outnumbered the Ivies by a very big margin.[10]

Meanwhile, he was improving his living conditions. Poking around Tulagi, Jack found a thatched hut hidden behind a bank of huge refrigeration units on the edge of the jungle. "Let's you and me clean it up and go live there," he suggested to a friend from Melville, Johnny Iles. His executive officer, former football player Lenny Thom, joined them there. It wasn't the Waldorf, but it was tolerably clean and not so close to the latrines. Jack installed his portable manual Victrola. "That Old Black Magic" and "All or Nothing at All" blended with the tropical birdsong high in the canopy at seventy-eight revolutions per minute.[11]

During his free time, Jack kept up his huge correspondence, writing to a wide variety of people from Lem Billings to Inga Binga, Joe Jr. to Clare Luce. While others played cards or softball, he stretched out on his thin Navy mattress stiffened with a five-ply board and opened a book, or he went looking for people who liked to talk about politics or world affairs. He asked the Melanesian houseboy he'd hired, a young man called Lani, to teach him the basics of pidgin English. And one night, in a rare moment during which he freely expressed his deepest feelings to another person, Jack had a long talk with Iles about his tottering religious faith. Yet he hadn't abandoned the struggle to believe. He intended to see Bishop Fulton J. Sheen—America's most glamorous Catholic cleric—about his spiritual crisis once he returned home.[12]

After each patrol, Jack went up to the Lingata Plantation to be debriefed by a naval lieutenant from Boston, Nick Wells. It was always the same: no sight of the enemy, nothing much to report. After the debriefing, Jack stood on the veranda for a long time, gripping the white railings of this elegant representation of civilized life, gazing thoughtfully or nostalgically out to sea.[13]

His feelings about the war had been sharpened rather than changed. Everybody—himself included—was terrifically homesick. "The only people who want to be out here are the people back in the United States— and particularly those in the Stork Club," he told Billings. Yet he wrote to Inga, "I'm extremely glad I came—I wouldn't miss it for the world."[14]

By June the action in the Solomons was moving rapidly away from Guadalcanal, as Allied forces prepared to fight their way towards the Japanese stronghold at Rabaul, two hundred miles to the north. New Georgia, roughly midway between Guadalcanal and Rabaul, was assaulted on June 30 by the Army's Forty-third Infantry Division and a regiment of marines. The Forty-third was poorly trained and badly led.[15]

In mid-July two of the Army's best divisions, the Twenty-fifth and the Thirty-seventh, took over from the battered Forty-third. At roughly the same time, the PT boats at Tulagi were shifted to the Russell Islands, fifteen miles from New Georgia. Their mission was to block Japanese attack transports—really, modified destroyers—and steel-hulled barges from reinforcing New Georgia's beleaguered garrison.

For Jack Kennedy, taking his boat north meant that all his machinations to secure a combat role were about to pay off. And yet . . . He had such a probing intelligence he almost certainly realized by now, as other Navy officers did, that the PT boats weren't a true weapon of war. Their plywood hulls could be easily pierced, with the risk of igniting their highly volatile hundred-octane fuel; their engines weren't robust enough for the South Pacific; they lacked speed; and their main armament, the Mark VIII torpedo, was almost useless thanks to a faulty exploder. Until the exploder problem was fixed, in the fall of 1943, the Mark VIII dented a lot more Japanese ships than it sank.[16]

The Japanese attack transports and barges making the run into New Georgia transited the Blackett Strait. Night after night the PT boats patrolled the strait, moving slowly, stalking the Imperial Japanese Navy, but sought in turn by Japanese floatplanes flying low and looking for the boats' phosphorescent wake. Then the floatplanes swooped, dropping flares and hundred-pound bombs. The night of July 19, *PT-109* finally saw action under Jack Kennedy's command. A floatplane spotted the boat and nearly sank it. Its bombs straddled the zigzagging craft, wounding two crewmen and pitting the hull.[17]

The boat was patched up, and the crewmen were checked into a field hospital. Then came orders to move to Lumbari, a small island west of

New Georgia and much closer to where the "Tokyo Express"—the attack transports, that is—came barreling through in the middle of the night.

On July 30, with a big operation in the offing, Jack did what warriors have done for centuries on the eve of inevitable combat—he went looking for more firepower. He scrounged a 37-millimeter antitank gun from an Army depot. The 37-millimeter was a virtually useless object that the Army had mistakenly bought in large numbers before Pearl Harbor. Since then, most had gathered rust and dust. Against a Japanese barge or destroyer, though, he thought it might prove useful.

Next day, Jack had his crew lash a coconut log and a huge piece of timber, roughly ten feet long and four or five inches thick, to the bow of *PT-109*. He mounted the antitank gun on the timber and the log. From her skipper on down, *PT-109* was as ready now as she would ever be to meet the foe.[18]

≡

It is eleven o'clock, the night of Sunday, August 1, 1943, and Lieutenant (j.g.) John F. Kennedy is in the cockpit of his boat, peering into the darkness of Blackett Strait, alert for the least sign of movement. His hands are on the wheel and he is wearing a life jacket, or Mae West, and from time to time he puts his helmet on, but it is too heavy to be worn for long.

Under the life jacket, hanging from his neck, are his identification tag and the lucky gold piece given him by Clare Luce. There is also a lanyard around his neck, leading to a Smith & Wesson .38 revolver stuck into his waistband. On his belt he has fixed a sheath knife.

Despite the support he wears, his back is sore. The pounding of the boat is a constant strain, and earlier in the day there had been an air raid on Lumbari. Jack had taken a dive into one of its waterlogged slit trenches and another officer had jumped in, landing on top of him. Jack is suffering, too, from hemorrhoids, but he hasn't mentioned it to anyone aboard the boat or in the squadron. He has become a master at denying, even to himself, the pain that gnaws at his body nearly every day.[19]

Naval cryptanalysts have become adept in recent weeks at breaking Japanese signals and several days earlier learned that the Tokyo Express will be heading for New Georgia the night of August 1. It will have to pass Kolombangara Island on its way. Captain Arleigh Burke, commanding a destroyer division, is preparing to ambush the enemy at the northern end of Kolombangara. Meanwhile, the commander of the PT squadrons at

Lumbari, Lieutenant Commander Thomas G. Warfield, has put all fifteen of his operable boats out here to attack the Express at the southern end, in Blackett Strait.

Both Burke's destroyers and Warfield's PT boats are trying to cover a lot of water in the darkness of what is, beneath the Southern Cross, one of the longest nights of the year. To make things even tougher for Warfield's crews, only four of his boats have radar, and even these are of limited use because he has ordered radio silence in every situation short of an emergency.[20]

Jack Kennedy strains every nerve as his boat moves along on one muffled engine at a leisurely six knots. He is trying to avoid kicking up a wake that would make him an easy target for the floatplanes that can be heard buzzing menacingly, sometimes near, sometimes far away. *PT-109* lacks radar, and he is relying on his forward lookout, a burly ensign named George "Barney" Ross, to look deeper into the darkness than he can from the cockpit.

Ross is not really a member of the *PT-109* crew. After his own boat was sunk by a Japanese plane, he volunteered to come on this mission with Jack and man the 37-millimeter gun. Ross is a brave young man who had become friendly with Jack in touch-football games back at Melville, but he suffers a serious defect as a lookout—he has almost no night vision. Staring into the stygian Blackett Strait when there is no moon or starlight, he is virtually blind.[21]

Suddenly, a searchlight sweeps over *PT-109* and the booming of a heavy gun rings across the water. Jack calls down to the engine room for maximum power, and as the three Packard engines spit, then roar, the bow goes up, the stern of the boat seems to dig into the water, and Jack, spinning the wheel this way then that, zigzags away from the searchlight's glare. The firing stops. The light goes out. He orders two engines shut down and by midnight is back to a six-knot pace.

What he has mistaken for a shore battery and searchlight is, in reality, a brush with the Tokyo Express. The four Japanese destroyers, modified to carry troops and supplies, are already racing south through Blackett Strait. They have eluded Arleigh Burke's destroyer force, which is still moving towards the northern end of Kolombangara, by arriving an hour earlier than expected. His six destroyers are not yet in the area. Nine of Warfield's boats have made contact and fired a total of twenty-four torpedoes; striking nothing, sinking nothing, achieving nothing. For their pains, several boats are now under attack from Japanese floatplanes.

A little after midnight, the four radar-equipped boats and those operating with them are ordered to withdraw. That leaves just three boats still on patrol, one of which is *PT-109,* but no one informs Jack Kennedy or the skippers of the two other PT boats that they, too, should pull out of the strait.

Unaware of this, and in visual contact with the two remaining boats, Jack resumes his patrol. The three boats try to establish a picket line, still hoping to block the Express, believing it will soon be inbound, when in fact it has already delivered nearly a thousand reinforcements plus food and ammunition. A little before two in the morning of August 2, the four attack transports that comprise the Express are on their way out at high speed.

It is close to half past two, and Jack can see almost nothing. He is trying to keep station with the other boats, when the seaman manning the starboard machine gun, Harold Marney, shouts, "Ship at two o'clock!"[22]

Jack calls out to Lenny Thom, his second in command, "Sound general quarters!" and spins the wheel, turning *PT-109* towards the oncoming ship. He is getting into position to fire his torpedoes, and he calls down to the engine room, "Full power!" But the big Packards are still spitting and coughing to life as the bow of a Japanese destroyer, the *Amagiri,* looms suddenly out of the blackness of sea and night. Looking up at the bow and the mast towering above it, now nearly on top of him, a thought flashes through Jack's mind: So *this* is how it feels to die! He is slightly apart even now, even from himself.[23]

The *Amagiri* rips through the plywood hull, shearing off a large portion of the starboard side of *PT-109.* The air is suddenly filled with the heady smell of red-dyed aviation fuel as the tanks rupture and nearly two thousand gallons spill onto the sea. Moments later, a sheet of orange flame erupts like a volcanic explosion.

The collision has thrown Jack hard against the side of the cockpit, and he lands on his back. Instantly, he is on his feet again. "Everybody into the water!" Quickly tearing up his codebook, he scatters the pieces overboard, grabs a life belt, then jumps into the sea.[24]

Nearly half the hull is still afloat, with much of the bow above water, but it is ringed by flame. The men floundering around it seem doomed to both burn and drown. Yet the danger almost miraculously passes. The *Amagiri*'s powerful, churning wake sucks most of the blazing fuel away from the shattered carcass of *PT-109.* The aviation fuel burns fiercely on the sea some distance away, casting a phantasmagoric light on the wreckage as Jack, Lenny Thom and Barney Ross swim from man to man. "Are you okay?" Four seamen are missing. Jack and eight survivors grab on to the railings and ventilators of the upturned portion of the boat's hull and pull themselves out of the water.

Two men call out from nearby. Jack strips off his boots and pants and swims out to them. One of them is Charles A. Harris, a twenty-year-old seaman from Boston and normally proud of his swimming ability, but he is in trouble from an injured knee and a waterlogged life jacket. The other is the boat's engineer, Patrick Henry McMahon, who has been badly burned.

Jack takes Harris's life jacket and gives the seaman his own life belt. Harris begins swimming slowly towards the hull, and Jack sarcastically tries to egg him on. "For a guy from Boston, you're certainly putting on a great exhibition."

"Go to hell," Harris replies.[25]

Turning his attention to McMahon, Jack grasps the straps of the engineer's life jacket, tows him over to the hull and gets him onto it. Only two of the crew have perished.

There is a Very pistol, loaded with a flare, that Jack might fire to signal both the loss of his boat and the presence of survivors. *PT-109*'s lantern has also been saved. But he chooses not to fire a flare or use the lantern. As far as he knows, the Express has just gone through and will soon be coming back. A flare or a flashing light could bring death, not rescue, to all his men. He and the other ten cling to the bobbing fragment of the hull, wet and frightened, waiting for daybreak.

=

It had been a typical PT-boat operation. In the course of nearly four years of naval warfare in the Pacific, only one operation was a success, and that was Bulkeley's daring rescue of MacArthur from Corregidor in March 1942. Every combat action, however, was characterized by bad planning, faulty equipment, inept leadership and absurd expectations. PT boats represented no threat to anyone but their own crews and, according to Japanese records, did not sink a single enemy warship.[26]

The amateurishness of PT command extended even to rescue operations. Following the sinking of *PT-109,* no effort was made to look for survivors. Compared to the efforts the Army Air Force made to rescue downed pilots, such indifference is both incredible and inexcusable. But for now, it meant that no one was going to rescue Kennedy's crew. They would have to do it themselves.[27]

By dawn on August 2 the men clinging to the shattered hull felt exposed to a thousand Japanese on Kolombangara, less than three miles away. The hull itself was a danger, filling up with water and shifting beneath them. If it sank in the night, it might take them down with it. In the early afternoon, as it began to turn turtle, they struck out for a small island several miles away. Nine of them clung to the large timber that had been lashed to the hull to mount Jack's 37-millimeter antitank gun. They moved away, feet paddling steadily.

McMahon's badly burned hands made it impossible for him to hold on to the timber. Jack gripped one of the straps of McMahon's life jacket between his strong, even teeth and towed him away, swimming the breast-stroke. After four hours in the water, he, McMahon and the others stumbled onto tiny and circular Plum Pudding Island, home to thousands of seabirds and slimy with their droppings.[28]

The survivors from *PT-109* had no food, no water. Next day Jack had his crew swim over to Olasana Island, which sported a large stand of coconut trees. They might subsist for a long time on coconut milk and meat. Once again he towed McMahon, carrying him more or less on his back. Several times he swam out into the shark-infested waters hoping to flag down a PT boat.[29]

On August 5 Jack and Barney Ross swam to yet another small island, this one called Naru. Here their luck turned around. They found a box filled with Japanese crackers and candy and, better still, a small barrel of fresh water. As they explored Naru, they also spotted two Melanesians in a canoe, examining a Japanese wreck on a reef a couple of hundred yards offshore. At the sight of the two Americans—whom they mistook for Japanese—the Melanesians paddled away.[30]

After yet another dangerous and futile swim in hopes of intercepting a PT boat, late at night on August 6 Jack swam back to Olasana, where he had left the rest of the crew. The exhausted Barney Ross remained fast asleep on Naru.

To Kennedy's astonishment, the two Melanesians—Biuku and Eroni—were sitting on the beach at Olasana with the crew. "We've been saved!" said Lenny Thom. "Two locals have found us." Jack put down the barrel of water and box of candy to throw his arms around both men, who had jumped up to greet him.

They took him in their canoe back to Naru to collect Barney Ross. Using his sheath knife, Jack carved a message into the yielding husk of a green coconut: NAURO ISL NATIVE KNOWS POSIT HE CAN PILOT 11 ALIVE NEED SMALL BOAT KENNEDY. Then he gave Eroni the knife to scratch out the message if they ran into the Japanese.[31]

That night Jack and Ross climbed into a small canoe the two Melanesians had given them and made one more attempt to see—or be seen by—a PT boat. As they tried to cross the reef offshore, the pounding surf tipped them out of the canoe. They struggled back to the beach, their feet cut up by coral.

Shortly after sunrise on Saturday, August 7, a large war canoe carrying eight Melanesians landed on Naru. One of the Melanesians, speaking excellent English, handed Jack a letter on notepaper headed *On His Majesty's Service.* It was addressed to "Senior Officer, Naru Is."

"Have just learned of your presence," said the letter. "I strongly advise you return immediately to here in this canoe. . . ." It was signed by Lieutenant A. R. Evans of the Royal Australian Navy. Moved, elated, relieved, Jack passed the letter to Ross. "You've got to hand it to the British."[32]

The canoe was carrying enough food to provide a small banquet. Jack had himself paddled to Olasana, where he and his crew ate their first real meal in six days.

That afternoon the canoe took him across the dangerous waters of Ferguson Passage, where both Japanese and Allied aircraft operated day and night. Jack was hidden beneath palm fronds. In midpassage, Japanese fighters buzzed the canoe. The Melanesians stood up and waved and smiled, looking as friendly and relaxed as possible, and the Japanese flew on.

It was early evening when Jack stepped out of the canoe and walked up to Lieutenant Evans, who was waiting for him on Komu Island. Jack was almost as yellow as a lemon and painfully emaciated, but his right hand was outstretched and he was grinning a grin that millions one day would know. "Hello, I'm Kennedy."[33]

CHAPTER 11

Full Circle

After six days in the sick bay on Florida Island, Jack found himself back at Tulagi. Walking away from the dock, he limped from the deep coral cuts still healing on his feet. For the next few weeks he remained in a downcast, introspective mood.

In the regular Navy, losing one's ship was usually enough to kill a career, and *PT 109* was the only U.S. Navy torpedo boat ever rammed and sunk by a destroyer. "I'm nobody," he told a fellow officer, Theodore Robinson. "But my father did have a pretty responsible job and so I've had a little experience with reporters. I'm afraid that someday, somewhere, perhaps after I'm dead, somebody who doesn't know the Blackett Strait and those appalling conditions will misunderstand." If his war service was remembered for anything at all, it might be as the tale of a fool, maybe even a coward.[1]

Tulagi itself now had a jaded, melancholy air that was even stronger than the feculent smell still wafting from the open-air latrines, and the glory days of the torpedo boats were gone forever. "They were rotten, tricky little craft for the immense jobs they were supposed to do . . . improvised, often unseaworthy, desperate little boats. They shook the stomachs out of many men who rode them, made physical wrecks of others for other reasons. . . . None of my gang ever sank a Japanese destroyer. It was just dirty work, thumping, hammering, kidney-wrecking work. Even for strong tough guys from Montana, it was a rugged living," wrote James Michener in *Tales of the South Pacific,* catching the essence of the PT-boat experience as Jack Kennedy had come to know it.

Shortly after arriving back on Tulagi, Jack sat outside the tent occupied by the squadron CO, Lieutenant Commander Alvin P. Cluster, and described the sinking of *PT-109,* with the loss of two men. Suddenly Jack's eyes filled with tears. There had been other PT boats in the area that fatal night. "If only they'd come over to help me, maybe I might have been able to save those other two," he said bitterly, and wept. Cluster recommended him for the Silver Star and the Purple Heart.[2]

Jack went up to the Lingata Plantation, as he'd done many times before, to be debriefed by Lieutenant Nick Wells from Naval Intelligence, but this time he carried rather than wore the blue sacroiliac belt that normally supported his back. He had been wearing it throughout the *PT-109* drama, and it was badly ripped and torn.

"Do you know anybody who's got a needle and thread?" he asked Wells. Later that day, Wells showed up at Kennedy's billet with an official Navy sewing kit in blue and gold. The worst of the damage was rapidly and skillfully repaired. Jack had learned to sew alongside his sisters.[3]

He resumed his correspondence with family, friends and former lovers, including Inga Binga. Like almost everyone else serving overseas, he could not get enough letters from home. And nearly every letter he sent out carried roughly the same message—I'm okay. He assured his parents there was nothing to worry about—"We have the boat going very fast. We can always get away."[4]

For him as for others, the war gave special significance to keepsakes and souvenirs. Before returning to Tulagi, Jack had given Clare Luce's lucky gold piece to Biuku; Eroni already had his sheath knife as a souvenir. In his free moments, he made a keepsake for Clare Luce from a Japanese machine-gun bullet and a small fitting from *PT-109.* He was trying to make a letter opener, but what he actually fashioned was, he told her, probably better suited for digging up weeds.[5]

He was as homesick as any man in the South Pacific, but he had one military ambition left—to strike back somehow, to make the Japanese pay for what they'd done to his men. He thirsted for revenge as keenly as he had ever lusted for a girl. But Jack found himself in the backwater of a secondary theater. Tulagi was now far in the rear, and the PT boats had no record of success to justify their existence.

The Japanese had pulled out of New Georgia between the sinking of *PT-109* and the rescue of its crew. Their ten-thousand-man garrison had been evacuated, and the Navy's strategy had altered dramatically. After the summer of 1943, the focus of naval operations until the end of the war was the drive across the central Pacific, all the way to Tokyo Bay.[6]

Cluster had been trying to think up some way to keep his PT boats in action. His answer was to turn them into gunboats, and in Jack Kennedy he found the right skipper, one who'd already experimented by mounting a 37-millimeter antitank gun on his boat.

On September 1 Jack assumed command of *PT-59,* an obsolescent seventy-seven-foot PT boat, and began a dawn-to-after-dark conversion project. The four torpedo tubes were taken out. He installed three 40-millimeter antiaircraft cannon, seven .50-caliber twin-mount machine guns and two smaller .30-caliber twin mounts. It might have been wiser to dispense with most of the machine guns and put some armor plate around the fuel tanks instead, but a modification like this—all menacing muzzles and bristling firepower—bespoke Jack's anger, his frustration and his determination to strike at the foe. What he was striving for was the great-est barge killer the Imperial Japanese Navy had ever seen.

While turning *PT-59* into what he and Cluster liked to call "Gunboat Number One," Jack was also creating a crew. There were only two men assigned to the boat when he assumed command. Eight survivors from *PT-109* had emerged from the sick bay, and five of them volunteered to serve with him again. Sailors are notoriously superstitious. The fact that these five men were still prepared to trust him with their lives was an accolade in itself. The rest of his crewmen came from *PT-21,* a written-off craft that Cluster had once commanded.[7]

Because it had so many guns to man, Gunboat Number One had a much larger crew than other boats. The boat itself soon assumed the over-crowded, slummy appearance of a junk in Hong Kong harbor housing a large Chinese family. Laundry flapped from the gun muzzles and the radio mast. Mattresses and blankets were spread across the decks. Cook-ing smells—fried Spam, fried onions—rose into the air; Jack Kennedy could be heard complaining, "What in hell kind of hash is making that god-awful smell"; and skinny, sunburned figures in shorts and go-to-hell caps could be seen bent or crouched, day and night, beavering away at obscure tasks.[8]

As the transformation of *PT-59* proceeded, Jack made numerous visits over to Guadalcanal to scrounge equipment and materials from the dumps and depots there. One day, however, he visited the cemetery, where there was someone he knew, Lieutenant George H. Mead, Jr. He and Mead had a number of mutual friends and used to play touch football and softball together. When the marines landed on Guadalcanal, Mead had been in the first wave. A machine gun bullet hit him square in the face, killing him instantly.[9]

Jack Kennedy stared down at the mess tin that had been flattened out to provide a grave marker. Someone—evidently one of those who had served with him—had managed to carve into its hard, metallic surface, "A great leader of men. God bless him." Tears once again made glistening tracks down Jack's thin, bronzed face.[10]

Admiral William "Bull" Halsey, the commander of the South Pacific theater, chose not to attack the ten thousand Japanese now dug in on Kolombangara. Instead, he chose to seize lightly held Vella Lavella, twenty miles farther north, isolating rather than attacking Kolombangara.

In mid-October 1943, PT-boat operations were shifted from Tulagi up to Lambu Lambu, on Vella Lavella, which was now in American hands. Their mission would be to support Halsey's push to the most northerly islands in the Solomons—Choiseul and Bougainville—by intercepting the barge traffic that sustained the enemy garrisons there.[11]

On October 18, when Jack arrived at Lambu Lambu, he was ordered to take his boat out that same night. This time he would have the advantage of radar, but like most small radars of the time, it was good only at showing up objects moving across a body of water and was useless at monitoring aircraft. Shortly after midnight, Gunboat Number One was attacked by a floatplane that appeared out of nowhere to drop two hundred-pound bombs. Both missed by a large margin.

Jack took his boat out on patrol most nights but encountered nothing. Then, on November 2, he was ordered to help evacuate a small party of marines whom the Japanese had trapped on Choiseul. The PT boats and several small landing craft went in at midnight to pick up the marines, fresh from a firefight. Gunboat Number One took ten marines out, but one of them, a badly wounded corporal, died in Jack's bunk.

Several nights later, close to dawn, he came across three beached—

possibly abandoned—barges and opened up on them with his boat's formidable firepower. Frustrated still, he proposed making a daylight run up the principal waterway on Choiseul, the Warrior River. Had he gone ahead with it, this venture would have been a kamikaze attack by PT boat. Cluster vetoed Jack's wild idea.

Shortly after this, Jack was felled again by problems with his stomach. Back in Tulagi, X rays showed he was almost certainly suffering from a duodenal ulcer. It was the kind of illness that might get him evacuated to a hospital in Australia and a long period of sick leave. He somberly informed his father that he probably would not be home until the war in the Pacific was over.[12]

For now he was recuperating at Tulagi. During these weeks, Jack became friendly with another PT-boat skipper, Paul "Red" Fay, who tried to teach him how to play poker. Jack proved as inept at poker as he already was at bridge. In return, he tried to get Fay involved in political discussions about how the war, with its blunders and sacrifices, could be justified only by creating a better world once it was over. Fay proved as interested in international politics as Jack was in mastering five-card draw. Even so, the late fall of 1943 was when their close lifelong friendship was forged.[13]

Cluster, who thought highly of Jack as both an officer and a man, was cooking up a wheeze to get the lieutenant sent home. There was nothing left for the PT boats to do to win the war, and it was obvious that they, and the primitive conditions of the Solomons, were destroying Jack Kennedy's health. Without any authority to do so, Cluster had orders cut transferring Jack to Melville. No higher headquarters bestirred itself to intervene. So on January 7, 1944, Jack arrived in San Francisco Bay, skeletal, a citrus shade of yellow, his back hurting as usual, physically weak and emotionally exhausted, yet home in one piece and rich beyond his father's knowing.[14]

≡

Inga Arvad had moved to Los Angeles, where she filled in for Sheila Graham, a movie columnist who was also F. Scott Fitzgerald's lover. While Graham was trying to keep Fitzgerald from drinking himself to death, battling to save a genius, Inga got her chance to make a reputation in Hollywood. Instead of heading straight for Palm Beach to see his family, Jack flew south to Los Angeles to see Inga again.

Whatever there had once been between them was dead. She had a different life now, and another man, a rich Jewish doctor with writing ambitions, William Cahan. Inga introduced Cahan to Jack, who got the message. He didn't tarry in Hollywood long.

His next stop was the Mayo Clinic in Rochester, Minnesota, where his father met him, anxious to know the state of his son's frighteningly troublesome bowels. This time the clinic's doctors finally came up with the correct diagnosis—Jack suffered from irritable bowel syndrome. It is a condition in which severe bowel disorders occur without any evidence of infection or injury to explain them; a disease associated with stress that is likely to vanish once the precipitating circumstances disappear. Joe Kennedy finally had a diagnosis, but one lacking the reassurance he wanted.[15]

Jack flew on to Palm Beach, where he spent a few weeks lounging by the pool during the day and hitting the nightclubs after dark, but his preferred scene was always New York. Four weeks after returning from the Pacific, he was back in the Stork Club with a fashion editor, Flo Pritchett, on his arm. He also met up with his old flame, Frances Ann Cannon, and her husband, John Hersey.

In the space of a few years, Hersey had become one of America's most popular and admired writers. His limpid prose was infused with a poetic sense of the fragmented nature of memory and a fascination with the ambiguities of lives shaped by war. The more important the meaning of an extreme situation seemed, the more uncertain it became.

Jack talked to Hersey about the sinking of *PT-109,* sensing that here was somebody who might understand, somebody who might get the story about Blackett Strait right and, in doing so, serve as a bulwark against phantoms taunting him from out of the future. Talk to my crew, he urged Hersey. Ask them what they think happened, find out what they remember.

Returning to snowy Boston in February 1944 for Honey Fitz's eightieth birthday, Jack agreed to be the principal guest speaker at a war-bond rally and, for the first time in his life, gave a speech. With the Navy now driving across the central Pacific and the Japanese on the defensive everywhere, expectations of a rapid end to the war in the Pacific were rising from week to week. Jack Kennedy wasn't much of a public speaker, but like many a returning veteran, he was irritated by the complacency he found at home. "Things seem to be going fast," he conceded in his brief speech. "Then I look at a map and think how long it took us to get from Guadalcanal to Bougainville, and I realize it's going to be a long war."[16]

Taking advantage of being back in Boston, he checked in to the Lahey Clinic for yet another physical. Its doctors repeated what they had told him a year earlier—he needed an operation on his back. During Jack's hospitalization, John Hersey came to see him, having interviewed most of the survivors from *PT-109.*

Hersey was enthralled as Jack Kennedy talked. Jack didn't present the loss of his boat and the rescue of his men as a tale of heroism. The whole event became a modern morality play, with surreal, unpredictable yet somehow significant elements. As he spoke, his own part turned into a chronicle of how an exhausted, inexperienced naval lieutenant caught in powerful and circular currents, in a state half awake, half asleep, at a time when death seemed almost as welcome as life, had somehow survived and in the mere fact of doing so had lived long enough to set in motion a train of unseen events that allowed his men to survive, too. Nothing heroic, nothing historic, but a web of blind chances that allowed life to assert itself over the maw of oblivion.[17]

Hersey called the resulting piece "Survival" and submitted it to *Life* magazine, which had published most of his journalism. *Life* turned it down. At fifteen thousand words, it would take up half the amount of space the magazine normally provided for text. He then submitted it to *The New Yorker,* which published it in June 1944. *The New Yorker* had a readership barely a tenth that of *Life,* and while Jack felt a little disappointed, Joe Kennedy was dismayed.[18]

Here was an opportunity to spread his son's fame and reap additional prestige for the Kennedy name. It might also help blunt the barbs of "draft dodger" and "coward" embedded in his own reputation. *Reader's Digest* had an even bigger circulation than *Life;* Joe Kennedy not only got the piece into the *Digest* but had an extra hundred and fifty thousand copies printed for free distribution.[19]

Jack was assigned to the Naval Training Center in Miami while the Navy's medical bureaucracy decided what to do with him. This time it agreed the operation could go ahead.

The Navy had rejected Cluster's recommendation that Jack should receive both the Silver Star and a Purple Heart. Joe Kennedy thought his son deserved at least the Navy Cross, second only to the Medal of Honor, and Clare Luce agreed with him, but that was unrealistic. The Purple Heart came through fairly quickly, but the Silver Star was ruled out.

The Navy's handling of gallantry awards in World War II was abysmal. The guidelines it followed were narrow and invited misinterpretation. The mechanism for approving awards was also clumsy, accident-prone and slow. The awards board at Halsey's headquarters eventually found that because Jack hadn't fired his torpedoes at the Japanese destroyer, he had not been in "actual combat," a conclusion that defied common sense.

What he got instead was the Navy and Marine Corps Medal, an award for lifesaving that he undoubtedly had earned. Scores of men who applied, after the war, for their lifesaving awards to be converted into combat decorations eventually got them. For others such as Jack Kennedy, there was a tenacious resistance that suggested what really counted against him, even years afterwards, was the loss of his boat.[20]

On June 22, shortly after he received his Navy and Marine Corps Medal, Jack underwent back surgery at New England Baptist Hospital. It soon became clear the operation had not simply failed: it had made his condition even worse. His back pain was now so intense he needed large doses of painkillers every day.

His stomach, too, was giving him hell, but this time it wasn't his irritable bowel syndrome. He had swallowed large amounts of seawater following the loss of *PT-109* and almost certainly some aviation fuel as well. "His present abdominal discomfort is different than that noted previous to his enlistment," recorded a Navy doctor. "He spent over 50 hours in the water and went without food or drinking water for one week. Following this experience, his present abdominal problems started."[21]

Jack spent much of that summer at Hyannis, where Joe and Rose were anxiously awaiting the return of Joe Jr. from overseas. Their eldest son had managed to become a Navy pilot and was currently flying from a base in southern England. Learning to fly at age twenty-seven would not have been a great challenge had he been going into civil aviation, but military standards were so high he was hard-pressed to keep up with the twenty-one- and twenty-two-year-old hotshots in his class.

Shortly before Joe Jr. went overseas, his father's friend the former Boston commissioner of police Joe Timilty told him about Joe Kennedy's fifty-fifth birthday party. Joseph P. Kennedy had been toasted as "the father of our hero, our own hero, Lieutenant John F. Kennedy." Sitting on the edge of his Navy bunk, Joe Jr. had wept bitter tears. "Not a word about *me*." He waved his arms in the air in frustration and anger. "By God, I'll show them!"[22]

The best Navy pilots were assigned to fly fighters. The second-best pilots flew torpedo planes and dive bombers. The rest, like Joe Jr., flew transports and patrol planes. And there was virtually no action, little glory and not much chance of a medal when he began flying antisubmarine patrols over the Bay of Biscay. The U-boats had already lost their war. Few put out to sea anymore, and the German day-fighter arm was being blasted out of the sky. It counted for nothing after April 1944.[23]

At the end of June a bored and restless Joe Jr. flew his thirtieth mission. His tour of frontline service should have ended there, but he volunteered for an extra ten missions, still hoping to sink a U-boat, a feat almost certain to win him the Silver Star. He was disappointed all over again. Shortly after this, he read "Survival."

Powerfully moved by both pride and jealousy, he wrote Jack a letter of congratulations with a cutting edge to it. Going straight for the sore point—the loss of the boat, one of the cardinal sins in the Navy—he said, "What I really want to know is, where the hell were you when the destroyer hove into sight, and what exactly were your moves, and where the hell was your radar?" These were the principal issues that would have been addressed by any court-martial into the loss of *PT-109*. Joe Jr.'s letter would have made uncomfortable reading, as it was meant to do.[24]

The Eighth Air Force, meanwhile, had come under immense pressure to attack the V-1 sites in the Pas de Calais. It was a mission that Army Air Force commanders considered a waste of airpower, but Allied political harmony required that they do something.

A program was devised to pack "war-weary" bombers—mainly obsolescent models of the B-17—with explosives and crash them into the V-1 sites, using radio guidance to get them on target. The Navy came up with its own plan: to fly war-weary B-24s to the Belgian coast and crash them into the V-3 "supergun" installation under construction there. Joe Jr. volunteered to fly one of these B-24s over the Channel. He and his copilot, Lieutenant Wilford J. Willy, would bail out just before their B-24 crossed the Belgian coast and be picked up by a fast patrol boat. If this mission succeeded, he would get the Navy Cross.[25]

Joe Jr. took off with ten tons of explosives and a primitive and balky electronic control system at six P.M. on August 12, two days after writing to Jack. As his plane drew near the English coastline, still on a long, slow, awkward climb, it blew up in an enormous explosion that caused structural damage to fifty-nine houses several thousand feet below. No piece of the B-24, Joe Jr. or Willy was ever found.[26]

The afternoon of August 13 a Navy chaplain and a Catholic priest drove up to the Hyannis house. Jack was at home that day, as were Bobby and Teddy, Eunice, Jean and Patricia, plus Joe and Rose. The priest broke the news to Joe first. Joe told Rose, then had the children gather on the long porch overlooking the two-acre lawn that sloped down to the water. "Children, your brother Joe has been lost. He died flying a volunteer mission." Bobby and Teddy had been planning to take part in a sailing race that day. Their father, his eyes filled with tears and voice cracking, told them to go ahead—that was what Joe would have wanted, he said.[27]

For Jack, his brother's death was both the agony of loss and a new competition. Rivalry is itself a bond; in this case one so close, so tight, it had defined his existence almost from birth. And in a way, his brother's death only represented a new phase of the rivalry. "I'm shadowboxing in a match the shadow is always going to win," he told Billings. Even so, his irritable bowel syndrome vanished, never to return.[28]

Jack sought to come to terms with his grief by compiling a memorial in printed form for Joe Jr. Overtly and consciously, he was putting together a touching tribute to his brother, an act of love and acceptance. Less obviously, though, the resulting book, *As We Remember Joe,* allowed him to have the last word.

After gathering the recollections of twenty people who had known his brother, Jack provided an introductory essay that began with an admission: "I suppose I knew Joe as well as anyone and yet I sometimes wonder whether I ever really knew him. He had always a slight detachment . . . a wall of reserve which few people ever succeeded in penetrating. . . ."[29]

He conferred on his dead brother the greatest praise he could—he compared him to Raymond Asquith, his own *beau ideal.* He quoted from John Buchan—his "debonair, brilliant and brave" description of Asquith—and Winston Churchill, who had written about Asquith's heroic death in 1915: "The War, which found the measure of so many men, never got to the bottom of him, and when the Grenadiers strode into the crash and thunder of the Somme, he went to his fate, cool, poised, resolute, matter-of-fact, debonair."

While he worked on this tribute to his brother, Jack was in and out of Chelsea Naval Hospital in Boston, undergoing two minor operations—one for hemorrhoids, the second for a small hernia—and seeking relief from his failed back operation and tormenting stomach pains. On December 27, 1944, he finally appeared before a Naval Retiring Board in Washington. From there he traveled to Palm Beach, where the family celebrated Christmas.

Joe Kennedy had suffered agonies following the death of Joe Jr. He never really came to terms with it. Yet grief dulled neither his burning dynastic ambitions nor his implacable will. That fall he told Jack it was his duty to go into politics, to step into Joe Jr.'s shoes.

Jack initially resisted. It must have seemed like a summons to live his brother's life, denying him all hope of creating one truly his own. And yet . . . His heart wasn't fixed elsewhere. No cherished ambition would have to be sacrificed if he followed his father's wishes. Besides, his father could hardly be ignored. "I can feel Pappy's eyes on the back of my neck," he told his friend Paul Fay, who was staying with the family that Christmas.

"It is your responsibility to go into politics," his father told him. Sometime around New Year's Day, 1945, he finally agreed to do as his father demanded—he would try to become the first Catholic President.[30]

CHAPTER 12

I'm Jack Kennedy

It wasn't just his father's dynastic hopes that now stretched deep into the unknowable future. So, too, did the shadow of back braces, walking canes, wheelchairs, expensive doctors and nurses in white stockings. If he was going to run for anything, he first had to get well.

February 1945 found Jack Kennedy the medical pilgrim heading for Arizona as he'd done nine years earlier, not so much in search of good health as in hot pursuit. Racked with malaria and looking deathly ill, he checked into Castle Hot Springs, a health resort sixty miles north of Phoenix.[1]

The resort had been built around a collection of springs that gushed water at 140 degrees. A former marine employed as a masseur assured Jack, "I'll have that back fixed in a couple of weeks," but Jack begged off. The other health seekers were gray-haired or bald, and nothing stirred after dark.[2]

This sojourn gave him the time to complete *As We Remember Joe*. He also wrote an article on how to secure peace once the war ended. Jack could no more stop thinking about international politics than he could stop thinking about girls. Perhaps inevitably for the author of *Why England Slept,* he thought it all came down to a question of armaments. He was heavily influenced, too, by the post–World War I peace movements, which assumed that arms caused wars and rejected the realpolitik view, that wars cause armaments.

As he pondered the looming postwar world, Jack concluded that if the United States, Britain and the Soviet Union chose to arm themselves at a level that allowed each country to defend its legitimate security interests but stopped short of arming to a point where any one of them could be seen as a threat to other countries, a stable peace would then become possible.

He did acknowledge that there was a joker in the pack: long-range missiles, or V-weapons. If such weapons were ever equipped with truly powerful warheads, "One does not have to be a Jules Verne to visualize the death of the human race, a victim of science and moral degeneracy," he wrote. Calling his three-thousand-word article "Let's Try an Experiment in Peace," he sent it to his father, who promptly submitted it to *Reader's Digest*. The *Digest* turned it down. *The Atlantic Monthly*, however, agreed to run it.[3]

The one health seeker at the resort with whom he became friendly was businessman Patrick J. Lannan, who was seeking relief in the thin mountain air from a chronic lung complaint. They went riding together, and Jack was the same daredevil descending a mountain on a horse that he was behind the wheel of an automobile.

They spent many hours talking about politics and what the end of the war would bring. It was already unleashing a wave of labor unrest. Dozens of strikes erupted every day as American workers, fearful of being ousted once the military demobilized, agitated for job guarantees. Jack got his father to send him a crate of books on labor issues. To Lannan's astonishment, he sat up into the early hours until he had read them all.[4]

Books on labor law are, as a rule, monuments to turgidity, but from World War I to the 1950s, the picket line, the lockout and the union shop were the battlefield of class war, the place where social, racial and political conflicts were fought and the toll in dead strikers and cracked skulls was high. As an aspiring politician, Jack needed to grasp the labor-law conflicts that had completely poisoned relations between Roosevelt and Congress in 1944. But it was important, too, that he understand the class issues that made strikes so violent. All this talking and reading and thinking had an effect: Jack Kennedy would prove to be one of the best friends organized labor ever had.

He was planning to stay in Arizona for up to six months, but recovery among rich, middle-aged *malades* soon became boring. With Lannan in tow, he headed for Los Angeles after only five weeks as a health pilgrim. Jack's friend Charles Spalding was currently in Hollywood. The film rights to a book that Spalding had written about being a naval aviation cadet, *Love at First Flight,* had been optioned by Gary Cooper.

Hollywood was crowded with people who fascinated Jack Kennedy. There was Inga, for one, but she was busy trying to reel in Robert Boothby, a Member of Parliament. Loquacious and smooth, Boothby was also bisexual, a pedophile and one of the most corrupt figures in British political life. Inga's hopes of marriage to this aristocratic con artist were sabotaged when the FBI spitefully revealed her Nazi connections to Boothby.[5]

During the few weeks he was in Hollywood, Jack met gorgeous female movie stars such as Olivia de Havilland, whose sexual allure knocked him sideways. He also became friendly with a young actor named Robert Stack, who had a small apartment in the Hollywood Hills. Stack's apartment featured the "Flag Room," which was so small it was almost entirely filled by a double bed. The ceiling was decorated with the flags of all nations. His dates—and Jack's—were invited to lie on the bed and play a game of identifying the various flags. The penalty for a wrong answer was kissing your date, a penalty always likely to produce further developments.[6]

The serious side of this Hollywood sojourn was Jack's intense interest in male movie stars such as Gary Cooper, Spencer Tracy and Clark Gable, who projected an exciting, captivating presence. That was something he had not given much thought to, until now. But if he was going to pursue a political career, he needed to fathom the secret, whatever it was. At first Jack was mystified. He had dinner with Cooper and found him yawn-inducingly boring. Yet the lanky and laconic Cooper had only to step onto the street and an adoring crowd would appear.

How does he do it? Jack asked Chuck Spalding. Do you think I could learn how to do it? It was the beginning of a long, unremitting personal quest for a movie star's charisma.[7]

As Jack tried to unearth the secret behind the obviously contrived yet somehow convincing glamour of Tinseltown—struggled, that is, to grasp the alchemy by which otherwise ordinary people were transmuted into celebrities—his back remained as problematic as ever.

On April 21 he and Patrick Lannan set off again for the Mayo Clinic in Rochester, Minnesota. The doctors there took yet another look at his back and advised him to have a spinal fusion operation. As for his other problems—the skeletal appearance, the yellowed skin, the malaria—there was no quick fix.

While he was in Rochester, delegates from forty-six nations were gathering in San Francisco to write the charter of the United Nations, a venture that Roosevelt and Churchill had created shortly after Pearl Harbor. Thus far, the UN had been little more than a wartime alliance, but with victory in sight and the postwar nearly at hand, it was time to establish a permanent structure.

After Jack checked in to the Mayo Clinic, he received a telephone call from the editor of the Chicago *Herald-American,* a Hearst newspaper. How would he like to report on the UN conference, covering the story "from the point of view of the ordinary GI"? This invitation had been engineered by Joseph Kennedy, a longtime friend of William Randolph Hearst, and it was a clever idea. Getting Jack's name in the newspapers would not only put him in front of millions, but being present at the conference would provide a chance to see how political history was made.[8]

Jack flew to San Francisco on April 25, the day the conference opened. Over the next week, the cautious optimism of "Let's Try an Experiment in Peace" ebbed away. The Russians, in dismal serge suits of blue and brown and sporting terrible haircuts, looked like the kind of cheap hoodlums who bumped off law-abiding citizens in gangster movies that starred Edward G. Robinson.

The Soviet foreign minister, Vyacheslav Molotov, was not simply wary —something Jack had expected—but brusque and confrontational. When he failed to get his way, Molotov staged a melodramatic walkout that did not halt the conference, but signaled trouble to come. Jack advised *The Atlantic Monthly* that he had changed his mind about the Russians and asked the editor not to run his piece.[9]

Eventually Jack became convinced that it was not the Soviets alone who were wrecking the UN's chances of success. The structure that was being created was flawed. The real power in the organization was vested in the Security Council, with its five permanent members (the U.S., Britain, France, China and the U.S.S.R.), each holding a veto. This institutionalized the tension that already existed between East and West, instead of providing a mechanism to resolve it. The UN, Jack grimly informed his newspaper readers, "will be the product of the same passions and selfishness that produced the Treaty of Versailles."[10]

During the month that Jack spent in San Francisco, his friend Chuck

Spalding came up for a visit. Jack finally told him the reason for all those discussions about "personal magnetism" in Hollywood a few weeks earlier. "Charlie, I can't do what other people do. I can't just do what I like, and I'm sure now that Joe is dead, I'm going into politics."

"That's terrific! You'd be just perfect for it," said Spalding. "You can go all the way!"

"Really?" said Jack.

"All the way!"[11]

As the charter-writing conference drew to a close, Jack's thoughts turned to events elsewhere. His last column from San Francisco was devoted to the British election that had just been called for July 5. The outcome was vital to the United States, he wrote. It would determine "whether we are going to be doing business with a capitalist or socialist state in the critical months ahead. The British Labour Party is out for blood. They are not compromising with any left of center prescriptions. They are going all the way—Public ownership of the Bank of England; Government control of rents and prices, gradual Government ownership of mines, transportation, planned farming—the works."[12]

The Hearst newspapers asked Jack to go to Britain and report on the election, an offer he promptly accepted. He could not stand to be alone, however. Throughout his life, Jack Kennedy had to have a friend with him to chew the fat, keep him amused, share in the adventure. There was in him both a distance that he needed and a deep dread of loneliness. So now he asked his new friend Pat Lannan to join him as he covered the British election. Lannan, who had published a few articles in business magazines, managed to obtain some press credentials and traveled to England.

In London, Jack met up with his sister Kick, who had ignored his advice not to marry an Englishman and had married into one of the grandest aristocratic families in the country. Her husband, the Marquess of Hartington, was a high-church Anglican. Her marriage had wounded her father and left her mother almost bereft. And when Jack saw Kick, she was already a widow: Hartington had been killed in action while serving with the elite Coldstream Guards.

Kick loaned Jack her car, a tiny Austin 7. Cramming his six-foot frame into it must have been torture for his back as he and Lannan drove around England. For the budding politician, following Winston Churchill around on the hustings turned out to be an education in itself. A British campaign was unlike its American counterpart. Ambitious set-piece speeches and huge gatherings were rare. The candidate spoke for only a few minutes, then devoted twenty minutes or so to questions and answers.

Churchill—pugnacious, defiant, quick-witted and funny—was a master of this cut-and-thrust style honed in numerous meetings that were comparatively small, often in the open air under dripping umbrellas, and heckling had an honored role in the process. Anyone with an aptitude for this low-key, occasionally thrilling and often lighthearted approach to politics was likely to do well in the House of Commons, where short, dramatic exchanges by opponents debating face-to-face could make or unmake a political career.

Personal attacks were also much rarer than in American politics. British political parties were permanent national institutions, not coalitions that came together every four years. The parties debated ideas furiously within and between themselves to a degree that was unusual in the U.S.

Fascinated though he was by Churchill, Jack also sought to understand the Labour party. The more he learned about the way it operated in Parliament, and the more he saw of how the trade unions were run, the more dismayed he was by left-wing authoritarianism. "You wonder about the liberalism of the left," he told his diary. He was especially disenchanted by Harold Laski, whom he expected to be a beacon of high-minded idealism. What he discovered instead was an angry, insecure man embittered and radicalized by the fact that, as a Jew, he would never be accepted as a social equal by the English upper classes. Jack deplored Laski's pretense of seeking justice for the many when his real goal was revenge on the few.[13]

He had anticipated a Labour victory before he left San Francisco, but facing up to that prospect as he drove around in Kick's cramped Austin 7 was something else. His dispatches reflected this ambivalence. On July 6, as the British went to the polls, Jack filed his last dispatch on the election: "Although the Conservatives should win this time," he wrote, "it will only be a question of time before Labour gets an opportunity to form a government." Labour won in a landslide.[14]

Two weeks after the election, Jack traveled to Eire. His motives were undoubtedly mixed. There was a story to be covered—the Irish were deeply divided over their country's continued membership in the British Commonwealth. Besides, a trip to Ireland would play well in Boston, whatever office he ran for.

Jack held a long conversation with Eamon De Valera, the highly controversial President of the Irish Free State. De Valera had spent the war hoping for a Nazi victory and expressed his condolences to the German legation in Dublin when news came of Adolf Hitler's death. De Valera's hatred of the British made him too fanatical in spirit and too narrow in outlook for Jack Kennedy's taste. The piece he wrote on Ireland was even-handed. In his diary, however, he coolly dissected the wrongheaded, legendary "Dev."[15]

From Ireland, he traveled to Paris, where he found President Charles de Gaulle unpopular, food in short supply and the quality of French perfume in precipitous decline. On July 29 he boarded the C-54 that had just brought his father's friend James V. Forrestal, Secretary of the Navy, to France. Forrestal was on his way to Berlin and invited Jack to join him.

Flying over Germany, Jack felt uneasy and depressed at the sight of German cities, their centers little more now than huge ash-gray scars on the landscape. Over the next few days, his characteristically rapid, long-legged stride carried him, deep in thought, through the rubble that was Berlin. He also saw the shattered ruins of Hitler's bunker, its interior black with scorch marks. Jack stood in the room where Hitler and Eva Braun had committed suicide, then went into the small courtyard where their bodies had been burned.

Americans and Germans alike had the same story to tell about the Red Army: the Soviet troops who had taken the city were set free to rape and loot for three days after it fell. The combat units were then withdrawn and an occupying force was brought in. It, too, was given several days for rape and pillage. Children, women over fifty and all the old men in the Soviet zone of occupation were then driven out and took refuge with the Americans or British. The Soviet soldiers Jack saw were "short, stocky and dour looking. Their features were heavy and their uniforms dirty." What they represented in Germany was not a fresh start but Stalinist terror.

Forrestal wanted to see Bremershaven, the big German naval base near Bremen. Jack made a beeline for an E-boat, the German equivalent of the PT boats he knew so well, and found "the German E-boat was far superior."[16]

From Bremen, Forrestal's plane flew to Frankfurt, where Eisenhower had his headquarters. Jack liked Ike. "It is obvious why he is an outstanding figure," he enthused. "He has an easy personality, immense self-assurance and gave an excellent presentation of the situation in Germany."[17]

Next day, he and Forrestal flew to Salzburg and were driven up into the mountains to Berchtesgaden and then to Hitler's famous "Eagle's Nest." The views were breathtaking, Jack acknowledged, but his mind was less on the scenery than on the psychological drama for which this was merely a setting.

History made sense to him almost entirely in terms of personalities. "Within a few years," he decided, "Hitler will emerge from the hatred that surrounds him now as one of the most significant figures who ever lived . . . he had a mystery about him in the way that he lived and in the manner of his death that will live and grow after him. He had the stuff of which legends are made."[18]

Back in London the next morning, Jack was felled yet again by stomach pains, complicated by fever. He spent two days in the U.S. Naval Dispensary in London, where he was diagnosed as having acute gastroenteritis. The fever suggests he also may have been suffering from malaria. Rebounding quickly, he was ready to leave with Forrestal when the Navy Secretary's plane took off from London on August 6.[19]

As the C-54 droned westward through the night, on the other side of the world a B-29 was dropping the first atomic bomb on Hiroshima. Jack Kennedy arrived home on August 7, the first day of a new age and a different, more dangerous world.[20]

=

That fall and winter of 1945 he was running for something but did not know what. Joe Jr. had planned to start his career by becoming lieutenant governor, so Jack assumed he'd do the same. At the last minute, Joe Sr.'s most astute political adviser, his cousin Joe Kane, told Jack that was a bad idea. He could do better running for Congress. Joe commissioned a poll, and it confirmed Kane's judgment. After that, he concentrated on buying James M. Curley, who was both mayor of Boston and congressman for the Eleventh District while living in neither place.

While his father was negotiating with Curley, Jack was getting to know Boston. He hadn't lived in Beantown since he was nine years old. He knew far more people in New York than in Boston, and when he went back in 1945, he had to be shown how to get from one part of the city to another.[21]

Starting in October 1945—five months before he declared his candidacy for Congress—Jack began making himself known to the voters, addressing crowds on behalf of the Greater Boston United War Fund, talking to veterans' groups, speaking at the Brighton Women's Club and giving interviews to the Boston newspapers to warn of the dangers of disarming too enthusiastically now that the war was over. He hardly ever mentioned the Russians, but he didn't have to. "If we are strong, no one will bother us [so] we must remain strong," he insisted.[22]

In February 1946 Joe Kennedy and Curley finally cut a deal. Curley had diabetes and some huge medical bills. He was also facing a federal indictment for mail fraud. Joe Kennedy offered to pay off all his medical and legal bills and finance his campaign for reelection as mayor if he'd quit his congressional seat. There was one thing Curley would not do, though—he would not endorse Jack. Curley announced he was "neutral."[23]

The Eleventh congressional district included Harvard and MIT, yet it was also one of the poorest districts in New England. The bulk of its population consisted of blue-collar and immigrant Irish and Italians. The Eleventh was so Democratic that success in the primary was tantamount to winning the seat.

The Boston Democratic party already had a potential successor to Curley when Joe Kennedy opened his checkbook—Mike Neville, the mayor of Cambridge. Neville had come up the hard way. He'd been shining shoes and delivering newspapers when Jack was being chauffeured around in a Rolls-Royce. He served in the state legislature and on the Cambridge city council before becoming mayor. Neville was hardworking and popular, and Cambridge was the key to the election. He was also seriously ill from diabetes and was going to die before the election in November.[24]

There were eleven candidates in the race, and for Jack Kennedy to win the primary, he had to stop Neville from running up a huge vote in Cambridge while the rest of the field divided what remained of the pie. The party regulars were not simply loyal to Neville; they resented Jack, whom they derided as a carpetbagger and a boy. They feared that if Joe, with his immense wealth, got Jack into Congress, Boston would soon belong to the Kennedys, not the Democrats. The Democratic machine made it almost impossible for Jack to campaign at fire stations, police stations and other city-owned property.

In response, Joe Kennedy talked to the chairman of the Boston school board. Jack was allowed to address meetings in schools across Boston. Archbishop Richard Cushing made the parochial schools available to him, too.[25]

Joe Kennedy also talked to his old friend William Randolph Hearst about Jack's bid for Congress. After that, the Hearst-owned *Boston American* made Neville a kind of nonperson—it didn't run any stories about him and wouldn't accept his ads. Joe rented every good billboard site in Boston for the duration of the campaign and had reprints of the *Reader's Digest* version of "Survival" mailed to every house and apartment in the district.[26]

Although the other candidates could only be dismayed at the money Joe was spending, political history in the United States is replete with instances of people spending staggering sums to win elections only to come up empty-handed. Money in politics works synergistically, adding strength to a strong candidate, but often makes a weak one look stupid. Jack possessed advantages his father's money could not buy.

Above all, he was a veteran, and there were nearly a hundred thousand war veterans who had returned to Boston and registered to vote. Neville had never served in the military, and the few issues in the campaign were all veterans' issues: Jack's turf, not Neville's.[27]

Joe Kennedy wisely remained in the background. He sold off all his liquor interests to improve Jack's chances and got his cousin Joe Kane to be Jack's front man. It was Kane who thought up Jack's campaign slogan, "The New Generation Offers a Leader." But Jack couldn't resist turning for advice to his adored Grampa, Honey Fitz, who knew the Eleventh District as well as anyone—he had represented it in Congress and had lived there for nearly forty years.

Joe Kane, however, could not stand the old man. Kane had been the right hand man of Peter Tague, the politician who had convinced Congress in 1919 that Honey Fitz was guilty of poll rigging. As a result, Honey Fitz was unseated and Tague took his place in the House.

When Kane found the old man at a strategy session early in Jack's campaign, he screamed, "Get that son of a bitch out of here!" Honey Fitz departed, but no one could stop Jack from talking to him. He had an impact on the campaign because Jack was determined to win the seat the way Grampa had done—taking it one hand at a time.[28]

One evening at the start of the campaign, he said to one of his campaign workers, Tom Broderick, "What do you think we should do tonight?" Broderick had an idea—"Why don't we take a ride in the trolley car?" They boarded a two-car trolley that ran from Oak Square out to Brighton. Jack, in his only suit, the navy blue pinstripe tailored for him in London in 1939, worked his way from one end of the trolley to the other, shaking hand after hand, swiveling from one side of the car to the next, from one person to another, smiling, self-assured. "Hello . . . I'm Jack Kennedy. Nice to meet you . . . Hello, I'm Jack Kennedy . . ." And Broderick shuffled along behind, explaining to the puzzled faces turning his way, "He's running for Congress . . . This fellow's running for Congress. . . ."

Jack felt it had been such a success that they rode back into Boston to do it all over again, and when they reached Park Street, he was so high on it that he and Broderick rode the subway out to Harvard Square. He shook another hundred hands or thereabouts, took an ice-cream-soda break, then rode the subway back into Boston, still reaching out for hands. He loathed being touched by other people, but would touch them—for their votes.[29]

Honey Fitz had featured house parties in his campaigns, but they had virtually died out since then. Why don't we have some house parties? Jack suggested to his young volunteer staff. The first one was a big success, so they scheduled entire evenings of house parties, with one every hour. While Jack worked one house, a girl singer, stroking a musical saw gripped between her knees, was entertaining the people at the next house on the list, getting them in a jolly mood for when Jack arrived. When he came into the house, the girl—with her saw—departed for another.[30]

The entire Kennedy family was involved in the campaign, apart from Kick, who was still in London, and Teddy, who was still at school. Jack also surrounded himself with old friends such as Torby Macdonald, Lem Billings and Red Fay. All of them had a role in the campaign, as did his new valet, George Taylor.

There were others, too, young lawyers and advertising men, people who—like him—still had careers to make. He also got the services of an expert on Boston politics at street level, Patsy Mulkern, whose myopia foisted on him a huge pair of spectacles. With his battered fedora, large, pockmarked nose, a prominent Adam's apple and a habit of talking out of one corner of his mouth, Mulkern looked like a B-movie plug-ugly. Joe Kane asked him to take Jack around.

The first time they met, Jack was wearing sneakers. Mulkern looked at them balefully. "For the love of Christ, take 'em off, Jack. You think you're going to play golf?" Shortly after, he was in Jack's small suite at the Bellevue Hotel—directly below the much larger suite where Jack's grandparents lived—and told him bluntly, "You're new at this game and your daddy's rich, so you are wondering right now who is widja and who is against ya. Well, I want you to know, if you wasn't a millionaire's son,

I wouldn't be widja." Jack chortled with delight. He loved the company of people who were colorful or funny. Patsy was both.[31]

Mulkern took Jack around Faneuil Hall and Quincy Market, Roxbury and the South End, ushering him into bars and drugstores, pool halls and homes, stopping people on the street, holding conversations in doorways and whispering in Jack's ear, "The hard way is the best way."

Jack laughed. "I don't know about the best way, but I know it's the hard way!"[32]

Kane got a recently returned Air Force veteran, Dave Powers, a man with a phenomenal memory for football scores, baseball scores and election results, to take Jack around Charlestown, the poorest, toughest part of the district. Powers took him into the cramped, depressing homes on the hills around the Charlestown Navy Yard, and there Jack came face-to-face with people so poor and living in homes so small the toilet was in the kitchen.[33]

One evening he addressed the Gold Star Mothers of Charlestown. Rose went with him. Every woman there was grieving for a dead son—killed at Pearl Harbor or on Guadalcanal, in North Africa or along the Rhine, in places with strange names, far from home. They stared at him when he stood up to speak, whispering to one another, "He reminds me of my own son." He talked for a few minutes, then looked around the room, obviously moved, and said, slightly awkwardly, "I think I know how you feel. My mother is a Gold Star Mother, too." When he sat down, the audience rushed forward to embrace both mother and son.[34]

The strain of climbing the hills of Charlestown and ascending the steps into people's houses hurt his back, and as the pain grew worse, his face turned the color of putty. One night one of the volunteers who was with him said, "You don't look good."

Jack retorted emphatically, "I feel great!" and climbed the steps to yet another house.[35]

Joe Kennedy checked into his suite at the Ritz-Carlton one night a week so he could grill the campaign staff and confer with Joe Timilty, the former commissioner of police. Timilty knew everybody who mattered in Boston. Then Joe gave orders for what the staff would do in the week ahead.

Around ten P.M. Jack showed up to talk to his father and gulp down a bowl of clam chowder or a plate of scrambled eggs before walking across the Common to the Bellevue, where "Cooky" McFarland, a physio who had spent years working on professional boxers, was waiting to rub his back. He relaxed and stretched out while Cooky gently worked on him, and Cooky, who was a superb raconteur, would regale him with some of the million fight stories he seemed to have stored in his memory. Then Jack swallowed some aspirin and went to bed or curled up on the floor, wrapped in a blanket.[36]

Each morning he climbed into a hot bath and held a staff meeting with his "Junior Brains Trust." Only those who really were close friends, like Lem Billings and Red Fay, were allowed into the bathroom. Jack would eventually dry himself off, pull on a pair of pants and his hip-length cream-colored Harvard cardigan with a big crimson H on the left breast. The meeting was likely to resume again in the small living room, where he and his pals sat and talked, tossing a football back and forth.[37]

After lunch and a nap, Jack got out to meet the voters. His style on the stump was a four- or five-minute speech delivered haltingly, followed by a few questions and answers in which he was confident and knowledge-able, then a brief reminder for people to vote. It was the British style of campaigning. The few long speeches he gave were about his war experi-ences, and then he hardly mentioned himself. He talked mostly about how well his crew had performed after their PT boat was rammed.

When some of his opponents freely attacked him, Jack was hurt and bewildered. He talked about the issues, or his family, or his PT-boat crew. If he refrained from making personal attacks on people, why should they do this to him?[38]

Inexperienced Jack Kennedy was decades ahead of other politicians. He was one of the first to spot the crucial importance of the female vote in what until then had been the whiskey-sodden, cigar-smoking macho world of politics. "Woman power," he'd say to his staff and at public gath-erings. "The untapped resource." It was an unpredictable offshoot of his deep, abiding interest in recreational sex that he should take women seri-ously as voters, but he did.[39]

Engraved invitations were sent to the two thousand registered female Democratic voters in Cambridge, to come have tea and meet the candi-date the afternoon of Sunday, June 15, two days before the primary. Rose or Eunice had signed every invitation. The Sheraton Commander had a room that could hold four hundred people, but more than fifteen hundred women showed up. The tea party ran late into the evening. Eunice and Rose were there as cohosts, with the skinny orgasmatron standing between them. Joe Kennedy was there, too, lurking in the background. So many women . . . impossible for him to stay away.[40]

During the campaign, Jack marched in several parades. He invariably set off walking down the middle of the street, at or near the head of the marchers, and just as invariably gravitated to the sidewalk where the people were, to shake hands, ask what they thought of the parade, smile at them, look into their eyes. Once, as he strode down the street, looking painfully thin, head up, carrying a hat, dressed in his pinstripe suit, a voice rose above the hubbub—"Hey, pal! Try facing the sun and you might cast a shadow!"

The crowd laughed and Jack's stride broke as he half turned in the direction of the voice and flashed that million-dollar smile, then turned back and strode on, swinging his hat easily in his left hand as people laughed and applauded. Money couldn't buy that.[41]

The day following the tea party, however, he marched in the Bunker Hill Day parade. The temperature rose into the nineties, and the parade route was five miles long, most of it on cobbled streets. At the end of the parade, Jack collapsed from exhaustion. Worried campaign aides quickly gathered around, and few people saw him on the ground. He was carried into a nearby house and a doctor was summoned.[42]

The primary was held the next day, and by then he had recovered. That afternoon, dressed in his blue pinstripe suit and a red tie with white polka dots, Jack voted, then took his grandparents to see *A Night in Casablanca*. As the sun went down, they walked over to campaign headquarters at the Kimball Building on Tremont Street while the votes were being counted.

Joe and Rose arrived and shook hands with everybody, smiling their toothy smiles as any proud parents might. Once the results began to flow in, it was clear that Kennedy was going to win. He had piled up twice as many votes as Mike Neville. The rest of the field was nowhere.

Honey Fitz climbed onto a table, danced a jig as only a spry eighty-three-year-old can and burst into "Sweet Adeline" but got so choked up he had to quit halfway through. Then Jack got onto the table and began to express his gratitude, but he, too, got choked up and burst into tears. No matter. He had overcome both physical weakness and mental doubts, willed himself to become something he did not think he could ever be, picked up the torch fallen from his dead brother's hand and was rushing with it now towards a future still more dark than bright.[43]

CHAPTER 13

Golden Boy

With victory number one, they were already rewriting the rules, something the Kennedys would go on doing for the next fifteen years. Jack Kennedy altered the way campaigns were run, remolding American elections, even changing the way people thought about politics. Yet he was so exhausted at the end of the primary that he spent much of that summer recuperating at Hyannis. Not that it made much difference—the campaign for the Eleventh congressional district rolled on.

Joseph Kennedy had created the Joseph P. Kennedy, Jr., Foundation as a memorial to his dead son. Between the June 1946 primary and the November election, Jack handed over large checks to Catholic charities in ceremonies that the Boston papers covered, and his narrow face beamed across their front pages. It was a groundbreaking example of how to campaign without actually campaigning—cynical yet almost beyond criticism; compassionate yet self-serving; charitable yet political. Other people had done similar things, but never on this scale or with such skill.

Joe Kennedy also used his clout to get a new Boston post of the Veterans of Foreign Wars established, named in honor of Joseph P. Kennedy, Jr.

Jack was the post commander. And it was almost certainly Joe Kennedy's doing that the forty-seventh annual Encampment of the VFW was held in September 1946 in Boston, with Jack as chairman of the event. This allowed Jack to present himself not just to Boston's voters but to people across the country as a spokesman on veterans' affairs.

At the election on November 5 Jack Kennedy picked up 73 percent of the vote without having to expend much of his limited strength. On Armistice Day he spoke at an American Legion post. He had included in his text a quote from the Bible—"Greater love hath no man than this, that a man lay down his life for his friends." But he suddenly broke down in tears, too choked up to speak before he reached "friends." Jack sat down, engulfed in grief, head bowed and struggling to get his feelings under control.[1]

After being sworn in as a member of the Eightieth Congress in January 1947, he went over to the National Press Club, where a reception was being held for the new Congressmen, and there met someone whose destiny would be entwined with his own—Richard M. Nixon. Like Kennedy, the thirty-four-year-old Nixon was a Navy veteran from the South Pacific. A complete unknown without any political experience or money, Nixon had ousted Jerry Voorhis, one of the most powerful figures in California politics. It was a race that had left Kennedy deeply impressed. "So you're the guy who beat Jerry Voorhis!" he said, reaching for Nixon's hand. "How's it feel?"

"I suppose I'm elated," Nixon cautiously responded.[2]

The following day, Jack was installed on the third floor of the old House Office Building, in a standard set of four rooms—one for himself, three for his staff. He carefully placed his coconut shell—enshrined now in a plastic container—in a prominent spot on his desk and hung some nautical prints of Kennedy sailboats on the walls. Otherwise, his office was almost as bare as a monk's cell. And he continued to wear his only suit, with a personal refinement—a pair of old tennis shoes.[3]

In the Eightieth Congress, the Republicans not only controlled both houses for the first time in a generation but were locked in a bitter, unrelenting struggle with the dead Roosevelt, the living Truman and the heritage of the New Deal. For a freshman Democrat like Jack Kennedy, there wasn't much that he would be able to accomplish in this Congress, and probably not in the next one, either.

The best he—or any other freshman on the Hill—could do was to concentrate on the few issues that mattered to him, which is precisely what he did. He staked out his territory almost as soon as he took office—labor legislation; housing and jobs for veterans; Communist subversion at home; Communist expansion abroad.

He got two committee assignments: the District of Columbia, which offered little excitement, and the House Committee on Education and Labor, a slot that pitched him right where he wanted to be, in the biggest domestic political dispute of the Eightieth Congress, the fight over the Taft-Hartley Bill. This legislation aimed to curb union power by reducing collective bargaining and eliminating the closed shop.

Jack's maiden speech in the House, on April 16, 1947, roundly condemned Taft-Hartley. The Republican majority on the committee—including Richard Nixon—was pushing the bill vigorously. The Democratic minority was equally adamant in opposition. Jack, however, had entered a dissent that was entirely his own. He welcomed Taft-Hartley's guarantee of democratic procedures in union elections and denounced "union feather bedding and racketeering." All the same, he thought the bill so punitive it would make labor truly antagonistic to business and labor disputes more likely, not less.[4]

The immediate result of this strict party-line split within the committee was the first Kennedy-Nixon debate. In April 1947, as Congress prepared to vote on Taft-Hartley, the two congressmen agreed to debate it in McKeesport, a steel town in western Pennsylvania. Nixon tenaciously argued the Republican case for curbing union power and privileges, concentrating on the blue-collar steelworkers in the audience. Kennedy made his pitch to the businessmen present, arguing that Taft-Hartley would poison labor relations for a generation. His charm and friendliness won him the debate, but Nixon shrugged that off.

They returned to Washington that night aboard the "Capital Limited," sharing a stateroom and sitting up into the early hours talking about the risks and responsibilities of standing up to a heavily armed and expansionist Soviet Union.[5]

Back in Washington, Kennedy told labor leaders they stood no chance of stopping Taft-Hartley: even if Truman vetoed it, Congress would pass it over the veto. And they were responsible for that. Labor had lost public support by tolerating subversives and gangsters. Organized labor had to reform itself, and until that happened, big business would dictate American labor law. What Jack said proved right: Taft-Hartley was eventually passed over the President's veto.[6]

Organized labor credited only six out of the twenty-five members of the Committee on Education and Labor as being sympathetic to its cause, and Jack Kennedy felt proud to be one of the six. Nevertheless, he was as strongly anti-Communist as any Republican on the committee, including Nixon.

Shortly after becoming a congressman, Kennedy clashed sharply with Russ Nixon, who had once taught him economics at Harvard and was, in 1947, working for the Congress of Industrial Organizations (CIO). Nixon admitted under questioning by the committee that some CIO officials were Communists, but he refused to concede Kennedy's point that they were therefore a threat to national security.

But wasn't it true, said Kennedy, that the policy of the Communist party was "to resort to all sorts of artifices, evasion and subterfuges only so as to get into the trade unions and carry on Communist work in them?"

"I didn't teach you that at Harvard, did I?" said Nixon, smirking at his own cleverness.

"No," said Kennedy. "I am reading from Lenin." Nixon, suddenly dumbfounded, had underestimated the boyish-looking plutocrat's son.[7]

Following this hearing, the Education and Labor Committee chairman, Fred Hartley (coauthor of the Taft-Hartley Bill), decided to create a sub-committee that would investigate Communist infiltration of organized labor. The subcommittee was chaired by Charles Kersten of Milwaukee, and its membership included Jack Kennedy.

Jack and Kersten were both interested in a strike that had broken out six years earlier. In the spring of 1941 the Allis-Chalmers plant in Milwaukee was shut down for eleven weeks. The plant produced machinery for destroyers and cruisers. Forrestal and any number of admirals were infuriated by this strike, which had occurred as the nation sought to build up its armed forces in case the United States was pushed or dragged into World War II.

The strike had been masterminded by a United Auto Workers official, Harold Christoffel, a secret member of the Communist party. The workers voted not to strike, but Christoffel and his friends falsified the result by producing two thousand fraudulent ballots in favor of striking. The Nazi-Soviet Pact of 1939 had inspired Communists throughout the free world to sabotage the defenses of Western democracies.

Christoffel was interviewed in Washington in March 1947, and Jack Kennedy was convinced almost from the start that he had committed perjury. Kennedy introduced a motion to seek Christoffel's indictment.

Before his motion could be acted on, the subcommittee traveled to Milwaukee, where Christoffel testified again, and denied everything again.[8]

Jack's motion was now approved and Christoffel was duly convicted, but the conviction was overturned on a technicality. Tried and convicted yet again, he eventually spent nearly four years in prison. Over the next few years, it gave Jack Kennedy immense satisfaction to remind people that he had nailed Christoffel long before Richard Nixon unearthed Alger Hiss. But after Joe McCarthy disgraced congressional efforts to expose and prosecute Communists, Jack rapidly drew a veil over the Christoffel case.[9]

The predominant foreign policy issue of the late 1940s was the onset of the Cold War. When Britain informed the Greek government in March 1947 that it could no longer finance its war against Communist guerrillas, Truman proposed to Congress that the United States step into the breach and provide military and financial aid to any country facing a military threat from Soviet Communism, starting with Greece and Turkey.

Jack did not need persuading. "If Greece and Turkey go down," he told reporters, "the road to the Near East is open. We have no alternative but to support the President's policy." The Eightieth Congress came around, reluctantly, to supporting the Truman Doctrine, a defining event of the postwar.[10]

While Congress was still debating the issue, in May 1947 Jack found himself under pressure to support the release of James Curley from the federal prison in Danbury, Connecticut. Despite the money lavished on his defense by Joseph Kennedy, Curley had been convicted of mail fraud and given a six-to-eighteen-month stretch. A petition for a presidential pardon was started almost immediately by John McCormack, who was the most powerful Democrat in Massachusetts and Democratic leader in the House; and by a Republican congresswoman of exemplary probity, Edith Nourse Rogers.

Almost every political figure in the state signed it, regardless of party. Joe Kennedy was in favor of it, as was Cardinal Cushing. But Jack wouldn't sign it, regardless of intense arm twisting by his father. He wouldn't do it, he told his staff, because to do so would upset Grampa, who still blamed Curley for thwarting every attempt he had made at a political comeback since 1919. But the justification Jack gave to journalists and his fellow politicians could hardly have been more disingenuous. "The petition begins, 'Those who have served with James M. Curley do hereby petition the President. . . .'" Jack would give his little half shrug and half smile. "How could I sign it? I never served with him." Truman rejected the petition. It was Christmas before he commuted Curley's sentence to time served, which by now totaled six months.[11]

Meanwhile, Jack strongly criticized the British administration of Palestine and ardently supported creation of a Jewish state. There were few Jewish votes to be won in Boston, but like Honey Fitz, Jack courted the Jewish vote. In June 1947 he rose in the House to demand "the establishment of a free and democratic Jewish commonwealth in Palestine, the opening of the doors of Palestine to Jewish immigration and the removal of land restrictions" that blocked Jewish purchases in heavily populated areas.

As he lambasted the British, there was nothing in what he said that suggested the Palestinian population had any rights at all. Jack Kennedy considered himself something of an expert on Palestine, having spent some time there before the war. It was a subject he had thought about long before the horrors of the Holocaust changed every calculation. Over the years, just as he proved a friend of organized labor, so, too, would he prove a friend of Israel.[12]

Nevertheless, he squirmed whenever anyone tried to pin a label on him, whether it was "conservative" or "liberal." Throughout his life he saw himself as a free agent, picking and choosing his own course. No group was ever allowed to assume he was one of them. When, during his first term in Congress, a group of liberal Democrats tried to co-opt him to support liberal legislation, he brushed them off by telling journalists what he thought of the liberal reform group in the House: "Those goofs are really obnoxious," said Jack.[13]

That summer, as Congress went into recess, newspaper columnist Drew Pearson published his appraisal of the Eightieth Congress. The best thing about it, he concluded, was the presence of some promising new congressmen. Jack Kennedy was at the top of his list.[14]

===

In the bright sunshine that he loved, Jack chased the tan that bespeaks vitality and youthful good health, but he got more from it than that. His skin shone at times, making him look like a gilded statue from classical and pagan Rome, a new Augustus sprung amazingly to life, tall, slender, confident and handsome, a golden boy, half god, half man. That amazing hue did not show up in the grainy black-and-white photographs of the time, but it floored many who met him. What is it, journalists and politicians asked Kennedy's aides, that makes him shine like that? Malaria, they said, something the war hero had picked up in the South Pacific.

It was true that Jack had malaria, and like countless other veterans of the Pacific war he took Atabrine tablets to control it. True, too, that Atabrine gave the skin a yellow tinge. Yet his glow was something else, something different, something for which the medication was merely a base coat.

With Congress in recess, Jack arrived in Ireland on September 1 to spend some time with Kick at Lismore Castle—owned by her in-laws, the Duke and Duchess of Devonshire—to meet some of Kick's English friends and to make a search for his family's Irish roots. Ostensibly he had come to Europe to look into Communist infiltration of trade unions, but that could wait until his Irish vacation was over.

He was introduced to one of Kick's friends, Pamela Digby Churchill, the blond, vivacious and pretty daughter of an English baron and, until recently, married to Randolph Churchill, the son of Jack's hero. She was what the French call a *grande horizontale,* cheerfully sleeping her way from one powerful man to the next, much like Clare Luce. Inevitably, given her promiscuity and his, they were soon in bed together.[15]

After a couple of weeks at Lismore, he and Pamela set off for New Ross, a village nearly sixty miles away, in Kick's station wagon. The result was predictable—the American stranger wanders around the whitewashed cottages of the auld sod, telling people his name is Kennedy and he is looking for the ancestral hearth. "Which Kennedy would that be?" ask the bemused locals. There were any number of Kennedys from New Ross and environs. Pamela found it all terribly tedious and pointless, but to Jack, a romantic when all else was scraped away, it was an enchanting day, walking across a landscape that was both strange but his, among people whom he'd never seen before but felt a kinship with, under gray skies that he knew were somehow part of himself. He had not found half of what he'd come looking for, but he would be back.[16]

A few days later he flew to London, where he intended to meet up with a couple of members of the Labour subcommittee. They planned to travel across Europe looking into Communist infiltration of trade unions. Jack suddenly fell seriously ill. He had felt unwell much of the time in Ireland, but now he was vomiting and feverish. Shortly after checking in to Claridges, he was rushed into the London Clinic on Devonshire Place. There, one of the stars of the British medical establishment, Sir Daniel Davis, diagnosed his illness as Addison's disease, the disease that had killed Jane Austen at the age of forty-one.

Addison's, which progressively destroyed the adrenal glands, was usually fatal. As they deteriorated, the adrenal glands produced ever-diminishing secretions of various hormones essential to good health, especially those that affected the heart and other large muscles. The disease was caused by a virus, although that wasn't known in 1947. Given the incubation period, Jack would have contracted it about a year earlier. He may well have had a genetic predisposition to this and similar viral infections, because his sister Eunice also contracted the disease. One of the effects of Addison's was to make the skin shine like burnished gold if it was deeply tanned or Atabrine yellow.[17]

Rose Kennedy hastened to London to be at his bedside, while in New York a distraught Joe Kennedy broke down in tears as he confided in his old friend Arthur Krock that Jack was in the hospital in England, dying. He had been given the last rites. But the story told to the press was that the Congressman had been stricken by "a recurrent attack of malaria."[18]

Anne McGillicuddy, a beautiful former Navy nurse who had looked after Jack in 1944—and whom he'd dated for a while—was flown to England. On October 18, after nearly four weeks in the London Clinic, Jack was loaded into an ambulance, still in his pajamas, and taken to Southampton, where he was carried aboard the *Queen Mary*. He spent the entire five-day voyage to New York in the ship's sick bay, attended by Anne, reading as voraciously as ever and talking eagerly with Barbara Ward, an English economist married to a Labour politician. He grilled her intently on the British government's recent creation, the National Health Service.[19]

Once the ship docked, Jack was taken by ambulance to La Guardia Airport, where a chartered plane flew him to Boston. He spent the next six weeks recuperating, with periodic visits to New England Baptist Hospital. There he became a medical guinea pig for a new treatment for Addison's disease—cortisone.[20]

The first of what became known as "miracle drugs," cortisone almost certainly saved Jack Kennedy's life, but it involved a teeth-gritting regimen. Every two months a cut was made in each thigh and the lower back. A small pellet of cortisone was pushed into each cut, which was then sewn up and bandaged. This treatment kept him going for the next four years, until a cortisone tablet that could be swallowed became available.[21]

During those four years he made regular payments to a church in Boston's North End for Masses to be said in his name. And he told his friend the journalist Joe Alsop his days were numbered. "The doctors say I've got a sort of slow-motion leukemia," he said one day. "They tell me I'll probably last till I'm about forty-five."[22]

He began asking his friends, "How do you think you'll die?" And when they asked how he expected *his* life to end, he told them, "In an automobile. Killed in an automobile accident." An anticipation, clearly formed, of a premature and violent death. To the poetic, Byronic side of Jack's soul, that seemed better by far than wasting away in a hospital bed, chained to a body that was dying miserably of Addison's disease, with himself the helpless witness to an early but uninteresting exit.[23]

CHAPTER 14

The Representative

O n the Hill, the young congressman was a hyperkinetic force, unable to remain at rest in committee meetings or conclaves with his staff, tapping his left foot constantly while playing a pencil on his knee nonstop, drumming silently, a one-man rhythm section. He looked different, too. Billy Sutton, one of his aides, told him shortly after they reached Washington that the blue pinstripe had to go. The seat was crosshatched and the elbows worn out. Besides, it did not fit him any longer. Jack bought a new suit, but instead of choosing a dark one, as any other congressman would, he went for light gray, which emphasized his youth and his apartness. He wasn't like them; wouldn't look like them.[1]

During the Eightieth Congress, he rented a small house in Georgetown that he shared with Eunice—currently working as a volunteer in the Justice Department—and Billy Sutton. After Jack's uncontested reelection in November 1948, Joe Kennedy bought him a more imposing Civil War–era house in the same neighborhood, but one with an English basement, servant's quarters and reception area. The first floor offered a wood-paneled library, dining room, kitchen and an extensive patio shaded by mature trees. There were two bedrooms on the second floor, a drawing room that held Eunice's baby grand piano, a third floor with two more bedrooms and a large bathroom and porch.[2]

His father not only provided Jack with a nice house but sent the family cook, Margaret Ambrose, to Washington to look after him. Each morning she made a hot lunch that Jack's valet, George Taylor—formerly employed by Arthur Krock—delivered to his office at noon.

One of the first friends Jack made in Congress was a tall, handsome congressman from Florida, George Smathers, aka "Gorgeous George." Jack was so physically weak after his Addison's crisis that for the rest of the Eightieth Congress, Smathers had to help him cross Independence Avenue when the bell sounded in the House Office Building for a floor vote.[3]

He and Smathers hit it off because neither one took politics with the seriousness that most congressmen did. It did not fill their entire lives or circumscribe their sense of self. Jack's office was itself a gentle mockery of the august establishment he'd joined. There was always a golf club propped up in a corner, and he could often be seen standing next to the desk, practicing his swing while dictating a letter or report. There was also a dartboard hanging from the door. He liked to sit with his feet on the desk, throwing darts. Jack's boredom with the House was no secret. It was too slow, too inward-looking.[4]

Each Thursday when Congress was in session, he flew up to Boston to check in with his office there. Sunday evening he flew back to D.C. All his life, Jack Kennedy loved to fly.

In Boston he maintained a small apartment at 122 Bowdoin Street that was a model of disorder, with discarded clothing on the floor and under the furniture. It consisted of four small rooms, with a painting of *PT-109* on the living room wall. He slept in his underwear and did not rise before nine A.M. if he could help it. Breakfast was invariably the same—in Boston or anywhere else—but here it was prepared for him by the building superintendent. He had four ounces of orange juice, fried eggs, two strips of bacon and some buttered toast.[5]

In 1948—a Leap Year—Jack was rated the nation's sixth most eligible bachelor (just behind J. Edgar Hoover!) in a newspaper poll. He told reporters he wasn't in love with anyone, "But this could be my year. There are ten months left."[6]

More than ever now, Jack could effortlessly sweep young women off their feet and onto the bed. His conquests included movie stars such as

Gene Tierney, Arlene Dahl and Ava Gardner. There also may have been a one-night stand with Clare Luce in the summer of 1947.[7]

With so much time spent in the air, he met countless stewardesses. They more or less displaced the models and starlets who had received so much of his attention before. Yet his problematic health ruffled the waters of true lust. Many evenings he lacked the energy to do more than eat dinner off a tray in bed, with his date sitting in a chair beside him, eating from a tray balanced on her knees.[8]

When he was feeling better, his preference was to take his date to a movie, then go home and read. If coitus did take place, it didn't hold his attention long. In his casual approach to recreational sex, he probably disappointed the hopes of countless young women but devastated the emotions of none. In all the later revelations about his busy sex life, what was missing was even one account by a woman who claimed to have been manipulated or exploited. His attitude prefigured the unwritten rule of professional basketball—no harm, no foul.

Busy as he was with the opposite sex, Jack Kennedy spent most of his evening hours in the library, where he seems to have read nearly every book on veterans and their problems published in the years after 1945. He reviewed some of them for *The Boston Globe*.[9]

Shortly after he was sworn in as a congressman, he was featured in the "Did You Happen to See . . . ?" column that was still running in the Washington *Times-Herald* long after Inga Arvad left town. Asked what he hoped to achieve now that he was in Congress, Jack replied, "For a long time, I was Joseph P. Kennedy's son. Then I was Kathleen's brother; then Eunice's brother. Some day, I hope to stand on my own two feet."[10]

=

Jack Kennedy was careless and messy wherever he lived, yet at work he was a clean-desk man. This, his overworked and highly capable secretary Mary Davis explained, was because he didn't do much work. There was a story circulating around the Hill that one day John McCormack, the Minority Leader, encountered him in a House corridor. "Nice of you to stop by and see us, John," said McCormack.[11]

Even so, as a congressman whose party was in the minority and who lacked even the least trace of seniority, there was only so much impact Jack Kennedy could hope to have in the House. Unlike some recently elected legislators, he did not bother to try to impress his constituents by introducing bills or tabling amendments to legislation, knowing they stood no chance. Whether he would have acted as he did with a narrow majority and a strong opponent in the wings is open to doubt.

Between 1947 and 1951 Jack limited himself to pursuing the handful of political issues that interested him. The most important, in the early years, was moderate-priced housing for veterans. During the Depression, housing starts had fallen to 1900 levels. There was some improvement during the war, but by 1946 the deficit ran into millions of units. To his mind, no one deserved decent housing at reasonable prices more than war veterans, who were demobilized in the millions, eager to make up for lost time, get married and raise families.

Jack Kennedy estimated 1.5 million homes were needed for veterans. The fact that government guidelines established preference for vets on home sales wasn't the answer. "Veterans' preference is a joke. A veteran can't afford to pay the prices asked for houses today."[12]

On this issue he was agitated, committed and well informed. Kennedy created a nonpartisan veterans' committee to lobby for passage of the Taft-Ellender-Wagner Bill, or TEW, that Truman was trying to push through the Eightieth Congress. To generate publicity for his committee, he arranged to be photographed talking to the nation's most decorated World War II hero, Audie Murphy, about the housing problems that veterans faced.[13]

The purpose of the TEW Bill was to build 1.5 million low- and medium-cost homes with federal subsidies and to ensure that veterans would get preference to buy them. The bill also provided money for something most cities desperately needed—slum clearance. The real estate lobby—aided and abetted by the American Legion—fought TEW as bitterly as the American Medical Association was fighting Truman over health care reform.[14]

Jack's lobbying group organized a National Veterans Housing Conference in Washington at the end of February 1948. Three thousand veterans gathered from across the country to demand that their representatives vote for TEW. Every important veterans' group was there but one—the Legion. He vehemently criticized the Legion as a reactionary force (even if he was a member of it). The Legion's leaders just as fiercely criticized him as being a congressional novice out of his depth.[15]

The number of congressmen who signed the discharge petition to get TEW onto the House floor rose overnight from 52 to 150, but the bill remained blocked in committee. An indignant Jack denounced the committee's inaction on the floor of the House as "a sellout to the real estate and building lobbies."[16]

Jack not only wanted moderate-priced housing but pushed hard, and often, to retain wartime rent controls, something that would benefit low-income families across the country. This was another battle he lost. But he did score one significant success. He and John McCormack teamed up to get a federal aid program for slum clearance—with Boston as the first city on the list.[17]

At times he described himself as "a conservative liberal," and many people assumed wrongly that he was as right-wing as his father. He was one of the few Democrats who favored limiting the presidency to two terms. This was a Republican amendment that amounted to spitting on the grave of Franklin D. Roosevelt, the four-term President. The two Democratic leaders in the House, John McCormack of Boston and Sam Rayburn of Texas, pleaded with him not to vote for the amendment, but he did so, probably out of loyalty to Dad. Then he sought to make amends by helping Rayburn buy a luxurious new automobile.[18]

Although his father had some influence over Jack's economic views, the congressman was not particularly conservative on economic issues, unlike, say, Massachusetts Republican Edith Nourse Rogers. Nor was he a tax-and-spend Democrat like John McCormack, who was ready to vote for any bill that promised increased government spending, and voted against every bill that would cut it.

In 1948 he voted against tax cuts. The money was needed, he insisted (and rightly), to rebuild the country's defenses following the headlong demobilization at the end of the war. Jack Kennedy's votes as a congressman were split almost evenly between economy and spending. And when Truman vetoed a bill that would increase federal public assistance to the blind, the aged and dependent children, Kennedy voted to override the veto. Jack voted, by and large, on what he saw as the merits of a piece of legislation.[19]

He was eager to be seen as a national spokesman on veterans' issues, but when House Democrats started proposing a more generous pension bill for veterans than the one the Truman administration wanted, Jack derided it as a cheap political stunt. And when a congressman with Legion backing began praising the proposal on the House floor, Jack interjected, "The American Legion hasn't had a constructive thought since 1918!" His detachment from party ideology over time would encourage an impression that he lacked passion or belief when, in truth, what had happened was that by the time he emerged from six years in the House, he had learned that controlling his feelings enabled him to pursue larger ambitions.[20]

For now, though, his temper showed. On July 7, 1949, Joe Kennedy's friend the right-wing columnist Westbrook Pegler testified before the Education and Labor subcommittee investigating subversion in organized labor. Charles Kersten had been defeated in November 1948, and the new chairman was Andrew Jacobs of Indianapolis. When Pegler denounced the leaders of the major unions as "despots, criminals and Communists," Jack was enraged. He tried repeatedly to get in a rejoinder, but Jacobs wouldn't recognize him.

Frustrated and angry, Jack burst out, "Why don't you let somebody else ask some questions?"

"You've got your ideas and I've got mine," said Jacobs contemptuously.

That was too much. Jack sprang to his feet and announced, "I'm getting off the subcommittee."

"That's okay by me," Jacobs responded.[21]

Jack's beliefs were also to the fore when it came to the interests of the Catholic Church. In 1948 the Education and Labor Committee was close to recommending a bill that the Truman administration favored to provide federal aid to education. It was a bill that Jack's friends in organized labor favored, too. The committee was split, though: twelve (mostly Democrats) in favor, twelve (mostly Republicans) against. Because the bill did not guarantee money for parochial schools, Jack effectively killed it with his vote against. Virtually the same bill came around again in 1950, with exactly the same result.[22]

In the winter of 1948 Jack agreed to appear with a group of Protestant ministers at a housing rally in Philadelphia. At the last minute he pulled out without explaining why. But afterwards he told Drew Pearson the reason—the Catholic hierarchy had ordered him not to attend an event where no Catholic clerics would be present.[23]

He took an interest, too, in questions of civil liberty. In 1949 he offered legislation that would curb government wiretapping, which he said was getting out of control. Jack denounced wiretapping as "one of the most fundamental violations of human rights and privacy." But his legislation never made it to the House floor.[24]

The following year he spoke to the 348 students graduating in January 1950 from Notre Dame, which honored him with a Doctor of Laws degree, the first of more than twenty honorary degrees he eventually collected. He warned the graduates to beware "the great leviathan—the state." They needed to be alert to "the ever expanding power of the federal government," which was now so pervasive it threatened individual liberties.[25]

Jack had not wanted to be assigned to the House committee that oversaw the District of Columbia, but he soon became an ardent supporter of District home rule. It was a moral issue, he argued, not a political one. Why should citizens' rights be denied to people simply because they lived in the nation's capital? It was a good question, and the people of the District are still waiting for an answer.[26]

When legislation was introduced in the House to impose a sales tax on D.C., he led the fight to kill it, to the astonishment of another member of the committee. Joe Kennedy was an outspoken proponent of sales taxes.

Jack explained his position this way: "The fact that I come from a wealthy family had nothing to do with what I did. I was elected by a lot of little people in low income brackets. They are against sales taxes, and as their representative, I am against them too."

"But what about your father—won't he be sore?"

Jack retorted impatiently, "I haven't asked him and I'm not interested."[27]

He also took a close personal interest in appointments to West Point and Annapolis, convinced they should be taken out of the hands of politicians. Jack felt vindicated in August 1951 when a cheating scandal erupted at West Point, to national dismay and amazement. He introduced a bill that would have created a twelve-member selection committee drawn from Congress, the executive branch and leading nonpolitical figures in American life. The present system, Jack argued, did not attract the bright young men who would be drawn to a system based entirely on merit. But academy appointments were a rich source of patronage. His bill went nowhere.[28]

For his own appointments, he required prospective applicants to take a physical examination as tough as West Point's. That weeded out a third of them. Those who passed then took federal civil service aptitude and achievement tests. Those with high scores on these tests and the SAT provided a short list whose members were interviewed by a panel consisting of a former Army doctor, a former Army chaplain and a psychology professor from Harvard Medical School. The panel made the final selection.[29]

His interest in women went beyond running up the score. Jack Kennedy may have been influenced by the fact that all his sisters were expected, like their brothers, to do something with their lives. For whatever reason, he was one of the earliest male politicians to urge women to pursue political careers. He appreciated better than most men the immense attractiveness of women who were both bright and beautiful, women such as Inga Arvad and Clare Luce. Utterly confident in his own brains and physical appeal, he did not feel threatened by them. In the fall of 1948, delivering a speech at Trinity College, a women's school in Boston—surrounded, that is, by adoring young women—he urged college-educated women to seek political careers.[30]

For all the interest he took in some domestic issues, nothing so fired Jack's imagination or challenged his intellect as the life-and-death realm of foreign policy and national security.

He was lukewarm towards the Marshall Plan when it was first proposed by George Marshall at Harvard's 296th commencement exercise in June 1947. At the same time, he recognized that something needed to be done to prevent a Communist takeover of Western Europe. He traveled to England, France and Italy in the summer of 1948 to see things for himself.

Jack was appalled by the British attitude towards the prospect of a new war in Europe—people and government alike dismissed it as unlikely for years to come. The Royal Air Force was training and reequipping on the assumption that it wouldn't have to fight the Soviets this side of 1955. He publicly ridiculed the RAF for being shortsighted and unprepared, much as he'd derided it in 1940 for being unready to stand up to the Luftwaffe.[31]

When he reached West Berlin, the Berlin blockade was under way. Stalin was trying to starve and freeze the city into submission. The commander of the American zone, General Lucius D. Clay, was confident nonetheless that the Allied airlift would ultimately prevail. More than that, said Clay, "The Russians—by their actions—have given us the political soul of Germany on a silver platter."[32]

Even so, Jack returned home convinced the Marshall Plan was already in deep trouble. It had not done anything to make Western Europe secure against Communism. Worse, the Europeans were cynically exploiting it to extract large sums of money from a dumb and generous Uncle Sugar. "They've got to realize that American aid is not going to be given them forever," he fulminated to newspaper reporters.[33]

As the Cold War evolved, he became increasingly agitated. In September 1949, when the Soviets achieved their first atomic detonation, Jack sent an impatient letter to Truman, demanding to know what civil defense preparations had been made to ride out an atomic attack. The answer, when it came, was nothing much. He was shocked and indignant to discover that the federal civil defense agency consisted of one person without a plan. "If an atomic bomb were dropped on one of our cities tomorrow," he announced, "all would be panic and confusion." The fact that it would be many years before the Soviets could make a nuclear attack on an American city did not seem to occur to him. On the other hand, given the surprise attack on Pearl Harbor less than a decade before, his anxiety was widely shared. Bernard Baruch, who had been charged with trying to keep the Cold War arms race from turning nuclear, praised Jack for his efforts to educate the nation on the lack of civil defense. "More power to you!" said Baruch.[34]

By 1950 Jack was almost as critical of Truman's leadership in the Cold War as the Republicans. He railed against the "loss" of China to Mao Tse-tung's Communists. "The basic question that must be answered is not whether the Chinese did their best to save themselves, which they most certainly did not," he argued, "the question is whether we did our best to save China."[35]

With China now under Communist rule, he was convinced the arena of struggle in the Far East would shift inevitably to Indochina. There would be a major war there, he warned, "within five years." Three weeks after he delivered this prediction to the Holy Name Society in Pittsfield, Massachusetts, there *was* a major war—in Korea.[36]

There was little clarity or consistency to his views on foreign policy in these immediate postwar years. In one speech he was likely to present the Far East as more important to the United States than decadent, left-wing Europe. In the next, he would present Europe as essential to American security, much more so than the Far East. The single unifying thread to his thought was an urgent, competitive response to the Communist threat at home and overseas.

It wasn't necessary to be a conservative to be opposed to Communism. Some of the staunchest anti-Communists were liberals. Yet in 1950 Jack contributed generously to Richard Nixon's campaign for the Senate against a liberal Democrat, Congresswoman Helen Gahagan Douglas. Following Nixon's victory, he told a discussion group at the School of Government at Harvard how glad he was that Mrs. Douglas had lost.

He also derided America's European allies—"We have to get these foreigners off our backs." Fighting in Korea didn't make any sense, he insisted. And Dean Acheson ought to resign as secretary of state. Not enough had been done to root the Communists out of government. While he despised Acheson, he stood up for Joseph McCarthy and his witchhunt at the State Department. "I know Joe pretty well and he may have something," said Jack.[37]

His failure to recognize McCarthy for the evil drunk and bully that he really was would haunt him for years to come.

=

After the death of her husband in 1944, Kathleen Kennedy had decided to stay in England. She had fallen in love not only with Billy Hartington but with his family and his country. She remained estranged from her mother, but Jack never held her marriage to a Protestant against her, and neither did her father. To both of them she remained what she had always been— the high-spirited, highly intelligent Kick, the star among the Kennedy daughters.

By 1948 she had fallen in love with another English aristocrat, Peter Milford, eighth Earl of Fitzwilliam, who was not only an Anglican but already married. On a trip to the United States in April 1948, Kick told her mother that Fitzwilliam was going to divorce his wife to marry her, and that any children they had would be raised as Anglicans. Rose went berserk, denouncing her daughter, screaming that she would be cut off from Joe's money and excommunicated and would spend eternity in Purgatory.[38]

A month later, on May 15, Jack was at the Hyannis Port house listening to a recording of *Finian's Rainbow* when the phone rang. Billy Sutton answered the phone. It was NBC calling. They had a report that Kick had died earlier that day in a plane crash in France. Did the congressman have anything he'd like to say? Sutton, still holding the phone, relayed the message.

"Has it been confirmed?" asked Jack. It hadn't. "Tell them to call back when they know one way or another." He went back to listening to *Finian's Rainbow.*

The phone rang again a few minutes later, as Ella Logan was singing "How Are Things in Glocca Morra?" Sutton picked up the telephone, then told Jack that Kick's body had been identified.

"That Ella Logan sure has a sweet voice," said Jack. He looked away as his eyes filled with tears. "First Joe," he said bitterly. "Now Kick."[39]

The sense of doom, never distant, clung to him for weeks afterwards. One day, walking under the cherry trees around the Tidal Basin with Ted Reardon, another member of his staff, he asked, "What's the best way to die?"

Reardon found the question embarrassing, but Jack persisted. Reardon finally said he thought dying of old age would be all right.

"You're wrong as hell," snapped Jack. "In war—that's the best way to die. The very best. In war." He strode on, grimly satisfied.[40]

CHAPTER 15

Globe-trotter

Jack Kennedy arrived in London on January 11, 1951, and as he descended the steps to the tarmac, close behind him came a tall, beefy figure. He rarely traveled alone, and on this trip—as on many others—he had the company of his old friend, college roommate and former Harvard football hero, the slightly flaky Torbert Macdonald. A believer in astrology and horoscopes, Macdonald was convinced that his friendship with Jack was written in the stars—both were Geminis.[1]

NATO had been organized in the fall of 1949 to discourage Soviet adventurism and deter a Soviet attack, but it still lacked a firm foundation in Western public opinion and was militarily weak. The purpose of his trip, Jack told reporters, was to see whether or not the United States should send more troops to Europe. At present, there were only two American divisions stationed in Germany. General Dwight D. Eisenhower, NATO's military commander, was asking for six.

Under leaden winter skies, with piles of rubble still common in London and basic foodstuffs stringently rationed, England seemed weary and impoverished. It had emerged from the war with a national debt more than three times its gross domestic product. The country seemed to stagger under this oppressive weight. One serious policy mistake, British politicians told Jack Kennedy, and this country could go bankrupt. To them, his repeated assertions that Britain must call on its people to make even greater sacrifices, tolerate more poverty and run up even bigger debts, were naive.

No one denied that Britain's armed forces were currently in a parlous state, but when Jack asked what would happen if a war suddenly broke out, British officials told him the people had learned so much from World War II that the whole country would be ready to respond. "This is no doubt B.S.," Jack told his diary.[2]

Emanuel Shinwell, the British Minister of Defence, told him it might take another year before the armed forces were ready for war. But Shinwell said he wasn't worried. The Russians, he assured Jack, were in even worse shape militarily than NATO. Besides, the Soviet leadership now consisted of old men—hardly the kind of people noted for risking everything on a single throw of the dice. Wishful thinking, thought Jack.[3]

At present, the British military told him, NATO could field ten divisions. In another year, it would field twenty. But stopping a full-blooded Soviet attack would require at least thirty-five, maybe as many as fifty-five. That figure could be achieved only if Germany was rearmed—and the French would not agree to that.[4]

From London, Jack and Torby flew on to Paris, where Jack was gratified to learn that the French had just increased the term of conscription from twelve months to eighteen. Yet he also found an ingrained resistance to serious rearmament. The French were fearful that if NATO seemed about to become strong too quickly, the Soviets might be provoked into launching an attack on Western Europe while it was still weak. The trauma of Nazi occupation had left the French, Jack sensed, with an unshakable defeatism.

The American ambassador, the French-speaking and elegant David Bruce, was convinced that NATO was Europe's best hope. But as things stood, Bruce told Jack, there was a glaring weakness on NATO's southern flank. "We have to get Spain into NATO."[5]

In Germany, which had almost no national debt—the democratic governments of postwar Germany felt morally free to repudiate Hitler's war debts—Jack was impressed to see a country that was rapidly removing its piles of wartime rubble and frenetically rebuilding its shattered cities. And wherever he went, he found a flourishing black market that offered just about everything.

Yet despite the evident buoyancy of West Germany, Jack was surprised to find the long shadow of Korea darkening the mood of the people. From news films and what they had read about the Korean War, being defended by the Americans seemed to many Germans almost as devastating as being defeated by the Russians. Some seemed tempted to think that it would make more sense not to fight at all.[6]

Flying from Berlin to Belgrade by way of Zurich, Jack crossed a Europe that was, in various ways and at varying speeds, recovering from the aftermath of the most destructive war in history. Belgrade struck him as a city thronged with young people, yet the atmosphere was subdued. There were few stores to be seen and none had anything much to sell. Armed soldiers appeared on nearly every street, in caps adorned with large red stars. They were evidently well fed, in contrast to a civilian population that was poorly dressed and bore the pinched gray faces of the malnourished.

Jack Kennedy was fascinated to meet with Tito, the partisan leader who had crushed all his domestic rivals and defeated the Germans. Tito was both a Communist and a staunch nationalist. It was his will, his troops and his prestige that held together the fissiparous and historically antagonistic peoples of Yugoslavia.

Over an hour-long talk around a small coffee table in Tito's beautiful Italianate villa, the aging, paunchy marshal chain-smoked his way through a pack of cigarettes, wielding a cigarette holder in one hand, smiling readily, laughing often. Jack took an immediate liking to him.

As they talked, everyone in the room patted and stroked Tito's pet, a large brown hunting dog called Tiger. Do you need arms? Jack asked the marshal. How big an army could you field? Do you think the Russians are likely to launch a surprise attack? And as Tito answered his questions, the young congressman, head down, scrawled notes, like the journalist he had briefly been.[7]

"I am not a prophet," said Tito, in response to the question about a surprise attack. But suppose the Soviets conquered Western Europe, what would they do with it? It was too big, too complicated, for them to run. They were hard-pressed to control what they already held. Besides, Communism preached the inevitability of class struggle. It had never preached the inevitability of war.[8]

What the Soviets really wanted, Tito said, was to see the United States waste its strength in a war with China. In time, the present Sino-Soviet alliance would crumble. But for now the Americans were playing the game that Moscow wanted—getting bogged down in an unwinnable Far Eastern war.

Probably hoping to impress Tito with his knowledge of European politics, Jack talked about the Munich Crisis and the political misjudgments that had led up to it. Tito brushed all that aside. If anyone had blundered, he said emphatically, it was the Czechs. If only they had possessed the nerve to stand their ground—and they were well armed and had built strong defenses—they would have forced Britain and France to fight alongside them. The power of decision was with the Czechs, and they had lacked the guts to take the right action. Yugoslavia would not make the same mistake: it would fight the Soviet Union if necessary. Jack, however, would not budge—not now, not ever—from the view that he had formed as an undergraduate, that Munich was the bitter fruit of appeasement, the failing not of the Czechs, but of the democracies.

From Yugoslavia, the two Harvard men flew on to Italy, where they had a private audience with Pope Pius XII. They knelt and dutifully kissed the huge ring on his shriveled, arthritic hand, the skin like parchment as old age advanced. Pacelli spoke English fluently now, unlike his halting attempts during Jack's last meeting with him in 1937. He asked after Joe and Rose and Jack's brothers and sisters. He gave Jack and Torby rosaries and religious medals and pronounced a special blessing on each of them.[9]

In Spain they found a country with only two classes—the stupendously rich and the desperately poor. Franco and his followers had killed or imprisoned much of Spain's small, prewar middle class, forcing the rest into exile to avoid the same fate.

Jack was impressed by the Spanish military leaders he met. Staunchly anti-Communist, they seemed more than ready to fight, but their weapons were obsolete. He became the leading advocate in Congress for Spanish membership in NATO and military assistance to Spain.[10]

On his return to the United States, Jack Kennedy was eager to impart what he had learned. As far as American security was concerned, "Europe is not essential," he told his diary. "We could survive without it." He ridiculed every democratic country in Europe for being weak and deluded. The only countries he expressed any admiration for were Yugoslavia and Spain, both dictatorships.[11]

It irked him that American troops in Europe were less a deterrent than hostages to fortune, there to embroil the United States in the event of a Soviet attack. For each division America committed to the defense of

Europe, he decided, the Europeans should be told to put up six of their own.

The day he arrived back in Boston, February 6, 1951, he spoke to yet another gaggle of scribbling journalists. "If Europe is to be saved, Europe must make the necessary sacrifices," he said. "But Europe is not making those sacrifices." At moments like this, he sounded much like his father on an isolationist rant.[12]

Two weeks later Jack put in a long appearance before the Senate Foreign Relations Committee. He was already beginning to take a more emollient line. "Europe is our first line of defense," he conceded. Senator Walter George reminded him that his father had recently made a speech that was critical of the Marshall Plan, NATO and all other foreign entanglements. Jack repeated what he'd just said about the importance of Europe to American security and added, "I think you should ask my father directly as to his position."

What did he think was the chance of a major war, the Senators wanted to know. "The bomb is still as much of a deterrent as it was," Jack replied. Besides, "Stalin is an old man and old men are traditionally cautious." He'd evidently reconsidered Emanuel Shinwell's "wishful thinking."

When the hearing got around to Eisenhower, Kennedy told the committee that when the general had testified before it two months earlier, he "was not completely frank." In fact, Jack went on, he had so little faith in Eisenhower's judgment that surely Congress should control the buildup of American forces in Europe. The committee stared at him, incredulous. The chairman asked him, "Are you a lawyer?"

"No, I am not."

The chairman then reminded him that the Constitution made the President—not a committee of Congress—commander in chief. Eisenhower answered to President Truman, not to congressmen. What Jack was suggesting was probably illegal and practically impossible.

"We should send the four divisions to Europe," Jack said, but the Europeans ought to be required to put up thirty-six divisions of their own. That kind of commitment would "require a considerable reduction in their standard of living," he agreed, but it was a price they should be willing to pay.[13]

His proposal would have condemned Western Europe to being a doppelgänger of the Soviet Union—permanent war economy, endless, grinding poverty, political sterility and social immobility. This stood in sharp contrast to the vision of Marshall and Eisenhower, Acheson and Truman, in which a restored and vibrant Europe would present a stronger challenge—militarily, economically, politically and morally—to the backward Soviet Union and its East European satellites. It was a vision that Jack Kennedy at this point couldn't even glimpse. His outlook was still, in its fundamentals, not so much pre–Cold War as pre–World War II. That summer he offered an amendment to the foreign aid bill that would have cut it by 20 percent.[14]

On April 11, Truman fired General Douglas MacArthur for sabotaging the President's efforts to negotiate a cease-fire in Korea. Truman called him home. It was a morally courageous act, even if it was long overdue. Half the country seemed to be outraged by Truman's decision, and nearly all of it reeled from the shock.[15]

When the news reached Capitol Hill, there was pandemonium. Politicians scurried up and down the echoing corridors, in and out of one another's offices, asking, "Have you heard? What do *you* make of it?"

Jack Kennedy was in the House lobby when journalists rushed in. He instantly came to MacArthur's defense. "MacArthur suffered from lack of direction from the UN," said Jack. "Secondly, MacArthur's views of the struggle differ from the administration, which is determined to localize the conflict, which MacArthur evidently doesn't think is possible. It is regrettable that we should not now have at this critical time the benefit of MacArthur's experience."[16]

Some weeks later he and William H. Bates, a Republican congressman from Massachusetts, had a two-hour talk at the Waldorf Towers with MacArthur. When MacArthur met Jack Kennedy, the general was still basking in the glow of his triumphal homecoming and his stirring "Old Soldiers Never Die" address to Congress.[17]

Even so, he was smarting, not only from his recent recall but from the Chinese Army's victory over his troops during the winter of 1950. Blinded by rage, MacArthur told Jack Kennedy and William Bates that Europe was of secondary importance. "Our first line of defense is not the Elbe or the Rhine river, but the Yalu. If we do not win in Korea, we can lose in Europe." It was a proposition that was absurd: China could not be defeated and occupied, so talk of winning in Korea was nonsense.[18]

MacArthur himself indirectly acknowledged as much. He told the two Congressmen that he feared the war would remain stalemated, "no matter how many Chinese Communists we kill." The vital centers were in Manchuria, and so long as they remained untouched, the war would grind on.[19]

Jack Kennedy was deeply impressed by the general's belief that the Far

East was essential to American security. He began planning another long trip, this time focused on Asia.

=

In May 1951 Robert Kennedy was planning to marry Ethel Skakel, of Greenwich, Connecticut, the exuberant blond daughter of a family as rich as his own. Jack would be best man, but first, like many an arriviste, he felt constrained to study Emily Post's writings on how upper-class weddings, and prewedding gatherings, were managed. At times like this, the Kennedys' place in society stood in stark contrast to their wealth and their fame. No one in the family possessed the manners, the refinement or the sensibilities of the Anglicized East Coast upper class of old (or old enough) money.

As if to underline a certain coarseness that seemed to dog the Kennedy family, the bachelor dinner that Jack hosted for Bobby at the Harvard Club of New York turned into a brawl, with fistfights, drunken stumbling, shattered crockery, ruined furniture and, afterwards, red-faced apologies. Jack had to send the club a check for $1,090 to pay for the damage to its Slocum Room.[20]

At the wedding several days later, Jack was the best man, but it was a blazing-hot day in Greenwich and he sent a shiver through the assembled wedding guests by fainting at the altar. Afterwards, he and his secretary, Mary Davis, drove back to New York. Jack seemed almost awestruck by what his younger brother had done. "He's really made a big commitment. It's a very big responsibility."[21]

Jack's shaky health ruled out foreign travel that summer. He suffered from blinding headaches and pharyngitis, as well as back pain and the debilitating effects of Addisonism. His projected Asian trip slipped back from August to October.[22]

He arrived in Paris on October 3, with Bobby and their sister Patricia for company. Next day Jack visited with Eisenhower, whose headquarters were then in Paris (France had not yet pulled out of NATO's military command structure), and he was surprised to see how fit and buoyant Ike appeared. The resentment that Eisenhower probably felt at Jack's unfounded assertion that the general had misled Congress was suavely disguised. If there was one way to infuriate Eisenhower, it was to impugn his honesty, and it seems a fair bet that he would have been well aware of Jack's testimony before the Foreign Relations Committee.

Eisenhower—pacing and smoking—said he thought Jack's plan to visit the Middle East was a good idea. "It would be a mistake to write off the Muslim world," he said. American attitudes towards the Arabs were foolish and dangerous. Egypt was the key to the region, but it was now politically unstable, thanks largely to a hostile Western press and an uncomprehending American public.

When they got around to talking about NATO, Jack asked Eisenhower if there was a risk of war. "Isn't there a great danger of the Russians being frightened by our preparations and attacking?"

Ike responded, "There are only two chances of a deliberate war." One was if the Russians thought a quick, cheap victory was possible. The other was a long but ultimately victorious war of attrition. "They can't do either of these now. But I don't eliminate the possibility of an accidental war."

And what did the general think of de Gaulle? "A son of a bitch," snapped Ike.[23]

The people who impressed Jack most on this trip—as on others; as, indeed, on his own fulgurant journey through life—were those with the big personalities, such as David Ben-Gurion, the Israeli premier, and Jawaharlal Nehru of India. In Israel, Jack, Bobby and Pat got a kaleido-scopic view of huge refugee camps filled with Palestinians, spent a day in Lebanon—which seemed to be populated entirely by traders—and drove along roads where the charred remains of burned-out Arab villages appeared every few miles.

And there was dinner in Jerusalem with Ben-Gurion. The other guests included several cabinet ministers and Franklin D. Roosevelt, Jr., an old friend of the Kennedy family.

Jack was charmed and thrilled to meet Ben-Gurion, who wore his sixty-five years defiantly. With his massive head, deep tan, glittering eyes and great shock of white hair, Ben-Gurion was a powerful man who clearly relished the life-and-death challenge of forging a new state from a traumatized, largely immigrant population who found themselves in a new land and surrounded by enemies.

What chance is there of a permanent peace? asked Roosevelt. Ben-Gurion responded that peace depended on the Arab countries eventually recognizing Israel. In the meantime, he was going to make Israel into a military power.[24]

From Tel Aviv, Jack flew to Teheran, which was in ferment. Here, as so often before and so often later in his life, he possessed a knack for being an eyewitness to history. The Iranians had long been outraged that their country gained almost nothing from its oil. British Petroleum, having created the Iranian oil industry, took nearly everything the oil fields produced and gave almost nothing in return. Only days before Jack's arrival in Teheran, the government of Dr. Muhammed Mossadegh had ordered Iranian troops to seize the oil fields.

The British had appealed to the UN to intervene, but Jack feared the Soviets would exploit the current turmoil to move into Iran. The American ambassador, Loy Henderson, told him, "The British have been extremely shortsighted here. Almost stupid." Yet the British officials Jack met professed unconcern. Iran was broke, they said, the Soviets were bluffing and Mossadegh was a buffoon who would not last long. Jack couldn't help but feel a stirring of sympathy for the Iranians, yet, as he told Bobby and Pat, "If we get into a serious disagreement with the British, it will endanger our chances in the Cold War."[25]

Flying south across the Iranian desert to Pakistan, Jack gazed, fascinated, at the blue-tiled dome of the large mosque dominating the "holy city" of Isfahan, appearing suddenly on the horizon. Made of sunbaked mud, with a winding defensive wall all around it, Isfahan appeared timeless; a creation of the Earth as much as a creation of man. It must have looked just like this hundreds of years ago, Jack mused. Reaching for his diary, he penciled a note to himself: "Check on history of this city."

Landing in Pakistan, he had a long interview with the Pakistani premier, Liaquat Ali Khan. The only subject that seemed to interest Ali Khan was the ownership of Kashmir, which both Pakistan and India claimed was rightfully theirs. To Jack, the solution was obvious—partition. But neither India nor Pakistan would ever agree to that. The dispute was about more than territory—it was about national identity and an ancient, sectarian struggle.[26]

India next. Invited to lunch at the presidential palace with Jawaharlal Nehru and his doe-eyed daughter, Indira Gandhi, Jack found the beauty of the palace seductive and Nehru's personality compelling. Cambridge-educated, suave and highly intelligent, Nehru was given to making provocative observations and testing the mettle of the people he met.[27]

During lunch, he paid virtually no attention to Jack or Bobby but worked his charm on Pat, to Bobby's irritation. Afterwards, however, he and Jack talked alone at length. Nehru angrily talked about how Churchill had ordered him imprisoned during the war and then had wanted to know if he was comfortable. Jack came to his hero's defense. "Don't you think that was something special of Churchill, who had so much to worry about during the war, to send such a message?"

Nehru thought about this for a moment but shrugged it off. "It was only because we had both gone to Harrow." Jack found this tribute to the old school tie amusing.[28]

Nehru was not a fine-detail man, and proud of it. Whenever Jack asked him a question on something concrete and specific, such as the number of divisions the Indian Army could field, Nehru leaned back in his chair and blew smoke rings at the ceiling before responding "I don't know" in a tone of voice that suggested he had no desire to find out, either.

Nehru came alive, though, when Jack pressed him to defend India's neutrality in the Cold War, something that Jack suggested was both impolitic and immoral. The alternative to peace, said Nehru, was war. "But war will not stop Communism. Rather, it will enhance it, for the devastation of war breeds only more poverty and more want."[29]

Jack left India profoundly impressed by Nehru. As a rule, he was scornful of people who did not appear to have studied essential questions down to the details. Personality, however, meant so much in his mental universe that Nehru got the benefit of every doubt. "He is interested only in subtler and higher questions," Jack informed his diary. There was something else, too: "Generally agreed Nehru is everything in India—the works. Tremendously popular with the masses."[30]

In Bangkok he met the prime minister, visited the royal palace and gaped at the huge reclining Buddha, covered in gold, nearly as long as a football field and surrounded by shaven-headed tourist monks in saffron robes, drawn to this site from all parts of Asia.

In Malaya there was a guerrilla war under way to end British rule. The British had recently offered independence once the guerrillas were defeated. This pledge split the insurgent movement and made it possible, eventually, to defeat it. But in 1951 the terrorist threat was still at its height. Only a few days before Jack arrived, Communist guerrillas had ambushed and killed the high commissioner, Sir Henry L. G. Gurney. When Jack Kennedy visited a tin mine only ten miles from the capital city, Kuala Lumpur, it took an armored car and a truckload of police to assure his safety.[31]

This brief excursion into Malaya prefaced the part of his globe-circling journey that was destined to have the most important consequences for him and his country: the time he spent in Indochina, from October 15 to October 25.

When he arrived at Tan Son Nhut Airport in Saigon, Jack was delighted to be greeted by the number-two man at the U.S. embassy, Edmund Gullion. When the Korean War began, Jack had asked the secretary of state, Dean Acheson, to provide him with guidance on foreign policy. Acheson had Gullion, a rapidly rising Foreign Service officer, explain Far Eastern policy to the young congressman.

As they drove into Saigon, the sound of gunfire erupted nearby. "What's that?" asked Jack.

"Small-arms fire," said Gullion. "Another attack by the Viet Minh."[32]

Kennedy's confidence in Gullion was only deepened during this visit. Gullion seemed intellectually superior—and by a wide margin—to the ambassador, Donald R. Heath. Jack also turned for advice to Seymour Topping, the AP bureau chief in Saigon. Gullion and Topping told him the French were going to lose the war against Ho Chi Minh's Communist guerrillas; Nehru had said much the same thing. The only hope the French had, said Gullion and Topping, was to do what the British had done in Malaya—promise independence once the fighting had stopped. Jack agreed. "This is going to cost me some votes with my French Catholic constituents," he told Gullion, "but it seems like the right thing to do."[33]

He dined at the palace with Bao Dai, the fat, fun-loving emperor of Indochina. Dozens of armed guards patrolled the corridors to thwart potential assassins. Bao Dai struck Jack Kennedy as an intelligent man and "a unifying force" linking North and South Vietnam. Yet there was no doubt he was a puppet under the control of the French. If a free election was held, Robert Kennedy noted grimly, "Ho Chi Minh would win it."[34]

The political appeal of the Communists was unmistakable, and their military strength was growing rapidly. France's hopes were riding now on a World War II hero, General Jean de Lattre de Tassigny, who was dying of cancer. De Lattre assured Jack that France was committed to seeing the struggle through to final victory, but Gullion and Topping knew better.[35]

France, they told him, had no stomach for this fight. The country was fighting not to hold Indochina, but to retain its North African possessions —Morocco, Algeria and Tunisia. If the French did not fight here, those colonies, much closer to metropolitan France, would soon break away. With so little commitment to Indochina, Jack reflected, "There is a danger that the French may drop Indochina into our laps." And what would the United States do then?[36]

A tour of Hanoi and the delta region, where the French had created elaborate defenses, did nothing to reassure him. Nor did the French colonel who assured Jack that the war would be won, "But not in my life-time, monsieur."[37]

Jack returned to Saigon, then flew on to Tokyo via Singapore. Hardly arrived in Tokyo, he fell seriously ill from a crisis in his Addison's disease. Hurriedly flown by military aircraft to Okinawa, where there was a large U.S. Navy hospital, his temperature rose to 106 degrees and he became delirious, lapsing into a coma. Jack's vital signs were failing remorselessly. For the second time in his life, he received last rites. Within a few days, however, he not only recovered but was ready to move on to Korea and Japan.[38]

The ghastly ruggedness of the terrain in Korea came as a surprise to him and helped explain why the fighting there was so difficult for the U.S. Army, which was equipped and trained for wars of movement, not prolonged trench warfare. He was convinced, too, that the great weakness had been in the air: given enough planes, MacArthur never would have been exposed to the huge, successful counterattack that the Chinese had launched against his forces in November 1950.

When JFK returned home, his mind was teeming with all he had seen, the people he'd met and the conclusions he'd drawn. Foremost among them was this: "Foreign policy—in its impact on our daily lives—overshadows everything else." Hardly a sentiment most Americans would have agreed with, but that had been the core of his thinking about politics before he even set off. His conviction was unshakable now that he had visited so many Cold War hot spots and seen the struggles to come.[39]

His long-standing fascination with airpower had also taken on a new urgency. The United States was on the short end of an airpower gap, according to Jack. It would produce only forty-five hundred airplanes in 1951, while the Soviet Union produced twelve thousand. He called the disparity "alarming."[40]

Military weaknesses such as this were too dangerous to ignore. He ridiculed Eisenhower's judgment that the Soviets would not deliberately attack Western Europe. War was possible in the near future, Jack told journalists, before NATO became strong enough to halt Stalin's armies.[41]

His trip had convinced him that the Voice of America was almost useless. Nearly all its broadcasts were in English, which most of the world's people did not speak. He was also appalled by nearly all the diplomats and State Department people he had met. Joe Kennedy's blundering adventures as an ambassador had produced many a parental tirade against professional diplomats, the most WASPish group in government. Joe

Kennedy blamed many of his failures on Foreign Service officers, whom he scorned as being personally hostile to him and useless in representing their country.

Some of that prejudice rubbed off on Jack. He told journalists that the diplomats "seem to be a breed of their own, unconscious of the fact that their role is *not* tennis and cocktails." Few showed any serious interest in the countries to which they were posted. Was it any wonder that the United States confronted a rising Communist tide, declining American prestige and an outpouring of nationalism in strategically critical parts of the globe?[42]

During his travels, another part of his spirit was asking questions of a different kind. On the long, slow airplane flights of the propeller age, he had plenty of time to read. And whenever he came across a passage that appealed strongly to his essentially romantic imagination, he wrote it down in the diary he kept of his travels.

In his recollections of David Ben-Gurion, he inserted the first stanza of Shelley's scathing portrait of Castlereagh, which he probably had just read: "I met murder on the way—he had a mask like Castlereagh. . . ."

Not surprisingly, he had to write down some lines of Andrew Marvell's poem "To His Coy Mistress," for they must have seemed addressed directly to him:

> But at my back I always hear
> Time's wingèd chariot hurrying near . . .

He was also reading a recently published war memoir that paid tribute to the Polish divisions that fought in Italy during World War II. The Polish war cemetery at Cassino now bore a plaque at the entrance declaring:

> We Polish soldiers
> For our freedom and yours
> Have given our souls to God
> Our bodies to Italy
> And our hearts to Poland.

Deeply moved, Jack copied out these lines. They form the last entry in his 1951 travel diaries. This was the Jack Kennedy the world never saw or understood in his lifetime. But there was one person who would.

CHAPTER 16

Ladies—I Need You

The House was a girdle, strangling his talents, making him seem smaller than he knew himself to be. He felt that almost from the first day on Capitol Hill. After his unopposed reelection in November 1948, he wasn't looking forward to more of the same—he was looking beyond it. One day he had Dave Powers put up a large map of Massachusetts on his bedroom wall at the Bowdoin Street apartment. He gazed at it for a moment. "You know, Dave, when I have been to every one of the thirty-nine cities and three hundred and twelve towns, then I will run statewide."[1]

Over the next three years he had a speaking engagement in Boston nearly every Friday night. On Saturday, he made an appearance somewhere in western Massachusetts. There were Holy Name Societies in small towns across the state that were flattered to have him as a speaker; ditto the Friendly Sons of Saint Patrick, the Knights of Columbus, American Legion posts and Veterans of Foreign Wars. He shook the hands of hundreds of thousands of people and wherever he went, if he met anyone he thought might be useful in a future political campaign, he noted the name and phone number on a three-by-five card that he turned over to his staff. Sunday evening he caught the train back to Washington.[2]

By 1951 the itch to move on was becoming unbearable. George Smathers and Dick Nixon, who had entered the House when he did, had been elected to the Senate in 1950. Jack Kennedy felt he was lagging behind, and he of all men had no time to be a laggard.

The traditional route to the White House was by way of the statehouse. The only senator to become President in the twentieth century was Warren Harding, back in 1920. His friends and supporters, even his father, thought the governorship was the way to go; that was the road Joe Jr. had planned to take. But Jack wasn't convinced; it didn't seem right for him.[3]

A few days after his return from Europe in February 1951, he had an independent political consultant, Van Ness Bates, come and talk to him at his father's Beacon Hill apartment. "I'm going to run for senator or governor," he told Bates.

"If you want to be a senator, perhaps you'd better be a governor first." That would not only make him a statewide political figure, it would also give him a chance to demonstrate his executive ability, Bates explained, adding, "But if you haven't got executive ability, don't run for governor."

Jack was slightly taken aback. "I don't know whether I've got executive ability or not!"

"Well, perhaps you had better find out."[4]

Being a governor didn't appeal, though. What was the main business of almost any governor? Handling patronage to keep his pals and his party in power. From his tiny Bowdoin Street bachelor's pad, Jack could look across the street to the office of Governor Paul Dever. "Sitting in that corner office," he mused aloud one day to Powers, "saying I'll do this if you do that. . . ." It was a different life—a more interesting one—being a senator.[5]

The question came down to Dever: would he run for reelection in 1952 or make his own Senate bid? Jack couldn't challenge him in the September 1952 primary for either governor or senator without splitting the party, and that was unthinkable. But Dever wasn't sure what to run for or whether to run at all.[6]

While Dever dithered, Joseph P. Kennedy had two experienced political operators scouring the state, taking the pulse. If Jack ran for the Senate in 1952 he would be up against the tall, elegant, handsome and popular Henry Cabot Lodge, who had won the 1946 Senate election by more than three hundred thousand votes. Joe Kennedy's polls showed Jack might just beat Lodge, but Dever would be thrashed in a contest with Lodge.[7]

Everything depended on whether Dever wanted to run for governor again or make a bid for the Senate. The afternoon of April 6, 1952, Palm Sunday, Jack walked over to Boston's fanciest hotel, the Ritz-Carlton, where Dever was going to tell the press what he'd decided. Dever came over and told him before he spoke to anyone else—"Jack, I'm a candidate for reelection."

"That's just fine!" said Jack eagerly. "I'm glad to hear it!" Next day he made his own announcement.[8]

=

The pattern was clear by now: as he became increasingly conservative on national security, he was becoming increasingly liberal at home. During his last term in the House, however, Jack pursued his greatest interest— national security issues—with a zeal and confidence that owed something to his 1951 travels. He had finally come around to unequivocal support for NATO and the Marshall Plan. His criticisms of the Truman administration these days were about implementation, not policy. He also accepted that Europe would always be more important to American security than Asia.

Jack's interest in aviation was keener than ever. The House was in a budget-slashing frame of mind as Congress struggled, in an election year, to finance the Korean War without adding to the tax burden on American voters. The Air Force appropriation was cut. Jack Kennedy was outraged.

There was an airpower gap, he insisted again. The Soviets were at least three years ahead of the United States, he argued, in both development of new designs and airplane production. They possessed not only more but better combat planes than the United States Air Force. Jack introduced legislation to increase Air Force appropriations, but it was swiftly voted down.[9]

He had tried to persuade the Eightieth Congress to finance the creation of an aerial equivalent of the Merchant Marine—a large fleet of huge cargo planes that would be of value to the nation in peace and war. This proposal got nowhere.[10]

His fascination with airplanes went back to childhood. "If he could do it, Jack would catch an airplane to cross the street," said aide Billy Sutton.[11]

The legislative assistant he had hired when he went to the House—the staff member, that is, who would draft legislation for him—was Langdon Marvin, someone he had known at Harvard. During his wartime service in the Navy, Marvin had revolutionized its logistics by organizing an air-express system that rushed crucial parts and equipment to the front lines.[12]

One of the two bills Jack Kennedy got passed as a congressman was a law that Marvin drafted to abolish the overly generous subsidies that went to a few big airlines. The favored few were making hundreds of millions of dollars a year without much effort, while wartime pilots eager to start up new airlines couldn't get financing because they had no assured revenues. Pan Am tried to buy him off, then tried to apply political pressure. But Jack was so rich, and had such a secure hold on his congressional seat, that he could shrug off both bribery and threats.

Thanks to Jack Kennedy, federal money for carrying airmail was spread more widely. This money then stimulated the establishment and expansion of numerous small airlines and helped finance the construction and development of airports across the country. For Jack, America's future seemed real only when it had wings.[13]

≡

This was a fight that had visceral appeal to Jack Kennedy. Honey Fitz and Henry Cabot Lodge's father had been political and personal enemies. Neither man could stand the other. Honey Fitz had died in 1950, to Jack's great distress. But here was something he could do for both himself and Grampa. "I'm going to get that son of a bitch Lodge out of the Senate," Jack told a friend.[14]

Like a good general, he had a clear view of the battle ahead and a real-istic strategy for winning it. There were seven hundred twenty thousand registered Democrats, six hundred fifty thousand Republicans and roughly a million Independents. "All we have to do to win," he told Dave Powers, "is get the Democrats, give Lodge the Republicans and break even with the Independents." If he could do that, he would win by seventy thousand votes.[15]

There was one potential snag: the core Republican vote had a very high turnout, much higher than the Democrats'. But on the few occasions when the total vote had approached two million, nearly all the extra votes went to the Democratic candidate. Jack Kennedy launched a vigorous voter-registration drive, and his campaign workers were zealous about getting people to the polls.

Although his campaign was ostensibly run in tandem with Dever's bid for another term as governor, the Kennedy campaign had its own organization, techniques and philosophy that distanced it from the Democratic party machine. Jack did not appoint local campaign chairmen. There were already local Democratic party chairmen. Not only would it be confusing to have two groups of chairmen, but it might appear the party was split. Instead, Jack appointed "campaign secretaries" all over the state. The secretaries reported to Bobby Kennedy, Jack's campaign manager, with headquarters at 44 Kilby Street, in Boston's financial district.

The place was swamped with eager young women more than ready to stuff envelopes, make phone calls, type letters, organize voter registrations. Because Jack cannily developed a habit of dropping by around ten P.M., many came early and stayed late. All told, the Kennedy campaign attracted roughly twenty-three thousand volunteers, overwhelmingly female.

There was a pattern to campaigning in Massachusetts that every politician understood. The campaign began about six weeks before the election. The entire party ticket would show up for a rally at which everything was taken care of by local party activists. The candidates gave short set-piece speeches, kissed a few babies, shook some hands, waved goodbye and drove on to the next town, the next rally.[16]

Jack Kennedy did not campaign like that. He began running eighteen months before the election, before he even knew whether he'd be making his bid for governor or senator. The most important factor in politics, he was convinced, was a name that had become something like a brand, with a brand image to match. If that worked for Coke or Cadillac, why not for Kennedy?[17]

And his style was that of Honey Fitz. Grampa had believed in meeting everybody and shaking their hands. Jack had tried to do the same all over his district. Now he seemed determined to do it all over the state, wearing a campaign button that Honey Fitz had worn fifty years before. Although Jack was not normally an early riser, the 1952 campaign yanked him out of bed before six in the morning. By eight he was out campaigning, and he plugged away until late at night. Not even back pain so acute that he needed crutches for several weeks slowed him down.[18]

The biggest concentration of industrial plants in the state was around Everett. The Kennedy secretary for Everett, Joseph Curnane, suggested that Jack campaign in the plants. Jack was astonished. "How the hell can we get in there? No plant manager's going to let his people take time away from their work just to shake hands at a political rally." Curnane said he thought it could be done. "Well, all right. But you make certain that you have it cleared. We don't want to get rebuffed at the gates!"

Curnane told the plant managers that the congressman, an influential member of the House committee on Education and Labor, was conducting a study of industry. They were delighted to have him visit their plants. They got a photograph of themselves looking important as they greeted the congressman, and he got to shake hands with hundreds of workers at each plant he visited. Political campaigns inside factories or on board fishing vessels were almost unknown, in Massachusetts or anywhere else.[19]

Like Honey Fitz, Jack sought to reach out to minorities and ethnic groups. In January 1952 there were physical assaults on blacks and Jews in Florida. Jack immediately put out a statement saying he was "incensed" and introduced legislation that would force the federal government to take over the investigation of hate crimes. It was killed in committee, as he surely knew it would be. But there was no mistaking his anger.[20]

There wasn't much of a Jewish vote in Massachusetts, and it seemed unlikely he would get it anyway. His father's contempt for most Jews was well known, and Lodge was a fervent supporter of Israel. Jack Kennedy had unwisely voted to cut aid to the Middle East less than a year before the election. It wasn't that he was against Israel—far from it—but he was indignant that Truman was allowing government spending to soar without introducing price controls.

John McCormack came to Jack's rescue. McCormack was such a favorite with Boston's Jewish voters that his nickname was "Rabbi John." He told his Jewish friends that Jack had acted as he did only to head off a bigger cut that the real foes of Israel were planning to push through if the aid bill Jack voted on hadn't been passed.[21]

That contained the problem, but it was not going to be enough to swing the Jewish vote Jack's way. For that, he needed outside help and got it. American Jews idolized both Franklin D. Roosevelt, Jr., and his mother, Eleanor Roosevelt. Franklin Jr. came to Massachusetts to campaign enthusiastically for Jack, while Eleanor warmly endorsed him.[22]

The black vote was probably even smaller than the Jewish vote. No matter. Jack wanted it, so he joined the NAACP. While he campaigned in Boston's black neighborhoods, the Joseph P. Kennedy, Jr., Foundation was making large contributions to black charities.[23]

When it came to appealing to the French and Italians, Jack was in trouble. He was never able to do more than jabber a few stock phrases in French. Yet there were entire towns in Massachusetts dominated by French speakers, and Lodge spoke French fluently. Lodge also had a sister-in-law who was fluent in Italian and loved campaigning.

Jack struck back by having Rose, who spoke French fluently but with an execrable accent, talk to the French speakers. Rose also spoke passable Italian. Meanwhile, Jack made much of the fact that he had convinced the Truman administration to amend the Italian peace treaty. Italy was restricted to an army of a hundred and seventy-five thousand men and could not send troops abroad. Yet Jack believed that NATO needed a strong Italy, just as Italy needed a strong NATO. The Italian government was so grateful it awarded him its highest civilian honor, the Star of Solidarity, a fact widely touted in Boston's Italian-dominated North End.[24]

Kennedy's campaign slogan was "He can do MORE for Massachusetts." His speeches were mainly attacks on Lodge's voting record in the Senate—something that his assistant Ted Reardon had researched minutely. Yet Jack did not have much to work with. Lodge was a firm believer in collective security, NATO, the Marshall Plan and the need to meet the Communist challenge at home and abroad.

Jack had to cover the local bases—the fishing industry, organized labor, the hard-pressed textile mills, the need for the states of New England to start operating as a political bloc, much like the Solid South. But the thread that ran through his major speeches was national survival in the nuclear age. The key to that, he argued, was finding the right leaders. And Lodge wasn't one of them.

He and Lodge participated in a radio discussion in July, and the main question they had to address was who would make the better President, Dwight Eisenhower or Adlai Stevenson. Lodge was far more impressive than JFK, if only because he was genuinely enthusiastic about Eisenhower. Jack felt no enthusiasm whatever for Stevenson.

After that, Lodge challenged him to debate the issues. Jack, caught by surprise, was wary of falling into a trap. Yet he could never resist a flung gauntlet. If anything, he found direct challenges stimulating. There is a two-word formula for getting the most out of life—"Live dangerously." Cautious on many political issues, Kennedy was nonetheless a man who almost lived for risk.

The League of Women Voters organized a debate that would take place in Waltham on September 16, half an hour after voting in the senatorial primaries ended. By then it would be down to just the two of them in the election in November.

Lodge and his supporters were confident he would demolish JFK in debate. Jack himself was afraid of that. Yet his spirits were buoyed by the reaction he got from the audience before the debate began. The hall was filled almost entirely with women. "He came onstage looking like a prince of the blood, fiddling with his tie but totally self-possessed," reported journalist Mary McGrory, and as he smiled shyly at them, the women almost swooned.[25]

Debates like this had become a rarity in American politics. They hearkened back to the nineteenth century, to Abraham Lincoln debating Stephen Douglas. Kennedy and Lodge argued mainly about foreign policy and national security.[26]

When it was over, Jack didn't feel he'd won the debate—he thought he'd broken even. But that was inspiring, given Lodge's fame, looks, popularity, impressive war record and closeness to Eisenhower. After the Waltham debate, Jack began to feel confident he would win the election.

There were lots of thirty-second radio spots. Some might feature Jack talking to labor leaders; others had him talking to people who made shoes or textiles or fished for a living. What excited him much more than radio, though, was television.

Joe Kennedy had asked one of the country's leading advertising agencies to look into ways to use television in a political campaign. Thomas Dewey was the first politician to try using television, in his 1948 presidential campaign, which had finished with an eighteen-hour "telethon" the day before the election.

The question Joe Kennedy wanted answered was whether TV was worth spending a lot of money on. The study he'd commissioned said it was, because TV generated a lot more publicity in the newspapers. Editors and journalists did not want television becoming a rival for political coverage. They fought back by running more political stories and photographs. Joe urged his son to use TV in his challenge to Lodge.[27]

There was no doubting that Jack's charisma came across on the small, grainy black-and-white screens of the early 1950s. After appearing on a show called *Chronoscope* in March 1952, he received an enthusiastic letter from a viewer named Alfred M. Lilienthal: "Resign from that seat in Congress and become a Television Idol!"[28]

That was going to happen one day, but only after a shaky beginning. During his first political broadcast in May 1952, there were two Tele-PrompTers to help him, but he was completely flummoxed when the one he was reading from broke down. He froze, unable to improvise without a live audience. A phone-in session did not redeem matters.[29]

During the summer he spent a day at the CBS television school in New York, learning how to look—and be—confident on camera. But a second television broadcast was also a flop. He groped his way through a turgid twenty-minute speech that consisted of political clichés delivered in a monotone. There was another phone-in, but it was dull and meandering.

On October 5, in the closing stages of the campaign, Jack Kennedy and Henry Cabot Lodge conducted the first televised political debate. Like the Waltham confrontation, the result was a draw, but one watched by hundreds of thousands of people who saw the underdog challenger easily hold his own against the more experienced Lodge.[30]

In retrospect, this campaign was the thematic forerunner of the campaign JFK would run in 1960 in his bid for the White House—Massachusetts was in crisis, its economy was faltering, the state had lost its way, only new leadership could reverse the decline and get the state moving again, and he alone could offer the kind of youthful, dynamic, forward-looking leadership that was so desperately needed.[31]

When he was studying Lodge's 1946 victory, Jack had come across an interesting fact: female registered voters were projected to outnumber male registered voters by 1952. When he mentioned this to Eunice, she proposed holding tea parties.

These followed the same formula established at the famous 1946 tea in Cambridge. In 1952 there were thirty-five teas, usually held on Sunday afternoons. The most successful one attracted fifty-five hundred women. And Jack appeared at all of them to make a direct appeal—"Ladies, I need you!"[32]

Rose had also hosted two installments of a morning television program, *Coffee with the Kennedys*. She chatted about her family, helped by one or two of the girls, and any viewer could make a toll-free phone call to put questions to Rose or her daughters. Both programs drew nothing but praise, and they represented once again a Kennedy willingness to push the envelope, to change the way a candidate campaigned.

≡

Back in 1946, when Jack was trying to establish himself as a Bostonian, his parents had spent nearly all their time in Palm Beach and New York. Hyannis was as close as they came to Boston, apart from an occasional fleeting visit. Their geographic remoteness from Boston only underlined his tenuous connections with the city.

Joseph P. Kennedy had an easy answer to the problem this time: he rented a large apartment on Beacon Hill, Boston's toniest district, a year before the 1952 campaign began. Once it was launched, he oversaw the campaign, although Jack couldn't resist twitting him. A lot of money would be needed from somebody. "Dad, we concede that role to you."[33]

Joe Kennedy oversaw not only his son's Senate campaign but Paul Dever's bid for reelection as governor. He helped finance it, chose Dever's campaign manager and coordinated both campaigns, something that probably worked more to Jack's benefit that Dever's.

When Jack was in so much pain he had to cancel an important speaking engagement, his father substituted for him. It was Joe Kennedy who made Bobby the campaign manager, and while Bobby controlled the volunteers, Joe controlled Bobby. It was also Joe Kennedy who told Jack that television was going to dominate politics in the future. Jack didn't need much persuading. He'd long loved the camera, aware that the camera loved him.[34]

When he learned shortly before the election that the *Boston Post,* long a pro-Republican newspaper, was about to endorse Lodge, Joe called the paper's publisher, John Fox. Under Fox's erratic direction, the once mighty *Post* had lost many of its readers and was burdened with huge debts. Joe Kennedy was well aware of Fox's tribulations and offered him a loan of $500,000 on the condition that the paper endorse Jack. Two days later the *Post* endorsed one Democrat—Jack Kennedy. All the rest of its endorsements were for Republicans. To Fox's dismay, the loan really was a loan—not a bribe. Joe Kennedy demanded his money back.[35]

Massachusetts law placed strict limits on how much a candidate could spend in most elections, but a Senate race was different. The state's law had to be followed in conjunction with federal election law, and the result was a vast gray area in which neophytes might get into trouble but a smart operator like Joe Kennedy felt at home. Fuzzy was good; untested limits even better. He spent freely, like a man without a care.[36]

However much he owed his father for the commitment in time, energy and money, Jack nevertheless imposed his own stamp on this campaign, in small ways as well as big ones. There were some things he would not do and some things he would not say, no matter how strongly his father felt.

Lodge became increasingly desperate to find a killer issue. He tried Jack's poor attendance record in Congress and got nowhere, because his own turned out to be not much better. Near the end of the campaign, he tried to cash in on his war record. He claimed Jack had led such a privileged life that he had no idea what ordinary people had to endure when their cities and towns were turned into battlefields. But he, Lodge, had seen it—been part of it—in Europe.

Jack was hurt and outraged at Lodge's assertion. His father told him to hit back and wrote out a personal attack on Lodge, for Jack to deliver in a speech. It portrayed Lodge as someone who had spent the war safely in headquarters far from the fighting while Jack was at the front facing the enemy. Jack refused to get into anything so tasteless.

Lodge had uncharacteristically descended into the gutter because his campaign was in deep trouble. He had spent so much time helping Eisenhower secure the nomination for President that he had scarcely been seen in Massachusetts before the primaries. He was in trouble, too, because in aiding Ike, he had infuriated the very conservative Robert Taft wing of the Republican party. Many, possibly most, of the die-hard Taft supporters were going to vote for Jack Kennedy just to spite Lodge. Billboards across the state proclaimed IKE NEEDS LODGE. It was really the other way around.

The night of the election, November 3, Jack and Torby Macdonald went to a movie. Afterwards Jack and Torby walked across Boston Common towards 81 Beacon Street, his parents' apartment, where Joe Kennedy was making phone calls and watching several television screens. "I wonder what sort of job Ike will give Lodge," mused Jack. It was a typical offhand remark, a way of saying he knew he would win without seeming boastful.

Most of the television coverage was focused inevitably on Eisenhower versus Stevenson. The coverage of Massachusetts's results was fitful, and it had Kennedy and Lodge neck and neck most of the time. At eleven o'clock, Stevenson conceded victory to Eisenhower. A few minutes later, Ike and Nixon appeared, holding their hands aloft in triumph. "Imagine that!" said Jack. "Dick Nixon and I came into Congress together, and now he's Vice President of the United States!"[37]

Long past midnight the Kennedy-Lodge contest was still too close to call. It was seven A.M., and dawn was breaking, before Kennedy was finally declared the winner over Lodge. His margin of victory was seventy thousand votes, and he'd carried Boston, taking all twenty-two wards.

A weary Jack Kennedy walked back to his Bowdoin Street digs, had his usual breakfast of orange juice, eggs, bacon, coffee and toast, then crawled into bed, elected.

CHAPTER 17

Alliance for Progress

The hair told a story. That vigorous, slightly unkempt mop so redolent of youth—was it really fitting for a United States senator? Obviously not. It undermined the gravitas of someone who was now a national rather than a provincial figure. So every few days Jack had a hairdresser stop by his office and tend the exuberant growth. It became part of the brand image he was seeking to establish. The JFK Look.[1]

He needed something else, too—a wife. During his Senate campaign, Jack had told people, "If I win, I'll get married." Once in the Senate, next stop—the White House. But no bachelor, be he ever so bright or witty, handsome or rich, stood much chance of being elected President.[2]

Still, there was the money question. With most of the young women he knew, whether he bedded them or not, "I think they see a dollar sign," he told his friend Ed McLaughlin. Even so, he had proposed marriage to at least three women before he met Jackie—towel heiress Frances Ann Cannon; a Hyannis Port neighbor, Betsy Finkenstadt; and fashion editor Florence Pritchett. There was just possibly a fourth, Alicia Purdom, half Jewish, Polish by birth and divorced from an English actor, Edmund Purdom.[3]

In 1950, however, Arthur Krock drew Joe Kennedy's attention to Jacqueline Bouvier, a beautiful twenty-one-year-old with an excellent pedigree. Jacqueline was the daughter of Janet and John Bouvier III. Her father resembled Ronald Colman, but with a swarthy Mediterranean cast to his handsome features. His looks accounted for his nickname—Black Jack—and made him a successful seducer of scores of women and, reputedly, various men, including Cole Porter. He was also a right-wing Republican who hated Roosevelt, the New Deal and all those associated with it, not least Joe Kennedy, the first chairman of the SEC. Bouvier was a stockbroker who had become a millionaire on the unregulated stock markets of the 1920s, only to lose nearly everything in the Depression. He blamed Joe Kennedy and Franklin Roosevelt in more or less equal measure.

Black Jack was not just broke most of the time and a libertine all of the time but an alcoholic as well. Janet referred to him as "that no-good drunk." To him, she was "that bitch." When Jacqueline was eight, her mother moved out and filed for a divorce. In 1942, when Jackie was thirteen, Janet married an investment banker, Hugh Dudley Auchincloss, or "Hughdie." He owned a large estate, Merrywood, near Washington, and an even bigger estate, Hammersmith Farm, in Newport, Rhode Island. As a child, Jackie was told she had to be good or that wicked man Franklin D. Roosevelt would get her. She had grown up in luxurious surroundings, but the money that provided her privileged lifestyle was Hughdie's, not Daddy's.[4]

At about the time Arthur Krock was extolling her beauty and brains to Joe Kennedy, Jackie was in Paris and madly in love with John Marquand, Jr., son of the novelist John Marquand, a man whose work both mocked and memorialized the WASP upper class he'd been born into. In Paris she surrendered her virginity one night to Marquand Jr. They were half drunk and stuck in the antique elevator of a small hotel. Yielding hastily, before the elevator started operating again, Jackie's first coitus was a knee trembler, with her skinny backside pressed up against open art-deco grilles. It was memorable and romantic, a cut above most sexual initiations. There was a snag, though—Marquand *fils* had no money. Janet made her end this liaison.[5]

On the rebound, Jackie began dating a young New York stockbroker, John G. W. Husted, Jr. At roughly the same time, in the spring of 1951, Joe Kennedy was telling Arthur Krock to arrange for Jack to meet Jackie.

Krock in turn persuaded Charles Bartlett, Washington correspondent for the *Chattanooga Times,* and his wife to host a dinner party so that Jack could meet Jackie. The Bartletts proved to be willing matchmakers. But when the dinner party broke up, Husted arrived to collect Jackie. Shortly after this, he proposed marriage and she accepted.[6]

Janet had drummed it into Jackie and her sister, Lee, that while they enjoyed the best of everything now, it wasn't going to last. What money Hughdie left would go to his own Auchincloss offspring, but the family fortune was spiraling down. There might soon be nothing left. Janet's father wasn't going to leave much to her children. It wouldn't be enough for Jackie and Lee to marry nice boys. They had to marry "real" money. Poor John Husted wasn't rich, merely well off. Not good enough, Janet told Jackie, not rich enough. Jackie broke off her engagement.[7]

In May 1952, a year after the first dinner, the Bartletts invited her and Jack back again, and this time it worked. Jack Kennedy asked her out. "I leaned across the asparagus and asked her for a date" was how he described it.[8]

She was highly intelligent as well as beautiful, and restless. After two years at Vassar, Jackie had spent a year at the Sorbonne. Back from Paris after the affair with Marquand ended, she enrolled at George Washington University. Artistically talented and in love with literature, she really didn't know what to do with her life except find a rich man and marry him. In the meantime, Krock obligingly arranged a job for her at the Washington *Times-Herald.* By the time of the second Bartlett dinner, she had a byline. Her column, "The Inquiring Camera Girl," was Inga Arvad stuff, but with even fewer words and bigger pictures.

Joe Kennedy investigated the background of any woman his sons showed a serious interest in. Yet he did not seem to discover that Jackie's roots were Jewish as well as French. Her mother pretended—like the Bouviers—to be descended from French aristocracy. But Janet's father's name was Levy. He had changed it to Lee in order to become a partner in an investment bank and thereafter claimed his ancestors were Irish.[9]

As for the Bouviers' assertions that they had arrived in America as part of Lafayette's coterie of idealistic young aristocrats to fight for the Revolution, that was *de la merde.* The Bouviers had immigrated to the United States long after the Revolution and were provincial tradespeople. Their descendants, trying to establish themselves in New York society, shamelessly began claiming descent from the Bouviers de la Fontaine and the de Vernous de Borneuil, ancient nobility with whom they had no connection at all. But Joe Kennedy himself was famous for saying, "It's not what you are that matters. It's what people think you are."[10]

When Jack began to press his suit on Jacqueline Bouvier, he was trying to win Lodge's Senate seat. Traveling around Massachusetts that summer and fall, he called Jackie on the weekends from pay phones in diners and small-town restaurants, receiver in one hand and a fistful of quarters in the other, his Anglo-Bostonian tones cutting above the ambient noise.[11]

Back in Washington during the week, he'd take her to the movies—Westerns, Civil War battle dramas, action films. Instead of courting her with candy and flowers, he gave her two books that meant a lot to him, showing her the kind of man he was or wanted to be. One was a biography of Sam Houston, *The Raven,* by Marquis James. Houston was a war hero, a politician and a poet. The second book was the inevitable choice—John Buchan's *Pilgrim's Way.* Jack probably drew her attention to those pages that described Raymond Asquith. Jackie reciprocated by offering him works that were both sweet and unique: charming small books that she had written just for him and illustrated herself.[12]

In November 1952 the Inquiring Camera Girl took the photograph of the newly elected senator for Massachusetts and wrote a brief, flattering comment to accompany it. Nevertheless, she sometimes found it hard to take him seriously. His constant fussing with his hair was irritating, but worse was his vanity. "If we go to a party or a reception and no one recognizes him," she told her cousin John H. Davis, "he sulks for hours."[13]

Jack took her to Hyannis Port for the July 4 weekend. All that competitiveness, noisy busyness and maniacal stress on winning got on her highly strung nerves. Touch football seemed almost a religion at the Kennedy compound, and no game was allowed to end in a draw. By her standards, the Kennedys possessed exuberance instead of sensitivity, believed in energy rather than thought. "They never relax; not even when they're relaxing," Jackie later grumbled.[14]

She managed to get on with Rose without ever liking her, a feeling that Rose reciprocated. The hostility between Jackie and Jack's sisters—plus the boisterous Ethel, Bobby's wife—was almost palpable. Jackie dismissively called them "the Rah-Rah girls." They called her "the Deb," and it was easy to make fun of her—eyes too far apart, shoulders too broad, chest too flat, feet too big and legs like sticks, and there was that ditzy baby-doll voice. But her slightly breathless, bubbleheaded way of speaking camouflaged a quick mind and a cutting wit.[15]

Joe, however, liked her from the start. While everyone else was watching a movie in the basement, he took Jackie into Rose's doll museum, with its hundreds of cute figures from all over the world. Surrounded by exotic small faces staring blankly, he talked to her in a language that he knew Jackie and, even more, Janet would understand. Joe told her about the trusts he had established for all his children. Jack would never want for money no matter what he did; he already had the income from a $10 million fund. Jackie was satisfied with that, yet afterwards, a doubt nagged at Joe. The girl's terrific, he told his friend Morton Downey, "But I don't think porcelain can carry babies."[16]

Jack Kennedy, unbridled skirt chaser that he was, never seemed threatened by women. He was so confident in himself that the brighter they were, the better he liked them. Although in time he would be held up as a prime example of the kind of man who uses women merely for sexual gratification, it was never as simple as that. He felt, for example, that American history was less interesting than English history and its public life poorer because American women were "either prostitutes or housewives, adding little to cultural and intellectual life."[17]

While he was in the House, Jack introduced legislation that would have required equal pay for equal work by women. It was killed in committee, as he probably anticipated. Even so, he didn't believe the struggle was over. On the contrary, it would only grow, becoming increasingly urgent and eventually unstoppable. In February 1953 he told Jackie he agreed with Philip Wylie's assertion in his current bestseller, *A Generation of Vipers,* that "the trend of the times is towards equality for women." And, he added, "That is what I have been fighting for for many years."[18]

=

It is April 24, 1953, towards the end of a hot afternoon, and Jack Kennedy sits at his desk in a mood of pleasant surprise and incipient lust. He has been allotted a steamy, uncomfortable office down in the basement of the Senate Office Building. As one of the newest members of the Senate, he does not rate anything better and does not even have air-conditioning.

That hardly seems to matter at the moment, though, because he is being interviewed by Margaret L. Coit, who is as pretty as she is attractive. Miss Coit won the Pulitzer Prize in 1951 for her biography of John Calhoun and is presently researching a biography of Joe Kennedy's friend Bernard Baruch. That is why Jack has agreed to this interview.

Washington's master of multitasking, Jack dictates letters to his secretary, takes phone calls and autographs dozens of glossy movie-star-style photographs of himself while Margaret Coit talks to him about Baruch. In the course of their conversation he throws in a remark that is both a compliment to her and a window on his own ambitions—"I would rather have the Pulitzer than be President." And in an attempt to impress her, he motions at the hundreds of books on his bookshelves. "Ask me about any of them. I've read them all."[19]

When the interview ends, he offers to drive her back to the boardinghouse where she is staying. She accepts his offer and they depart the building, with Kennedy on crutches. What follows is a hair-raising ride across the District.

These days, the senator drives a dented and none-too-clean green Buick convertible. Always a wild driver, he has acquired some worrying new habits at the wheel, such as reading a magazine as he drives. Kennedy also has his own way of getting through the rush-hour traffic quickly: he uses the streetcar tracks as if they were his own private road.

As he races up behind a streetcar, the conductor shouts angrily at him from the rear platform to get off the goddamn tracks. Jack shouts back, unleashing a torrent of profanity before swerving off the steel rails and back onto the street.

"Why are you in such a hurry?" asks a shaken Margaret Coit.

"I'm going to grab everything I want," he says. "You see, I haven't any time." A few minutes later, as they pass the White House, he jerks his thumb in its direction. "I'm going *there*."

Jack invites her to a cocktail party at the house he shares with Eunice. His sister is soon going to marry Sargent Shriver, who runs the Merchandise Mart in Chicago for Joe Kennedy. During the party, Jack pays almost no attention to Margaret Coit. He stands in a corner talking for nearly three hours with Stuart Symington, the rich, handsome and glamorous junior senator from Missouri.

A few days later, Jack calls Margaret and asks her out. When she arrives at his office, he tells her he's too tired to go anywhere. How about a quiet evening at her place? Once there, he propositions her urgently while pawing her freely. "Don't be so grabby," she protests. "This is only our first date." He ignores her protests and continues groping. "Listen to me," she tells him firmly. "I have standards, just like your sisters."

Jack laughs that off, telling her he doesn't care what his sisters do or don't do. Margaret tries another tack. "What about your priest? What will you tell him?"

"Oh, he'll forgive me," says Jack, grinning.

She continues to fend him off, and Jack suddenly gives up, flopping onto her couch. He starts talking about international affairs—"We can't provide milk to every Hottentot in the world. . . . What these countries need really isn't our money but our know-how. . . . Indochina is the next hot spot. . . ."[20]

Margaret Coit gazes at him, bemused. How can he act like a horny college boy one moment yet talk like a graying foreign-policy expert the next? After a while he stops talking about politics and starts talking about himself. He can't understand his own moods sometimes, he tells her—exuberant one moment, dejected the next. Then he drives himself home through the darkness, on yet another wild ride.

≡

In May 1953 Jackie departed for England to report on the coronation of Elizabeth II. Jack had talked about marriage without actually proposing. "I'm not ready yet," he told her. "But you are my choice."

"How *big* of you," she retorted.[21]

While she was gone, Jack sent her a telegram: "Articles excellent, but you are deeply missed. Love, Jack." Then he sent another one asking her to marry him. It seems typical somehow. Having been turned down three times, why risk another face-to-face rejection? Jackie's absence was perfect. When she returned to the United States, having signaled her acceptance, Jack was at the airport to greet her.[22]

Even now, Jackie wondered just how committed he was, as did he. Jack confessed his own doubts to Red Fay: "I'm both too young and too old for all this [and] it means the end of a promising political career, as it has been based up to now almost completely on the old sex appeal."[23]

He also told John Droney, a friend in the Massachusetts state senate, that marriage would probably cost him a lot of votes among women. Droney said Jack should forget about that: being married meant he'd probably have children, and one day he'd realize being a father brought more happiness than anything in politics.[24]

It was early June when Jack and Jackie agreed to get married, with the wedding to take place in September. However, there was a caveat. "Don't tell anyone until after June thirteenth," said Jack.

"Why not?"

"Because the *Saturday Evening Post* is running a story called 'Jack Kennedy: The Senate's Gay Young Bachelor.'" Their engagement was announced in *The New York Times* on June 25.[25]

Jackie was now wearing an eye-smackingly expensive engagement ring of emeralds and diamonds, an example of what Janet Auchincloss had in mind when she talked about "real" money. There was also a typically exuberant engagement party, which involved a scavenger hunt. First prize would go to whoever brought back "the largest object." Patricia Kennedy went into Hyannis, hot-wired a bus and drove it home.

In late July, to his fiancée's chagrin and embarrassment, Jack flew to France with Torby. They were going to rent a yacht and cruise the Riviera for what Jack called "girling." Like other masculine pursuits such as golfing and bowling, the object of girling was to run up an impressive score.

There were orgies on the boat and casual encounters ashore. In Cannes one day Jack ran into an English friend, Gavin Welby, who introduced him to a pair of Swedish lovelies. Welby dated one, Jack the other, twenty-one-year-old Gunilla von Post. In all probability, part of her fascination for him was the imperishable memory of Inga Binga: the blondness, the eager air, the Scandinavian accent.

Gunilla believed in astrology and asked him what his sign was, then wanted to know, "Do you believe in destiny? In fate?"

He smiled his characteristic wry smile. "Oh, I think my destiny is whatever my father wants it to be," he said lightly.

He took her to one of his favorite places on the Riviera, the Hôtel Eden Roc at Cap d'Antibes, and they huddled together in the darkness, waiting for dawn to break. "I'm going back to the United States next week to get married," he told her. She said nothing, hugging her hurt feelings in silence. "If I had met you one week before, I'd have canceled the whole thing." He said it only to make her feel better, but she was too young to realize that.[26]

Days later, he returned to get married; ironically, to a girl with dollar signs in her eyes. To cultivate good relations with his prospective father-in-law, Jack watched boxing on television with Black Jack Bouvier. They had something else in common, too. Black Jack had suffered for years from a ruptured disk. Sympathizing with Jack, he suggested various treatments that might help alleviate the pain. Yet they were never close. Jack still addressed him as "Mr. Bouvier" long after he had married his daughter.[27]

The wedding had its own unique role in Joe Kennedy's plans to put his son in the White House. Not only would there be five hundred people at the ceremony and twelve hundred at the reception; six hundred bottles of champagne and a five-tiered wedding cake; he had also arranged for front-page coverage in *The New York Times* and *The Washington Post*.

Jackie was aghast to discover there would be journalists present. It seemed vulgar to turn a private occasion into a public display, with herself as one of the two main exhibits. But what could she do? It was Joe who was paying for nearly everything, not Black Jack and not Hughdie.

Archbishop Richard Cushing, a man of imposing mien and risible self-importance, would conduct the ceremony in Newport. Jackie was a nominal Catholic; the kind, that is, who appears in church only to be "hatched, matched and dispatched." She did not attend Mass, had not been educated by nuns, had not grown up in a Catholic household. Her father was ostensibly a Catholic, but Janet was an Episcopalian married to an Episcopalian. Jackie had enjoyed the upbringing of a WASP princess, not a Catholic one, which was why, in marrying her, Jack was marrying up, while she was marrying money.

The evening before the wedding, Jack and Bobby and Teddy and various pals such as Red Fay played touch football. For Jack there were no ludic distractions. At the movies, he tried to divine the secrets of celebrity and charisma. So, too, in sports, he was trying both to win and to learn. When he played baseball, he thought of himself as Ted Williams at the plate and tried to swing the bat like Ted Williams. When he played touch football, he was invariably the quarterback, and for that role, he studied the throwing action of Y. A. Tittle of the New York Giants. During the game the evening before his wedding, Jack skidded into some briars. Next day—September 12—he showed up at the church immaculately attired but with angry red scratches crosshatched on both cheeks.[28]

Jackie expected her father to give her away. Janet conspired, however, to get Black Jack drunk. He would be so drunk, if her plan worked, that he would be unable to stir from his hotel room. Drunk but determined, Black Jack nevertheless managed to get to the church, although the ceremony had already started. Creeping into the church, he sat inconspicuously near the back.

When Jackie arrived she found that her stepfather, Hughdie, would be escorting her down the aisle instead of her father. She was indignant—but helpless. During the wedding service, she was comforted to see her father arrive, but by then something else was troubling her—Jack was in agony. Kneeling at the altar, standing up, kneeling again . . . The pain from his back was martyrdom, and he uttered his vows through gritted teeth.

Cushing, a longtime Kennedy family friend, relished his starring role. He conducted the ceremony in the benign, meandering style that had glazed the eyes of Bostonian Catholics for years. "I had the feeling that

Cushing thought he was number one," Jack told Red Fay later. "Jackie was number two, and I was number three."[29]

The whole day was turning into an ordeal for both bride and groom. The reception was held in a huge marquee erected on the expansive lawn overlooking the sea at Hammersmith Farm. Uncomfortable and edgy during the reception, Jackie ducked behind the drapes whenever she saw anyone she disliked moving inexorably towards her in the receiving line.[30]

The newlyweds headed for Mexico the next day. Jackie had been to Acapulco on vacation with her mother and sister in 1951 and liked it so much she wanted to go back. For Jack, the highlight of the honeymoon was catching a sailfish. Jackie had it stuffed and placed it on the wall in his Senate office. It eventually ended up hanging on a White House wall, raising a small question mark over Jackie's famously exquisite taste.

She sold off the wedding gifts she didn't like or need. Joe Kennedy's money was in trust for his children and grandchildren, she had no inheritance of her own to count on, and she would get nothing if Jack died. Whenever she had the chance to put some money away, as now, Jackie made the most of it. Over time, she developed an obsession with money. Instead of making her feel financially secure at last, marriage seemed only to deepen her anxieties.[31]

After the marriage, Jack carried a picture of Jackie in his wallet, but she had no illusions about his ability to commit himself to her or any woman. And she had seen time and again the effect the young Senator had on women. That narrow, beaming face radiated happy augury.

In a way, she had rehearsed this life. Jackie's father had boasted to her about his conquests, which only made her love him the more because she would always be, he told her, "my best girl." Married, then, to a man whose favorite hobby was girling, she tried making gentle fun of his charm, especially when he turned it on to full effect, dazzling women. She called it "Jack's incandescence" and gave him a nickname—"Magic."[32]

But that did not make the burden much easier to bear. She asked a friend, "How can you live with a husband who is bound to be unfaithful, but whom one loves?" Puzzled and anxious, her agonizing self-doubt only too obvious, Jackie told another friend, "But I'm so different from the girls Jack usually finds attractive."[33]

Shortly after the wedding, she was confronted with the unpalatable truth about her marriage, a truth she surely knew but yearned to deny. Jackie overhead Joe, Jack and Bobby talking about her role in Jack's quest for the White House. Her blood was chilled by the way they talked. "They spoke of me as if I wasn't a person," she told Eleanor McGovern, one of the few congressional wives she liked. "I was just a thing, just a sort of asset, like Rhode Island."[34]

She was angry at Jack's infidelities some of the time; bore up under her lot most of the time; but was wounded in her self-esteem all of the time, as Rose had been. Unlike Rose, she didn't flee into faith. She resorted to some revenge affairs, including one with William Holden. Mostly, though, she adopted an attitude that was both stoic and forgiving, much like W. H. Auden's:

> If equal affection cannot be,
> Let the more loving one be me.

Even so, she cried easily. Jack found her tears baffling, irritating, unendurable. She was also given to prolonged periods of moody introspection. As she turned in on herself, he tried to talk her into a better frame of mind. Sometimes that worked, but when it didn't, he became difficult himself. Tears and gloominess bewildered him. Kennedy women weren't supposed to cry. His mother didn't do it; nor did his sisters. Still, she wasn't really a Kennedy. Not now, not ever.[35]

Making the challenge even harder, most of their interests were divergent rather than convergent. He was allergic to horses, just as he was allergic to dogs, yet Jackie could not imagine life without horses. JFK liked to play backgammon and Chinese checkers, both of which Jackie found boring. Whenever they went to a party, he would usually go home early, and she went home late. He had something to get up for in the morning; she didn't. Jackie had no interest in politics. Besides, she had grown up in the bosom of Republicanism. Becoming a Kennedy meant marrying out.

She was younger than most Senate wives, and they were too suburban and stuffy for her anyway. Nor did Jack try to convince her that being a senator was exciting. Being in the Senate could be as tedious as being in the House. It wasn't unusual for him to sum up a morning of Senate business in two words—"Bored shitless."[36]

Jackie excelled at the party games the Kennedys loved, such as a version of hide-and-seek called "sardines," or "categories," which called for choosing some weird or esoteric subject. The winner was the first person to come up with twenty-six relevant names, starting with A and ending with Z. Jackie proved better at such diversions than any of the Kennedys. One evening, entertaining a group of Spanish diplomats at their Georgetown house, Jack got a game of categories going. Jackie beat him every time. He asked her to come into the kitchen.

"Gosh, Jackie. You can't afford to do this to your husband when he is in public like this."

She smiled sweetly. "Why, Jack, I thought *all* the Kennedys liked competition."[37]

Jack was proud of his wife's artistic talents, and shortly after their wedding, he gave Jackie an easel, a paint box, a palette, some brushes and several square yards of canvas. Soon, however, she found he was using them himself. He began by painting scenes that looked vaguely like representations of the Irish countryside—little houses without much character or charm, smoke curling lazily from small chimney pots. Jack moved on to copying works by French Impressionists. Convinced after a few weeks that he was a natural artist, he challenged Teddy to a painting competition. The family provided a judging panel. Teddy had never painted anything in his life, so Jack awaited the result calmly. Teddy's painting won.[38]

In Jackie's dream life, she was a movie star, much as Jack was a screen hero in his. For a time, she nursed serious hopes of becoming an actress. Jack soon disabused her of that idea. If she pursued it, that would hurt him politically. She would be in Hollywood, removed from her main role, the loyal, loving political wife. Their strongest shared interest was a love of books and an admiration for great writers. Jackie memorized passages from one of Jack's favorite long poems, "John Brown's Body," so she could recite them to him.[39]

Jackie's own taste ran in a different direction, towards the introspective and offbeat. She loved works such as Charles Baudelaire's *Les Fleurs du Mal,* the kind of mocking introspective verse that meant almost nothing to him. Jack Kennedy's love of poetry was less an exposure to those truths about the human heart that only great poets can express than a need for hortatory verse, the kind that generations of sensitive and book-loving young men have relied on to inflame their courage and reinforce their tenacity.

He found comfort and inspiration in poems such as Alfred Lord Tennyson's "Ulysses," with its clarion call to defiance of implacable fate:

> Death closes all; but something ere the end,
> Some work of noble note, may yet be done. . . .
> Come, my friends,
> 'Tis not too late to seek a newer world. . . .
> [T]hat which we are, we are,
> One equal temper of heroic hearts,
> Made weak by time and fate, but strong in will
> To strive, to seek, to find, and not to yield.

Jack was given especially—and understandably—to memorizing mournful poems and ballads about brave men who die for noble causes, such as Thomas Osborne Davis's lament for the seventeenth-century Irish resistance hero Owen Roe O'Neill. JFK was deeply moved whenever he recited its closing lines:

> Sheep without a shepherd when the snow shuts out the sky,
> O why did you leave us Owen? Why did you die?

When Jack and Jackie returned to Hyannis from their honeymoon, he told her there was something important that she had to know. "*This* is my favorite poem," he said at the threshold to their new home and their new life, in a small house adjacent to his father's property. Standing there, he slowly recited a poem by Alan Seeger. Tall and thin and brilliant and handsome, Seeger had graduated in the Harvard class of 1910 and had joined the Foreign Legion to fight for France in World War I. He was killed in action on July 4, 1916, in an attack to recapture a German-held village in northern France, not long after writing his most famous poem:

> I have a rendezvous with Death
> At some disputed barricade . . .

Jack intoned it solemnly, flawlessly, to its conclusion:

> And I to my pledged word am true,
> I shall not fail that rendezvous.[40]

Joe and Rose

There had never been a father and mother like Joe and Rose in the history of the Republic. They weren't famous because their son became President; they were famous long before their son became President. Well-known figures in their own right, their present dismal reputations cast long, deep shadows over Jack's.

Joe Kennedy has become the embodiment of evil—a liar, a master criminal, a corrupt fixer and manipulator, an anti-Semite, a debaucher of teenage girls, a man without shame or honor, a draft-dodging coward, someone who would sell his country for an advantage, a father whose sole interest in his offspring was as instruments of a weird, vainglorious ambition. As for Rose, she is the archetypal icebox mother, incapable of loving her children, especially Jack; a self-deceiving woman who ignored her husband's infidelities and absences in exchange for haute couture and diamonds.

Such characterizations are cartoon versions of the realities, and they turn Jack Kennedy's life into an expression of the malign forces generated by the two damaged people he called Mother and Dad. This, though, is historical determinism. It tells us nothing about someone with a hinterland as deep, strange and surprising as Jack Kennedy's. The comic-book view also decontextualizes him, yet he was the product of an age as well as a family; of a country as well as a religion; of his own will and desires as well as those that others projected onto him.

His parents had reached a modus vivendi in their marriage years before Joe Jr. died. After that, Joe and Rose spent less and less time together. Rose clung to the illusion that some romance still existed between them, writing Joe letters that told him she loved him and calling herself "Rosa," something she did only in her letters to him.[1]

Yet when they were in the same city, they stayed in different hotels. After World War II, Joe couldn't be bothered with Hyannis. Even in the summer, when most of the family was there, he remained in New York, flying up to the Cape now and then for a day or two. Hyannis was really Rose's domain, and Palm Beach was his.[2]

To most of JFK's friends, his father was "Big Joe," a man with a piercing gaze, a cutting tongue and a powerful presence. That gimlet gaze behind, and beyond, the glitter of his spectacles amounted to a sharp probing of the world, in which every human weakness was obvious and the essential truth—that in the end, humanity is ruled by ideas—was obscured. Wherever he was, Palm Beach, New York or Hyannis, he began the day at a breakfast table covered with every important newspaper from Boston to Miami. His appetite was always stronger for the news than it was for eating.[3]

After breakfast, he exercised by riding a large, powerful horse for an hour or so. Then he went into his poolside hut. Joe Kennedy had a kind of office-cum-cabana erected next to the Palm Beach swimming pool. Roughly a hundred feet square and open to the sky, it contained a couple of small tables and several wicker chairs in which he would sit, stark naked and coated in suntan oil. He spent the rest of the morning making telephone calls across the United States and Europe, tracking his investments, barking commands, as rivulets of sweat flowed down his red, freckled face, threatening to fall from his chin onto the notebook cradled in his lap. After lunch he took a nap, went to the golf course, came home again and sat listening to music or read until dinner.[4]

This carrot-topped paterfamilias demanded that his children excel. Whatever other people's children did, his children had to do better. But the people who worked for him at Hyannis Port remained sturdily unimpressed. Behind his back, they made fun of him, like the man who remarked, "Old Joe wants the world to think Kennedy shit don't smell." They watched the parade of expensive whores he brought home and knew that throughout the 1950s he was sleeping with his secretary, Janet Des Rosiers, who was the same age as his youngest daughter, Jean.[5]

Joe Kennedy more than once remarked, "I don't want to be bored. Ever!" Not all of the legacy was bad. And there's no doubt he succeeded in some crucial father roles: as an example of success, as a strong, powerful male and as a bridge to the wider world. Above all, his interest in his sons was intense. In various ways, Joe was the kind of father a lot of adolescent boys yearn for. In the end, he bound them to him with a force greater than money, for his way of winning their love didn't call for riches, but it did call for commitment. Any articulate middle-class father could have pursued the same strategy and achieved a similar emotional bond with his children.

Most young people have secret lives that their parents know almost nothing about. In the case of Joe Kennedy and his sons, there was very little that was truly secret. He created an intense, familial and masculine world where each son was intensely loyal to his brothers and all were devoted to him. What secrets the Kennedy men possessed were held against the world; what lies they told, they told to the world. To one another, they were true, and that was sincerity enough. No hypocrisy at home, no pretense.

Unlike other fathers, Joe Kennedy did not hide his failings from his sons or pretend he was something that he was not. He made them accept his weaknesses much as he'd made Rose accept them, by sheer force of personality. If he heard that Jack had taken an interest in a girl, he would invite her to dinner so he could judge what she was after and, if he took a fancy to her himself, to see how far he could get. Most sons would deeply resent that. Jack found it amusing, telling people, "I hope I'm just like him if I get to be sixty-five."[6]

Joe liked to think his greatest achievement was producing such a dynamic family, but the Kennedys would not have become a dynasty without Joe's stupendous wealth. His own view of businessmen was dismissive. Most of them weren't very bright, he told his children, and he knew that as able as he was, he owed a lot to luck. "Six or seven times in my life, the pendulum swung my way," he told an old family friend one day. "If it hadn't fallen favorably for me, life could have been quite a bit different."[7]

He discovered, too, that after a while, being rich wasn't particularly interesting. "Money isn't important in itself," he concluded. "It's the power it gives you to do something that matters."[8]

His greatest business coup came at the end of World War II, when he bought the twenty-four-story Merchandise Mart in downtown Chicago. What was remarkable wasn't so much the fact that he bought it, but the way that he bought it.

The Marshall Field family had built the Mart, and when it opened in 1930, it offered ninety-three acres of covered space. Impossible to fill during the Depression, it proved to be a huge and costly white elephant. Many of its occupants were federal agencies and departments of the Illinois state government. The Fields couldn't wait to unload it.

Joe Kennedy, on the other hand, knew the federal government intended to depart. Betting that the war would be over soon, he put in a bid for the building in early 1945. The Mart would need to be cleaned up and renovated once the federal and state bureaucrats left, but Joe was certain he could fill the place with tenants desperate for space once the war ended. From 1941 to 1945 Americans had saved hundreds of billions of dollars. That money was going to flood across the country once the shooting stopped, and Joe was going to be in the path of the floodwaters with his very own reservoir ready to fill up.

He borrowed $13 million at a time when interest rates were around 2 percent. The deal went through in July 1945, and less than a month later Japan surrendered. Within a year, the Mart had been refurbished and rapidly filled with high-paying tenants. Buying the Mart cost him only $1 million of his own money, and he soon earned that back. Over the next twenty years it generated a reliable cash flow that provided working capital for Joe's business interests and financed Jack's campaigns.[9]

Joe's circle of acquaintance was a mid-twentieth-century *Who's Who*. There was hardly an important figure in government or business whom he did not know. And those few movers and shakers he had not already met could be counted on to take a telephone call and listen carefully to whatever he had to say.

While he relished his role as a Big Catholic Layman, Joe was the most detached kind of Catholic this side of lapsing. It seemed enough that he could buy the favor of the Church; he did not have to submit to its demands. Joe Kennedy did not go to Mass or confession, say his prayers or seek any of the consolations of religion. Whatever he wanted, he paid for rather than prayed for.[10]

He knew he was widely disliked and sometimes feared, but that never bothered him. Nor was he a man to agonize over a problem. Joe Kennedy was convinced most problems came down to money. And "anything that can be settled with money is not worth losing a night's sleep," he told his daughter Patricia.[11]

Joe Kennedy not only bankrolled his son's political ambition but was assumed to control it. Jack was a fiscal conservative, much like his father, but on the foreign policy and national security issues that were his overriding interest, they had almost nothing in common.

Jack was always mildly irritated at the way his father was portrayed as the dominant force in his life and career. Jackie scoffed at such ideas. "You'd think he was a mastermind playing chess," she retorted, "when actually he's a nice old gentleman who we see at Thanksgiving and Christmas."[12]

In truth, he was something more than that while remaining something far less exalted than Jack's mastermind. Just before Jack was elected to the Senate, his father was pushing him to introduce a congressional resolution supporting "captive peoples" under Communist rule. Joe hired a legislative expert on Capitol Hill to produce a draft, and the expert warned him not to get his hopes up. "Jack, with his accustomed independence, will probably make his own changes or not follow this line of thought at all." Which was precisely what happened.[13]

Unlike most isolationists of his generation, Joe never could acknowledge that his earlier attitudes had been mistaken. Rose called him "infallible," and he took much the same view. Long after the war ended, Joe Kennedy remained an isolationist, convinced that American involvement in World War II had achieved nothing except to send three hundred thousand young Americans to their deaths.

He never doubted that Communism was an unmitigated evil but drew back from engagement even in the Cold War with a kind of irritated indifference. As far as he was concerned, those countries such as France and Italy that tolerated strikes and anti-American sentiments got what they deserved and deserved what they got.

There was also a risk of America going broke, he believed, if the country had to fight the Cold War before paying off what it had cost to fight Germany and Japan. In 1947 he damned the Marshall Plan and aid to Greece and Turkey—"a horrible waste of money. People keep talking about what will happen if Russia takes over the countries of Europe. What is going to happen if Russia takes them over after we have poured billions of dollars into them?"[14]

Joe convinced himself that the Korean War was due to the presence of American troops in the Far East. He was therefore hostile to NATO, the UN and any other international body the United States belonged to. He considered every dollar spent on foreign aid or mutual security a dollar wasted.

Not only were he and Jack far apart on the issues that fueled his son's political passions, they were completely unlike in their temperaments. In 1953 Joe Kennedy, Jack and a dozen friends went to watch the Harvard-Yale game. Teddy was playing. Joe organized a small motorcade of four cars, heading from Boston over to Cambridge, with a police car leading the way.

Joe wanted to play a joke on Jack. Turn the siren on, he told the police just before the motorcade set off. Getting into his limousine, Joe told his friend John Droney what he'd done. "I'm not trying to get there any quicker. Just look behind, and Jack will have his head down on the floor." The cars set off and the siren wailed. Droney looked at the automobile behind and saw Jack Kennedy bend over so far he couldn't be recognized. "I don't know what's wrong with him," sighed Joe. "If I were a senator and going to a football game, I'd have them use the sirens so people could see me. Jack hates anything like that."[15]

Even as his son moved steadily towards the presidency, Joe Kennedy's dynastic project was fatally flawed. It was a personal ambition whose seeming ineluctable success was going to be undermined by the mercurial elements that went into its making.

The Kennedys lacked bourgeois solidity and stolidity. In the 1950s, while Joe Kennedy was forging his dynasty, in next door Connecticut, Prescott Bush was forging *his,* and the end result would be no accident. The Bushes were sufficiently ordinary to endure. But in the Kennedy home there was a strongly antibourgeois sensibility at work, a scorn for dullness and routine, an invigorating idiosyncrasy and a passionate intensity. Greater even than these, though, was the tribe, the clan, the family— these set the boundaries of Joe Kennedy's ambition, and within those limits were all the reasons for its brief, dazzling success and ultimate fall.

=

Jack Kennedy famously—and bitterly—remarked, "My mother is a nothing." This comes close to saying, "My mother is nothing to me." Nevertheless, he also told people that while he got his charm from his father, he got his brains from his mother, and intelligence meant more to Jack Kennedy than almost anything else. He put it on a par with physical courage, above which nothing rated more highly.[16]

He had used his mother to help him get elected to the House and later to the Senate, but as he advanced on the presidency, Rose's value dwindled. In time, he cut her out of his life; revenge, it seems, for her having cut him out of hers when he needed her most, as a lonely and sickly boarder in private schools.

Jack might have respected her more had she deployed her undoubted intelligence in the rough-and-tumble debates at mealtimes. When the children were growing up, Joe and Rose and the older children sat together. The younger ones sat at another table with a governess. At the grown-up table, there was endless talk, dominated by Joe. Rose might occasionally try to say something, but she rarely managed to make herself heard.[17]

As the children grew up and prepared to strike out on their own, so did she—by going into internal exile. In the fall of 1941, with Joe Jr. and Jack in the military and the United States edging ever closer to war, Rose built a retreat for herself at Hyannis Port. In a way, it was her version of Joe's Palm Beach poolside cabana; redolent, too, of the convent cell she had occupied in Holland in her youth. It contained a desk, a chair, a cot and a small closet. Over the years, it was blown down twice by hurricane winds and was rebuilt a little sturdier each time. She was likely to head for her hut after breakfast, carrying a bathrobe and a book.[18]

After a walk along the beach and a swim, she retreated into her clapboard cell and stayed there, reading, thinking, possibly even praying, for most of the day. Then she'd return to the house for dinner and afterwards sit alone at her baby grand piano, playing show tunes.

Another escape was long-term retail therapy. Rose shopped enthusiastically all over the Western world, especially for clothes. She went to Paris each year for the fashion shows at the major houses, and throughout her long life, she was immensely proud of her expensive, handmade wardrobe. Yet hers was the kind of aesthetic that made Coco Chanel once remark that she had learned what good taste was by looking at how rich women dressed—almost anything was better. Rose favored flowered silk dresses under big flowered hats.

Although she was admired and envied by millions of women, Rose remained socially insecure. As the wife of the ambassador to the Court of St. James, she had mingled with royalty. But that wasn't because she was considered well-bred and sophisticated. It was because she was the wife of one of the more important ambassadors, and they always got invited to the palace.

Rose liked to imagine that she was descended from the Italian aristocracy, but she lacked aristocratic refinement. She was likely to pull out her compact and powder her nose in the middle of a meal, seemingly unaware that this was a habit associated with shopgirls and showgirls. While Rose was proud of her ability to speak French, she spoke it with an excruciating accent that only excited derision and laughter among the French. A stickler for correct grammar and punctuation, she was an abysmal speller.

In truth, to the WASP elite of New England and New York, she was a "mick." So was Joe; so were the four sons; and so, too, were all five daughters. The Kennedys didn't entertain for various reasons, including a sense of social inferiority that fame and money couldn't erase. After leaving London in 1940, Joe insisted for the rest of his life that people call him "Ambassador." Such tics invariably emphasize pose over poise.

Rose seems to have felt truly herself only when she was on her own or on her knees. She hoped for years that Teddy might become a priest and—who could tell?—possibly a cardinal one day. Then he ruined her hopes by getting married.[19]

In 1951 Rose had the Joseph P. Kennedy, Jr. Foundation give $2.5 million to the Home for Underprivileged Children, which the Catholic Church maintained in the Bronx. The home was one of the favorite projects of the politically astute Francis Cardinal Spellman of New York. In December 1952, to Rose's immense delight, she became a papal countess.[20]

Meanwhile, she continued lobbying for the beatification of Mother Cabrini as America's first saint and for the elevation of Richard Cushing to cardinal. In 1957 Cushing received a cardinal's hat. By then he was known throughout New England as "the Kennedys' parish priest." Rose's efforts on behalf of Mother Cabrini took longer, but they, too, paid off.[21]

The great secret and shame in her life was the destruction of her oldest daughter, Rosemary. Easily the most attractive of the Kennedy girls, Rosemary was shy and withdrawn. Rose spent many hours teaching Rosemary to read and write, but it was a struggle. One of her biggest problems was getting Rosemary to write from left to right. The child insisted on going from right to left. This is what is known as "mirror writing" and can be a sign of dyslexia.

Both Joe and Rose were frustrated by Rosemary's learning difficulties.

Nevertheless, in 1938 she was presented at court with her sister Kathleen. She was also entrusted with looking after her sister Eunice when the two of them traveled alone through Switzerland.

Yet by 1941 Rosemary was becoming increasingly difficult. She threw temper tantrums and would not, or could not, act as a Kennedy daughter was expected to act. She had a worrying habit of leaving the house late at night and not returning for hours.[22]

Rose and Joe feared some wastrel or fortune-hunter might impregnate her. She might even be kidnapped and held for ransom. According to the authorized history of the family, Rosemary "had the body of a 21-year-old [and] the mentality of a four-year-old child."[23]

Rosemary's diary tells a different tale. Here is a sample entry, from a day when she and Kick and Jack were together in Washington: "Went to luncheon in the ballroom in the White House. James Roosevelt came in and took us in to see his father, President Roosevelt. He said, 'It's about time you came. How can I put my arm around all of you? Which is the oldest? You are all so big.' "[24]

There were ways that a rich family could cope with her erratic behavior. Joe and Rose might have hired a nurse-companion, preferably one used to dealing with the mentally disturbed. If that didn't work, there were psychiatric hospitals in tranquil settings that catered to the rich.

Instead, they decided to have their daughter lobotomized. Rosemary was not a danger to herself or to anyone else. Nor had she been diagnosed as suffering from any serious form of mental illness such as schizophrenia; that is, she did not qualify as a suitable patient for a lobotomy. Every Boston surgeon who was approached declined to perform the operation.

Never a man to be thwarted, Joe found two doctors in Washington who were looking for guinea pigs on whom they could practice a new technique. It did not involve cutting into the skull but instead called for inserting an instrument similar to an icepick through the eye socket and forcing it up into the frontal lobe of the brain. After agreeing to this ghastly medical assault on her daughter, Rose left the country while the operation was performed.

Having been reduced by surgery to the mentality of a four-year-old, Rosemary was placed in a Catholic home for the mentally retarded in Wisconsin. She was allowed to come back to Hyannis Port for brief visits every few years, although never when Joe was there.

After Rosemary's lobotomy, Joe Kennedy took an interest in mental retardation that he had never shown before. Guilt? Perhaps, although he was not a man to whom a sense of guilt came easily. Now, though, he decided that the Joseph P. Kennedy, Jr. Foundation should devote most of its considerable resources to alleviating the suffering of mentally retarded children. In time, thanks to Rosemary's sister Eunice, the foundation would also organize and finance the Special Olympics.[25]

Whether Jack Kennedy knew or understood what had happened to Rosemary will probably never be known. He was so sensitive to nuance, to atmosphere, however, that this brutal attempt to erase his oldest sister for the greatest failing of all—her inability to fit in as a Kennedy—can hardly have passed without wounding him somewhere. He would become the first President to launch a federal program for the treatment of mental retardation.

CHAPTER 19

Patient Profile

B eetling Joe McCarthy, with his bushy eyebrows and glittering dark
eyes, a permanent five o'clock shadow emphasizing his jowls, was
a gift to cartoonists. Drawings that portrayed McCarthy with huge,
hairy knuckles scraping the ground were funny yet convincing.

After failing as a chicken farmer, he had bounced back to become a
county judge and had served in the Marine Corps during World War II. In
1946 he had won a Senate seat in Wisconsin, a state better known for its
radical politicians than its reactionaries. Grasping all the notoriety his
show-off's nature craved, in February 1950 McCarthy addressed three
hundred Republican women in Wheeling, West Virginia, brandishing a
piece of paper. "I have here in my hand a list of 205—a list of names that
were made known to the Secretary of State as being members of the Communist party and who nevertheless are still working and shaping policy in
the State Department."[1]

With a scrap of paper that no one was allowed to examine, thus did Joe
McCarthy get the attention not only of three hundred women but of the
entire country, eager to have those names. At the same time he ushered in
the stalking fear known as McCarthyism.

He was already a friend of the Kennedys, and if anything, Joe Kennedy liked him even more after the Wheeling speech. Although McCarthy was a Republican, Joe gladly gave $5,000 towards his reelection in 1952. Jack, too, liked McCarthy. During Jack's time in the House, they had disagreed openly and sharply over low-cost housing for veterans. But that was political, not personal. Each regarded the other as a friend.[2]

In 1951 Joe McCarthy was a guest at Robert Kennedy's wedding to Ethel Skakel. Half of the Kennedys—including Jack—attended McCarthy's wedding two years later, and Eunice was a bridesmaid. Ethel Kennedy's closest friend was Jean McCarthy, Joe's wife, and Joe McCarthy became godfather to Bobby Kennedy's first child, Robert Francis Kennedy, Jr.

Following his overwhelming reelection to the Senate in November 1952, McCarthy chaired the Committee on Government Operations. Its members included Jack Kennedy and three noted liberals, Henry "Scoop" Jackson, Hubert Humphrey and Margaret Chase Smith.

None of these normally outspoken liberals openly criticized Joe McCarthy's outrageous attacks on figures of absolute probity, such as George Marshall. Yet there were limits to what any decent person could stomach. Jack was disgusted after watching McCarthy ranting on the Senate floor one day in the fall of 1953. Leaving the chamber, he remarked to Tristram Coffin, a young and very liberal journalist, "Joe's nothing but a faker!" He'd just glimpsed the obvious, late.[3]

In February 1954 Eisenhower publicly deplored what he called the "excesses" of McCarthy and fellow red-baiter Senator William Jenner of Indiana. Days later, when this issue came up on *Meet the Press,* Kennedy was asked how he felt about Eisenhower's comments. Kennedy said both McCarthy and Jenner were guilty as charged.[4]

That summer, television broadcasts of the Army-McCarthy hearings exposed to millions just how unscrupulous and reckless McCarthy was. With the tide of public opinion turning irreversibly against McCarthy, Senator Ralph Flanders of Vermont introduced a resolution in the Senate to censure him. A Senate select committee was formed to consider whether the Flanders resolution should go to a vote.

As these events unfolded, Jack Kennedy felt deeply torn. The family was so close to McCarthy that if he condemned him outright and publicly, it would deeply upset his parents, Eunice, Bobby and Ethel. McCarthy was also popular across Massachusetts. There could be a heavy political

price to pay. Even so, Jack felt McCarthy deserved censure. He had his
principal assistant, Ted Sorensen, whom he had hired after being elected
to the Senate, write a speech in support of the Flanders resolution, but he
was only going to use it if it came to a vote on the Senate floor.

As he debated the McCarthy issue with himself, Jack's mind turned
inevitably to the past, and an idea came to him. In April 1954 he tried it
out on Cass Canfield, publisher at Harper & Row. He had a feeling, he
told Canfield, that there was a book waiting to be written about senators
who had risked their careers for the sake of principle.

Nothing came of this discussion, partly because throughout the summer of 1954, Jack's back pain became unendurable. By September he was
on crutches most of the time. His staff had to carry him up and down stairs
in buildings that lacked elevators.

The only hope seemed to be another spinal fusion operation, much like
the failed surgery Jack had undergone in 1945. This time the doctors at
the Lahey Clinic advised strongly against it. Because of his Addison's disease, there was a fifty-fifty chance that a postoperative infection would
kill him. The cortisone he needed to stay the menace of adrenal deficiency
thinned his blood, impeding healing and increasing susceptibility to disease.[5]

Yet Jack knew of a fate even worse—if he carried on as he was, the back
brace and crutches would be followed before long by a wheelchair, and
once in a wheelchair he might never escape. Death had more appeal. He
couldn't slow down—there wasn't enough time, or a good enough reason.

Besides, the great venture spun like a steel net from his father's implacable will held him fast, and his brothers along with him. The creation
of a Kennedy dynasty would go on even without him. "If I died," he once
remarked, "my brother Bob would want to be a senator. And if anything
happened to him, my brother Teddy would run for us." Jack was never
allowed to be just himself, for himself; he was part of something bigger.
That was a curse, yet within it existed a rare kind of freedom. Not for him
the quotidian banality that grays most of human existence.[6]

Boston had failed him, but in New York there is always hope. If there's
anything you want to buy and you can't find it in New York, then chances
are it doesn't exist. As he probably expected, Jack found doctors there
who would perform the operation despite the risk.

He told his father, "I'm going under the knife."

Joe begged him not to risk it. Even if he needed a wheelchair, he told his son, he could still become President. Franklin Roosevelt had done it; Jack could do the same.[7] But not even Joe Kennedy could talk him out of the operation. The image of Jack Kennedy as the embodiment of health and fitness was at risk, and without that, he could survive physically only to die politically. "It might be well for all of us to have the same story concerning your hospitalization," one of his staffers, Ted Reardon, suggested. So what did he want them to say? Surgery for an old war injury, responded Kennedy. That was the story. Period.[8]

On October 10, 1954, he entered the New York Hospital for Special Surgery on East Forty-second Street. After more than a week of tests, X rays and earnest discussions with the patient, his wife and his family, the surgeons agreed to go ahead on October 21.

The Senate select committee was expected to report any day now on the Flanders resolution censuring McCarthy. An hour or so before he was due to go under the knife, Jack's old friend Chuck Spalding came by to wish him good luck. Jack stared at the ceiling for a while, tapping his teeth. "You know," he said at last, "when I go downstairs, I know exactly what's going to happen. Those reporters are going to lean over my stretcher. There's going to be about ninety-five faces bent over me with great concern. And then every one of those guys is going to say, 'Now, Senator, what about McCarthy?' And I'm going to pull the sheet over my head and yell 'Ow!'"[9]

Shortly before noon he was wheeled into the operating theater. Three days later his vital signs failed. Infection was about to kill him. Jackie sent for a priest to administer the last rites. Joe Kennedy went to see Arthur Krock and burst into tears: "Jack is dying!" Jackie, the nominal Catholic, did something she had never done before—she got down on her knees and prayed. "Help him, oh Mother of God. Oh, help him," she pleaded.[10] "The first time in my life," she told a friend, still slightly bemused that she'd done it at all.

For the third time in his eternally youthful existence, Jack Kennedy drifted into that penumbral zone where life seems almost indistinguishable from death. He hovered there for nearly two days, then drifted out again on the side he'd gone in. By surviving, he made medical history. Jack Kennedy was one of the first sufferers from Addisonism to undergo major surgery and live.[11]

Over the weeks that followed, Jackie spent her days by his bedside, and much of each night. She helped the nurses bathe him, feed him and get him in and out of his hospital gown. Jackie brought him tidbits of gossip about his family and friends, read to him, recited poetry, played checkers with him and told him about the new movies that had just been released.

Seeking to please while buoying Jack's depressed spirits, Jackie's sister, Lee Radziwill, put up balloons in his room. Jackie bought him a toy shotgun that fired corks so he could try popping some of the balloons. A few months before he was hospitalized, Jack had met Marilyn Monroe, now the hottest new Hollywood star. To Jackie's dismay, Jack got someone to tape a poster featuring Monroe in *Gentlemen Prefer Blondes* to the ceiling, directly over his bed. Monroe, dressed in a tight sweater and short shorts, with her legs splayed, gazed down at him like a promise.[12]

The doctors discouraged all but close relatives from visiting, but Jackie made an exception for Grace Kelly, another of the movie stars Jack had dated. One of Jack's old girlfriends, Florence Pritchett Smith, got Grace Kelly to dress up as a nurse. Grace slipped into the room and whispered in Jack's ear, "I'm the new night nurse." There was absolutely no response. He stared at her blankly, his mind clouded by sedatives. She stepped back into the corridor, abashed. How did it go? Jackie asked. "I must be losing it," Grace said, sighing.[13]

All the while, the resolution to censure McCarthy was being thrashed out by the Senate select committee. Jack had his wife read him biographies—the life stories of Massachusetts senators who had risked their careers over principle. Men such as Daniel Webster, whose integrity was almost as famous as his oratory; Charles Sumner, the vehement foe of slavery who had been bludgeoned nearly to death by an incensed Congressman from South Carolina in 1857; and George Frisbie Hoar, widely considered the best lawyer of his generation. Just as he looked to Y. A. Tittle on how to throw a football and Gary Cooper on how to project a charismatic presence, so Jack Kennedy examined these figures from his home state for clues on how to be a great senator and do the right thing that was hard instead of the wrong thing that was easy.[14]

By the end of November he was out of bed but still on crutches, and *The New York Times Magazine* was asking him to write an article on "the New Isolationism." He made a counterproposal. Here was a chance to test the waters for his book idea on courageous senators. *The New York Times Magazine* agreed: it would accept a piece on the importance of courage in politics.[15]

He was going to need a lot of help. Jackie herself conducted some of

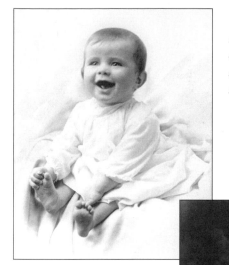

A happy President in the making clutches his foot and laughs as if he already knows the camera will always love him.

Rose Kennedy poses with, from right to left, Joe Jr., Jack and their sister Kathleen at the end of World War I, not long after she tried to leave her philandering husband, and failed.

Joseph P. Kennedy poses with his two eldest sons as the bull market of the 1920s reached its frenzied peak. Following the October 1929 Wall Street crash, Joe, thanks to inside information, unregulated markets and lucky guesses, managed to hold on to the millions he had amassed, unlike many of his contemporaries.

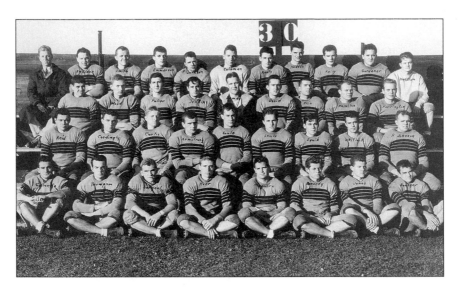

A skinny but eager John F. Kennedy sits third from the right in the front row in this 1937 picture of the Harvard Junior Varsity. Desperate to win his father's admiration and to prove himself among his peers, Jack Kennedy yearned for football success, without ever showing much ability at the game.

His physical courage and a youthful desire to show off were displayed during Jack's motoring vacation in 1937. Here he hangs by his fingertips above a dry moat at Carcassonne; the ground is more than twenty feet beneath him. When this picture was taken, he had no difficulties with his back; less than two weeks later, a lifetime of problems began.

The United States ambassador's son helps fill sandbags in Scotland four days after Britain declared war on Germany in September 1939. It was a statement, in effect, that while Joseph P. Kennedy was a staunch isolationist and appeaser, Jack at once identified himself with Britain's defiant response to Hitler's invasion of Poland.

Palm Beach, December 1940: Jack poses on the beach outside his parents' winter home with two friends and their dates. At the right is his lifelong friend from Choate, Lem Billings.

An emaciated Lieutenant John F. Kennedy is reunited with Lem Billings in 1944, after commanding *PT-109* in the South Pacific. Billings, like Kennedy, had not been able to pass his Navy physical without the intervention of Joseph P. Kennedy, a man powerful enough to fix almost any problem except Jack's precarious health.

Always a sun worshiper, Jack Kennedy tries to regain his health and strength by basking in the Florida sunshine in the winter of 1944 with his adored eldest sister, Kick.

In June 1946, congressional candidate John F. Kennedy (far left) leads the Bunker Hill Day parade. A politician was expected to wear a hat in those days, but Kennedy loathed hats and did not even own one—here, he carries a hat borrowed from a campaign worker. Minutes after this picture was taken, he collapsed from exhaustion; nevertheless, he won the primary election the following day.

A skeletal and almost weirdly youthful congressman takes up his duties in Washington, January 1947.

Christmas 1948 at the Palm Beach mansion, and Jack Kennedy seems to have recovered from his various ailments and put on a little weight. He has recently been reelected to the House and is reading a new book, *The Gathering Storm*, which lies open in the right of the picture. This was the first volume of Winston Churchill's account of World War II; Jack Kennedy devoured nearly every word that Churchill ever wrote.

The congressman faced the prospect of life in a wheelchair. Kennedy often had to use crutches, although these were rarely seen by anyone outside his family or his staff. On this occasion, a 1952 meeting of the House Labor Committee, however, someone has forgotten to put them out of sight.

Onward and upward: Jack Kennedy, a pioneer in the use of television in politics, campaigns for election to the Senate in 1952. And as in all his campaigns, this was a family affair. Here, his sister Eunice sits loyally beside him, ready as all his sisters are to convince the world that Jack is the one.

It looks like a wedding ceremony as staged for a movie, and it came close to being that. In 1953, former movie producer Joseph P. Kennedy wanted, and got, a wedding—and a marriage— that would promote his own ambitions for his son. As Jack Kennedy kneels, he is in agony. Getting to his feet after praying was like torture.

Kennedy visited Vietnam long before it entered the awareness of most Americans. He arrived at Tan Son Nhut airbase in 1954 at the same time as the new French commander in Vietnam, General Jean de Lattre de Tassigny, shown talking to him here. It was a critical moment: the Viet Minh were besieging the French bastion of Dien Bien Phu. Its surrender brought the withdrawal of French forces and a growing American involvement.

Had he not gone into politics, Kennedy would probably have been a career writer. But like his hero Winston Churchill, he wrote books when he could, and he won a Pulitzer Prize in 1956 for *Profiles in Courage*. He claimed he would rather have the Pulitzer than the presidency, but in truth he intended to have both.

As part of his attempt to establish himself as an expert on national security, the senator visited Camp Dix in 1959, and although he refused to wear silly hats, he donned a helmet liner to be photographed with a machine gunner suitably festooned with .50-caliber ammo.

Jack and Bobby confer while interrogating a hostile witness before the Senate Rackets Committee in 1959. This is a rare photograph—it shows JFK wearing his glasses.

March 1960, and the senator hits the primary trail in Nashua, New Hampshire. History was against him. No senator had been elected to the presidency for nearly one hundred years. After Kennedy's election, many a senator suddenly saw himself as a potential president.

On the campaign trail in Wisconsin, and this, too, is an unusual picture. Farmers distrusted Kennedy as a rich, pampered urbanite. He considered them hicks—"square faces, square bodies, square feet and standing in square fields." It was almost like campaigning in a foreign country, but if a Kennedy campaign was nothing else, it was thorough.

Jackie loathed campaigning, but she was a frustrated actress. If she chose to, she could pretend she was enjoying herself, as she did here, in 1960.

His father was afraid that anti-Catholic bigotry would ruin Jack's efforts to become President. Cartoons like this circulated widely during the 1960 campaign; had it not been for his religion, Kennedy would probably have won by a convincing margin.

Kennedy's choice of Lyndon B. Johnson as his running mate stunned the Democratic party. In this picture, taken at Hyannis Port days after the convention ended, Johnson's unhappiness at having accepted second spot is writ large all over his rubbery, expressive features.

The fulfillment of two ambitions, his own and his father's, achieved by two wills, the newly inaugurated President chats with his Vice President. And although Kennedy had decreed silk top hats, neither he nor Johnson actually wanted to be seen wearing them.

A lover of convertibles throughout his life—sunshine, speed, style, sexy—JFK rides down Pennsylvania Avenue to the White House from his inauguration in an eight-year-old Lincoln. One of his first actions as President was to order an enlarged version of the new Lincoln Continental, a lineal descendant of the first car he ever owned.

April 22, 1961: three days after the Bay of Pigs operation ended in humiliation, Kennedy and Eisenhower met at Camp David (named for Ike's grandson). Eisenhower uttered no criticism of Kennedy's leadership in public, but in this picture, the body language of the two men speaks volumes.

Jack and Jackie almost instantly became the smiling embodiment of stylishness, enthralling millions not only at home but around the world. Here, in September 1962, they leave a performance of the Irving Berlin musical *Mr. President* at the National Theatre in Washington, the biggest acting couple ever.

October 23, 1962: Kennedy faces the press the day after the Cuban missile crisis ends. "We have won a great victory," he says in private, but orders his staff, "Don't gloat."

A proud father—and powerful swimmer—JFK teaches his two-year-old son, John-John, to swim in the pool at Joe's mansion in Palm Beach. The children's nanny, Maud Shaw, sits with Caroline on her lap.

He loved military music, military displays, military uniforms and military bands. On November 13, 1963, Jack and Jackie looked on from the White House porch as the pipe band of the Argyle and Sutherland Highlanders paraded and played on the South Lawn at his request.

The President and his wife arrive at Love Field, Dallas, on *Air Force One,* **shortly before noon on November 22, 1963.**

the research and enlisted the research assistance of a former history professor of hers at Georgetown University, Professor Jules Davids. Joe Kennedy got his old friend the former dean of Harvard Law School James Landis to lend a hand. But the principal researcher would be Ted Sorensen, who drafted a piece on political courage and submitted it, in Jack's name, to *The New York Times Magazine*.[16]

Like Kennedy, Ted Sorensen saw the magazine article as the foundation of a book and informed the senator he was more than willing to do most of the work, sending him a long list of potential Senate heroes. Like his boss, Sorensen was plainly a frustrated writer.[17]

As research materials piled up, Jack began working on his own rough draft, flat on the bed, writing almost upside down on a board over his head. His back was still so bad he could not sit up, even with firm support.

In early December the Flanders resolution came to a vote on the Senate floor. It passed, 76–22. Every Democratic senator but one voted for it. The sole exception was John F. Kennedy, still in the hospital. Had he wanted to vote, there was a way to do it. He could have been brought to the Capitol in an ambulance and carried into the Senate to cast his vote from a stretcher. Other sick senators had done that. Jack was metaphorically disappearing under a bedsheet and screaming, "Ow!"

He took his notes with him to Florida on December 21, when he at last left the hospital, two months after his operation. He was going to recuperate in the warmth of Palm Beach, where the family had already gathered for Christmas.[18]

Jack arrived weighing 115 pounds. There was an eight-inch suppurating wound in his back. From time to time, it opened up, revealing to horrified friends and family the dull gray glinting of a sinister-looking steel plate, inserted to brace his damaged spine.

The drugs he needed for his Addison's disease impeded healing. His wound also required a fresh dressing every few hours. Jackie sometimes cleaned it out and applied the new dressing.

Dressed only in shorts and boat shoes, Jack and his friend Chuck Spalding took a brief stroll along the beachfront property each day. Low in spirits and proceeding haltingly, Jack often asked Spalding to take a look at his back. "How is it now? Is stuff running out of it?"

"Still oozing, Jack."[19]

Stretched out by the pool in Palm Beach, Jack also continued trying to turn Sorensen's draft for an article, plus the research notes that kept flowing in from Washington and elsewhere, into a book about courageous senators. Besides writing on a board tilted over his head, he also dictated long passages based on his reading.[20]

Jack wrote two chapters and combined these with another draft that Sorensen worked up. He decided to call his book *These Great Men,* then submitted the chapters, the outline and the proposed title to Cass Canfield at Harper & Row. While Canfield was pondering the manuscript, Jack returned to New York and the Hospital for Special Surgery.

On February 15 he underwent his third back operation. The plate was removed, and this time the surgeons tried a bone graft. The technique worked. But almost the first thing Jack read when he came around after the operation was a rejection letter from Cass Canfield, who informed the senator that he and three other editors had found the material confusing and trite.[21]

It was hardly the kind of letter to be read in a hospital bed. Within twenty-four hours, however, Evan Thomas, the senior editor, talked Canfield around. Jack Kennedy was famous, glamorous and the author of a bestseller. Given the right kind of help, a competent and potentially profitable book could almost certainly be produced. Jack hardly had enough time to digest Canfield's rejection before he received a letter from Thomas that was nothing but enthusiasm and encouragement.[22]

When Jack left the hospital a few weeks later, he and Jackie returned to their narrow but charming Georgetown house, and he tried to make progress with his book. He had Jackie shuttling between the house and his Senate office, carrying documents, memos, correspondence.

One day in May he felt strong enough to drop by the office and say hello to the staff. Word that he was on his way went around the building, and the occupant of the office facing his own sent over a gift. When Jack went into his office, there on his desk was a basket of fruit. There was a card, too. It read, "Welcome Home! Dick Nixon."[23]

Although his back was finally healing, Jack still had trouble walking. There was characteristic pain radiating down the left leg from his spinal injury, and his right knee, which had been problematic for years, was becoming increasingly stiff and painful. He was referred to a female physician in New York, Dr. Janet Travell. When he reached her office at 9 West Sixteenth Street, he could not even manage to climb the two steps to her front door without help.[24]

She applied a vapocoolant spray to his knee, and within minutes, as he swung the leg up and down in a sitting position, it became more flexible and less painful. Travell then gave him a shot of Novocain in the lower left quadrant of his back. The muscle spasms that caused much of the pain down his left leg quickly ceased. Here was Jack's kind of doctor—an attentive, attractive female, handy with his idea of good medical treatment: the quick fix, applied without fuss. After a few days back in a New York hospital for tests on his back and knee, he returned to Washington ready to pursue *These Great Men* again.

As he and Sorensen worked on the manuscript, the title changed every few weeks. Eventually, Evan Thomas informed him, "I have changed the title to *Profiles in Courage.*" Jack was lukewarm but could live with it. Thomas also told him firmly that some of his courageous senators had to be Republicans: they couldn't all be heroic Democrats.[25]

Much of the manuscript was undoubtedly the work of Ted Sorensen, and Jack Kennedy did very little of the research. Who, then, really wrote *Profiles in Courage*? Sorensen himself referred to the book as "our monumental work," and Jack acknowledged Sorensen's contribution by paying him a bonus of $6,000, the equivalent of four months' salary. There's also no doubt that much of what originated with Jack Kennedy was heavily rewritten.[26]

Yet he was seen writing parts of the book, and there are recordings of him dictating portions. In the end, the fairest judgment seems to be that it was really a work of joint authorship—Kennedy and Sorensen—even though only one author's name appears on the spine.

The spirit that infuses *Profiles,* however, is Jack Kennedy's. It represents a stirring of idealism generated after his having thought long and hard about the way Joe McCarthy had degraded American politics and driven good people out of political life.

Jack wrote an extended prologue for the book in which he debates his case with a character called "Senator J. P. Oldtimer." The prologue took the form of eleven letters supposedly exchanged between Jack Kennedy and Oldtimer. The young senator argues that there are times when a politician has to put the nation's interests above his own political career. At first Oldtimer scoffs at anything that resembles idealism. This correspondence ends with Kennedy finally winning Oldtimer to his point of view, that a senator has a duty both to represent his constituents and to lead them . . . regardless.

Thomas made him remove the prologue. The book opened instead with a reference to Ernest Hemingway, a man much like Jack wanted to be—a literary figure of enormous talent noted for his physical courage. The theme of his book, Jack said, followed Hemingway's definition of courage— "grace under pressure."

Why this banal phrase struck such a chord with him is a mystery. First, it was little more than the civilian's version of the soldier's "courage under fire." Second, there is no evidence that Hemingway coined "grace under pressure." It appears in none of his writings.[27]

Profiles can be read, too, as a mea culpa. Jack Kennedy had failed to show courage over Joe McCarthy, and he knew it. But since he was unable to express directly what he truly thought and deeply felt, those thoughts and feelings came out—in typical fashion—indirectly and by implication.

That is the force that brings his book alive. It is no masterpiece of historical scholarship. Intellectual insights are thin on the ground. Nevertheless, a spirit that confesses past failure while seeking to aim higher animates it. What most people—the young, especially—get from *Profiles* is less information than inspiration.

Still, irony is sometimes just another way of spelling "history," and there is no gainsaying the slightly sordid way the book was promoted. The book became a bestseller, in part because Joe Kennedy had his cousin Joe Kane buy enough copies from the right bookstores to get it onto the *New York Times* bestseller list. Meanwhile, Harper & Row submitted the book for the Pulitzer Prize in two categories—history and biography. Joe Kennedy urged Arthur Krock to use his influence with the members of the Pulitzer board.[28]

It was not chosen as a history finalist, and although it became a finalist in biography, the selection committee picked a different book to receive the prize. Not for the first time, or the last, the Pulitzer board exercised its right to overrule the committee and substitute its own choice. *Profiles in Courage* won the 1957 Pulitzer Prize for biography.[29]

Three years earlier Jack had told Margaret Coit he would rather have the Pulitzer than be President. That was then and this was now. He still intended to be President.

CHAPTER 20

Losing

W hen Jack Kennedy returned to the Senate in May 1955, his hair was starting to turn gray. Unthinkable. He began dyeing it brown, but hair coloring wasn't an exact science and he, like many others, had to live with variable results. As he stood outside the Capitol that day in bright sunlight, his hair seemed almost blond. At other times, in a different light, it looked almost red.[1]

His Senate colleagues applauded warmly as, on crutches, he made his way onto the Senate floor to resume his accustomed place at a desk in the back row. Yet now as much as ever Jack seemed more a visitor to these halls than a part of them. He was present only in body much of the time; his mind was elsewhere.[2]

One of the first things Jack Kennedy had done following his election to the Senate was apply for assignment to the Senate Foreign Relations Committee. He got Labor instead, while the place he coveted on Foreign Relations went to another freshman senator, Mike Mansfield of Montana. The Senate Majority Leader, Lyndon B. Johnson, knew that Mansfield was both conscientious and a party loyalist.[3]

Jack was never going to become a member of the Senate club, the informal group of eight or nine senators who ran things. He regarded it with a wry detachment that barely disguised an underlying contempt. When his gossipy, gay journalist friend Joe Alsop asked what it took to be accepted into the Senate club, that sardonic grin bloomed slowly as Jack explained, "The ticket of admission is being willing to make deals that you ought to be ashamed of without the smallest sign of shame."[4]

But when the Eighty-fourth Congress convened in January 1956, he tried once again for a seat on the Foreign Relations Committee, bombarding Johnson with analyses produced by Ted Sorensen showing Jack Kennedy being treated less generously than senators junior to him. Johnson shrugged them off, and Kennedy staff members remarked bitingly that "LBJ" stood for "Let's Block Jack."[5]

By this time, though, his thoughts were turning an exciting new possibility. In September 1955 Eisenhower had been felled by a nearly fatal heart attack. At first, most people assumed he would not run for reelection. During that winter, Democratic hopes for the 1956 election rose like a rocket, Jack's among them. Adlai Stevenson seemed almost sure to be the Democratic presidential candidate again. Jack wondered what chance he would have of becoming Stevenson's running mate.

He had a poll taken of Democratic party activists on their preferred choice for VP. The poll was conducted so it couldn't be traced back to him, and the results weren't particularly encouraging. He was well down the list, mainly because those polled thought his religion would be a handicap.[6]

At about the same time that Jack was pondering the results of the poll, a journalist named Fletcher Knebel came around to talk about stories *Look* magazine might be running on the young senator. As they chatted, Jack couldn't help revealing what was on his mind.

"You know, you guys have got this Catholic thing all wrong. I think a Catholic would run better for Vice President. Maybe not President, but he'd run better for President than a Protestant would on the Democratic ticket."

"Oh. Do you have any figures?"

"No," Jack admitted, "but let's get some. Let's research it."

Ted Sorensen put together a report that supported Jack's hunch. He titled it "The Catholic Vote in 1952 and 1956." Its thrust was that in every national election since 1928, the Catholic vote had nearly always gone to the Democrats, and in the one year it didn't, 1952, a Republican became President. In effect, as the Catholic vote went, so went the nation.[7]

In a none too convincing attempt to disguise its origins, Kennedy persuaded John Bailey, the Roman Catholic chairman of the Democratic party organization in Connecticut, to circulate the report as the "Bailey Memorandum." Copies were sent to all two thousand delegates and alternates to the forthcoming Democratic convention. The ever-helpful Arthur Krock devoted an entire column to the so-called Bailey Memorandum in *The New York Times.*[8]

All this effort might be in vain, Jack mused aloud one day. "Unfortunately the presidential nominee decides who his Vice President is going to be. And there's nothing you can do."[9]

On February 29 Eisenhower announced that he would run again. At this point, Jack discovered he had gone too far to turn back. Politics at this level provided more excitement than anything he was going to find in the Senate. Hooked and looking for some cards to play, he set out to gain control of at least half of the Massachusetts delegation and improve his credibility with Stevenson.

A week after Eisenhower's announcement, Jack met with the eighty members of the Massachusetts Democratic Committee to seek their support. The committee was largely under the control of an onion farmer, William "Onions" Burke, a protégé of James Michael Curley, an admirer of Joe McCarthy, a good friend of John McCormack and a man who hated Joe Kennedy.

Many of the Massachusetts party regulars shared the Burke-Curley-McCormack resentment towards the way the Kennedys had elbowed the organization aside to win the support of Democratic voters. During the overwrought meeting in March 1956, one member of the committee called Jack "a fool" and another, a woman, spat on him.

Seething but outwardly calm, Jack Kennedy tried to cut a deal in which half the delegates to the convention in Chicago would support Stevenson and the other half would support McCormack as a favorite-son candidate. Burke sabotaged the proposal.

Jack had only one card left: take control of the state committee. Burke was up for reelection in May, and for two months Kennedy money, Kennedy organizational skill and Kennedy anger were directed at getting him out. A former mayor of Somerville, Massachusetts, John M. "Pat" Lynch, agreed to run against Burke. Former governor Paul Dever also came on board. When the vote was held, it wasn't even close. Lynch beat Burke by forty-seven votes to thirty-one. The upshot was that John Kennedy would control the entire Massachusetts delegation at the convention. Maybe Stevenson would take him seriously now.[10]

=

In April 1954 Patricia Kennedy married an English actor, Peter Lawford, and they set up home in a large house on the beach at Malibu. The marriage came at almost the moment Lawford's career as a screen idol fell apart. Although he was exceptionally handsome, Lawford had nothing but journeyman talents: he wasn't big enough or deep enough to carry a film on his own. The studios stopped sending him scripts. Joe Kennedy bankrolled various television series, such as *The Thin Man* and *Dear Phoebe,* to keep his son-in-law employed and Patricia happy.[11]

Lawford became Jack Kennedy's new link to Hollywood. Joe's connections were with an older generation of directors, producers and actors. It was Lawford who knew the exciting new stars and introduced Jack to Marilyn Monroe. Through Lawford, too, he was asked to narrate a thirty-minute documentary on the history of the Democratic party that was being made for the 1956 convention by Oscar-winning writer and producer Dore Schary. Jack spent a pleasant week in July at the Lawford beach house, working on the film by day, coupling by night.

Called *The Pursuit of Happiness,* Schary's film was largely a hymn to the New Deal. Rumors were rife that Joe Kennedy had put up $500,000 for the film on the condition that Jack did the narration. Dore Schary insisted that wasn't so, but Joe Kennedy knew how to hide his hand. The selection of Jack instead of someone venerated across the party, such as Eleanor Roosevelt, seems too fortuitous to take at face value.[12]

On August 11 Jack arrived in Chicago for the convention at the head of the Massachusetts delegation. Tip O'Neill, Jack's successor as congressman from the Eleventh District, had been planning to go to Chicago as a member of the state delegation, but Jack had pressured him to get Bobby named as a delegate. "You know, lightning may strike at that convention, and I could end up on the ticket with Stevenson. I'd really like to have my brother on the floor as a delegate so he could work for me." O'Neill surrendered his own place on the state delegation to Bobby.[13]

Jack was also accompanied by Jackie. Nearly eight months pregnant, she would stay with Sargent Shriver and his wife, Eunice, well away from the frenzied atmosphere of Jack's suite at the Stockyards Inn, two blocks from the Chicago Amphitheatre.

Passing through Boston shortly before the convention, Stevenson had praised Jack's record in the Senate and said he'd make "an excellent choice" for VP. Jack had responded by getting Sorensen to send a four-page letter to one of Stevenson's advisers, Ken Hechler, that stressed the advantages to Stevenson of having Jack Kennedy as his running mate.[14]

Even so, Jack continued to tell journalists, "I am not a candidate. I am not campaigning for office." Who then *did* he think would be Stevenson's running mate? "I think it will be a Southerner." Whatever he said to the press, Stevenson's comments nonetheless could only lift his hopes higher.[15]

The Democratic party nominating convention of 1956 was typical of all conventions from the pre-Kennedy era: virtually every delegate was a professional politician or had been handpicked by professional politicians to do the party's bidding. But the star that first day was Jack Kennedy.

At a reception for Eleanor Roosevelt the afternoon before the convention opened, Jack had stood almost unrecognized at the end of a long line of party dignitaries waiting to shake her hand. The next few days changed all that.[16]

His narration of *The Pursuit of Happiness* was the first time most Democratic party activists had heard that distinctive accent, easy to mock, impossible to forget. There were also the tens of millions who encountered it for the first time. The conventions of 1952 had reached about eight million homes, thanks to TV. In 1956 that figure rose to forty million.

Here, then, in grainy black and white from Chicago, Jack Kennedy was revealed to his countrymen in his immortal incarnation, the ideal politician for the celebrity age; at ease with himself, as relaxed in the spotlight as others are in candlelight, confidently careless as to what the camera might catch, reveal, betray.

Cameras of all kinds invariably add something that isn't there, or take away something that is. For him they did both, making him look much younger than he did in the flesh, and healthier than he had ever been or might hope to be.

Some months earlier, Joe Kennedy had wanted to see Jack secure the vice presidential nomination, provided the presidential nominee was Lyndon Johnson. He calculated that LBJ would run and lose narrowly. That wouldn't do Jack any harm. On the contrary, it would make him the almost certain presidential nominee in 1960.[17]

Stevenson, however, would not simply lose—he would be buried. And in that case, Jack and his Catholicism would be blamed for the drubbing. With Johnson out of the frame, all that Joe Kennedy wanted from the 1956 convention was a blaze of publicity that would kick-start Jack's drive towards the presidency in 1960.[18]

Once he began running for something, though, Jack Kennedy didn't know how to stop. Almost from the moment he arrived, he circulated freely with delegates from other states, shaking hands, looking them in the eye, trying to connect—"Hi, I'm Jack Kennedy." Bobby prepared for an open bid by getting hundreds of KENNEDY FOR VP badges made.[19]

The public reaction to Kennedy's narration of *The Pursuit of Happiness* and his overwhelming telegenic appeal had an impact on Stevenson. After breakfast on Wednesday, Stevenson sent word that he'd like to talk to Jack. They met in Stevenson's suite at noon. Whom did Kennedy favor for Vice President? asked the governor. "Humphrey."

Would he be willing to nominate Stevenson for the presidency?

Gladly, Jack replied. "But does that mean I will thereby be disqualified for being nominated for the vice presidency?"

"Not necessarily," Stevenson replied.[20]

That afternoon Jack had a short meeting with Eleanor Roosevelt, hoping she might support him as a potential running mate for Stevenson. But when she asked him why he hadn't taken a firm stand against McCarthy, he equivocated. Despondently, Jack returned to his hotel, convinced he stood no chance of being on the ticket.[21]

Stevenson's speechwriters had already written the nominating speech, but Jack and Ted Sorensen wrote a different speech, one that sounded a lot more like Jack. He was still writing it in the car that took him to the Chicago Amphitheatre on Thursday afternoon. When he intoned, "Our candidates will be up against two of the most skilled campaigners in history—one who takes the high road and one who takes the low road," convention delegates whooped, clapped and cheered for nearly a minute.[22]

Having secured the presidential nomination, Stevenson agonized over a running mate. He didn't want to take Estes Kefauver, the junior senator from Tennessee, who was favored by his advisers. That would only alienate Kennedy, whose star was rising fast. Yet he couldn't bring himself to accept Jack as his running mate for three reasons: youth, religion and Dad.

The way out of this dilemma, Stevenson decided, was to have the convention make the choice. Besides, the Republican convention—held in San Francisco several weeks earlier—had seen Nixon forced on a reluctant party. The Democrats could show they did things differently and better. A little before midnight Stevenson returned to the amphitheatre to announce he wanted the convention to choose his running mate.[23]

Jack told Bobby to get hold of Dad, who was vacationing on the Riviera, and tell him what was happening in Chicago. Bobby made the call, informed his father that Jack was going to try to win the vice presidential nomination, flushed red and hurriedly replaced the telephone on its cradle. "Whew, is he mad!"[24]

By dawn a Kennedy organization directed by Bobby and Jack's brother-in-law Sargent Shriver was tracking down delegates and making the pitch. The badges whose need Bobby had presciently foreseen were widely distributed. KENNEDY FOR VP blossomed on hundreds of suit lapels and dress fronts.

Jack was too exhausted after four days with only a few hours of sleep each night to plunge into the fray. Throughout the balloting on Thursday, he looked gray and drawn and spent much of the time sprawled on his bed in nothing but his underpants or easing his back in a hot bath. At one point, Sorensen rushed into the bathroom: "You've got it!"

He glanced up. "Not yet."[25]

On the first ballot, Kefauver had 483½ votes, Kennedy had 304 and Albert Gore—the senior senator from Tennessee—had 178. The remaining 13½ went to Hubert Humphrey.

When voting on the second ballot reached Texas, Lyndon Johnson grandiloquently declared, "Texas proudly casts its fifty-six votes for the fighting sailor who wears the scars of battle—Senator John F. Kennedy!" That put Jack well in front. But a string of border states voted next, and all went heavily for Kefauver. So did much of the West. Kennedy got most of the votes from the South and the Northeast, but that wasn't enough.

He stepped out of the tub, dressed and went down to the convention floor to make his concession speech. It was charming, gracious and utterly spontaneous. No one watching him in the amphitheatre or on television would have imagined they were looking at an exhausted figure living on his nerves.

Returning to his suite, Jack called his father. "We did our best. I've had some fun and I didn't make a fool of myself." Then he sat down and began picking at a sandwich. Weariness and the disappointment of defeat seemed to weigh on him. He had never wanted the second spot on the ticket as much as he wanted it now.[26]

≡

When Gore Vidal was growing up, his mother was married to Hugh D. ("Hughdie") Auchincloss. As a child, Jackie had slept in the same small room over the front door, even slept in the same narrow bed, where a few years earlier Vidal had dreamed of sex with lithe, golden young men.

In effect, Vidal became the brother Jackie never had. When he learned of her engagement to Jack Kennedy, he told her it didn't make any sense. "Of course I don't like politics and he's a lot older than I am," she admitted. "But life will always be more interesting with him. And there's the money."

"But what on earth is going to become of you in that awful world?" Vidal protested.

"Read the newspapers."[27]

As she soon discovered, an interesting life did not include a close relationship with Jack. He was always in a hurry, always impatient; there wasn't a moment to waste, an hour to lose. The space and time needed for an ever-deepening, steadily maturing relationship didn't exist.

That quick, humorous smile made him look like the man who always got the joke first, and it disguised a latent irritability. That volatility flared often enough with men—including his friends—but the usual targets were women. Tempest Storm, a long-legged, busty stripper who fueled countless masturbatory fantasies in the 1950s, was one of Jack's conquests. She was astounded by his reaction one night when she chatted with a club manager for a few minutes before getting into Jack's car. "Goddamn it," he screamed, "you kept me waiting!"[28]

Not even Jackie was spared such eruptions of anger. One day Jack was stretched out in the bathtub of his Georgetown town house, gossiping with his friend Chuck Spalding about people they knew in New York. Suddenly, Jack raised a finger to his lips, carefully stood up, stepped out of the bathtub and in a single swift movement yanked open the bathroom door. There stood Jackie, framed in the doorway, startled in the middle of eavesdropping. Jack reached out and pulled her hair. "You fucking bitch!"[29]

There was also the burden of his infidelities. They surpassed anything Jackie had ever known or expected. Jack was a practitioner of hedonic psychology *avant la lettre*—will this be a fun thing to do? Will it be interesting? Will it make me laugh?

In hasty, affectless sex with what were, for the most part, strangers, the inward eye was distracted by glimpses of ecstasy away from the near and certain embrace of premature oblivion. Another man might have sought much the same escape in alcohol as Jack pursued in sex.

Jack Kennedy was nonetheless striving for something besides pleasures sharp enough to balance his emotional wounds, the pain in his back and the psychological burden of looming death. What he sought was what we all need—connection. But his ambition directed those inchoate powers at millions rather than one.

While Jackie loathed Rose, and Rose loathed her right back, Jack tried to win over Janet. He spent a week or so at Hammersmith Farm in Newport each summer, playing at being the dutiful son-in-law. Yet every minute he was there, he had to beat down an intense yearning to get away. The Auchinclosses' milieu was WASPish Newport society, all navel gazing and gossip about people too dull to be worth gossiping about.

The Kennedy with whom Jackie got on best was Joe, yet he had no real interest in her. What mattered to Joe Kennedy was what he wanted—grandchildren. It was dynastic ambitions that counted, not Jackie's emotional needs. And Joe knew how important money was to her. He would set up a million-dollar trust fund, he told her, for her first child. But if she couldn't have children, she would get the million dollars for herself.

Jackie accepted his terms, but with a stipulation. "The price goes up to twenty million if Jack brings home any venereal diseases from any of his sluts."

"If that happens, Jackie, name your own price."[30]

Far advanced in her pregnancy during the 1956 Democratic party convention, Jackie expected Jack to remain at home once the convention ended. Instead, he chose to go to the south of France, ostensibly to bring his father up to date on events. In truth, he intended to spend a month or so as he had spent other Riviera vacations, girling. He, Teddy, Torby Macdonald and a railroad lobbyist who shared his taste for orgies, Bill Thompson, rented a yacht, which they filled with pulchritudinous examples of the European demimonde. Jackie was distraught.

She returned to Hammersmith Farm, seeking the solace of her mother. On August 23, however, she began hemorrhaging and was rushed to the hospital in Newport for an emergency cesarean. She had been hoping for a girl and intended to name her Arabella, but the baby was stillborn. When Jackie awoke from the anesthetic in the early hours, it was Bobby who sat at her bedside, not Jack. Bobby also arranged for the funeral of baby Arabella.[31]

Bobby advised his father not to tell Jack about the loss of the baby. Jack would rush home, Bobby told Joe, and find Jackie so depressed and angry at his absence that relations between them would become worse, not better. So Jack was sent a message that said Jackie was not well, without any hint that the baby was about to be buried.[32]

Jack did not make any immediate plans to return home until his friend and Senate colleague George Smathers called him and told him how serious the situation was. If he remained on vacation, Smathers said, he'd be making a serious mistake. "If I go back there, what the hell am I going to do?" Jack protested. "I'm just going to sit there and wring my hands."

"If you want to run for President," said Smathers, "you'd better get your ass back to your wife's bedside or every wife in the country will be against you." Jack flew home.[33]

He told reporters he had not rushed back sooner because he was at sea aboard a yacht that lacked ship-to-shore radio. The fact, though, was that his Washington office was able to get hold of him at any time.

Jackie, grieving and incensed, wanted to end the marriage right there. He had wounded her beyond any excuse or reason when she was at her most vulnerable. All she wanted now, she told Jack, was a divorce. But then she made a discovery—she wasn't tough enough to go through with it.[34]

"You can't beat them," she told Chuck Spalding, close to tears and clutching her head in her hands. "They're just too strong."[35]

CHAPTER 21

Running, Always Running

Following his tardy return from France that summer, Jack was in low spirits for weeks. After leaving the hospital, Jackie took refuge with her mother, while Jack returned to their Washington home. Although the death of what would have been their first child hurt both of them deeply, he and Jackie were unable to comfort each other in their grief. Such was the price of separate lives.[1]

Jack worked his way out of despondency by campaigning for Adlai Stevenson, traveling widely, speaking often (if briefly) and shaking many of the party activists' hands he would need to shake all over again when he made his own bid to win the nomination in 1960. And when Stevenson lost to Eisenhower by an even bigger margin the second time around, no one was surprised, least of all Jack Kennedy.

From time to time that fall, he received letters and telegrams from his editor, Evan Thomas, charting the soaring sales of *Profiles in Courage*. Following the Democratic convention, Jack's book had become a bestseller all over again, getting back onto the *New York Times* bestseller list and reclaiming the number-one spot.[2]

A year later, as its sales faded to almost nothing, it was revived again, this time by controversy. Columnist Drew Pearson was the guest Saturday, December 7, 1957, on ABC's *The Mike Wallace Interview*. Pearson, the most feared journalistic gadfly of his generation, eagerly tore into Jack Kennedy—"The only man in history that I know who won the Pulitzer Prize on a book which was ghostwritten for him, which indicates the kind of public relations buildup he's had."

Pearson also remarked that Jack's fellow senators mocked the high-minded pretensions of *Profiles in Courage*, supposedly telling him to his face, "Jack, we wish you had a little less profile and more courage."

On Monday, December 9, 1957, Jack asked Clark Clifford to come and see him at his Senate office immediately. Clifford had been one of Truman's closest assistants and was now a Democratic party statesman and a $1-million-a-year Washington lawyer.

When Clifford arrived an hour or so later, an agitated Jack Kennedy angrily denounced Pearson's claims on Saturday night—"I can't let this stand. It is a direct attack on my honesty and integrity." He wanted Clifford to file suit against ABC, Drew Pearson and Mike Wallace.

The phone rang. It was Joe Kennedy. Jack handed the telephone to Clifford, and from Palm Beach, Joe Kennedy bellowed, "I want you to sue the bastards for fifty million dollars. Get it started right away. It's dishonest and they know it. My boy wrote that book. This is a plot against us."

Clifford studied Jack's notes, manuscript drafts and correspondence with Evan Thomas. By the time he had finished, he was convinced that Jack Kennedy was indeed the author of *Profiles in Courage*. He had little trouble persuading the chairman of ABC, which ran a retraction and an apology a week following the original broadcast. In time, Drew Pearson, too, concluded that Jack had written *Profiles*. This controversy kept interest in the book alive and put Jack Kennedy in the unusual position of appearing to be a victim of modern journalism.[3]

===

After years of protesting that he wasn't a liberal, the young senator finally joined the Americans for Democratic Action, or ADA. He could now be counted on to vote with other liberal Democrats on legislation they favored, but he still would not give speeches on the Senate floor for anything but his own pet projects.

There were other limits, too. Jack Kennedy did not eat in the Senate Dining Room or socialize with other senators; nor did he lobby them in favor of this bill or that. He rarely took an interest in the detailed work of drafting legislation or getting it passed.[4]

Yet there were some domestic issues he cared deeply about. One of the first measures he pushed after being elected to the Senate was an increase in the minimum wage from 75 cents to $1 an hour, but the AFL-CIO was pressing for $1.25, and he wouldn't go along with that. It seemed inflationary. It took two years of patiently promoting the issue, but the minimum wage was eventually raised to a dollar. What the AFL-CIO had been demanding was unrealistic and he knew it.[5]

He was one of the principal advocates of federal aid for medical research, and legislation that he proposed in 1956 led eventually to the creation of the U.S. National Library of Medicine. That same year Jack Kennedy introduced legislation to amend the Social Security Act and abolish mandatory retirement at sixty-five. It got nowhere. This initiative was a generation ahead of its time.

The great burgeoning domestic issue of the late 1950s was civil rights. The first *Brown* v. *Board of Education* decision, in 1954, had struck down the doctrine of "separate but equal" education. The second decision came a year later and called for school integration "with all deliberate speed."

Jack Kennedy limited himself to saying what he truly felt and believed: bigotry was not just wrong but wicked. He denounced racial prejudice in general terms and played a prominent part in raising money to rebuild a black school that had been destroyed by racist vandals. Beyond that, he was careful not to do or say anything that would alienate the South.

He was hoping that the strong support he had received from southern delegates in 1956 could be carried over to the 1960 convention. There was no willingness to acknowledge just how little that support owed to his own appeal and how much to southern contempt for Estes Kefauver.[6]

Kennedy did not expect civil rights to become a national issue before the 1960 election. He suddenly had to recalculate when, following his second inauguration, Eisenhower submitted a comprehensive civil rights bill to Congress. No civil rights bill had been passed since 1865. Southerners, who dominated the relevant Senate committees, made sure the bills never came to a vote.

Yet Eisenhower's prestige was so high and Lyndon Johnson's presidential ambitions for 1960 so urgent that there was a unique opportunity to get a bill passed. Johnson, the Senate Majority Leader, needed to recast himself as a national, rather than a regional, figure. He would get a civil rights bill onto the Senate floor.

Ike's bill would create a nonpartisan commission on civil rights to recommend future legislation and oversee implementation; establish a civil rights division in the Department of Justice; give authority to Justice to intervene whenever it deemed someone's civil rights were likely to be violated; and provide federally enforced guarantees of voting rights.

Numerous amendments to the administration's bill were advanced in Congress. Most got nowhere, but Jack voted in favor of the most contentious of all, the jury trial amendment.

The new Civil Rights Act was designed to stamp out the kind of civil rights abuses that were common across much of the South, such as preventing black people from registering to vote or engaging in lawful protests. Those who ignored the new law could be enjoined by the courts to cease violating other people's rights. If they persisted, they would be prosecuted for contempt of court. The jury trial amendment required jury trials for people cited for contempt in civil rights cases.[7]

Civil rights organizations vehemently opposed this part of the law. Black people generally did not believe that southern juries would convict white defendants in civil rights cases.

To Jack Kennedy, and others, accepting the jury trial amendment was essential to getting the bill passed. Besides, the amendment contained provisions that made it possible for black people to get onto southern juries. That in itself would be a breakthrough. Such half-a-loaf gradualism was characteristic of JFK, even though in this instance it alienated the leadership of the National Association for the Advancement of Colored People.[8]

Eisenhower himself was not happy about the bill and was tempted to veto it, even though it was his own legislation. The most important provision of all—giving the Justice Department power to intervene and secure people's civil rights—was struck down. That, too, was essential to getting the bill passed.

Meanwhile, Jack had become a member of a new Senate body, the Select Committee to Investigate Improper Activities in the Labor Management Field, better known as the Senate Rackets Committee. The new committee was nonpartisan, with four Republicans and four Democrats, and its chief counsel was Bobby Kennedy, whose only previous relevant experience was working on Joe McCarthy's committee.

This Select Committee had been created mainly to bring down Dave Beck, the president of the International Brotherhood of Teamsters, the epitome of union corruption. Beck and his union had close ties with organized crime. Yet the FBI under J. Edgar Hoover maintained there was no such thing as organized crime—which flourished in most big cities—

and devoted its energies to rooting out the greatly exaggerated menace of Communist subversion.

Senate Rackets Committee hearings were televised nationally and provided some of the most gripping broadcasts of the late 1950s, despite the fact that many witnesses wrapped themselves in the legal armor of the Fifth Amendment. "I decline to answer on the grounds," et cetera. Beck invoked it rather than admit to knowing one Dave Beck, Jr., his own son.

The Teamsters' vice president, Jimmy Hoffa, was even more brutal and corrupt than Beck, and he, too, invoked the Fifth repeatedly. At one point, Jack Kennedy remarked that innocent people rarely resorted to the protection against self-incrimination. Hoffa's lawyer protested; he was unaware, he said, that guilt could be inferred from invoking the Fifth Amendment. "Well," said Kennedy dryly, "I'm putting it forward as an original thesis." Jack and Bobby turned into television stars thanks to the Rackets Committee hearings.[9]

The revelations of criminality within organized labor called out for legislation. Jack Kennedy and another member of the Senate Labor Committee, Irving Ives of New York, drew up a bill that would tackle the most flagrant abuses. They wanted union decision-making and union accounts to become more or less transparent. George Meany, the president of the AFL-CIO, was calling for "a goldfish bowl," which was what the Kennedy-Ives Bill provided.[10]

However, two congressmen from Michigan were drawing up a bill in the House that responded to the National Association of Manufacturers' demands. This legislation, the Landrum-Griffin Act, sought to be more of a cage than a bowl, restricting labor unions in nearly every power they possessed. A conference committee was organized to stitch the two bills together. The result was a compromise between a bowl and a cage. Neither labor nor business was happy with it, and Kennedy and Ives refused to allow either of their names to be attached to this hodgepodge.[11]

As a fairly junior senator, and one who held himself aloof from the Senate club, there was not much chance for Jack Kennedy to make an impact on legislation, as this episode demonstrated. His involvement in the efforts to root out corruption in organized labor nevertheless identified Jack Kennedy more than ever with the liberal wing of his party. So, too, did his initiative on the National Defense Education Act of 1958.

Following the orbiting of Sputnik I in October 1957, there was alarm across much of the United States and strident calls for a large boost in military spending. Yet Eisenhower did not see Sputnik as a military challenge. His response was to funnel large amounts of federal money into colleges and graduate schools. He was certain the Cold War could be won only by brains, rather than with weaponry. This enlightened approach was threatened by Senator Lister Hill of Alabama, who introduced an amendment that would impose a loyalty oath on students who received NDEA money and on their professors.

This gave Jack Kennedy a wonderful opportunity to invite eminent liberal academics to Washington to testify against Hill's stupid amendment. His success in blocking it helped transform his image among professors who had believed until then that he was just a playboy whose odious plutocrat of a father had bought him a Senate seat.

His vote on the nomination of Lewis Strauss to become Secretary of Commerce had a similar effect. McGeorge Bundy, a young historian at Harvard, urged him to vote against Strauss's nomination. "It would require an extreme case to vote against the President," said Jack. After all, a President ought to be able to pick his own Cabinet. "Well, this is an extreme case," said Bundy.

He proceeded to educate the senator on Strauss's role as chairman of the Atomic Energy Commission in the inexcusable attack on the reputation of J. Robert Oppenheimer. The fact that Bundy was a Republican attested to his lack of party bias. He convinced Kennedy that Oppenheimer was indeed a martyr to Strauss's jealousy and pettiness. Strauss's nomination was rejected by forty-nine votes to forty-six, and Kennedy was among those who voted against confirmation.[12]

In 1958 he had to run for reelection, and he wanted to win big—by such a margin that the whole country would notice. When he learned that the Republicans were going to run an inexperienced and obscure candidate, Vincent Celeste, against him, Jack was dismayed. He pleaded with his friends in the Massachusetts Republican party, "Can't you get a stronger candidate against me?" Not only did he want to win big, but the victory had to be credible, not laughable.[13]

To help improve his vote, Jack got the Massachusetts legislature to redesign the ballot so that the names of the candidates for the U.S. Senate would appear at the top line of the left-hand corner, with the incumbent above the challenger. This was the most prominent spot on the ballot, the place where the eye—and the hand clutching the pencil or reaching for the lever—was naturally drawn.[14]

There was no doubt that one way or another he would secure reelection, and he did not intend to wear himself out chasing a certainty. He was going to spend that summer doing what he usually did—vacation on the Riviera.

Two of his campaign advisers, Larry O'Brien and Kenneth O'Donnell, protested. They told him he had to spend the summer campaigning if he was going to win by a huge, attention-grabbing margin. Joe Kennedy tried to contradict them—"You'll wind up with a dead candidate and you'll be responsible!" But Jack eventually did as they advised, and he survived the experience. That year he visited roughly half the cities and towns of Massachusetts.[15]

During his reelection campaign, his speeches were less about local issues than about national ones; less about domestic policy than about foreign policy; and throughout, he seemed compelled to speak up for politics as an honorable profession. He told numerous audiences that the original meaning, in Greek, of the word "idiot" was "a person who takes no part in the government of his country."

Jack Kennedy was hoping he might win by a million votes in 1958. He fell short of that, but his winning margin of 874,608 was the biggest win in the history of Massachusetts and by far the biggest victory in any Senate race that year.

=

In January 1957, after years of protesting and lobbying, he was finally given a place on the Senate Foreign Relations Committee. The almost certain Republican candidate for the White House in 1960 was Richard Nixon. The Vice President's strongest card, apart from Ike's endorsement, was his reputation as an expert on foreign policy. Nixon did not simply travel widely—he met the most important people in every country he visited. A place on the Foreign Relations Committee had never been so important to Jack.

His ideas, though, were still in flux. He seemed reluctant to put aside some of the pugnacious and immature judgments he had arrived at during his years in the House. In February 1957 polling expert Elmo Roper and Thomas Burke, the AFL-CIO's chief legislative expert, went to see JFK, asking him to support a strongly pro-NATO resolution at the forthcoming AFL-CIO convention. Kennedy's response was withering.

"I think you're barking up the wrong tree. For twenty-five years

Europe has been trying to flush itself down the drain." The Europeans weren't worth defending, anyway, because "Europe is no longer of any major importance in the world. We've got to recognize that fact and turn our eyes to our allies of the future—such as Indonesia."

Roper and Burke were astonished. Did his condemnation of Europe include countries such as England, with its long democratic tradition, and West Germany, with a booming economy? "You've picked two good examples of nations that are absolutely through—finished—washed up!" he snapped.[16]

He also remained convinced of the crucial importance of Vietnam. Eisenhower had resisted pressure from the Joint Chiefs and powerful figures in Congress for American intervention to save the French from defeat at Dien Bien Phu in 1954. After that, an international conference at Geneva provided a fig leaf for French withdrawal and called for elections in 1956, to be held in both the north and south on unification.

The United States refused to sign the Geneva Accords and encouraged the government of South Vietnam to block the projected elections. Kennedy's attitude was much the same as Eisenhower's. He argued that there should be no election on unification until the Communists allowed elections across East and West Germany and North and South Korea.[17]

Unlike the Eisenhower administration, he welcomed the burgeoning spirit of nationalism that was being ignited around the world with the decline of colonial rule. Jack Kennedy wanted the United States to identify itself with the new governments of new countries. The U.S. was, after all, not only a powerful and rich country, but a nation born of revolution. Within the ambiguous syntax of international politics, he read a text that was youthful and optimistic, idealistic and romantic, and yearned to translate it into policy.

On July 2, 1957, he returned to a theme that had concerned him deeply since his trip to Vietnam in 1951—French colonialism. This time he made an outspoken attack on French policy in Algeria, where France had unleashed what amounted to state terror against the terrorist tactics of Algerian guerrillas. "French insistence upon pacification of the area—in reality, reconquest—is a policy which only makes both settlement and cease-fire less likely." The only lasting solution, he went on, was for the United States to accept its responsibilities as a leader of the free world and a member of both the UN and NATO and push the French "toward political independence for Algeria."

This speech infuriated the White House, the State Department and the French government. Yet to most of those who heard it, this speech was one of the finest and most convincing delivered on Capitol Hill that year.[18]

A month after the Soviets orbited Sputnik I, the Gaither Report, a high-level, top-secret study into America's strategic posture, was submitted to Eisenhower. It made an alarming prediction that beginning in 1959 the United States would be increasingly vulnerable to a Soviet missile attack—a nuclear Pearl Harbor. The President was advised that the only way to preclude this might be to launch a preventive war while the U.S. still held its lead in the arms race.[19]

Two months later a second report, financed by the Rockefeller Brothers Fund, similarly portrayed a vulnerable America falling under the ever-lengthening and deepening shadows of Soviet intercontinental ballistic missiles, or ICBMs. Even so, the picture these reports offered was false.

The Soviets had test-fired several ICBMs into the waters of the Pacific, but they were years away from being able to guide a nuclear warhead onto a target. In warhead design, missile guidance and projected production, there was a gap of about four years between the U.S. and the U.S.S.R., and it was the Soviets who were lagging.

Jack Kennedy had issued clamorous warnings during the Korean War that the Soviets had snatched an airpower lead, putting America in peril. The fact that, in the skies over Korea, U.S. Air Force pilots shot down thir-teen MiGs for every lost American plane told a different story. But he never managed to get *Why England Slept* out of his mind.

It was hardly surprising, then, that he accepted without question the assertions being circulated by his friend Joe Alsop, the journalist, and Sen-ator Stuart Symington, a potential presidential candidate, that the United States was falling steadily behind the U.S.S.R. in the development of strategic weapons.

On August 14, 1958, Jack gave a speech in the Senate that asserted not only that there was a missile gap, but that it was growing alarmingly. Unless the United States responded effectively, and soon, "Their missile power will be the shield from behind which they will slowly but surely advance—through Sputnik diplomacy, limited 'brushfire' wars, indirect, nonovert aggression, intimidation and subversion . . . and the vicious blackmail of our allies."

He concluded with a clarion call: "Come then—let us to the task, to the battle and to the toil—each to our own part, each to our own station."

Kennedy was hoping to sound the tocsin much as Winston Churchill had done when he warned his countrymen in the 1930s about the dangers of a rearmed and Nazified Germany. Hardly anyone in America noticed or cared.[20]

≡

During these years, Jack and Jackie gradually put their marriage back together. She made picnic lunches when the weather was pleasant enough to sit outside the Capitol, and they ate on the grass or the steps, unnoticed among the tourists. She also started going to Senate Foreign Relations Committee hearings and organized crime hearings on days when Jack was going to have something to say. She freely admitted, "I wasn't interested in politics before I got married. But I'm learning by osmosis."[21]

In 1956 they had bought a charming small estate called Hickory Hill with six acres and stables. This was to be the home where they would raise their children, and Jackie had designed a nursery for Arabella. After losing the baby, she couldn't bear the thought of living at Hickory Hill. Jack sold it to Bobby, and he and Jackie bought 3307 N Street in Georgetown. Built of red brick around 1800, it was tall and narrow, and one side seemed slightly higher than the other—a lot, that is, like Jack. "My sweet little house," Jackie called it.

She became pregnant again and on November 27, 1957, gave birth to Caroline by cesarean section at New York Hospital. For them—as for countless other couples—having a child proved a transforming event in a troubled relationship.

Jackie learned to play golf, hoping that might mean she would get to spend more time with Jack, but it was in vain. Jack liked to play golf only with other men, and they had to tolerate an idiosyncratic approach to the game that shadowed his approach to life.

Jack Kennedy did not always play all eighteen holes on a golf course. If his back was troubling him or he felt pressed for time, he looked for the most interesting holes—say, the third, the sixth, the seventh, the ninth, and so on. Beginning on the third tee, he played the interesting holes in whatever order suited him that day.[22]

He also had a wide variety of nervous tics—pulling up his socks, tapping his teeth, drumming his fingers, patting his pockets. Jackie was much the same. Despite a photogenic appearance that made her seem matchlessly cool and poised, Jackie bit her nails to the quick and smoked forty

Pall Malls each day. She, like Jack, couldn't keep her hands still, and there were ashtrays all over their house.

Meanwhile, she became almost obsessively interested in her appearance. As a mother and the wife of a rising young politician, Jacqueline Kennedy began to put aside the windblown, outdoors girl look that Jack liked so much, probably because it was little more than the female version of his own casual and eternally tanned appearance. After years of spending almost nothing on clothes, she suddenly began spending lavishly.

In two of the most successful films of the mid-1950s—*Roman Holiday* and *Sabrina*—Audrey Hepburn brought the simple, straight-line European look of Balenciaga, Givenchy and Coco Chanel to America. Jackie took to it at once. For one thing, it oozed European chic. For another, she possessed even longer legs and a flatter chest than Audrey Hepburn. She might have been born to dress like this.

Jack's look, too, needed a makeover now that he was on the verge of middle age and required a degree of gravitas as ballast to his ambitions. Up until about 1957 he couldn't even handle a tie properly. It was usually twisted around his collar, and the end dangled too far below his belt. His brother-in-law Peter Lawford taught him how to tie a tie properly and urged him to stop wearing button-down shirts. "Looks juvenile."[23]

From 1957 on, Jack increasingly appeared in expensively tailored two-button suits with narrow lapels, custom-made monogrammed shirts and narrow, good-taste ties. He took to wearing dark bench-made shoes and, once he got interested in footwear, turned into a shoe enthusiast, buying dozens of pairs. In all of them, the left shoe had a special lift to compensate for the fact that his left leg was half an inch shorter than the right. For years, he had walked with an uneven gait. Thanks to the craftsmen at Church's, his walk suddenly evened out.[24]

Through Jackie he got to know Gore Vidal, and his acquaintance with writers thereafter grew wider. As someone who had always loved books, and as a writer himself, these were his kind of people in a way politicians would never be. No one else in the Senate could have gotten as much pleasure as he did from spending most of a day with Tennessee Williams. The playwright, too, enjoyed the day and mischievously told Gore Vidal, "He's got an attractive ass." Vidal passed on this information. Jack grinned. "That's very exciting."[25]

In the spring of 1957 he told Jackie he was going to run for the presidency. While she cannot have been surprised, she was nonetheless dismayed. "It isn't the right time for us," said Jackie. She was pregnant again and wanted to enjoy a normal family life before he made a presidential bid. "We're still young. We should be enjoying our children and having fun."[26]

When his publisher, Cass Canfield, asked him, "Jack, why do you want to be President?" he responded with a kind of hopeless candor typical of the man who finds himself in a situation that has become stronger than he is—"I guess it's the only thing I can do."[27]

≡

The invitations simply flooded in. During 1958 and 1959, Jack Kennedy received roughly a hundred requests a week to give a speech, and after his 1958 reelection to the Senate, he spent nearly every weekend on the rubber-chicken circuit, flying all over the country, on his own or with Ted Sorensen. In effect, he was conducting a rehearsal for a presidential campaign. There was a lot to be learned from these trips, not least how well he would stand up physically. As he told his old friend Red Fay, "I know I'll never be more than eighty to eighty-five percent healthy. But as long as I know that, I'm all right."[28]

His preparations included spending a day in the studio of Howell Conant, a noted photographer famous for his portraits of movie stars. Conant took hundreds of photographs, then had Jack study the contact sheets, picking out which were the best angles to be seen from, which the best expressions, which way to hold his head and just how far to look into the middle distance.[29]

With the inexorable clock running ever faster, Jack faced a mountain of material that had to be absorbed quickly—official reports and expert studies, legislative drafts, books, newspapers and magazines. Jack felt he was falling behind—the last place he would ever feel comfortable. So he, along with Bobby, completed a speed-reading course in Baltimore.[30]

He had also assembled his own Brains Trust, based mainly on people at Harvard. He had Henry Kissinger advising him on strategic affairs; Archibald Cox on labor legislation; Paul Samuelson, John Kenneth Galbraith, Seymour Harris and Walt Whitman Rostow on economics; and Arthur Schlesinger, Jr., on history.

Addressing the Nieman Fellows—journalists, that is—at Harvard on February 2, 1959, Jack said he no longer had a choice about running. Public expectations had grown too great. As of now, he was the front-runner, and you got to be the front-runner only once.

He didn't think the GOP would choose Nixon because the anti-Nixon candidates would mount a "Nixon Can't Win" campaign that would block him, the way the "Taft Can't Win" movement had kept Robert Taft from the Republican nomination in 1952. The candidate would be Nelson Rockefeller, who would be handicapped by having to defend the Eisenhower record. Yet on the major issues, there would not be much choice between Rocky and himself. It would be a campaign that turned on personalities.

Someone pointed out that the Senate was a bad place from which to make a presidential bid. Kennedy responded, "Not anymore. The big issues in government now are national security and foreign policy problems." Being governor of a state wasn't any advantage there.[31]

Meanwhile, whenever anyone spoke highly of Nixon or Humphrey, Symington or Johnson, Jack would ask, "What has he got that I haven't got?" He wasn't joking; he really wanted to know. The paradigm here was not just that of the aspiring actor envying another man's performance; it also had a hint of the pagan warrior who will eat an enemy's heart to capture his strength.[32]

Packing his Dansette and a selection of his favorite records, Jack traveled that year to nearly half the states in the Union, yet insisted he wasn't campaigning for anything. One of the must-visit places was Wisconsin, whose primary he'd need to win a year down the road.

The reaction he drew there in April 1959 was almost rapturous. He spoke in Madison, Milwaukee and four other towns, drawing huge crowds wherever he went. No one responded more than young people. "Students at Beloit College hung on his every word," reported *Life* magazine. "They followed him outdoors as if he were the Pied Piper, then stood in an ogling semi-circle until he drove away."[33]

Asked by a journalist if it didn't bother her to see how young women went into a frenzy in Jack's presence, Jackie said of course not. "Women are very idealistic and they respond to an idealistic person like my husband." As she spoke, she stared at her exiguous nails.[34]

These travels and speeches gave Jack the chance to try and draw the sting from the inevitable hostility to a Catholic seeking the White House. Addressing the Alfred Smith Memorial Dinner in New York, he observed, "I think it is well that we recall at this annual dinner what happened to a great governor when he became a presidential nominee. Despite his successful record as a governor, despite his plainspoken voice, the campaign was a debacle. His views were distorted, he carried fewer states than any candidate in his party's history. He lost states which had been solid for his party for a century or more. To top it off, he lost his own state. . . . You all know his name and his religion: Alfred M. Landon, Protestant."[35]

Jack's preparations also included a campaign biography, written by James MacGregor Burns, a Massachusetts Democratic party activist and professor of history at Williams College. Jack Kennedy cooperated closely with Burns, speaking to him freely and at length. Yet he was deeply unhappy when he read the first draft. What upset him most wasn't anything said about himself. It was Burns's description of Joe Kennedy as a coward, fleeing London at the height of the Blitz to seek refuge in the English countryside. "This is the worst, the most scurrilous and most false charge that could be made," Sorensen protested to Burns on Jack's behalf.[36]

This wasn't the only part of the book he objected to. It irked him to be portrayed as a nominal Catholic, and he contested Burns's description of him as being repeatedly and sometimes seriously ill during the four years at Choate. He insisted that it simply wasn't true.

Burns removed the references to Joe Kennedy's cowardice and Jack's illness and described his Addisonism as being a remarkably mild form, one without serious implications or complications. What troubled Burns far more than Kennedy's health was his seeming lack of commitment to anything beyond winning the next election. To Burns, Kennedy appeared to want the presidency as a kind of trophy. Burns could detect no moral imperative that might guide Kennedy's actions once the trophy was his.[37]

Jackie had her own objections, asking Burns, "Please—in the book—call me Jacqueline, not *Jackie,* which I loathe."[38]

Jack Kennedy feared that, far from helping him, the Burns biography was going to hurt his chances, but there was an even greater obstacle to his hopes—the opposition of Eleanor Roosevelt. Shortly after his reelection to the Senate, she had appeared on television and pointedly remarked that of all the potential presidential candidates in the party, only one—Hubert Humphrey—possessed "the spark of greatness." As for John F. Kennedy, his father was spending "oodles of money all over the country" to get his son into the White House.[39]

Jack protested that Mrs. Roosevelt really ought to avoid making such claims unless she was prepared to support them with hard evidence. He pursued the issue so desultorily, though, that his lack of appetite for a fight over his father's spending was obvious.

Her response came in an interview for *Look*. She said what troubled her was his failure to stand up to McCarthy. Her scorn was withering. She described Jack Kennedy as "someone who understands what courage is and admires it, but has not quite the independence to have it." That amounted to saying he hadn't challenged McCarthy because Dad wouldn't permit it.[40]

Jack struck back with an interview in *Harper's* magazine. The specter of McCarthyism continued to cast a shadow, he acknowledged. Then he tried to rewrite his personal record. "There were only four or five Senators who very vigorously attacked McCarthy [but] I opposed him," he said.[41]

In December 1959, at a charity ball in New York, an old friend, Nancy Coleman, said teasingly, "Now, Jack—you don't *really* want to be President." He bristled. "Nancy, I not only want to be, I am going to be." It irritated him that at this late date anyone might fail to take him seriously as a candidate, even in jest.[42]

=

That winter, as the family gathered for Christmas in Palm Beach, Jack prepared to announce his candidacy. One day, as he and Red Fay lolled in the pool chatting, Bobby started berating Jack for taking it easy; he ought to be working on the campaign. Jack murmured to Fay, "How would *you* like to have that high, whining voice in your ear for the next six months?"[43]

For his part, Joe Kennedy was having second thoughts after the years and the millions he had spent on bringing his son this far. "Jack's trying for the presidency too soon," he told Fay. "How does he have a chance? The economy is good. There doesn't seem to be a problem of war breaking out. He is too young. And besides, he is a Catholic. I hate to see him and Bobby work themselves to death only to lose."[44]

Once Christmas was out of the way, Jack and Jackie flew back to Washington to make his announcement. Ben Bradlee, a journalist at *Newsweek*, was by this time well on the way to becoming a friend. He and his wife, Toni, socialized with Jack and Jackie, and with Jack on the brink, Bradlee asked him, "Do you really think you can do it?"

After a long, thoughtful pause, Kennedy replied, almost in a whisper, "Yes, if I don't make a single mistake."[45]

On January 2, 1960, he made his way to the Senate Caucus Room, which was crowded with three hundred supporters, plus dozens of reporters and photographers. There was hardly enough room for him to stand with Jackie, dressed in a red suit, beside him. With slightly shaking hands, Jack read a brief statement. "I am announcing today my candidacy for the presidency of the United States. . . ." Jackie looked glum.

After a few anodyne observations about the reasons for his candidacy, he asked, "Are there questions?" There was a solemn hush as people absorbed what they felt was a moment in History. Then came the cheers and applause.[46]

The photographers started clamoring, "Look this way, Senator . . . Give us a smile, Senator . . ." Jackie gazed at them with an implacable remoteness while Jack, feeling self-conscious, tried to produce a smile. Then, to lighten the tense mood in the room, he said he'd read an article recently in *The New Yorker* about politicians who smiled too much—it showed how shallow they were. A photographer responded, "That's okay, Senator. Not everybody reads *The New Yorker.*" That ignited a short laugh and the full million-dollar smile.

CHAPTER 22

Jack Be Nimble

J ack was going to direct his campaign for the nomination towards the liberals in the party, as if they were his natural constituency, even though he had tried throughout his time in Congress not to be identified as one of them. Shortly after he was elected to the Senate, the *Saturday Evening Post* had quoted Jack Kennedy as saying, "I'm not a liberal at all. I never joined Americans for Democratic Action or the American Veterans Committee. I'm not comfortable with those people." Arthur Schlesinger, Jr., a Harvard historian whom Jack had gotten to know, promptly wrote to ask if he'd really said these things.[1]

Kennedy responded by criticizing the *Post* but at no point claimed he'd been misquoted. Instead, he insisted that he really was a liberal and was grateful for the support of ADA members.

Even after he'd joined the ADA—and he was the principal speaker at the 1958 meeting of the ADA in Philadelphia—JFK still wasn't at ease with the liberal label. Too many liberals struck him as people who preferred making gestures to making hard choices. He also thought they were likely to lack the toughness and realism that national security problems demanded. Yet he needed their support and was prepared to move in their direction to win it.[2]

Although he considered himself an expert on foreign policy, he appointed a Stevensonian liberal, Chester Bowles, to be his foreign policy adviser. Having announced Bowles's appointment, Kennedy thereafter had almost no contact with him. The last thing he really wanted was Bowles's advice.[3]

Like Franklin Roosevelt, Jack felt comfortable around intellectuals without being one. He had little interest in abstract thought and looked instead for ideas that would get him where he wanted to go. Most of his brain trust comprised high-profile, academic liberals.

Only sixteen states would hold primaries in 1960. Jack had little choice about entering the first, New Hampshire, because that was virtually a gift. So, too, was Massachusetts. And he had no say when it came to the last primary, Oregon, in May. Every declared candidate was automatically placed on the Oregon ballot.

The campaign for the nomination was to be guided partly by instinct, partly by advice from local experts and partly by opinion polls. Joe Kennedy had used market research extensively in building up the Merchandise Mart. He had come to believe that the same kind of polling helped identify those issues that determined people's votes. So far, Jack Kennedy had used polling more than any politician in American history. But that was nothing compared to the crucial role that polling was going to play in 1960, beginning with a poll, conducted by Lou Harris, that convinced Jack to run in Maryland, and yet another poll that persuaded him to stay out of Florida.[4]

The first chance to challenge Humphrey, who was the front-runner for the liberal vote, would come in Wisconsin. Most of Jack's staff didn't like the look of the battleground. Wisconsin was right next door to Minnesota and had much the same ultraliberal political history. Jack Kennedy was convinced all the same that ducking Wisconsin would count heavily against him. And if he could defeat Humphrey there, that might generate enough momentum to carry him through the rest of the primaries.

As the campaign began, Joe Kennedy provided his son with something no other Democratic hopeful had, his own airplane—a twin-engine eighteen-seat Convair Jack called the *Caroline*. It was noisy and vibrated fearsomely, but he loved it. "I could never see anybody running for President without an airplane!" he enthused.[5]

He had also learned an important lesson from his countrywide travels in 1959: many small town newspapers took their editorials from the North

American Newspaper Alliance. And it seemed to him that whenever he was mentioned, it was nearly always in a slighting way.

That fall Kennedy had Sorensen go to see NANA's chief editorial writer, Bruce Biessat, regularly. By the time the primary campaign began in 1960, Biessat had been tutored extensively on Kennedy's political beliefs, Senate voting record and presidential hopes. NANA's editorials were turning increasingly favorable as Kennedy packed for the snows of northern Wisconsin.[6]

=

Kennedy began with the toughest part of the state, the Tenth congressional district—solidly Humphrey territory. It was also bitterly cold. The temperature was barely into double figures, yet he stood in front of a meatpacking plant, hand extended, at six in the morning. "Hello, I'm Jack Kennedy. I'm running for President." He stood outside the plant for hours, shaking close to two thousand hands—still doing it the hard way.

Humphrey was counting heavily on labor to carry him in the industrial cities and towns, but much of the labor leadership was quietly backing Kennedy. So were the rank and file. Kennedy discovered that his role on the Senate Rackets Committee was a vote winner. The labor vote in Wisconsin swung firmly during the campaign away from Humphrey and over to Kennedy.[7]

He was also making some—but not much—headway on agricultural issues. At the end of the Wisconsin campaign, he understood the agricultural issues better. Talking to Walt Whitman Rostow one day, he held up his hand. "I have a big hand, Walt, but I have been talking to fellows with hands twice as big as mine. They get up at five in the morning, and because the milk price is low, they work these hours and live this life for too damned little."[8]

Most of the time Kennedy campaigned without a hat or an overcoat, although he wore long johns on the coldest days. He stood outside factory gates in darkness and below-freezing temperatures, smiling and shaking hands as the first shift clocked in at six in the morning. He grazed instead of eating proper meals and pushed himself so hard that a health crisis was inevitable. Countless times his left hand went up under his jacket so he could push on the brace that was supporting his back, trying to ease a torment that never really went away.

One day, while campaigning through various rural towns, his back suddenly went into spasm. The pain was excruciating, and he turned white in front of the gathering he was addressing. Helped into a nearby school, he stretched out on the floor of the principal's office for a couple of hours while the spasms subsided.[9]

A year earlier, Fletcher Knebel of *Look* had asked him if the rumors about his having Addison's disease were true. Kennedy had adamantly denied them. He said he had a minor glandular problem, but it was so trifling, he didn't even need medication for it. It was no problem at all.

To his surprise, Knebel showed up in Wisconsin in March 1960. Kennedy had thought he was still in Washington, working on a different story. When Jack encountered Knebel now, he said pointedly, "What are you doing here? It must be because we are going through Addison today."[10]

In the first month all the rallies were indoors. Although the candidates had no choice about campaigning in the cold, they could hardly expect voters to show up at outdoor events where they risked frostbite as well as boredom.

When the weather began to improve, open-air rallies became possible in the southern parts of the state. This was more his style—big signs reading JACK KENNEDY FOR PRESIDENT; red, white and blue bunting strung across the front of a small platform, a few tables piled with Kennedy literature, some attractive young women handing it out, a loudspeaker that boomed "Anchors Aweigh" into the frosty air, followed by Frank Sinatra singing "High Hopes," the sudden arrival of a motorcade, then a brief introduction from a local figure and the candidate himself coming forward, smiling, nodding, waving, tucking his right hand into a pocket as he stepped up to the microphone. A short speech, a few questions, then the motorcade got on the road again with the candidate sitting in the backseat, running a small Ace comb through his hair while being briefed on the next stop.

Humphrey grew alarmed as he sensed Wisconsin slipping away. He tried to blame it on Joe Kennedy's lavish spending, but Jack made a joke of it. "I've just received the following telegram from my generous father," he'd remark in an offhand way. "It reads—Dear Jack: Don't buy a single vote more than is necessary. I'll help you win this election, but I'll be damned if I'm going to pay for a landslide."

On polling day, April 5, Kennedy flew into the state aboard the *Caroline* with Ben Bradlee. He and Bradlee agreed to write down how they thought he would do and put the answers in a sealed envelope. Kennedy was by now convinced he would carry nearly all of the state's ten congressional districts. He wrote, "JFK 9, HHH 1."

Bradlee's forecast was "Kennedy 7, Humphrey 3."[11]

While the votes were still being counted, Kennedy appeared at the CBS studio in Milwaukee where Walter Cronkite was covering the election. During the broadcast, Cronkite asked Kennedy to comment on how he thought the Catholic vote was developing. Incensed, Jack mumbled a noncommittal reply. He later called the president of CBS, Frank Stanton, and pointedly told him that if he became President, he would be appointing members of the Federal Communications Commission and maybe Stanton ought to keep that in mind. He wasn't always Smilin' Jack.[12]

The Wisconsin result turned out to be a narrow win, six districts to Kennedy and four for Humphrey. Hubert was down but not out.

=

Back in Washington after Wisconsin, Jack and Hubert sat talking on the Senate floor one day. "Hubert, I don't think you can get the nomination." Kennedy's tone was objective and analytical. "I don't know why you want to go on with this battle. You're not going to get any of the New England states and you won't carry California." And so it went, across the country. There weren't enough states where Humphrey could win.

Kennedy was equally dispassionate about his own chances. "I think I've got some problems. Getting the nomination is going to be easier for me than for you. But the religious question will hurt me in the general election. I think you'd find it easier in the general election, but you can't get the nomination."

"Well, I think maybe you're right," said Humphrey.[13]

He had not yet decided whether to run in West Virginia, and Jack, too, had been forced to think long and hard about it. His father was completely opposed to the idea. "It's a nothing state and they'll kill Jack over the Catholic thing," he insisted during a strategy meeting in Palm Beach.

Jack responded, "Well, we've heard from the ambassador and we're all very grateful, Dad, but I've got to run in West Virginia."[14]

It seemed at times as if Joe Kennedy had come this far only to conclude that Jack's religion was too high a hurdle to jump. Yet by now Jack saw it as one more challenge that had to be met. If he showed fear, if he so much as blinked in the face of religious bigotry, it would bring him down. His best chance was to meet it head-on.

That meant he really had no choice about West Virginia. As he told Walt Whitman Rostow, one of his Brains Trust advisers, in the end, it sometimes didn't matter what the polls said or what his staff thought. "There is one simple, overriding point. I have no right to go before the Democratic convention and claim to be a candidate if I can only win primaries in states with twenty-five percent or more Catholics. I must go in there. And I am going in."[15]

Shortly before the West Virginia campaign began, when Kennedy had just triumphed in Wisconsin and Humphrey was still making up his mind whether to continue, a Lou Harris poll showed Kennedy leading the other declared Democratic presidential candidates in West Virginia.

What he needed was a credible opponent. To Kennedy's delight, Humphrey announced at the last minute that he would run there, too. The mood changed overnight. With a Protestant versus a Catholic, it turned into a race, stirring up all the elemental passions Joe Kennedy dreaded. Taken aback by the amount of hostility he encountered when he began campaigning in West Virginia, Jack told a journalist friend, "Boy, Lou Harris was down here, but I don't know who he talked to!"[16]

Outsiders running in West Virginia primaries relied on a tactic called "slating." This meant getting Kennedy's name onto the most promising Democratic slate in each county. He would be expected to give money to the other candidates—local judges, sheriffs, district attorneys and others who were on the same slate. Kennedy volunteers would distribute his literature along with theirs and try to make it appear that the Kennedy organization merged seamlessly with the local Democratic party.

As in Wisconsin, the huge margin by which Kennedy outspent Humphrey provoked accusations of buying the nomination. And the widespread corruption of politics in West Virginia encouraged rumors that much of the money came from mobsters; a bizarre idea, considering that Joe Kennedy had more money than anyone in organized crime.

Mob money was certainly being spent in some counties, and JFK was on the slate with a number of people who got backing from mobsters, but the only way to avoid that was to keep off the slate—and that was as good as kissing West Virginia goodbye. Humphrey went in for slating just as Kennedy did, and for exactly the same reasons.[17]

Parts of West Virginia looked promising, especially in the north, which had most of the larger towns, most of the Catholics and most of the industry. Farther south, in places like Logan County, Kennedy volunteers were almost impossible to find. The staff from his Washington office, plus various friends, were drafted to hand out leaflets and knock on doors. And the only way they could assure a decent turnout for a rally was to provide free hot dogs and sodas.[18]

He also had a Roosevelt card to play. Iconic photographs of Franklin D. Roosevelt were still venerated in shacks and poverty-stricken homes across the state. When Franklin D. Roosevelt, Jr., appealed for West Virginians to vote for Jack Kennedy, he was listened to in openmouthed awe. Unfortunately, he got carried away and gave a speech that characterized Humphrey as a World War II draft dodger, unlike heroic Jack Kennedy, who had gone and fought the Japanese in the South Pacific. When he heard about it, Kennedy reacted fiercely. "Get him out of West Virginia!"[19]

Coal was the state's economic mainstay and some of Kennedy's first campaign visits were to the mines. As he shook hands with weary, black-faced men after they finished their shift, one miner looked him straight in the eye and asked bluntly, "Is it true you're the son of our wealthiest man?"

"I guess it's true," replied Jack.

"Is it true, too, that you have never wanted for anything? You've had everything you wished?"

"Yes. That's true."

"And isn't it true you've never done a day's work with your hands your entire life?"

"Yes," said Jack. "That's true."

"Well, let me tell you this," said the miner. "You haven't missed a thing."[20]

The people here were poor but proud. Near the bottom of the table for disposable income, West Virginia was near the top of the list for the number of Medal of Honor winners. Kennedy appealed to that martial heritage in his challenge to religious bigotry.

"How many Catholics died at the Alamo?" he'd ask. "Side by side with Bowie and Crockett died McCaffrey and Bailey and Carey. But no one knew if they were Catholics or not because there was no religious test at the Alamo!" He also remarked—sometimes sounding melancholy, at other times sounding close to anger—"When my older brother, Joe, was killed on a wartime bombing mission, nobody asked if he was a Catholic."[21]

His back held up, just, to the strains of this campaign, but for several days he lost his voice and had to communicate with notes. Flying over the state in the *Caroline* one day, he passed a note to another journalist friend, Charles Bartlett. It read, "I'd give my right testicle to win this primary."[22]

But it soon began to appear that such sacrifice wouldn't be necessary.

Lou Harris's polls showed that Kennedy was making a comeback from his initial sharp drop against Humphrey, and Myer Feldman, one of his legislative assistants, overheard a couple of men talking at a Kennedy rally. One of them said, "You know, I normally vote three times in an election. This time it's two to one for Kennedy."[23]

The fundamental issue was a simple as could be: which candidate was going to do the most to alleviate the poverty that gripped most of the state? Humphrey was telling people, "I won't let your grandpappy die in the poorhouse," a pledge that probably offended as many people as it reassured. Kennedy chose to make a more dignified promise: if he became President, he would act to relieve the distressed parts of the state within sixty days of taking office.

Arriving in Welch, population five thousand, in the far southwestern corner of the state towards the end of the campaign, Jack spelled out what his promise meant. He was going to create a food-stamp program, something that would help many a family in West Virginia. "I think the people of this state need and deserve a helping hand, and I'm going to see that you get it!"

Gazing up at him as he spoke was Homer Hickam, Jr., a seventeen-year-old dressed in the suit he'd bought that morning—a suit that was orange in color. Homer's great passion wasn't clothes, but making and launching rockets he had designed. So when JFK asked, "How about some questions?" Homer's hand shot up.

"Yes. The boy in the . . . um . . . suit."

"Yessir. What do you think the United States ought to do in space?"

Kennedy smiled. "Well, some of my opponents think *I* should go into space. But I'll ask you, young man—what do you think we ought to do in space?"

"We should go to the moon!" The crowd seemed to think this was a good idea.

"Well, if I'm elected President," said Kennedy, "I think maybe we will go to the moon."[24]

The day before the vote, he was resigned to defeat. Kennedy thought the best he could hope for now was a 48 to 52 percent split; a narrow defeat. But if it really did turn out that close, he optimistically told himself, he might be able to survive it.[25]

The evening of voting day, May 10, Jack and Jackie went to the movies with Ben and Toni Bradlee. They saw a skin flick called *Private Property;* titillating rather than pornographic, but hardly Jackie's kind of film. When they returned to the N Street house, the phone was ringing. It was Bobby with poll results from West Virginia—Jack had swept the state. He was going to pick up around 60 percent of the vote. The two couples cheered, embraced, then downed some champagne and hurried to the airport for a flight on the *Caroline* and a midnight victory celebration in Charleston, West Virginia.[26]

The rest of the primaries proved anticlimactic. The Democratic party in state after state came over to Kennedy after West Virginia. The only unsettling incident occurred during the Oregon primary, when the official Vatican newspaper, *L'Osservatore Romano,* ran an editorial asserting the right and duty of the Church to tell Catholics how they should vote. Infuriated, Kennedy told Ted Sorensen, "Now I know why Henry the Eighth set up his own church!"[27]

In January 1959 Jack Kennedy had sent one of Sargent Shriver's assistants at the Merchandise Mart to talk to J. Leonard Reinsch. Since World War II, Reinsch had managed both Democratic and Republican conventions. He had more experience in this rarified field than any man alive. What Kennedy wanted to know was how a candidate ought to prepare himself and his staff for a convention.

Following this meeting, Reinsch went to see Jack Kennedy. There was one thing he needed to know before he could offer any really useful advice: were they talking about a VP bid? Kennedy's narrow face creased into his wry half-smile. "We ran for the vice presidency in 1956. In 1960 we go for the big one."[28]

≡

By the time the primaries ended, Kennedy calculated he was within a hundred delegate votes of the nomination. He was well ahead of his nearest rival, Lyndon Johnson, and even further ahead of Hubert Humphrey.

Yet it wouldn't be enough to be nominated—he had to win the nomination in just the right way if it was going to be worth anything come November. If he appeared to be the candidate of the South, he would lose the election. Jack's best hope was to run as the liberal candidate, which meant getting Adlai Stevenson to endorse him.[29]

On May 18, with the Oregon primary behind him, he flew to Illinois to meet with Stevenson at his home in Libertyville. Before their meeting, Kennedy talked to Stevenson's law partner, Newton Minow. "Why doesn't he come out for me?" he asked Minow.

"The governor says he intends to remain neutral."

"Don't kid me," said Jack impatiently. "That means he wants to get it for himself." He thought for a moment. "What about Secretary of State? Do you think I should say something to him about appointing him Secretary of State?"

Minow told him that would only annoy Stevenson, not bring him around.[30]

Kennedy met with Stevenson with no one else present. He said he needed to know whether Stevenson had any hopes of being nominated. Stevenson claimed he wasn't interested in the nomination, but he couldn't do anything about his supporters. He didn't control them.[31]

This kind of equivocation only irritated Kennedy. He bore down on Stevenson, demanding his endorsement. But Stevenson was evasive. Hadn't he already declared publicly that he wasn't going to endorse anyone before the convention? That meant he was honor-bound to hold back.

"Look, I have the votes for the nomination right now," said an exasperated Kennedy. "And if you don't give me your support, I'll have to shit all over you. I don't want to do that, but I can, and I will."

Stevenson said that from what he could judge, Johnson might still get it. Kennedy turned scathing. He dismissed LBJ as "that fucking bastard."[32]

His impatience and brusqueness at this meeting were uncharacteristic. Normally he conducted himself courteously with his elders, including the leaders of his party. His back may have been particularly painful this day, or maybe the drugs he was taking had produced a violent mood swing, but for whatever reason, this encounter was something neither man ever wanted to talk about. Both hoped the press would not find out it had taken place.

Jackie had played a decorative role in the primaries, and at one point Jack had pulled her leg, telling her the only way he could carry Wisconsin was for her to go there and be photographed milking a cow. She avoided that fate, but mostly she showed up in this town or that and was stared at, something she loathed.

With the primaries out of the way, Jack took her to Del Monte Lodge at Pebble Beach for a break. Each morning Jack talked for an hour or so to Hugh Sidey of *Time* before he and Red Fay played golf. After several days, though, Jack began to suspect Sidey was going to produce a piece that was really about Joseph P. Kennedy, power-crazed plutocrat.

"That's all they want to read in *Time* magazine," he burst out to Fay one morning. "That I'm a pawn in my father's hands; that it isn't really Jack Kennedy who is trying to be President but his father, 'Big Joe,' who is using him as the vehicle to capture the only segment of power that has eluded him." And he told Sidey to his face, "This is supposed to be a piece about a promising young candidate, not the kiss of death!"

In the end, the piece *Time* ran was broadly favorable while being mildly critical, but he took offense anyway. Kennedy was remarkably friendly towards journalists but hypersensitive about criticism, astonishingly frank about most things yet cynical and dishonest about his health and his marriage.[33]

The convention would be held July 11–15 at the Los Angeles Sports Arena. A month before it opened, Reinsch and the convention-management team set up shop in the huge and luxurious Biltmore Hotel in the heart of downtown. They had barely gotten down to work before Kennedy staffers moved into the Biltmore, too.

Bobby Kennedy's team were the first people to monitor the convention arrangements and get into the details—where is there office space? Secretarial help? Do we have enough typewriters? Pencils? Stationery? Telephones? By taking care of such questions now, they wouldn't be distracted by them later.[34]

On July 9 Jack Kennedy flew into Los Angeles on a commercial flight, seated next to Toni Bradlee. His throat had given out again, so he communicated with little notes. When she asked him, "What about Lyndon Johnson for Vice President?" Kennedy scribbled, "He'll never take it."[35]

As he settled in to the apartment where he would stay for the next week, he was still worrying about Stevenson. There was no chance of the governor getting the nomination, but "Stevenson could be a spoiler," he told his staff. If the liberal vote split between Stevenson, Humphrey and Kennedy, the nomination would go to Johnson; possibly even to Symington.[36]

And beyond that, he could not risk a fractured liberal vote if the nomination was going to be worth anything. A Kennedy candidacy that appeared to have been engineered by southern Democrats would go down in defeat in November.[37]

Kennedy's candidacy was almost tripped up not because of a split in the liberal vote or a challenge from Stevenson, but because two of Lyndon Johnson's strongest supporters, India Edwards and John Connally, were spreading the word that Kennedy had Addison's disease. His press secretary, Pierre Salinger, immediately denied the story, and when it was put to him that Kennedy was on cortisone, Ted Sorensen vehemently denied it. One of Kennedy's doctors, Janet Travell, loyally put out a statement that his adrenal glands were functioning adequately and that he was no more susceptible to infection than anyone else.

When this failed to kill the issue, Bobby Kennedy held a press conference. There was a minor problem with Jack's adrenal glands, he conceded, but he denied that his brother was suffering from Addison's "in the classic sense."

This nifty footwork—creating an entirely new and fictitious ailment and then denying John Kennedy had it—was the real contribution of Janet Travell. In truth, the reason why his Addisonism had been so quickly and accurately diagnosed in London in 1947 was that it was a perfect example of the disease. It could not have been more "classic."[38]

The working press accepted the flimflam and wandered away to cover other questions. At moments like this, Jack Kennedy's buddy-like relationship with reporters reaped a reward that money could not buy.[39]

The first day of the convention, Monday, July 11, was dominated by thousands of people flooding into the Los Angeles Sports Arena brandishing banners and signs for Stevenson. They paraded tirelessly for hours—women, children, young, old, in between—screaming, "We want Stevenson! We want Stevenson!" Eleanor Roosevelt was telling reporters what a wonderful ticket it would be: Stevenson for President, Jack Kennedy for Veep.

While the hysterical demonstration for Stevenson ran on, it provided images of genuine passion that came across powerfully on television, but there was no substance behind them. The *Newsweek* bureau chief, the highly experienced Kenneth Crawford, was studiously unimpressed. "Just look at the delegates," he said to Ben Bradlee. "They are not demonstrating." And they weren't.[40]

This synthetic concoction encouraged Stevenson, as it was doubtless intended to do. To Kennedy's disgust, Stevenson even went onto the convention floor to lead the demonstration. To make a serious bid for the nomination, however, he would have to carry the entire Illinois delegation with him, as his state's favorite son. Mayor Richard Daley of Chicago bluntly informed him that nearly the entire delegation was going to vote for Jack Kennedy. Stevenson had left it too late.[41]

During the first two days of the convention, Kennedy circulated among the delegations, urging them to vote for him. When he requested Lyndon

Johnson's permission to talk to the Texas delegation, LBJ neatly offered a joint appearance before the Texas and Massachusetts delegations in which they would debate each other.

Kennedy hadn't been looking for a debate, but he promptly accepted the challenge. Johnson was a fixer, an operator, not a debater, and the "debate" turned into a snide Johnsonian attack on "some people" who were seeking the presidency. He made reference to a variety of failings and shortcomings that were plainly intended to refer to Kennedy. Among friends, Johnson had a habit of calling Kennedy "that skinny little prick."[42]

Refusing to be provoked in front of so many delegates, JFK smiled. "I come here today full of admiration for Senator Johnson," he declared, "full of affection for him, and strongly in support of him—for Majority Leader." It was deft and it was witty. Even Johnson had to laugh.

The first ballot was scheduled for late afternoon on Wednesday. Even now Stevenson would not rule himself out. In a masochistic gesture that smacked of weakness and vacillation, he allowed his name to go forward to inevitable defeat. When the balloting began that afternoon, Jack Kennedy had at least 700 of the 761 votes needed to be nominated, and virtually everyone in the Sports Arena knew it.

When balloting reached the last state, Wyoming, Kennedy was leading with 750 votes, and Wyoming had 15 ballots to cast. Watching television with Dave Powers, Jack suddenly noticed something interesting—Teddy was standing just behind the chairman of the Wyoming delegation with a big grin on his face. "This could do it," Jack murmured to Powers.[43]

The Wyoming chairman, Tracy S. McCraken, savoring the moment, slowly declared, "Wyoming casts all fifteen votes for the next President of the United States. . . ."

Sorensen and other members of Kennedy's Senate staff had for weeks been urging him to offer the vice presidential slot to Johnson, but nothing had changed his feeling that Johnson would turn him down. Kennedy was tempted to offer it to Humphrey but had come around to preferring Symington. Hubert was good on domestic issues, but he was too inexperienced and pliable on national security for a potential successor. Symington, though, was a lot like himself—more or less liberal on domestic issues but fundamentally conservative on defense and foreign policy. Ten days before the convention, Kennedy had lunch with Clark Clifford, Symington's political mentor. Would Stu consider second place? The answer appears to have been yes.[44]

Now, only hours after being nominated, JFK encountered Symington in a Biltmore corridor. "You are my first available choice for Vice President," said Jack.

"What about Lyndon?"

"He isn't available." And at that point, he wasn't. Sam Rayburn was completely against it, and Johnson was not going to accept a place on the ticket without the blessing of his surrogate father, Mr. Sam.[45]

From the Biltmore, Kennedy was driven over to Chasen's restaurant, where the United Steelworkers were holding a buffet and cocktail party for him. Tip O'Neill showed up uninvited and whispered to Jack that he had just been talking to Rayburn. Then he got straight to the point. "Are you interested in Johnson for the vice presidency?"

Jack responded, "Tip, go outside and stand by the car, will you? I want to go over this whole conversation with you."

It was forty-five minutes before he could get away from the steelworkers, and when he stepped outside the restaurant, there was a throng of several thousand people crowding the sidewalks, so Kennedy had to hold a hurried, sotto voce conversation with O'Neill in the glare of klieg lights and cameras. Tip said Mr. Sam had changed his mind and told Lyndon that he would have to run if Kennedy offered him a place on the ticket.

JFK was thrilled. "Of course I want Lyndon. But I'd never want to offer it and have him turn me down. I'd be terrifically embarrassed. Lyndon's the natural choice, and with him on the ticket, there's no way we could lose." Next morning he went to see Johnson and made the offer.[46]

It wasn't a choice without risks for either of them. Johnson was giving up the immense power he wielded in the Senate in exchange for what another Texan, John Nance Garner, had once called a "a pitcher of warm piss" (bowdlerized ever after as "spit"). Kennedy was going to have to sell his decision to a lot of unhappy liberals and to members of his own family, who were still incensed that Johnson had raised the issue of Addisonism at the 1956 convention.

Arrangements had been made for the formal acceptance speech to be delivered in the Sports Arena. Kennedy insisted on doing it in the more imposing Coliseum, which held eighty thousand people—fifteen times the capacity of the arena—and provided a much more dramatic setting for a television audience of millions.[47]

Since 1946 a certain shyness and self-consciousness had undermined Jack's set-piece speeches. But now he showed something new—the skill to disguise such faults behind actorish tropes. The result wasn't completely satisfactory. It needed polishing, but he thrilled the devotedly partisan crowd before him.

"We stand today at the edge of a New Frontier, the frontier of the nineteen sixties," he told the crowd. As he closed with "Now begins another long journey. . . . Give me your help," cheers rolled over him in joyful waves. Kennedy extended his arms. "Give me your hand . . ." The roar from the crowd almost drowned out his final words: ". . . your voice and your vote."

CHAPTER 23

Too Close to Call

He needed the whole party behind him, beginning with Harry Truman and Eleanor Roosevelt. Truman was grumbling as only he could at the party's nomination of "this immature boy" under his father's thumb. A month after the convention, Kennedy flew to Independence to tell the former President that however dominating his father might appear, he really was his own man. They met at the presidential library for an uncomfortable half hour, then went outside and insisted to the assembled press that each was a lot happier with the other than he truly was or ever would be.[1]

A few days later Jack traveled to Hyde Park, where he and Eleanor Roosevelt spent an hour together, with no one else present, over lunch. He told her it had surprised him to discover just how fragmented the Democratic party was. At the end of the convention, the governor of Florida had come to him to let him know "I am a conservative and I am against integration and right-to-work laws." Kennedy had responded, "Then why don't you join the Republicans?"

Eleanor Roosevelt told him to keep in mind how useful Stevenson could be when it came to carrying New York and California, and without them, he didn't stand a chance, because the party could no longer rely on the Solid South—solidly Democratic, that is. After Jack departed, she dictated a memo of the meeting and conceded that she had misjudged him. "He will make a good President."[2]

Once the Republicans had nominated Nixon, Jack Kennedy could hardly wait to begin the campaign, but Johnson had arranged a summer session of Congress, anticipating that he would be the Democratic nominee. This extra session was intended to allow him to start campaigning from Capitol Hill a month before Labor Day. Kennedy was forced to spend much of that August in Washington. When the session finally ended, he rushed to the French Riviera for a brief vacation, then hastened home.

═══

The campaign began September 2 in Maine. Over the next ten days Jack crisscrossed the country. In California he told a press conference, "My wife is going to have a boy in November." A journalist asked, "How do you know it's going to be a boy?"

"My wife told me," said Jack, and they roared.

At some point, he knew, he was going to have to confront the question that haunted his father—Catholicism. Kennedy hoped, if not prayed, it could be pushed off until the last week or so of the campaign. He did not want it smoldering through the campaign, breaking out like a peat fire every time it seemed under control.

A week into the campaign, however, the country's best-known Protestant, Norman Vincent Peale, loudly let it be known that a Catholic had no choice but to be obedient to the Pope. And a Catholic who wasn't obedient was . . . well, little better than a hypocrite.

Peale was too highly regarded to be ignored, and Kennedy suddenly came under intense pressure to explain publicly how he could square the demands of his faith with the demands of the presidential oath. Some three hundred Protestant ministers were going to be meeting in Houston on September 12. They invited him to come to the meeting and address them on the questions that Peale had raised.

"I came home to find the campaign was not between a Democrat and a Republican, but between a Catholic and a Protestant," he informed his father's old friend Lord Beaverbrook. "This is going to be tough."[3]

Peale and the preachers who were heading for Houston were ignorant about the nature of Kennedy's Catholicism. Nor did they know how deep the split was in the Catholic Church over his candidacy. Most Catholic priests in the U.S. were thrilled by his presidential bid, but the church leadership was horrified, fearing it would only stir sectarian hostility. Besides, he was too liberal for the Vatican. Most cardinals and bishops were going to vote for Nixon.[4]

As for what kind of Catholic Jack Kennedy was, the studied detachment he brought to his faith was of a piece with the rest of his life. He fitted naturally into a tradition rooted in Voltairean skepticism: witty, sardonic, slightly aloof, yet permanently attached. He intended to have both the pleasures of his sins and the assurance of salvation.

While Bobby wore a gold religious medal around his neck, it was inconceivable that Jack would do the same. The only time he seems to have given questions of faith much thought was during the war. After that, he observed the rituals of observance, which seemed enough. But one day in the late 1950s, he asked Chuck Spalding whether he considered himself religious. Spalding told him he found it impossible to know what was true and what was false about religion, so he had given up trying even to think about it.

"Me, too," said Jack.[5]

Nearly everyone around him advised him not to accept the Houston invitation, and his own gut reaction was to turn it down. Yet to refuse would only make him seem afraid of the issue, and then it really would have to be faced—again and again—and Catholicism would become the biggest issue in the election. He agreed to appear, and would offer what he was best at—a short statement followed by questions and answers.

Kennedy spoke for less than ten minutes. The strength of his performance was in the smoothness of his response to even the most pointed questions. The substance of his answers was that he would be surprised, and affronted, if his church attempted to pressure him to do anything that conflicted with the duties of his office. He did not intend to resign if there was a conflict—he would tell the church leadership to back off.[6]

The three hundred ministers had given him a cool reception when he arrived but had warmed up—moderately—by the time he finished. Beyond the ballroom of the Rice Hotel, though, were tens of millions who saw edited versions of this meeting on television. And there, in people's homes, his polished, confident answers drew the sting from the religious issue. Some of the poison remained, but not enough now to kill his hopes, and he knew it.

A few days before the appearance in Houston, Jack Kennedy had received a telegram from David Sarnoff, the president of NBC. The networks were legally obliged, under recent legislation, to offer free time to the candidates of the two major parties. What NBC proposed was a joint appearance in which Kennedy and Nixon responded to journalists' questions, then commented on each other's responses.

Kennedy asked Len Reinsch, the Democratic convention manager and an expert on television in politics, to come to Hyannis. Over clam chowder, he showed Reinsch the telegram. "What do you think?"

"Send an immediate and unqualified acceptance," said Reinsch, "on the basis that you would be glad to meet the Republican candidate at any time and any place."

Kennedy made a few phone calls and went back outside, where Reinsch was still eating clam chowder. "Now, what sort of program will we have?"

"I'm really not concerned about the program. All I want is a picture of you and Nixon on the same television tube."[7]

Four joint appearances were arranged, split among the three major networks. CBS would broadcast the first from Chicago on September 26; NBC would handle the second from Washington; and ABC would do the final two from New York and Los Angeles. These joint appearances were billed as "debates."

Kennedy arrived in Chicago twenty-four hours before the first debate and spent most of the time rehearsing in a suite at the Ambassador East. His Washington staff had spent more than a year collecting a huge file of material on Nixon. Dubbed "the Nixopedia," it was revised almost daily, and by this time it almost filled a footlocker.

Every statement Nixon had made, on almost any subject imaginable, was filed and cross-indexed. Kennedy stretched out on the bed to study dozens of three-by-five cards filled with data from the Nixopedia, or took his aching back into a hot bath, where he practiced his responses to some of the more likely questions.

After nearly a month of campaigning, he felt exhausted. Some days he was rising at six A.M., and some nights he was still campaigning at ten o'clock. Chuck Spalding had been similarly low on energy and started getting injections, supposedly based on vegetable compounds, from a Dr. Max Jacobson, who had a profitable practice on Park Avenue. Kennedy summoned Jacobson to Chicago, and the doctor injected him in the back-side with a potent combination of amphetamines, steroids and vitamins.[8]

Within minutes Kennedy felt a surge of energy and optimism. Not for nothing was Jacobson known as "Dr. Feelgood." Jack felt suddenly re-vived as if by a magical potion. There was a knock on the bedroom door. "Come in."

The door opened, and there stood Langdon Marvin, one of Jack's leg-islative assistants, and with Marvin was a pretty girl. Marvin introduced them to each other and left. Jack put a Peggy Lee record on the Dansette. By the time he confronted Nixon, he was going to feel both energetic and relaxed.[9]

Nixon considered himself a champion debater and expected to show up Kennedy as an out-of-his-depth upstart, with little apart from good looks and his father's fortune to prop up his candidacy. Nixon, however, had a self-destructive streak that came out in small ways as well as large ones. Obsessively attentive to some kinds of detail, he was overly complacent about others.

For this appearance he chose to wear the same light gray suit he had worn for his famous and ultimately successful "Checkers" speech. It was a terrible mistake. He looked washed-out and exhausted against the light-colored background on black-and-white television. Kennedy, in a dark blue suit and light blue shirt—on Reinsch's advice—seemed the more substantial figure.

Reinsch was in the control room, pestering the director and producer to show reaction shots. The program was nearly over before they finally relented, but it was worth the wait. The first reaction shot showed Nixon nervously rubbing a sweaty brow while he listened to Kennedy. The next showed a slightly amused Kennedy listening to Nixon.[10]

To those who watched this first debate, Kennedy was clearly the win-ner. But to those who only heard it, on radio, Nixon's resonant, deep bari-tone sounded more authoritative and convincing. In this split was a glimpse of the future. For at virtually the exact historic moment when image became half of politics, Jack Kennedy showed that he possessed the two essential traits of the movie star—emotional power and psycho-logical authority.

The effect of this, and the remaining debates, was to make Jack Ken-nedy revise his opinion of Nixon. Unlike most Democrats, he had never felt contempt for Nixon. They had been friendly in the House and during

Kennedy's years in the Senate. Jack had admired Nixon's political skills and envied his spectacular rise from freshman congressman to Vice President in just six years. Yet the debates had revealed something Jack had not noticed before. There was an irreparable flaw, a deep, self-pitying streak. "Anyone who can't beat Nixon doesn't deserve to be President," he told Ben Bradlee.[11]

=

The 1959 rehearsal for a national campaign, followed by the primaries, had taught Jack and Bobby how to create and command a national organization that remained close to the grass roots. They recruited able people and relied on them to produce good results instead of trying to tell them how to do it. The Kennedy representative—the advance man—had wide latitude when it came to organizing events and scheduling the candidate. Much thought went into drawing up travel plans that produced a large number of appearances for every hundred miles traveled. That, too, paid off. Kennedy was able to appear in forty-four out of the fifty states and hold rallies in 237 towns and cities in the ten weeks of the fall campaign.[12]

As he had done ever since 1946, Kennedy carried a variety of speech themes in his head instead of feeling compelled to write a new speech for every town and city he visited. Other presidential candidates had done it the other way and spent their time traveling from one place to another writing speeches. He didn't. That gave him time to meet local politicians, have a motorcade and hold rallies in half a dozen places each day.[13]

A speechwriting team was laboring for him, but to their despair, he ad-libbed most speeches, using what they had prepared as an introduction, nothing more. What he was looking for was the memorable phrase—better known now as the "sound bite"—rather than the grandiloquent exposition of uplifting thoughts.[14]

He had also developed his own public-speaking style—pinching right thumb and forefinger together and making a chopping motion, up and down, with his right hand. Nobody else did that.

John F. Kennedy was singular, too, in a completely fortuitous way: his name galloped off the tongue with dactylic energy. Like "Anna Karenina," it was instantly memorable thanks to its internal meter. No presidential hopeful since Franklin D. Roosevelt had been so lucky in his name.

For all the careful scheduling, Kennedy was nearly always late, showing up long past his advertised arrival at one stop after another. This was because he couldn't resist talking to people, one-on-one, while fretting aides buzzed around, ostentatiously looking at their watches. But meeting people was what he liked. Campaigning was what he didn't like—the dull photo ops, the set-piece speeches, the glad-handing with local worthies.

During the course of the campaign he appeared time and again striking faux casual poses for photographs with local politicians. The way he held himself, the way he gazed at the camera, were projections shaped to suggest a bonhomie that did not exist, while concealing a disdain that did.

He also revolutionized the motorcade. For twenty years the approved style had been for the candidate to stand up in the automobile and accept the acclaim of the people. Jack remained seated, the way royalty did. Over the years he had taught himself not only how to excite a crowd or wave from a passing automobile but how to make a glance feel like an embrace.

His restrained, detached reaction to enthusiastic crowds only cranked emotions even higher. The more self-contained he seemed, the more hysterical people became. Languor has its own mysterious power, but it took a confidence that few politicians possessed to trust it.

People were charmed, too, by Kennedy's jaunty wit. He often finished a campaign speech by quoting from Robert Frost:

> But I have promises to keep,
> And miles to go before I sleep,
> And miles to go before I sleep.

A hush fell over his audience at such moments, and then he'd puncture the tense emotional atmosphere he'd just created by adding casually, "And now I go on to Brooklyn [or wherever]," and there'd be a howl of sheer delight.

Confronted by a 142-pound watermelon, he recoiled in mock horror. "Is it still alive?" And when Senator Albert Gore took him to see his prize-winning bull, Kennedy stared at it for a moment, then asked Gore in a voice loud enough for the journalists to hear, "Has he been getting much . . . um . . . recognition lately?"[15]

There were, inevitably, big disparities between police figures of crowd sizes and those being put out Kennedy's press secretary, Pierre Salinger. Ben Bradlee asked Kennedy just how his campaign staff came up with the figures it did. "Plucky [Salinger's nickname] counts the nuns, then multiplies by a hundred."[16]

Towards the end of the campaign, Bill Lawrence, the political editor of

The New York Times, informed Jack that the paper was going to endorse him, the first Democrat it had explicitly backed since Roosevelt. Kennedy was elated, but when he read the editorial a few days later, he threw the newspaper aside in disgust. "Damn little praise in that!"[17]

=

One result of a presidential campaign is that whoever the next President turns out to be, by the time he is sworn in, he is carrying the whole country in his head. As Jack Kennedy traveled the length and breadth of the land that fall, he couldn't help thinking back to how it had been in Honey Fitz's day. Grampa had put together an unprecedented coalition of Irish, Italian, black and Jewish voters to get himself elected to Congress, then did it again to become mayor.

By 1960 that kind of broad ethnic-based politics seemed to have taken over everywhere. And Jack felt uncomfortable with it as it was transposed from a city to the entire country. The Balkanization of American politics meant that a presidential candidate had to craft a pitch for the Jews, a pitch for the blacks, a pitch for Hispanics, a pitch for Italian Americans, a pitch for Irish Americans, a pitch for women and so on. Race and ethnicity and religion were taking the spontaneity and fun out of politics. Yet success would go only to those presidential candidates who learned how to navigate through this new political geography.[18]

Jews were going to vote for him, as were Hispanics, if only because by now both had a tradition of voting Democratic. The black vote was more complicated. The South had voted Democratic since the Civil War, yet the 1957 Civil Rights Act had rent the party.

The immediate challenge for Jack, as a candidate who stressed his liberal credentials, was to hold on to the southern support that had nearly delivered the VP nomination to him in 1956. At the same time, he couldn't present himself as a liberal if he addressed segregated audiences when campaigning in the South. Kennedy's solution was to talk mainly to university groups. On the campuses where he spoke, there were always at least a few black faces in the crowd.

That sufficed until nearly the end of the campaign, when Georgia police arrested Dr. Martin Luther King, Jr. Some time earlier, the minister had been given probation for a minor traffic violation. He was now being charged with violating his probation, and a county judge sentenced him to four months on a road gang.

King's wife, Coretta—five months pregnant—was alarmed. A black

man as well known as her husband would be an easy target for fellow pris-
oners and brutal guards alike. The road gang might be a death sentence.

At the end of a busy day campaigning in Chicago, Kennedy wearily
retired to a room at the Airport Inn at O'Hare to rest for a couple of hours
before catching a flight. As he undressed for a nap, Sargent Shriver came
into the room and told him about Martin Luther King and Coretta Scott
King's fears. "Give her a call, Jack," urged Shriver.

Kennedy replied, "That would be the decent thing to do." When
Shriver got Coretta King on the line, he handed the telephone to Jack. He
told her he had heard about her husband's misfortunes and sympathized
with her distress. "If there's anything we can do, please let us know."[19]

Few newspapers covered this story, and it passed almost unnoticed on
television. Shriver, however, got three million flyers printed, and they
were distributed at black churches across the country the following Sunday. For all the calculation that Kennedy put into the campaign, this was
the one important moment when he acted entirely out of what he was as a
human being and not out of what he thought would serve him as a politician.[20]

In addressing other domestic issues, he had to invent a situation that
did not exist and promise to redress it. The country was stagnating, he
insisted, and he was going to "get America moving again."

The image that he and some of those around him, such as Arthur
Schlesinger, were creating to advance Jack's cause was of the 1950s as a
period of stifling conformity and immobility. But how cool or cultured
was it to be deaf and blind to the liberating force of rock 'n' roll; to fail to
honor the most influential writer of the time, Jack Kerouac, whose *On the
Road* changed countless lives; to ignore the greatest expansion in college
enrollments in the country's history, a steady increase in College Board
scores and the creation of modern teen culture. This was the time when
the United States began to dominate the Nobel prizes. In art, Jackson Pol-
lock and Abstract Expressionism swept the world. And it took a dull soul
not to thrill to the automobile designs of the 1950s.

There was also, despite two recessions, an increase in living standards
in real terms of 30 percent between 1952 and 1961, the beginning of
urban renewal in the cities, the spread of the new interstate highway system, and the arrival of television in most American homes. Eisenhower
had created the daring and reforming Warren Court and pushed through
the enactment of the first civil rights act since Reconstruction. And there

was the arrival in American life of four people who still hold a nation's imagination—James Dean, Elvis Presley, Marilyn Monroe and Jack Kennedy; sex, sex, sex . . . and sex again.

As in any healthy democracy, there were always people who were quick to spot the flaws and missed opportunities. The great majority, however, were content with the way the country was run and the direction in which it was going, as opinion polls clearly showed.[21]

Had Eisenhower been allowed to seek a third term, he would have buried Kennedy or any other Democratic challenger. Acutely conscious of that, Jack Kennedy was at pains throughout his campaign not to criticize Eisenhower and attacked instead "the government."

Struggling to make headway on claims that most people shrugged off as mere rhetoric, Jack became exasperated. The press seemed more interested in running pieces about the handsome Senator and the handsome Senator's glamorous wife than it did about the platform he was campaigning on. "Why doesn't anybody ever report what I think about the issues?" he complained to a sympathetic reporter, Laura Bergquist.[22]

He was especially annoyed that so little attention was paid to his views on national security. While there was something to his claim that American prestige abroad was being challenged, his assertions that American military power was about to be eclipsed by the Soviet Union were demonstrably wrong. Kennedy believed that it was American intermediate-range ballistic missiles (IRBMs) deployed in Western Europe that were the deterrent to a large and growing force of Soviet intercontinental ballistic missiles (ICBMs) capable of striking the United States.

He was impressed, too, when Nikita Khrushchev visited New York that fall of 1960 and boasted that the U.S.S.R. was producing long-range missiles "like sausages from an automatic machine." His son Sergei, a rocket engineer, was horrified. "We only have two or three," he reminded his father. It was the Big Lie technique, and Kennedy fell for it.[23]

In truth, the Soviets did not have a single operable ICBM targeted on the U.S., but they did have dozens of IRBMs targeted on Western Europe. Eisenhower sent Allen Dulles, the head of the CIA, to give him the true picture, but when Kennedy asked him, "Where do we stand in the missile race?," Dulles said that was for the Pentagon to answer, not the CIA.[24]

With Kennedy still refusing to relent on what an infuriated Eisenhower considered a cheap attempt to win votes through false charges, the President ordered the Joint Chiefs to brief him. General Earle Wheeler of the

Joint Planning Staff arrived at Kennedy's Senate office on a hot day in September 1960 with a Navy captain, two enlisted men, a slide projector and a pointer.

Wheeler was to reveal just what America's military strength was, and what was known about Soviet strategic forces. Kennedy seemed to sense that he was about to hear something he did not want to know. Instead of telling his secretary to hold his calls, Kennedy let the telephone on his desk ring incessantly as Wheeler struggled to catch and hold his attention.

Kennedy chose to talk to people all over the country about how the campaign was going rather than listen carefully to authoritative informa-tion on the "missile gap" that he claimed threatened the very existence of the United States. When Wheeler eventually managed to point out that the United States had dozens of operational ICBMs capable of striking the Soviet Union, while the United States was still out of the Soviets' reach, Kennedy ridiculed that idea. "General, don't you have any doubting Thomases in the Pentagon?" That was tantamount to saying the doubters were right and the Joint Chiefs were wrong. His mind was not only made up. It was firmly closed.[25]

Kennedy's proposed solution to the asserted and imaginary missile gap was simple: spend more money. Lots more money. Security could only be found, Kennedy insisted, in more nuclear warheads, more long-range missiles.[26]

At moments like this, his inexperience showed, but there was a lot more to him than the callow young politician his inflated campaign themes suggested. It was going to take two remarkable minds, not one, to get him elected President; two implacable wills, not one—his own and his father's. Yet ultimately he was driven less by Dad's dynastic ambitions than by a personal quest: to be his own man, to arrive at his own vision of the world and eventually to impose that vision *on* the world. This is the archetypal life struggle of the writer and philosopher, the poet and painter. It is not the life struggle of the junior Senator from a middling state.

For him, the best moment of the ten-week campaign came late at night on October 13, when he flew into Ann Arbor, arriving—typically—nearly four hours behind schedule. There were still several thousand University of Michigan students waiting to greet him, and he addressed them from the steps of the Student Union at eleven P.M.

On the flight to Ann Arbor, Jack had read a memo drafted two weeks earlier by an associate professor at the university, Samuel P. Hayes. The memo was entitled "A Proposal for an International Youth Service." Hubert Humphrey had recently proposed legislation for something similar, and the British already had an organization working in newly independent countries called Volunteers in Service Overseas.[27]

Hayes's idea matched seamlessly with the argument JFK had been making for nearly a decade now, that what the world needed more than American money was American know-how. So it came naturally to Jack to stand on the steps of the Student Union close to midnight and talk about how he wanted to send educated young people like the students gathered here to help poor countries develop their potential. As he talked, his youthful, idealistic audience went into raptures. Here was a captivating vision— a chance to do good while seeing the world.[28]

———

Determined to prove he was a strong—and winning—political figure in his own right, Richard Nixon tried to succeed in his quest without Eisenhower. By the last two weeks of the campaign, Nixon seemed doomed to defeat. His campaign was inept and his personality unattractive. In those last two weeks, he finally relented and asked for Eisenhower's help. With only a few public appearances late in the race, Eisenhower started turning the election around.

The evening of Sunday, November 6, with voting barely thirty-six hours away, Kennedy rode the *Caroline* into Logan Airport. Merriman Smith, one of the journalists aboard, asked him, "How do you feel about it right now?"

"I feel that I'm going to win," he replied. "But I don't feel as confident as I did. We've had some polls that show Nixon coming up, and it's going to be close as hell."

"How do you think you'll take it if you lose?"

Kennedy grinned broadly. "I won't take it as hard as Nixon will." There was more to his life than politics, he went on, with a wide range of interests to pursue. But Nixon had nothing else; a politician was all he was, ever wanted or could be.[29]

Recently, Jack had been giving more and more thought to what he would do if he won. It would mean goodbye to summer vacations on the Riviera with orgies on a rented yacht. And he would miss out on many a casual impromptu encounter. "No more poon!" he thought wistfully.[30]

The morning of November 8, Election Day, Jack and Jackie went to the polling station in the West End Branch Library in Boston, near the state-house. Jackie had already voted by absentee ballot. She was simply there, heavily pregnant, to support Jack.

That evening they had dinner with the Bradlees before going over to Bobby's house in the Kennedy compound to follow the election returns. Just before they sat down to eat, Jack called Mayor Richard Daley of Chicago. According to television reports, the result in Illinois was too close to call. "Mr. President," said Daley, "with a little bit of luck and the help of a few close friends, you are going to carry Illinois."[31]

At midnight, with most state results now in, the outcome of the 1960 election still hung in the balance. Jack was ready to go to the National Guard Armory in Hyannis as soon as Nixon conceded, but the hours dragged by. At three A.M., there was a television broadcast from Nixon's headquarters in Los Angeles. Nixon acknowledged that if present trends continued, Kennedy would win the election. But he pointedly made no concession. In his rambling self-pity, Nixon rebuked his supporters for interrupting while he tried to read his statement, and Pat Nixon seemed close to tears.[32]

Jack Kennedy stood up and said he was calling it a night. "This will probably not be decided until morning. I think I'll go over to the house and get some sleep."[33]

Wearily, head down and shoulders slumped, he walked across the grass to his own home. He woke Jackie and told her he still didn't know if he'd won. Kennedy ate a sandwich, drank a glass of milk, read for a while, then crawled into his narrow twin bed and fell asleep, eight Electoral College votes short of victory.[34]

CHAPTER 24

Learning Curve

A t half past eight there was a gentle knock on Jack's bedroom door. It was Caroline's English nanny, Maud Shaw. She opened the door and Caroline rushed in, jumped on the bed and pulled the blanket that half covered her father's head. He groaned, but reached out, hugged her and gave her a kiss.

"Good morning, Mr. President."

"Well, now. Is that right?" said Jack, suddenly awake. He glanced at Maud Shaw standing in the doorway. "Am I in, Miss Shaw?"

"Of course you are, Mr. President."[1]

Michigan had clinched it. Even now Nixon could not bring himself to concede. His press secretary, Herb Klein, appeared on television at nine A.M. on the East Coast and acknowledged that with nearly all the returns in, Kennedy had won the election.

An hour later Jack Kennedy arrived at the Hyannis National Guard Armory looking physically drained and sounding emotionally flat. His eyes glistened with tiredness and tears that he willed not to fall. It was an anticlimactic finish to the closest presidential election of the twentieth century. He had won only a plurality, not a majority, of the popular vote.

His victory rested on 118,000 votes out of 68.5 million cast. In the Electoral College he was a clear winner, but there, too, victory was a story of razor-thin margins in nearly every state that he'd carried.[2]

Jack read out a telegram he had received from Nixon, and the telegram he had sent in reply. Jackie, eight months pregnant and in a purple coat, stood beside him, looking eager to leave from the moment they arrived. After answering a few questions, Jack managed a faint smile. "Now my wife and I prepare for a new administration and a new baby."

He was going to take office without a clear political mandate, which would make pushing his own program through Congress hard. Kennedy was touchy about the narrowness of his victory. "A margin of only one vote would still be a mandate," he insisted. Yet the lack of popular endorsement was reflected in the voting for Congress that November. The Democrats still controlled both the House and the Senate, but for the first time in living memory, an incoming President's party had lost strength on Capitol Hill rather than adding to it during the election. Instead of Democratic congressmen clinging to his coattails, across the country he had been clinging to theirs. They owed him nothing while he owed them his presidency.[3]

Right now, though, what really upset Jack Kennedy was finishing in a virtual dead heat with someone like Nixon. The voters didn't seem to have noticed or cared that he was far superior to his deeply flawed rival. That hurt.[4]

Returning to Bobby's house at the Kennedy compound after appearing at the Armory, JFK made his first appointment of the New Frontier. Calling J. Edgar Hoover, he flattered the old fraud shamelessly, assuring him that he wanted him to stay on as director of the FBI. Jack's friend Ben Bradlee, overhearing him on the telephone, was astounded. But as Kennedy later admitted to Timothy Seldes, an editor at Doubleday, he had to keep Hoover happy. The director still controlled the Inga Binga tapes.[5]

For the next three weeks he did little but recuperate at his father's home in Palm Beach. Then, at the end of November, he returned to Washington and went to meet with Nixon. His friend John Sharon asked him, "What are you going to see Nixon for?" Jack grinned. "Well, there are just some things we Democrats have to do." In truth, he was being both gracious and politic. Thirty-four million people had voted for Nixon. If he wanted to be President of the entire country, it was a good idea to make a gesture in their direction.[6]

On December 6 he saw Eisenhower. It was their first meeting since Jack had visited Ike at SHAPE (Supreme Headquarters Allied Powers Europe) in Paris in 1951. Not once during Jack's time in the Senate had he been invited to the White House. He was too small a player on Capitol Hill for the President to court.

At this meeting, the two of them spent an hour together in the Oval Office, talking about how a President does his job. Ike told him, "No easy matters will ever come to you as President. If they are easy, they will be settled at a lower level."

The most pressing problem was a ballooning balance of payments deficit and an unsustainable outflow of dollars. The dollar's travails reflected the postwar economic recovery in Western Europe, and to Eisenhower that meant it was time to start bringing the troops home. "America is carrying far more than her share of free-world defense."[7]

As Kennedy settled down to finding people for the top slots in the new administration, he faced challenges unlike any he had encountered before. So far he had relied on and drawn his strength from a small and utterly dedicated staff and a circle of old and trusted friends. When things were going badly, he was likely to cheer them up by telling them, "You were with me on St. Crispin's Day." Then, to drive home just how much that meant to him, he'd recite the rousing oration on the eve of the Battle of Agincourt from Shakespeare's *Henry V*:

> This day is called the feast of Crispian: . . .
> And Crispin Crispian's shall ne'er go by,
> From this day to the ending of the world,
> But we in it shall be rememberèd;
> We few, we happy few, we band of brothers;
> For he today that sheds his blood with me
> Shall be my brother. . . . [8]

Now, though, he would have to trust his hopes to more than the happy and dedicated few. He knew the presidency was going to be tough. All his experience—and that of the people around him—was in the legislature. The executive branch was unknown territory for him and for them.[9]

Just how tough became evident in trying to create a Cabinet. "You know, I always thought it would be kind of fun to pick the people that were going to be part of the administration," he told Mike Feldman, one of his legislative assistants. "But after sitting through these discussions, it strikes me that this is one of the most difficult parts of the presidency, and it carries with it the least pleasure."[10]

His first choice for Secretary of State was Senator J. William Fulbright of Arkansas. But Fulbright, for all his urbane demeanor, his Rhodes scholarship and pretensions to high-mindedness, never failed to solicit the racist vote. He attached his name and prestige to "The Southern Manifesto," a repellent screed that rallied southern resistance to the Supreme Court's 1954 decision striking down segregation in the public schools. Bobby pointed out that making Fulbright Secretary of State would be a gift to Soviet propagandists and was sure to outrage the leaders of developing countries across the world. Jack dropped the idea reluctantly. "It would be nice to have somebody in the Cabinet who I actually know," he said wistfully.[11]

Walter Lippmann, one of the country's most influential political commentators, urged Kennedy to make McGeorge Bundy, a forceful, highly intelligent dean and history lecturer at Harvard, his Secretary of State. Kennedy was intrigued, telling Ted Sorensen, "a forty-one-year-old Secretary of State might be a good idea." But in the end, Bundy was ruled out. He was not only too young, he was also a Republican. Kennedy was willing to have Republicans in the Cabinet, but not holding down most of the top posts. Bundy became Kennedy's National Security Adviser, which put him closer to the President than most Cabinet members.[12]

Several people suggested Dean Rusk, president of the Rockefeller Foundation. A Rhodes Scholar, a southerner but an integrationist, Rusk had served in the Army in Burma in World War II, been an Assistant Secretary of State during the Korean War and was an authority on the Far East. In early December, Kennedy, who had never met Rusk, called him and said he was looking for someone to take over the State Department. "Aren't you going to offer it to Adlai Stevenson?" asked Rusk.

"No. Adlai might forget who's the President and who's the Secretary of State," said Kennedy sardonically.[13]

When they met for the first time, on December 8, Kennedy found it hard to draw Rusk out. Rusk's diffidence in the presence of someone as glamorous as Kennedy betrayed his origins as a poor boy from Georgia, killing conversation. After an awkward half hour, Rusk left, convinced he would not get the job. Next day, however, Kennedy asked him to come over and told him State was his.

Kennedy had already told Stevenson that he would not be Secretary of

State but asked him to be ambassador to the UN. Kennedy had made it sound like the most important job in the government, bar the presidency. Upset at not being offered State, Stevenson said he would have to think about it. Kennedy was disgusted but not surprised. It only seemed to prove once again just how weak and vacillating Stevenson was.

Stevenson came to see Kennedy the afternoon of December 8 to tell him he would take the UN post, on condition that he did not have to report to Bundy or Rusk. Kennedy reassured him, "I'll be your boss. You can have a direct line to me."[14]

Kennedy's first choice for Treasury was Robert Lovett, someone highly respected on Wall Street, a Republican and a former Assistant Secretary of War. But Lovett said his health was not up to it. He was expecting to have a major operation soon. He suggested several people Kennedy might wish to consider for Treasury, including Robert S. McNamara, the new president of the Ford Motor Company.

While McNamara's name was being batted around, Kennedy also read a laudatory article about him in *Time*. McNamara was a statistical wizard and an intellectual and something of an athlete; a man who relaxed by mountain climbing and skiing. A millionaire businessman, he lived in Ann Arbor as if he were a professor and was content to drive himself to work in a small, inexpensive automobile instead of being chauffeured in a shiny new Lincoln.[15]

On December 8, shortly after his first meeting with Rusk, Kennedy had his first meeting with McNamara in the house on N Street in Georgetown. McNamara, a man who read widely, bluntly asked, "Did you really write *Profiles in Courage* yourself?"

Kennedy said he really had, and would McNamara be interested in being Secretary of the Treasury or Secretary of Defense? After thinking it over for a week, McNamara said he preferred Defense, but there was a condition—he would choose his own subordinates. "It's a deal," said Kennedy.[16]

The next day *The Washington Post* said he was going to make McNamara Secretary of Defense. "How did they get that story?" Kennedy fumed. He had not made any announcement yet. Then he realized who the leaker was—himself. He had played golf with Philip Graham, the publisher of the *Post,* two days earlier and talked so enthusiastically about McNamara that it wasn't too hard for Graham to figure out what would probably happen next.[17]

While trying to find the right people for State and Defense, Kennedy was also looking for someone for the Treasury Department. Almost the only connection he had with big business was his father, and Joe Kennedy had always been a lone wolf. Besides, JFK had something of the intellectual's disdain for businessmen. He remarked to Tristram Coffin that he did not understand why Eisenhower had so many businessmen around him. "I don't see how he stands those people. Business tycoons are awful bores most of the time. They can't talk about anything but money."[18]

But no President could hope to avoid economics, even if he managed to evade tycoons. Kennedy had tried to prepare himself by getting some intensive, if not remedial, instruction from three eminent Harvard economists: John Kenneth Galbraith, Seymour Harris and Paul Samuelson. Yet how much ground he still had to cover was revealed when the Organization for Economic and Cultural Development (the think tank for the world's richest countries) was established in the fall of 1960. Jack confessed to a friend that he hadn't a clue what the OECD was or what it was supposed to do.[19]

"We need a Secretary of the Treasury who can call a few of those Wall Street people by their first names," he mused aloud one day. The person his talent spotters suggested was C. Douglas Dillon, former chairman of the major brokerage house Dillon, Reed, currently serving as Eisenhower's Under Secretary of State.

The fact that Dillon was a prominent Republican was less a problem than a recommendation. Eisenhower's first Cabinet had included a Democrat as Secretary of Labor to reassure ordinary working stiffs that Ike had their interests at heart. Appointing Dillon as Secretary of the Treasury would reassure the bond markets that Kennedy wasn't another reckless tax-and-spend Democrat.

To win Dillon over, Kennedy made a personal pledge. "You will be my chief financial adviser." Thereby reassured that academic economists were not going to dictate government policy, Dillon accepted Kennedy's offer, but only after securing Ike's (grudging) blessing.[20]

The fourth big appointment was Attorney General, but that one seemed the easiest of all. One of the few close friends Jack had in the Senate was Abraham Ribicoff of Connecticut. Jackie regularly made lunch for three and took it to Jack's office, where Ribicoff would join them. "If Abe weren't a Jew," she used to tease Jack, "he'd be running for President, not you."[21]

In early December, Jack told his legislative drafting expert, Langdon Marvin, "Ribicoff can have anything he wants." Shortly after this, Ribicoff came into Jack's Senate office to tell him directly, "I'd like to be Attorney General." Jack said the appointment was his, and they shook hands on it. Then he flew down to Palm Beach, and at breakfast the next morning, as he and his father sat by the pool talking about appointing various people to various jobs, Jack mentioned Ribicoff.[22]

His father reacted fiercely. "Bobby's going to be Attorney General. He's given you his life, his blood, everything. He wants to be Attorney General, and I don't want you to have one thought other than that." The old man would not be dissuaded.[23]

Ribicoff was bitterly disappointed but gamely played along by telling everyone he had not wanted to be Attorney General, that his heart was set on becoming Secretary of Health, Education and Welfare, something that Jack was happy to give him. But HEW would not get Ribicoff onto the Supreme Court, which was his life's ambition, whereas being Attorney General probably would.[24]

Ben Bradlee was astonished when Jack returned to Washington and told him Bobby was going to be the Attorney General. Just announcing that would be problematical, said Bradlee. Kennedy smiled. "I think I'll open the front door of the Georgetown house some morning about two A.M., look up and down the street, and if there's no one there, I'll whisper, 'It's Bobby.' "[25]

Over Christmas and the New Year, Jack worked on his inaugural address at poolside in Palm Beach. He spent hours clacking away at a portable manual typewriter on a small table covered with notes. Jackie and Caroline kept to themselves indoors, while in an upstairs bedroom a nursemaid hovered over the Kennedys' new baby, John F. Kennedy, Jr., born three weeks after his father's election.

On January 19, 1961, with the inauguration only two days away, Kennedy, McNamara, Rusk and Clark Clifford met with Eisenhower and his Cabinet. First, though, the two men spent forty-five minutes alone in the Oval Office, during which Ike showed Jack a black vinyl satchel. Inside were a small telephone, a loose-leaf binder filled with thirty pages of nuclear options, codes to activate each, and what was, in effect, the first laptop computer.

Inserting a laminated presidential identification card activated the laptop. Once the card had been recognized, the President could use the attached phone to transmit the code. Within minutes he could launch anything from a limited nuclear strike to an all-out attack that would destroy more than a thousand targets in the Soviet Union. For Kennedy, as for anyone, it would have been a sobering experience to have placed in his hands—literally and physically—the instruments of Armageddon.

"I'd like to show you something else that goes with the Office of the President," said Eisenhower. He picked up a telephone and said, "Opal Drill Three." Five minutes later a Marine Corps helicopter landed on the lawn. That brought a smile to Kennedy's face and lifted the mood.

Then Ike took Kennedy into the Cabinet Room for the rest of the meeting, telling the men who were waiting there, "I've just showed my friend here how to get out in a hurry."[26]

The agenda had been set mainly by Kennedy, who had sent over a list several weeks earlier of the topics he wanted to discuss—world trouble spots such as Berlin and Cuba; how the NSC worked; how the White House was organized; and what Eisenhower thought of the three principal Allied leaders, Harold Macmillan, Charles de Gaulle and Konrad Adenauer.

The most urgent trouble spot was Laos, said Eisenhower. If it fell to the present Communist insurgency, it would be only a matter of time before Thailand, Cambodia, Burma and South Vietnam were taken over by Communist regimes. "Unilateral intervention would be our last desperate hope. This is one of the problems I'm leaving you that I'm not happy about. We may have to fight."

When they got around to Cuba, Kennedy asked, "Should we support guerrilla operations in Cuba?"

"To the utmost," Eisenhower replied. "We cannot let the present government there go on."

As the meeting broke up, there was one other thing Eisenhower wanted to impress on Kennedy: there was no missile gap, and there wasn't going to be one for years, if ever. The United States held the ultimate card in the strategic arms race—"You have an invaluable asset in Polaris. It is invulnerable."[27]

Jack returned to the small, lopsided house on N Street and worked on his inaugural address some more, rewriting drafts on a couch in the living room, or simply thinking about it while lying in his twin bed under a large triangular Harvard banner thumbtacked to a wall. He wanted to craft an eloquent, Churchillian call to make sacrifices in defense of liberty; a speech that would be memorable and short.[28]

CHAPTER 25

Fire and Ice

I t is seven o'clock on the morning of Friday, January 20, 1961, as John F. Kennedy awakes after only a few hours' sleep in his bedroom at the house on N Street. This is the day of his inauguration as thirty-fifth President of the United States.

In the wan light of a winter's dawn, the streets of the city are populated with the bent and busy figures of thousands of National Guardsmen in field jackets, heavy boots and thick gloves. Seven inches of snow have fallen over the past twenty-four hours and there are hundreds of abandoned automobiles on Pennsylvania, Constitution and Independence avenues, thoroughfares that must be opened before today's ceremonies can begin.

The Guardsmen are shoveling furiously and pushing the cars up and onto the sidewalks. At the East Front of the Capitol, where the inaugural stand has been erected, combat engineers with flamethrowers are blasting away the ice with blistering bursts of orange flame.[1]

Before he dresses, his personal physician, Janet Travell, gives him a shot of Dexedrine to carry him through the physical and emotional rigors of the day. A little before eight o'clock, Jack Kennedy's driver, Muggsy O'Leary, drops him off at Georgetown University's Holy Trinity Church.

A special Mass is being held to ask God's blessing on the new administration. Rose Kennedy is already there, but her son, entering the church alone, walks past his mother without even acknowledging her presence. She stares poker-faced at his back.[2]

Part of the burden of the presidency, Jack protests to friends, will be "Mass every Sunday for four years." As a senator, he could go to church as the spirit moved him. Not anymore.[3]

After church he returns home and has breakfast while Jackie gets dressed. At 10:45 Muggsy drives them to the White House, where they go inside to take coffee in the Red Room with Ike and Mamie and a handful of senior officials from the incoming and outgoing administrations.

At noon Kennedy and Eisenhower step onto the portico facing Lafayette Square, then climb into the 1950 Lincoln Cosmopolitan parade car. Descended from John Kennedy's first automobile—the 1937 Ford sedan convertible in which he and Lem Billings drove around Europe—this Lincoln is an anachronism. It can be used either as a convertible or as a sedan, but the Secret Service men hate it—three tons, fat whitewall tires, no power steering. One of Kennedy's first actions as President will be to order a new Lincoln, custom-built, modern and easy to drive.[4]

For his inaugurations, Eisenhower opted for homburgs and business suits instead of the more traditional top hats and morning coats, which he considered old-fashioned. Kennedy, however, is so eager to symbolize how much he rejects the Eisenhower style of government that he has reverted to toppers and morning coats.

Eisenhower is feeling depressed at having to give up the White House. A life of power and excitement yields to boredom and impotence. He is convinced that, despite his charm, Kennedy is too callow, too flashy to make a good President. And he deeply resents Kennedy's asserted "missile gap." This is close to saying that, instead of defending his country, Eisenhower has neglected the first duty of any President, assuring the survival of the United States. That rankles.

Not surprisingly, then, small talk between them is difficult as they ride up Pennsylvania Avenue to the Capitol, with Jackie and Mamie following directly behind in a Cadillac Fleetwood limousine. Kennedy asks Ike if he has read *The Longest Day*, Cornelius Ryan's recent bestselling account of D-Day. Eisenhower says he hasn't.

Kennedy will later tell Bobby this shows that Ike shuns serious books —"Doesn't do his homework" is how he describes it. What Eisenhower doesn't tell him, probably because it might seem immodest, is that he spent hours explaining the D-Day operation to Ryan and left out much that was secret.[5]

The Lincoln deposits them at the East Front. While Ike and Mamie go out onto the inaugural stand, Jack and Jackie are ushered into a small room and left alone for fifteen minutes. Do they pray together? Do they embrace? We will probably never know. One thing is certain: Jack Kennedy will arrive for his inauguration in his usual style—late.

Jackie had asked JFK to get Marian Anderson to sing "The Star-Spangled Banner" at the inauguration, a suggestion he had readily accepted. But when Stewart Udall, his incoming Secretary of the Interior, said he ought to get Robert Frost to read a poem, he had balked. "Oh, no," said Kennedy. "You know that Robert Frost always steals any show that he is part of." But Udall had persisted and gotten his way because, of every poet alive, there was none that Kennedy admired more than Frost.[6]

Following Marian Anderson's rendition of the national anthem, Cardinal Cushing delivers a typical Cushing invocation—turgid, meandering, oozing self-importance, tripping over the moment rather than rising to its height. And then, as if in answer to the silent prayer of millions, blue smoke begins curling from under the rostrum into the 20-degree air. His Eminence concludes hurriedly and the Secret Service closes in.

So does Kennedy's television adviser and convention impresario, J. Leonard Reinsch. The problem has to be an electrical short, he assures Jim Rowley, head of the White House Secret Service detail. Bending low, Reinsch peers through the hazy smoke and sees eight plugs inside the rostrum—one for the P.A. system, one for the lighting and so on. Taking a chance, he reaches in and pulls out a plug. The smoking stops. Reinsch has beaten the odds.

Eisenhower, who has been looking bored until now, finds this interruption amusing and turns to Kennedy. "You must have a hot speech."

Fidgeting nervously with his papers, Kennedy asks Reinsch, "Is it all right now?"

"Yes, sir."

"Then let's get going."[7]

The Chief Rabbi delivers a brief benediction, then it is Robert Frost's turn. The eighty-six-year-old poet has composed an ode for the occasion. Called "For John F. Kennedy His Inauguration," it consists of 350 years of American history crammed into seventy-six lines of Hallmark-style doggerel. The wind is wildly agitating the pages he holds in his shriveled hands, and the sun, reflected dazzlingly off the dome of the Capitol and the snow-covered roofs all around, is blinding.

Frost cannot read his poem and is having trouble just holding on to it. He saves himself from public humiliation by reciting from memory a poem that Kennedy, too, knows by heart—"The Gift Outright"—a poem more fitting than he could ever guess.

It is almost one o'clock. Chief Justice Earl Warren will swear in John Kennedy. Rising to his feet, the President-elect removes his overcoat and runs a hand over his chestnut hair, gestures that emphasize his youth to those millions watching on television and however many countless millions more who will watch, down the years, the film of this moment.

Beads of sweat cover his forehead—one result of the shot of Dexedrine, plus cortisone. As Kennedy takes off his coat, Eisenhower's doctor, Major General Howard Snyder, remarks to Admiral Arthur Radford, "He's all hopped up."[8]

At forty-three, he is the youngest man ever elected President, and on the screen, he looks it. In truth, Kennedy moves slightly stiffly, even on a good day. There are a few hints of gray in his hair, and when he dresses in a T-shirt and shorts to play touch football, white chest hairs poke impertinently into view just below his Adam's apple. His upper lip is serrated with numerous deep, vertical lines, the kind usually seen only in the old; a legacy, in his case, of lips pursed over years against pain and discomfort. The once sharp gray-green color of his eyes is turning opaque. Close up, he is youth and age at the same time.[9]

Yet as he moves towards the charred rostrum, clutching his speech, he becomes promise. Warren prepares to take him through the presidential oath and Kennedy places his right hand on the Fitzgerald family Bible—the Douai version that Grampa used to be sworn in as mayor of Boston and, before that, as a member of Congress. Jackie stands nearby, between Mamie and Lady Bird Johnson, entranced.

The sixteen-hundred-word rallying cry John Kennedy is about to deliver has been more than twenty years in the making. Its roots run deep into *Why England Slept*. Throughout his congressional career, he reprised its refrains—tyranny threatens, sacrifices are needed, appeasement is foolish, this is our hour. Churchillian rhetoric and Churchillian defiance shape Kennedy's response to the world.

He has prepared himself for this, in mind and imagination, since college. Ted Sorensen has crafted many of the words, but the tone—that is pure Kennedy. It is a tone that has been raised to a new pitch by a fresh apprehension. He does not expect to leave the White House alive.[10]

For years John Kennedy has talked of dying young and violently, probably in a car crash, while yearning for a more poetic, more heroic, death in war. Since his election, that premonition of an early death has taken a new form—a crowd . . . a man with a rifle . . . someone prepared to give life for life.

He had gone to the LBJ ranch shortly after the election and Johnson had, to his embarrassment, organized a deer hunt. Rather than show weakness, Kennedy killed a deer, but it was a depressing and distressing experience to look through a sniperscope at a beautiful and helpless creature and will himself to kill.[11]

When his friend and nominee as ambassador to Ireland, Grant Stockdale, came to see him in Palm Beach shortly before the inauguration, he found Kennedy in a somber mood, a rifle in his hands. "Stock, do you think I'll be assassinated?" It is a question he puts to various friends these days, a question that won't go away.[12]

He is what he has always been—stoic and fatalistic in the presence of danger—but when Kennedy looks out on a crowd now, he wonders if that man is there. A new sense of foreboding will lend urgency and immediacy to the speech he delivers this day. Time is short; there is danger at hand; we must act; we must not be afraid.

Standing in the sunshine, hatless and coatless, he gives a performance not even he could have foreseen. Although the temperature is 12 degrees below freezing, the wind chill makes it feel close to 0. The body has its own imperatives, and Kennedy's responds to the cold, to the cortisone, to the amphetamines and to the occasion by improvising a chopping motion with the left hand, the fingers pinched together, as he emphasizes each point—"The torch has been passed . . . tempered by war, disciplined by a hard and bitter peace. . . . Let us never negotiate out of fear, but let us never fear to negotiate. . . . Ask not what your country can do for you but ask what you can do for your country. . . . Bear any burden, pay any price. . . ."

As he turns away from the rostrum, Jackie takes a step towards him and touches him on the cheek. "Oh, Jack, you were wonderful. What a day!"[13]

When Eisenhower was sworn in as President, he had kissed Mamie, a gesture that millions of people found touching and somehow right. But Jack's response to Jackie is to turn away. And he ignores Rose again, even though she has come over to stand beside him. He shakes his father's hand and hugs his brothers. Becoming President is a male celebration, not a family affair.

Lunch is taken in the old Supreme Court chamber, now a part of the Senate. The new President and First Lady sit down, glowing, with Harry and Bess Truman and the congressional leadership. But before Kennedy can sit down, his assistant Fred Dutton gives him some papers to sign— the nominations of Cabinet members awaiting Senate confirmation. This is really how the presidency begins—prosaically, disposing of routine paperwork.[14]

After lunch, as the parade car pulls away from the Capitol to take Kennedy back to the White House for the inaugural parade, another convertible sets off ahead of them. In it he can see Walter Cronkite talking into a microphone and glancing back at the Lincoln. Kennedy and Cronkite disagreed heatedly during the election, over a television interview in which Kennedy performed miserably. He had insisted on doing the interview again, and Cronkite had refused. Now, though, all that is forgotten. Kennedy tips his silk hat to Cronkite, while Jackie gives him a dazzling smile and a friendly wave. It is spontaneous, charming, irresistible.[15]

The Lincoln moves slowly down Pennsylvania Avenue towards the White House and the reviewing stand. When the Lincoln reaches the stand, Kennedy notices his father already seated there, stands up, bows slightly and sweeps off his silk topper in an expansive gesture of esteem. Joe responds by rising and bows even lower, tipping his hat in return. It is almost a Japanese moment, one that marks a relationship suddenly and forever reversed.

The parade drags on until dusk—forty bands, thirty thousand marchers and almost a million cheering spectators, nearly all of them shivering. Jackie, soon bored and feeling the cold, leaves the stand and disappears into the White House. The display that pleases Kennedy most is a large replica of his old command, *PT-109,* and seated in the reviewing stand are some of his wartime comrades from the South Pacific.

He takes a close interest in all the military displays and is irritated as the Coast Guard contingent marches past. There is not a single black face to be seen. He tells one of his assistants, Dick Goodwin, to call the

Coast Guard commandant and tell him that the next time his men parade in front of the President, it will be with a contingent that resembles America.[16]

A little before five o'clock, the last of the marchers stride past and Kennedy goes into the White House for a family reception. Jackie remains upstairs, taking a nap. Downstairs, Bouviers and Kennedys mingle uneasily, parvenu egos clashing like cymbals.

Kennedy, too, takes a nap. When he rises, he gets dressed for the evening while Jackie gets her own shot of Dexedrine from Janet Travell. He and Jackie then go for a light dinner with some old friends in Georgetown, George and Jane Wheeler, and return to the White House, where Jackie gets into her white and silver ballgown glittering with diamanté. Kennedy approves. "You've never looked lovelier," he tells her.[17]

Eisenhower broke precedent by having two inaugural balls instead of one. Kennedy will easily beat Ike's record, with five. The first is at the Mayflower Hotel; the second is at the Statler Hilton, where Frank Sinatra—who has attached himself, leechlike, to the Kennedys—is holding a party. Kennedy slips away to visit with his Rat Pack pals.

The biggest affair of the night is the third stop, at the Armory. When Jack and Jackie enter the presidential box a thousand guests, the cream of Washington's political and social elite, applaud ecstatically for twenty minutes. The glamorous Kennedys of Georgetown and Capitol Hill are their own.

By now the effects of the Dexedrine are wearing off, and Jackie is fading. Besides, even at the balls, her husband has ignored her, leaving her to sit in the presidential box in order to mingle with his friends from the two worlds he has brought together forever, Hollywood and politics. Jackie tells him, "You go on, Jack." She is going to bed.[18]

A little after one in the morning, Kennedy leaves the fifth and final ball of the evening, but back at the White House, he is too elated to sleep. He tells his driver to take him to Joe Alsop's house—a few blocks from his own Georgetown residence—where he knows there is a party tonight. He decides to join it. Alsop, distantly related to Franklin Roosevelt, an ardent Cold Warrior and busy homosexual whose camouflage is a *mariage blanc,* is someone whose company and malicious gossip Kennedy has always enjoyed.

Alsop is astonished and thrilled to find the new President on his doorstep at two in the morning and invites him in for an improvised supper. A kind of turtle soup is concocted from frozen terrapin, a pound of butter and a bottle of sherry.[19]

Departing at three in the morning, Kennedy notices in the knot of people gathered on the steps to wish him farewell a beautiful woman in tears—a former lover, weeping at the thought that their fleeting sexual encounters will be no more. Half an hour later, President John F. Kennedy climbs into Abraham Lincoln's huge Victorian bed, alone.[20]

CHAPTER 26

Standard Operating Procedure

I t was all going to be different now, beginning with the Oval Office. Under Eisenhower it had been painted a shade that soldiers called "easy-eye green," which adorned Army barracks and headquarters around the world. The Navy preferred tasteful shades of white. One of Kennedy's first actions as President was to have the Oval Office painted ivory.

He also changed the look and feel of the place by installing a couple of red sofas with a coffee table between them. There was a desk in the basement that had been given to Rutherford B. Hayes in 1880 by Queen Victoria. It was historic, nautical and an objet d'art. Made from the timbers of Britain's last wooden frigate, HMS *Resolute,* the desk was used by every President from Hayes to Truman. Once the desk had been retrieved, it was graced with the piece of coconut shell—preserved in clear plastic—on which the young Jack Kennedy had carved the message that brought the rescue of his *PT-109* crew. His own history absorbed its.

In the furiously busy ten weeks between election and inauguration, he began to sense how burdensome his inexperience might be. In the excitement of the long pursuit, he had pushed such thoughts aside. Besides, a lack of experience can be a liberating force, provided it is served by common sense and uncommon intelligence. But now he found himself turning for advice to people such as Truman's Secretary of State, Dean Acheson. Kennedy had berated him unmercifully in the early 1950s and had called for Acheson's resignation, blaming him for the supposed "loss" of China and holding him largely responsible for the Korean War.

As President-elect, however, JFK found himself seeking Acheson's counsel and frankly confessed to him, "One of my troubles is that I've spent so much time knowing people who could help me become President that I now find I know very few people who can help me *be* President."[1]

He brought his Senate staff with him to the White House. The most important by far was Ted Sorensen, whom he called "my intellectual blood bank." There was also his secretary, the bright-eyed, birdlike and homely Evelyn Lincoln. There was a place in the White House, too, for a court jester, Dave Powers. And a onetime Harvard football captain who had proved a tireless and effective campaign worker, Kenneth O'Donnell, became the appointments secretary.

The new White House staff wasn't simply confident as it moved into 1600 Pennsylvania Avenue—it was exultant. "We felt that our team was the best in history," said Myer Feldman, one of Kennedy's principal assistants. Such self-regarding cockiness disturbed old hands like Clark Clifford. For any new administration, the past has lessons worth heeding, and the executive branch has ways of doing things that are worth discovering. For now, though, that didn't seem to matter.[2]

One of the first things to be junked was an Eisenhower innovation, the White House chief of staff. No one really managed the staff under Kennedy. He relied instead on the FDR model: a staff comprising a handful of people—such as Sorensen and O'Donnell and Feldman—whom he'd known for years and were ready to do whatever he wanted them to do, unconstrained by job titles. That had worked well enough for Roosevelt in the 1930s, but the federal government now had nearly three times as many employees, spent about five times as much money and was indescribably more complex in its responsibilities.

Throughout the executive branch, the relationship of people to the President was no longer going to be hierarchical. JFK made it almost entirely personal and direct. If he wanted somebody to do something, he sent for them and told them to do it, and they reported back to him. It was almost like something out of the nineteenth century. But by the 1960s the responsibilities of government departments and agencies tended to overlap. Who was going to ensure coordination between competing federal fiefdoms? Under the new arrangement, the answer appeared to be no one.

The Solicitor General, Archibald Cox, was only one of Kennedy's appointees who feared the new White House regime would permit the executive branch to drift along, rudderless, until it crashed into something. But when he told the President that the government needed a clearer definition of responsibilities, Kennedy shrugged it off. "There is no clearer definition."[3]

During the transition, Jack had established a variety of task forces, all of which reported directly to him. They dealt with domestic problems such as civil rights, and international affairs such as Latin American policy. Following the inauguration, many of the people assigned to these task forces segued into the administration as the President's major advisers on whatever subject their task force had tackled. JFK was creating, in effect, a small, parallel structure that would operate outside—and in some ways above—the federal bureaucracy, much as he'd created his own campaign organization, one that operated alongside and above the Democratic party in all of his political campaigns.

The philosophical underpinning of Kennedy's approach was much like the British one, which was based on responding to events rather than trying to anticipate them; putting clever people in charge and allowing them to improvise solutions; and trusting to a few first-rate generalists instead of recruiting a large number of second-rate specialists. "You can't beat brains," Kennedy was inclined to say, putting intelligence above experience or established procedure.[4]

The White House staff naturally felt encouraged to scorn anything that looked like red tape, zealously uprooting it at every opportunity. However commendable their enthusiasm, what looked like red tape to them was often the standard operating procedure by which the federal bureaucracy got things done—including things that Kennedy wanted to accomplish.

Yet no one was more willing than he to ignore chains of command (except where the military was involved) and standard operating procedures. In January 1961 there was widespread famine in China, the result of Mao's insane Great Leap Forward. Was there anything the U.S. could do to relieve such suffering? he wondered. He scribbled a note to one of his assistants, Ralph Dungan: "Ask Chet [Under Secretary of State Chester Bowles] and Bob Amory what they think of this." Amory was a high-ranking official at the CIA, and CIA director Allen Dulles was shocked when Amory showed him the note. "This is a policy question. We can't get into this," protested Dulles. "We're intelligence people."

Amory replied, "Goddamn it, Allen—it's a new President. He's going to do things differently [and] our first response can't be a bureaucratic 'No, somebody else.'"

Nothing came of Kennedy's impulse to help the Chinese; the cost he'd have to pay in Congress was simply too high. But incidents like this shocked and alienated senior officials in the executive branch.[5]

It wasn't long before JFK discovered just how great was their power to thwart him. "You know, I give an order around here and that order hits the outer desk," he told Red Fay one day, "and it just dies. Everybody thinks that I am the commander in chief, but there must be fifty guys outside that are really running the show." It did not seem to occur to him that his own way of doing things might be making the life of the obstructionists easier.[6]

At times Kennedy appeared to be depending on a support group composed of nearly everyone who had ever been close to him (allowing for the fact that some were a lot closer than others). Muggsy O'Leary had been a member of the Capitol Police before being hired as Kennedy's driver back in 1947. Muggsy had put him on the wrong airplane or the wrong train more than once, was always slightly disorganized and was not the world's most skillful driver. Nevertheless, JFK had no intention of letting him go. The President forced the Secret Service to make Muggsy an agent so he could still drive him around Washington.[7]

Other old friends—such as Rip Horton, Red Fay and Jim Reed—were persuaded to accept high-ranking government jobs at considerable financial sacrifice to them. But when Kennedy offered to make Lem Billings the Assistant Secretary of Commerce, Billings turned it down. He said he wanted their relationship to remain what it had always been. It seems more likely, though, that Billings was eager to avoid the FBI background check, which might have forced Kennedy to face up to the fact that Billings was a homosexual.[8]

JFK's *Henry V* "band of brothers" principle—with personal relationships as his core management tool—would, in a just world, have knocked flow charts and decision trees into a cocked hat and seen human warmth triumph over etiolated bureaucracy. But it didn't turn out that way. There was unnecessary friction and confusion and endless resort to ad hoc solutions for problems that better organization would have avoided. There was also something rotten in the woodpile.

The Oval Office has a door on either side, each opening onto an office, and French doors that open out onto the Rose Garden. Kennedy installed O'Donnell in one office and Evelyn Lincoln in the other. Most of the time, both office doors were open—as were the French doors—and JFK wandered into the adjoining offices from time to time to talk to O'Donnell or Mrs. Lincoln.

Nearly everyone who was not on the staff or a member of the Kennedy family was expected to go through O'Donnell to see the President, but he was so fiercely possessive it was hard even for Cabinet members to get in. As a result, most people—including Douglas Dillon and Robert McNamara—got in through Evelyn Lincoln's office. She was not only more accommodating, she was more sensible and had nothing to hide.[9]

Besides being a Harvard football star, O'Donnell had been a wartime "bombagator"—qualified, that is, as both bombardier and navigator on B-17s. He had flown thirty missions in Europe in 1944, including D-Day, and been awarded the Distinguished Flying Cross; Kennedy liked to be around people who had served in the military in wartime. As if to demonstrate that he still wasn't a man to be crossed, O'Donnell carried a handgun in a holster on his belt. A slightly creepy figure who was heartily loathed throughout the administration, he delighted in his nickname— "the Cobra."[10]

O'Donnell's office was the informal headquarters of what the Washington press mockingly called "the Irish Mafia." It was part of Kennedy's presidential style to play off other members of the staff—the cerebral types such as Ted Sorensen and Arthur Schlesinger and Richard Goodwin—against his streetwise, tough-talking political friends from Boston and their gun-toting leader, O'Donnell.

Given the self-absorption of people who considered themselves superior to all those who had served previous Presidents, arrogance was inevitable. O'Donnell and Dave Powers handled a lot of calls from high-ranking officials who thought the President ought to be informed of one thing or another. Sometimes they exchanged knowing glances while assuring the caller, "Well, the President has been informed about it." Putting down the telephone, they then shared a contemptuous laugh and returned to whatever they were gossiping about before being interrupted. They also thought nothing of calling government officials and telling them, "The President wants you to do such and such," when Kennedy knew nothing about it.[11]

Worse was the corruption. Far from being impressed by the Oval Office, O'Donnell was operating on the other side of the door like an old style pol ensconced and counting his money at Boston city hall. Diligently soliciting campaign contributions for future elections, O'Donnell was skimming off 50 percent for himself.[12]

Long before he went into politics, when he was still a student at Stanford, Jack Kennedy had a clear idea of how to make a tough political decision. His inspiration was Lincoln—"The true rule in determining whether to embrace or reject anything is not whether it have any evil in it, but whether it have more of evil than of good. . . . Almost everything, especially of Government policy, is an inseparable compound of the two. . . ." That principle guided many of Kennedy's actions in Congress and remained with him throughout his short presidency.[13]

The way he made decisions was also unchanged. At the college level, it was a dorm bullshit session, but in professional politics, it was elevated to the level of a Jacksonian Kitchen Cabinet or Rooseveltian Brains Trust. Kennedy collected whoever's view he was interested in. The result was a high-powered yet almost informal seminar. Everybody was placed on roughly the same level. Rusk and McNamara were discomfited to find themselves having to debate important issues in front of the President with middle-ranking people who did not run large departments and had never carried the burden of great responsibilities.[14]

Throughout the day there were small gatherings in the Oval Office with some of his principal advisers, but other than that, JFK loathed meetings. In his administration, Cabinet sessions were perfunctory affairs where little of substance was discussed and almost nothing important was ever decided. He simply did not see his Cabinet members as his principal advisers; apart, that is, from the Attorney General.

The three highest-ranking departments—State, Treasury and Defense —were all in the hands of Republicans. Rusk, Dillon and McNamara could as easily have been in Ike's Cabinet as in Kennedy's. Democratic liberals, such as Orville Freeman at Agriculture and Arthur Goldberg at Labor, held the secondary Cabinet posts. The makeup of the new Cabinet was a shrewd way of reassuring the country that whatever the rhetoric of the campaign, this was going to be a centrist government rather than a liberal one.

Where Ike had held a Cabinet meeting each week and took these sessions seriously, Kennedy considered them more or less useless and convened them infrequently. The most memorable thing that ever happened during any of them was a meeting in the spring of 1961 when five-year-old Caroline opened the door, walked over to her father and told him, "Mommy wants you." The entire Cabinet—and Kennedy himself—erupted in laughter.[15]

=

One day shortly after his inauguration, Kennedy made a heartfelt confession to Bobby Baker, the assistant to the Senate Majority Leader: "When I was a congressman, I never realized how important Congress was. But I do now!"[16]

He found himself that spring in a weaker position than he could have imagined during the campaign. The Democrats had lost twenty-two House seats in the 1960 election. Kennedy's Catholicism hadn't kept him out of the White House, but it kept more than a few Democrats out of Congress, and nearly every one was someone who would have voted with the administration.

In the Senate, Hubert Humphrey had hopes of succeeding Lyndon Johnson as Majority Leader, but Kennedy could not stand having someone that liberal controlling his legislation. Besides, Humphrey would just as soon lecture the southern Democrats who controlled key committees as work with them. Kennedy let the word go forth that he'd rather have George Smathers, a man not greatly esteemed by other senators, than the irrepressible Hubert.

Johnson meanwhile tried to persuade Mike Mansfield, the Senate Democratic whip, to take over. Mansfield said, as he was a Roman Catholic, that might hurt Kennedy rather than help. Within hours, he got a call from the White House—"What's this I hear about your not taking the leadership job? Well, I want you to take it."[17]

There were problems in the House, too. Ostensibly, the Democrats had an overwhelming advantage: 263 seats to only 174 for the Republicans. The Committee on Rules, chaired by Judge Howard K. Smith of Virginia, decided which legislation would go to a vote on the floor of the House. There were other ways of doing the same thing, but they were so time-consuming and difficult that they were hardly ever employed. Smith was an ultra-conservative Democrat, stiff-necked, strong-willed and jealous of his prerogatives as chairman of such an important committee. At present, it numbered eight Democrats and four Republicans, but two of the Democrats regularly voted with the Republicans, producing a six to six deadlock and making the chairman's position decisive.

Sam Rayburn, the Speaker of the House, promised Kennedy that he would find a way to break Smith's iron grip on the Rules Committee. He proposed adding two more Democrats (of a pro-administration persuasion) plus one more Republican, which would narrowly tilt the balance in JFK's favor.

The eventual vote, on January 31, 1961, was 217–212 for Rayburn's proposal. But although the President had won his first major fight in Congress, he had done so by such a small margin it only showed how vulnerable and fragile his core vote was in the House. There was no reservoir of goodwill for him to tap in to, no reliable majority he could count on when the going got tough.

After the struggle over the Rules Committee, Kennedy went out of his way to appease southern Democrats. Without them, he could not hope to get anything of substance through Congress. His biggest concession was to abandon any thought he might have had of promoting civil rights legislation. There were other gestures, too, such as increasing federal subsidies to cotton producers.

He had appointed the hardworking and competent Larry O'Brien to take charge of congressional relations. But O'Brien had no relationship with anyone on Capitol Hill when he began, and good relationships were an essential ingredient. It would take anyone, however charming or diligent, at least two years to learn how the Hill worked, and how to work the Hill.

The President meanwhile tried to charm Congress, although what it responded to best was personal persuasion, manipulation, deal making and strong leadership. But Kennedy, like Ike, could not bring himself to wheedle and bargain and plead with members of Congress for their votes. He expected Sam Rayburn to do that for him, but the Speaker was seriously ill that first year and died in the fall.[18]

Mansfield, too, was a disappointment. He was not an arm-twisting, ego-stroking, in-your-face kind of leader, for which most senators were immensely grateful. They had endured plenty of that from LBJ and were glad to have a respite from it. Mansfield was a conciliator and a man prepared to bide his time no matter how long it took. But from Kennedy's perspective, time was an enemy, not a friend.

What he needed above all was someone who could deal with Harry Byrd, the chairman of the Senate Finance Committee. Byrd was a Democrat, but he had not supported Kennedy for the nomination, and it couldn't be said he'd supported him in the 1960 election.

Kennedy was looking for ways to stimulate the economy. In his campaign pledge to get the country moving again he had wrung maximum mileage from the 1958 recession. By the time of his election, the recession had ended, but the recovery was still weak, the federal budget was running a sizable deficit and unemployment was stuck at 6 percent. JFK came into the White House intending to lower unemployment and promote economic growth as his surest route to reelection.

However, Byrd believed devoutly in balanced budgets as the bulwark of American prosperity. He could support the President only when his conscience allowed it, he told Mansfield. The implication was that his conscience was a grudging beast that wasn't happy often, if at all. Kennedy despised Byrd, but he was careful to show him nothing but respect, because without Byrd's cooperation he would never be able to get any important economic measure through the Senate. He felt constrained to court the senator, inviting him to spend a weekend at Palm Beach and accepting an invitation to visit his Shenandoah Valley home during a Byrd family gathering in April 1961. Such gestures, though, did not bring Byrd around. Kennedy's hopes of stimulating the economy had to be directed elsewhere, such as increasing spending on space and the military.[19]

The problematic state of Kennedy's relationship with Congress meant that his legislative goals for 1961 were modest rather than ambitious: federal aid to education . . . an increase in the minimum wage . . . an area redevelopment program to alleviate poverty . . . a housing program . . . and Medicare.

He got his minimum-wage increase in March 1961. His education bill had a huge price tag—$5.6 billion, much of which would go for college scholarships. But what attracted attention and stirred up emotions was the fact that there was no money for Catholic schools. The Church opposed the bill strenuously, but while a Protestant President might have been able to yield on aid for parochial schools, a Catholic President could not. "There isn't any room for debate on the subject," Kennedy declared at a press conference, and for him, at least, there wasn't.[20]

Despite his firm stand—and by a supreme irony—Kennedy's aid-to-education program was killed in July 1961 by the Rules Committee, the body he had struggled so hard to reshape. His legislation did not even make it to the House floor.

He got an area redevelopment program, but one much smaller than he'd hoped for. As for Medicare, he couldn't get that passed despite strong support in the Senate. To many of his supporters, it came as a surprise as well as a disappointment that Kennedy wasn't able to get more help from Johnson in dealing with Congress.

Shortly before his inauguration, JFK had assured Johnson, "Lyndon, you may be number two in the country, but I'll see to it that you remain number one in Texas." One way he was going to do that was to let LBJ control all the federal appointments in Texas.[21]

This was completely counter to established practice. Senator Ralph Yarborough, a very liberal Texas Democrat and one of Kennedy's strongest supporters, was incensed. He and Johnson had long been rivals, and the President had just undercut him. Kennedy's clumsy attempt to keep Johnson happy created a deep split in the Texas Democratic party that festered for years.

In the meantime, the Senate followed established custom and refused to confirm any of Johnson's proposed appointments, out of deference to the well-liked and very angry Senator Yarborough. There were virtually no federal appointments in Texas for the first year of the Kennedy presidency. In the end, he had to create a committee just to arbitrate appointment disputes between Johnson and Yarborough.

Neither the President nor the Vice President was happy with the way things were working out between them. Kennedy didn't help matters by calling Johnson "a crybaby. Always crying over something." The White House staff took that as license to treat the Vice President with disdain. And Bobby Kennedy never forgave Johnson for trying to make an issue of his brother's Addisonism at the 1960 Democratic convention.[22]

Johnson was hardly sworn in as Vice President before he started telling people what a terrible mistake he'd made. "If I speak one word of disagreement with the Cabinet or the White House staff looking on, they'll put it out that I'm a damned traitor. Oh, sure, Jack Kennedy's as thoughtful and considerate of me at those meetings as he can be. But I know his snot-nosed brother's after my ass, and all those high-falutin' Harvards. . . . I'm not gonna stick my head in the noose at Cabinet meetings. All Jack Kennedy's gotta do, if he really wants my opinion, is pick up the telephone." That was something JFK rarely did.[23]

Kennedy found Johnson so touchy, he once told *New York Times* reporter Tom Wicker, that even sending him a birthday telegram was filled with pitfalls. "It's like drafting a state document."

At Cabinet meetings, Johnson sat silent and depressed, a portrait of hangdog human misery. It got on Kennedy's nerves until George Smathers made a suggestion. "Send him off on a round-the-world trip. He'll get a lot of fanfare and smoke will be blown up his ass. Let him have a great time."

"You know, that's a damn good idea," said Kennedy. Shortly after, it was announced that Johnson would be taking a long trip to India.[24]

=

On the Monday night following the inauguration, Kennedy invited Charles Bartlett and his wife to the White House for dinner. Then he and Bartlett walked through the West Wing and into the Executive Office Building, next door to the White House. He wanted his old friend Charlie, a political reporter from Chattanooga, to show him around the room where Eisenhower had held his press conferences. Kennedy was already thinking about the best way to hold a presidential news conference and whether this was the right stage on which to appear not just before journalists but also in American homes.[25]

This was not the kind of decision he would leave to his press secretary, the rotund and ebullient Pierre Salinger. It was too important for that. Kennedy never seemed to take Salinger seriously and was always making fun of him. There was a slight undercurrent, too, to his mockery, because JFK was never wholly comfortable around people who were obviously overweight.[26]

If anything, his aversion was stronger now than ever, for it had acquired a personal dimension. The new form of cortisone that he was taking made him look jowly. On being elected President, JFK moved to the new dietary frontier and tried Metrecal.[27]

Salinger's White House press office became known throughout the executive branch for its atmosphere of barely controlled chaos. "An absolute madhouse and a mess" was a typical description.[28]

It hardly seemed to matter. As Salinger himself acknowledged, Kennedy had more ability to court journalists than any press secretary possessed. The President liked newspaper reporters, having been one himself, but that didn't mean he liked the newspapers. Kennedy felt they were out to make him look bad, distort his views, pick on small mistakes, tarnish his reputation and so on. He took reams of praise as his due, but the least criticism infuriated him.

"No one can be liberal enough for the *New York Post,*" he complained to Gore Vidal. And when *U.S. News & World Report* ran an article on the high cost of the presidency—Air Force One, a fleet of helicopters, a dozen expensive automobiles and the like—JFK was incensed. "That damn reactionary David Lawrence will do just about anything to undermine my support." Even so, he cut back on Air Force One, which O'Donnell had turned into a commuter aircraft for his cronies.[29]

Television offered a chance to reach out to the public directly. Only a week into his presidency, Kennedy decided his press conferences would be shown live. Eisenhower's had been filmed, and the film was shown on television, usually with nothing more than nominal cuts.

There was opposition from the White House staff when Salinger told them there would be live broadcasts. Ike had always been worried he might reveal secret information or precipitate some kind of crisis with an unwise choice of words; that was why they had been filmed. But JFK accepted the risks that spontaneity carried in order to harvest its gains. Besides, risk energized him. To skate up to, then along, the fine cutting edge of danger was for him life itself.[30]

The writing press was indignant at his decision. Since the founding of the Republic, journalists had explained the President to the people and the people to the President. Kennedy was pushing them aside. James Reston of *The New York Times* called Kennedy's decision "the goofiest idea since the hula hoop," and Kennedy got mad at him, but the decision stood.[31]

Most of the press conferences were held in the auditorium at the State Department. It was larger and had a more modern look and feel to it than the room Eisenhower had used in the Executive Office Building. Americans were fascinated to see their President in action and speaking as much to them as to the journalists. Yet while Kennedy was relaxed, often slightly amused, as if he'd just happened to stop by, he had in fact spent hours preparing for each press conference. The majority of questions raised had been anticipated, either by him or someone else in the administration, and many of his answers—including some of his joking replies—had been rehearsed.[32]

Once he got the hang of it, he turned these live press conferences into exercises in information management. Invariably composed, Kennedy gave almost nothing away. He was witty rather than open; clever rather than candid. Every appearance was really a performance. But he made his performances so agreeable that few—apart from reporters—noticed or cared about the dearth of substance.[33]

Yet as soon as they became routine and a pattern set in, JFK found them boring. There were too many journalists with too many long and tedious questions. And he had nothing but scorn for loaded questions parading as honest inquiry. Worst of all, Kennedy found, was his habit of turning to the right when standing. That meant he found himself facing two hyperactive and hypercritical reporters—May Craig and Sarah McClendon—time and again. He tried to look over or past them, but that did not stop them from jumping to their feet, blocking his view and shouting out questions.[34]

Kennedy's press conferences were a public relations success as great as Roosevelt's fireside chats. His approval rating climbed to 80 percent. The narrowness of his election made him weak on Capitol Hill, but popularity like this freed him to be strong in the world.

CHAPTER 27

Hands-on

Khrushchev liked to joke that he had elected John F. Kennedy. From the moment of Kennedy's nomination in Los Angeles, Khrushchev wanted to see him beat Nixon, someone he detested. Throughout the presidential election, Khrushchev did and said nothing that might hurt Kennedy's chances of winning, and he celebrated JFK's victory by releasing the crew of an American reconnaissance aircraft that had crash-landed in Soviet territory. Khrushchev had held on to the airmen because an earlier release might have helped Nixon.[1]

Such gestures encouraged Kennedy to think the Soviets were looking for a fresh start in U.S.-Soviet relations, and they were. But they also wanted to send a signal that while they were glad he had beaten Nixon, he could not take them for granted. On January 6, exactly two weeks before Kennedy's inauguration, Khrushchev delivered an ostensibly "secret" speech to senior party officials in Moscow: a two-hour peroration called "For New Victories of the World Communist Movement."

He asserted that in the modern world three kinds of wars were possible—a world war, which would be fought with nuclear weapons and probably bring the end of mankind; local wars, which might see millions perish over issues that could be settled by other means; and wars of national liberation, such as the present struggles in Vietnam and Algeria. Liberation wars were fights against oppression; they were "sacred" to good Communists, declared Khrushchev.

There was nothing new in what Khrushchev said; it was the timing that mattered. Shortly before his inauguration, Kennedy received a copy of Khrushchev's speech, and two days into his presidency, he directed members of the National Security Council to "Read, mark, learn and inwardly digest" what Khrushchev had to say.[2]

Khrushchev's challenge to American power, with the Third World as the battleground, was based not on Soviet strength but on Soviet weakness. Fomenting trouble in the Third World did not seem likely to cost the Soviets much and might prove endlessly problematic for the Americans. Khrushchev did not want to match the United States weapon for weapon. He wanted to wage the Cold War on the cheap.[3]

Meanwhile, Kennedy embarked on a comprehensive reshaping of the machinery by which he would respond to Khrushchev's challenge. He had nurtured a low regard for the State Department and its Foreign Service officers ever since his father's unhappy experiences at the American embassy in London in the 1930s. Disdain then turned into contempt during his journeys as a globe-trotting congressman and senator in the 1950s.

The State Department counted for little in the new administration, supplanted by Kennedy's revamped National Security Council. McGeorge Bundy, his National Security Adviser, completely overshadowed the Secretary of State, and Kennedy derided Rusk as "a good errand boy."[4]

Under JFK, as under Eisenhower, the NSC presented various options, developed by foreign policy and intelligence experts, to the President. However, the new NSC was much smaller. Its staff was cut overnight from seventy-one to forty-eight. By rights this should have been forty-seven, but the tally included a young woman with whom JFK had been having an affair when she was still a student at Radcliffe. Kennedy put her on the NSC staff, where she would still be available for recreational sex.[5]

The fact that Bundy had no foreign policy experience counted in his favor, as far as JFK was concerned. A former dean of Harvard College and a sometime history lecturer, Bundy seemed to the President to combine the best of the two worlds that mattered—a superior intellect and an inner toughness. Foreign policy professionals, in Kennedy's experience, lacked one quality or the other, sometimes both. He told Jackie one day, "Damn it, Bundy and I get more done in one day in the White House than they do in six months at the State Department." It was less a complaint than a boast.[6]

=

The first foreign policy crisis Kennedy had to confront came in the country he invariably called "Lay-os." In 1958 a left-leaning neutralist government had been elected in Laos, but it faced a strong challenge from the Communist guerrillas of the Pathet Lao. Armed by the Soviets and aided by the battle-hardened troops of North Vietnam, the Pathet Lao exercised effective control over much of northern Laos, which has a ninety-mile border with southern China.

In 1960 a disaffected anti-Communist general, Phoumi Nosavan, overthrew the neutralist government, confident he would receive American backing. Money, arms and twenty-two U.S. Army advisers arrived shortly thereafter. In January 1961, however, the Royal Laotian Army broke apart, and within a month the Pathet Lao, backed by airdrops of Soviet arms, launched a strong thrust across the Plaine des Jarres towards the Mekong River and the Laotian capital, Vientiane.

Kennedy went on television to inform Americans of the unfolding crisis and to pledge American support to Phoumi's forces. But in early March the Pathet Lao brushed Phoumi's troops aside. The general had boasted about taking back the Plaine des Jarres only to pull out when the real fighting began. "General Phoumi is a total shit," a disgusted Kennedy told his friend Ben Bradlee.[7]

The forces the United States could send into Laos on short notice amounted to ten thousand men at most; not enough to ensure the defeat of the Pathet Lao. And if the North Vietnamese pushed their own regular troops into the fight, the United States might have to commit up to three hundred thousand men. Even then, the CIA argued, the enemy would still possess numerical superiority.[8]

Kennedy recalled all too clearly how the French were defeated at Dien Bien Phu in 1954. He knew that if he pushed American troops into Laos and they, like the French, were isolated, besieged and ultimately forced to surrender, he would never be reelected. When he asked what might happen if American forces found themselves besieged, the Joint Chiefs told him he would have to use tactical nuclear weapons. It was the kind of reassurance that did not reassure.[9]

The more he thought about Laos, the less willing Kennedy became to intervene. The one ray of hope proved to be Phoumi's failure. It seemed to offer the chance to install a new government in Vientiane and start again.[10]

On March 23, equipped with three large maps of Laos and wielding a pointer, Kennedy appeared on national television. In the course of a compelling presentation, he struck a new note—"We strongly and unreservedly support the goal of a neutral and independent Lay-os." At that moment Eisenhower's policy of thwarting the Pathet Lao by fighting them was abandoned. Kennedy was seeking to neutralize the entire country under a coalition government. To go back, that is, to the situation before Phoumi's coup.

To secure a neutral government this time, however, the resurgent Pathet Lao had to be stopped from taking Vientiane. The CIA was already secretly airlifting American soldiers into Laos. Drawn mainly from Special Forces units, they were not advisers—they fought with and sometimes acted as spearheads for Royal Laotian Army units that had remained loyal to Phoumi Nosavan. Backed by two battalions of artillery from the Royal Thai Army and supported by thousands of Hmong tribesmen—who had a long history of antagonism towards the Chinese and Vietnamese—this hastily assembled force contested the Pathet Lao's advance on Vientiane.

Kennedy held a long, frank conversation in the Oval Office with Andrei Gromyko, the Soviet foreign minister. He left Gromyko in no doubt that whatever the outcome in Laos, it was going to shape Soviet-American relations for a long time to come.

For the Russians, this crisis was the diplomatic equivalent of a slam dunk. Only a few months earlier Khrushchev had told Llewellyn Thompson, the U.S. ambassador to the Soviet Union, that Laos wasn't worth a war. "Why take the risk?" said Khrushchev. "It will fall into our hands like a rotten apple." On April 1, barely a week after Kennedy's conversation with Gromyko, Khrushchev declared he was willing to accept a cease-fire and a neutral coalition government in Laos, although skirmishing continued on the Plaine des Jarres until formal talks began six weeks later.[11]

The Joint Chiefs were disgusted that the United States had abandoned Phoumi Nosavan. That seemed an invitation to disaster. "Mr. President, if you don't stand in Laos, you're going to have to stand someplace else," protested Admiral Arleigh Burke, the Chief of Naval Operations. "If it's not Laos, is it going to be South Vietnam? And if it's not South Vietnam, is it going to be Thailand?"

"I think you're wrong," said Kennedy.[12]

In the early 1950s he had often claimed that Southeast Asia was crucial to Western security. But now that he was President, Kennedy wasn't so sure. "Why do we need to hold it?" he asked Bundy's deputy, Walt Whitman Rostow, who was arguing strenuously for intervening massively in Laos. "Why can't we get out of there?"

Rostow's argument, like Burke's, was that if one Southeast Asian country fell to the Communists, all would eventually topple like dominoes. The dominoes reached all the way to Australia.

Kennedy thought such arguments ignored the great centrifugal force in Far Eastern politics—China. He worried often about what would happen once the Chinese Communists acquired nuclear weapons. "They are bound to get them at some time," he told Arthur Krock. "And from that moment, they will dominate Southeast Asia anyway."[13]

Far from seeking a confrontation with China over the fate of Laos or South Vietnam, JFK thought the United States ought to recognize the Communist regime in Peking. The current policy of nonrecognition was stupid and potentially dangerous. A two-China policy, recognizing both Peking and Taiwan, was the right way to go, but he could not see it happening while he was President.[14]

=

During the election campaign, Kennedy had criticized the Eisenhower administration for not doing more to prevent Fidel Castro from coming to power. Nevertheless, Eisenhower did him a favor by breaking American relations with Cuba several days before the inauguration.

Like many young Americans, Kennedy was intrigued by the youthful, charismatic Castro. And always interested in other people's sex lives, he asked Fletcher Knebel, who had reported on the Cuban revolution, "Who does Castro sleep with? I hear he doesn't even take his boots off."[15]

Eisenhower had not only severed relations with Cuba, but even before, he had ordered the CIA to promote economic sabotage and political instability in Cuba. He also encouraged the Cubans who had fled to the United States to form a government in exile.

If the CIA's operation succeeded, it might be possible at some future point to move that government into Cuba, grant swift American recognition and offer military support. To Eisenhower's disappointment, the sabotage-and-disruption program failed to produce results, while Castro appeared to move ever closer to turning Cuba into a Communist dictatorship. In the fall of 1960 the CIA director, Allen Dulles, and his deputy, Richard Bissell, chose to enlarge the project but did not bother to inform Eisenhower. Their aim now was to create "a significant strike force" composed of Cuban émigrés who would be given military training in Guatemala.[16]

During the Thanksgiving break in November 1960, Dulles and Bissell briefed Kennedy at his family home in Palm Beach. There was, they told him, a plan to land several hundred Cubans in their homeland. They would then move into the mountains, where they would become guerrillas and saboteurs.

By the time of his inauguration, "Operation Zapata" had become even more ambitious—to put fifteen hundred Cubans ashore in an amphibious assault. They would seize a beachhead, and if they could hold it long enough, the Cuban government in exile would be brought in. Alternatively, if it proved impossible to hold a beachhead, the Cubans would head for the mountains and wage a guerrilla war.

Three weeks into Kennedy's presidency, *The New York Times* carried a story on Operation Zapata, and he sent a memo to Bundy: "Has the policy for Cuba been coordinated between Defense, CIA and State?" It turned out that while the CIA was backing the operation enthusiastically, there were serious doubts about it in the State Department.[17]

The Chairman of the Joint Chiefs, General Lyman Lemnitzer, responded on behalf of the military. The entire operation hinged on whether or not air strikes flown by World War II B-26 medium bombers were conducted effectively and air superiority over the beachhead was secured. Without control of the air, Lemnitzer said, the operation would fail. Overall, he concluded, it had only "a fair chance of ultimate success."

The President, Bundy, Dulles and Bissell all managed to misinterpret what "fair" meant. They thought it amounted to an endorsement. In fact, it was exactly the opposite. Within the Army, an efficiency report that rated an officer as average, or even good, was enough to kill a career. In the military lexicon, the only rating lower than fair was poor.[18]

Kennedy was not really pinning his hopes on the invasion anyway. He was counting on murder. One day in the early spring of 1961, as he sat in the Rose Garden enjoying the sunshine with his old friend Senator

George Smathers, he asked Smathers what he thought the reaction would be in Latin America if Castro was assassinated.

Smathers considered himself an expert on Latin America, being close to various leaders such as the brutal and corrupt Rafael Trujillo of the Dominican Republic. He said he didn't think murdering another head of state was a good idea. The repercussions would be disastrous if it was ever traced back to the United States. It would be better to stage a fake attack on Guantánamo Bay, added Smathers, and use that to justify a full-scale invasion.

"Well, there is a plot to murder Castro," Kennedy told him. "Castro is going to be dead at the time the Cuban exiles trained by the CIA hit the beaches."[19]

He still could not bring himself to set a date for the operation and order it done. Bissell put the pressure on. "You can't *mañana* this thing. You can cancel it. In which case you've got a problem of disposal. What will we do with these fifteen hundred people?" Dulles, too, pressed him hard: "Do you want to be perceived as less anti-Communist than the great Eisenhower?"[20]

As Kennedy studied the details of the plan, he fretted about concealing the American role and began altering crucial elements. The landing site the CIA had chosen was close to the town of Trinidad. "Too noisy," he told Bissell. He wanted a successful invasion, but one that was "less spectacular . . . without the appearance of a World War II–type amphibious assault." The CIA moved the operation eighty miles west, to the remote, sparsely populated Bay of Pigs, where extensive swamps would hinder exit from the beaches.[21]

Lemnitzer penned another memorandum to the President, telling him bluntly that if the invaders failed to achieve surprise, the operation was doomed; and if a single Cuban Air Force fighter survived the opening air attacks, "it could sink all or most of the invasion force."[22]

Kennedy continued to fret over the planned air strikes and looked for ways to deny American involvement. Having altered the landing site, he demanded that the landing be made at night instead of at dawn. That way the invasion fleet would be a hundred miles away by the time the sun came up.[23]

He convinced himself such changes would not impair the chances of success for the Cubans—they would merely cloak the American role. Kennedy assured his Under Secretary of State, Chester Bowles, that if the operation went ahead, "It just won't amount to anything."

Bowles asked, "Will it make the front page of *The New York Times*?"
"I wouldn't think so."[24]

The President spent Easter in Palm Beach and returned to Washington on April 4 to hold a press conference at the State Department auditorium. When it ended, he went upstairs to a smaller conference room on the seventh floor, where the Joint Chiefs, Bundy, McNamara, Rusk, Dulles and Senator J. William Fulbright from the Senate Foreign Relations Committee were waiting for him.

Over the next two hours they debated whether to authorize the invasion of Cuba by what was now known as "Brigade 2506." Fulbright said the operation was both immoral and unwise. Rusk opposed it, too. Having spent much of World War II as an Army officer operating with guerrilla groups in Burma, he did not think this landing stood an earthly hope of success. The Joint Chiefs said almost nothing. The principal enthusiasts remained Bissell and Bundy.

Kennedy brought the session to a close. "Well, gentlemen, I think we'd better sleep on this matter and not decide it today."[25]

By now Kennedy felt nothing but scorn for doubters like Rusk and Fulbright. "I know everybody is grabbing their nuts on this," he told Sorensen. "But I'm not going to chicken out."[26]

He got a tip-off that *The New York Times* was about to run a story saying the CIA had spent the past nine months training a force of up to six thousand Cubans to invade their homeland and overthrow Castro. Kennedy called the newspaper's publisher, Orville Dryfoos, and tried to get the story spiked. Dryfoos called back after talking with the editors and told him that wasn't possible. Nevertheless, when the story did appear on April 7, it had been extensively edited to reduce its impact and was buried in the inside pages.

Even so, Kennedy was incensed. "Castro doesn't need agents over here," he fumed. "All he has to do is read our newspapers!" And Castro seemed to be doing just that—two days after the story ran in *The New York Times,* Castro appeared on television to call on Cubans "to repel any invasion attempt by the counterrevolutionaries now massing in Florida and Guatemala and who are sponsored and financed by the United States."[27]

On April 12 Kennedy held a press conference. The main subject of discussion was Yuri Gagarin, who had become the first man in space less than twenty-four hours earlier. When questions were raised about the story in *The New York Times,* the President skirted the issue by asserting that U.S. armed forces would not take part in any attack on Cuba.[28]

Two days later he sent for Bissell. The first air strike was going to be launched in less than twenty-four hours, on Saturday, April 15. Kennedy was still anxious about the air strikes. What he wanted, he told Bissell, was "a minimal attack." All along, the President had been hoping for a landing that he could pass off as the work of a handful of anti-Castro Cubans. But sixteen medium-range bombers—how would he explain them away? Bissell returned to CIA headquarters and cut the number of aircraft to eight.[29]

The attack by eight B-26s on Saturday lacked weight and napalm wasn't used. The B-26s relied on strafing, for which they were poorly equipped. Only five of Castro's forty operable combat aircraft were destroyed. Several more were damaged. First blood, but only a scratch.

Brigade 2506 was due to land in the early hours of Monday morning, and a second air strike would be launched at dawn as they started to move off the beach. Late Sunday night Kennedy canceled the second air operation. Meanwhile, Salinger was telling the world that what was happening at the Bay of Pigs was entirely the work of Cuban freedom fighters. There was no American involvement.

During Monday morning the Cuban Air Force found the ships that were carrying ammunition, vehicles and communications equipment to the Bay of Pigs beachhead. In less than half an hour, two were sunk. The rest fled.

By Tuesday morning up to twenty thousand Cuban soldiers were reported advancing on the beach, supported by tanks. When Kennedy stepped into the Cabinet Room for a scheduled Cabinet meeting at nine o'clock, he looked ashen. He sat down and talked for twenty minutes, musing aloud about the origins of the operation, the reasons why he'd okayed it and what was going wrong now. No one said anything. Then he stood up and walked out through the Oval Office and into the Rose Garden, lost in thought, close to despair.[30]

Returning to his office, Kennedy called Eisenhower and told him the Bay of Pigs operation was in trouble. Then he had the switchboard track down Barry Goldwater to tell him the President wanted to see him immediately. Goldwater was not only a key member of the Senate Armed Services Committee but had more influence with the hawks on the Hill than anyone else. He was also a likely GOP presidential candidate in 1964.

Kennedy was puffing on a small cigar and looking dejected when Goldwater arrived an hour later. The President glanced up. "So you want this fucking job, eh?"

He briefed Goldwater on what had gone wrong and said he'd made a mistake in canceling the second air strike. Goldwater was sympathetic, but only up to a point. "A great nation must be willing to use its strength," he told Kennedy. "Power belongs to those who use it [and] I would do whatever is necessary to assure the invasion is a success."[31]

The annual White House reception for members of Congress and their wives was scheduled for that evening. It went ahead as planned, and the President confronted a struggle he always dreaded—the white-tie affair. His valet, George Taylor, couldn't tie one, and Kennedy was left to fight it out alone.[32]

At midnight Kennedy and the Chiefs, Bissell and Bundy gathered in the Cabinet Room, while the Marine Band played on and congressmen and their wives wandered around the White House, enchanted and thrilled. It seemed for a time that Bissell was so stunned by the prospect of failure he was almost incoherent. After the discussion had gone on for a while and he had a chance to compose himself, Bissell said he wanted "two jets to shoot down the enemy aircraft."[33]

Kennedy responded emphatically. "No. I've told you over and over again, our forces won't engage in combat."

Arleigh Burke then argued for letting him send in a single destroyer. It would be able to knock out every tank that tried to make it onto the beach. Kennedy's temper flared and his voice rose. "Burke, I don't want the United States involved in this."

"Hell, Mr. President, we *are* involved!"[34]

After three hours of discussion, Kennedy finally relented. He would allow Navy fighters from the aircraft carrier *Essex* to fly top-cover for a single close air support mission by all sixteen B-26s to aid the hard-pressed invaders. The Navy pilots were not to fire unless fired upon.

When the meeting in the Cabinet Room broke up at four A.M., Kennedy walked out to the Rose Garden and paced up and down in his white tie and tails. It was a poignant sight. Bobby came out to console him. "They can't do this to you," he said, putting his arm around his brother. "Those black-bearded Communists can't do this to you."[35]

No one at the CIA or in the Navy noticed there was a one-hour time difference between Cuba and Nicaragua. The B-26 force arrived over the Bay of Pigs at dawn on April 19 without fighter escort. Castro's jet trainers, modified to carry 20-millimeter cannons, shot most of them down. The Navy fighters arrived an hour later.

By nightfall Castro's tanks were on the beaches at the Bay of Pigs.

Brigade 2506 was being overrun as the President attended a diplomatic reception at the Greek embassy that evening. He was composed during the reception, but on the return journey, Kennedy sat in the back of his limousine brooding on his failure and on the men who were dying at this moment under tank treads and artillery fire. He slumped forward, doubling up like a man in pain, and wept.

CHAPTER 28

Holding Fast

The Bay of Pigs brought long, testy letters from the Kremlin to the White House, yet it only encouraged both Khrushchev and Kennedy in their mutual desire to meet up. Hardly had the operation ended before a summit meeting was agreed upon for Vienna at the beginning of June.

The President looked to Llewellyn Thompson, a skilled career diplomat and U.S. ambassador to Moscow, as *the* expert on Khrushchev. Over the past three and a half years Thompson had gotten to know Khrushchev well, drunk and sober. Khrushchev's mercurial moods, his simmering resentments and maudlin affability, his obvious inferiority complex over a grade school education, his search for insight into the wider world by paddling in the intellectual shallows of Marxist-Leninism, were going to make him difficult to deal with.

Even so, Kennedy was impressed by the two elements that always impressed him: "He's not dumb—he's smart," Kennedy told Dean Rusk as he read up on Khrushchev. Then, making a fist and shaking it in the air, he added, "He's *tough*!" Smart and tough meant an adversary worth putting to the test in what Kennedy sometimes called the "Great Chess Game" of international politics.[1]

He was worried, though. What if Khrushchev thought he was too young, too inexperienced, to be just as smart, just as tough? To ensure that his adversary would take him seriously, Kennedy appeared before Congress on May 25. Returning to Capitol Hill so soon after his State of the Union address was extraordinary, Kennedy conceded, but "these are extraordinary times," he told Congress.

The President asked for an extra $2 billion for "new helicopters, new armored personnel carriers and new howitzers." The United States needed these so it could respond to the threat of conventional warfare and Communist-inspired guerrilla conflicts.[2]

The country needed something else too: success in space. After Soviet cosmonaut Yuri Gagarin became the first man in space, people around the world assumed the next Soviet triumph would be to put a man on the moon. As a senator, Kennedy had voted against the creation of the National Air and Space Administration. He accepted the arguments of scientists that there was nothing a man could do in space that could not be done better and more cheaply by instruments. As President, he had rejected pressure to mount a moon program and appointed the highly skeptical Jerome Weisner as presidential adviser on science and technology.

Yet with the meeting in Vienna looming, and the certain prospect of the pudgy, brash Soviet chairman gloating unmercifully over Gagarin's feat, Kennedy found himself helpless in the grip of testosterone and national pride. Before he went before Congress in May, he sent for Wernher von Braun, the nation's leading rocket scientist. "Can we beat the Russians?" he asked von Braun. "Can we put a man on the moon?"

"We have a sporting chance," said von Braun. "With an all-out crash program, I think we could accomplish this objective in 1967 or 1968."[3]

When Kennedy appeared before Congress on May 25, he said he was ready for Khrushchev. That brought a huge cheer. And near the end of his speech, he flung down a direct challenge to the Soviet Union: "I believe that this nation should commit itself to achieving the goal—before this decade is out—of landing a man on the Moon and returning him safely to the Earth. No single space project in this period will be more impressive to mankind." His audience jumped to its feet as one man, applauding wildly, cheering lustily, frantic to beat the Russians in space. If it had not been a race before, it was now.[4]

Four days later Kennedy went to Boston for the celebration of his forty-fourth birthday. He rode to the Armory that evening in the new presidential parade car, a Lincoln Continental convertible that was longer and heavier than the standard model and boasted two jump seats. Rain was falling steadily, but rather than disappoint the crowd, Kennedy had the Lincoln's bubble top removed.

As the Lincoln passed the statue of the renowned abolitionist editor William Lloyd Garrison on Commonwealth Avenue, Kennedy remembered that it bore an inspiring quotation and asked a state trooper to go over and copy it down for him. The trooper caught up with the President at the Armory and handed him a piece of paper. Kennedy finished his speech that evening by quoting Garrison's defiant utterance to his opponents: "I am in earnest. I will not equivocate. I will not excuse. I will not retreat a single inch. And I *will* be heard." Next day he boarded Air Force One and headed across the Atlantic, still reading up on Khrushchev, getting ready.[5]

=

There would be two days in Paris for the President to talk politics with Charles de Gaulle, for Jackie to delight in her Frenchness, and for the French to delight in her chic. The crowds that greeted the President and the First Lady were immense.

Kennedy was merely a President of the United States, like Woodrow Wilson and Dwight Eisenhower, who had visited Paris before him. Jackie, née Bouvier, onetime student at the Sorbonne, fluent in French and dressed by Givenchy, was one of their own. The clamor was overwhelming, the ecstatic screams of "Zhaa-kie! Zhaa-kie!" unforgettable, the sense of occasion almost unbearable.

That night they were de Gaulle's guests at a magnificent state dinner at Versailles: a giddying triumph of high fashion, blinding jewelry, military pomp, blaring trumpets and haute cuisine. Jackie was once again the star. For the first time in their marriage, Kennedy saw his wife as a person who might be interesting and important in her own right. "I'm dazzled," he told her, having finally seen her as millions did.[6]

Next day, in agony from his back, he needed a shot of whatever it was that Dr. Feelgood—Max Jacobson—was giving him. Bobby had been trying to get his brother to allow a government lab to figure out just what was in Jacobson's hypodermic, but JFK had brushed that aside. "I don't care if it's horse piss. It works."[7]

Kennedy had a long, wide-ranging discussion with de Gaulle before lunch at the Elysée Palace, with only their interpreters present. What the President wanted to talk about most was Indochina, which had been carved up into French colonies until 1954.

The President said he would welcome French assistance in his attempt to secure a neutralist coalition government in Laos. De Gaulle said he could help indirectly with the Laotian problem but warned, "There is no military solution to Vietnam. You will sink into a bottomless military and political quagmire, no matter how much you spend in men and money."[8]

Kennedy also wanted to talk about Berlin. For three years Khrushchev had been threatening to sign a peace treaty with East Germany, ending the state of war that technically continued to exist between the Soviet Union and Germany. The essential issues were access to Berlin—which was two hundred miles from West Germany—and movement within Berlin.

Once there was a peace treaty, Khrushchev asserted, East Germany would acquire control over air, road and rail access to Berlin, and the four-power (U.S., Soviet, British and French) agreement that had governed access since 1945 would expire.[9]

No one disputed that the arrangements made in 1945 were meant to be temporary. And in a sensible world, sixteen years was an absurdly long time to wait for a peace treaty. Nevertheless, Khrushchev's proposed treaty with East Germany was obviously a ploy to force out the Americans, the British and the French. Yet these nations over time had developed a moral obligation not to abandon the people of West Berlin to any Communist—and therefore illegitimate—regime.

Besides, any concession on Berlin would be seen as weakness and would be followed by even greater pressure from the Soviets to yield elsewhere. The future of NATO and the principle of mutual security were at stake in Berlin. Eisenhower had told Khrushchev in 1959 that any move blocking access to the city would provoke a war, and the issue faded away.[10]

With the arrival of a new President, Khrushchev revived his demands for new arrangements in Berlin. What worried him, Kennedy told de Gaulle, was that the United States and Soviet Union might blunder into a war. He was not going to surrender any rights of access to or movement within Berlin, but there might be minor issues that could be negotiated.

De Gaulle scoffed at that. "There is nothing to negotiate with the Russians. . . . Your job, Mr. President, is to make sure Khrushchev knows you are a man who will fight." He offered some advice for the Vienna meeting: "*Tenir bon*"—Hold fast.[11]

As they parted, Kennedy's mind went back to the impassioned welcome he, but especially Jackie, had received. He had been deeply moved and said so, if indirectly. "My most vivid impression of France is French vitality," he told de Gaulle. "I have never seen more vigorous people."[12]

For someone so dependent on pills and injections, a man who had brought his special horsehair mattress and crutches to Paris, there could be no higher or more heartfelt compliment.

=

Two days before he departed for Europe, the President received a memorandum from the Joint Chiefs of Staff intended to put clearly in his mind the overwhelming military strength of the United States. "Be assured," the Chiefs informed him, "that you may speak from a position of decisive military superiority . . . the military forces under your command . . . can achieve decisive military victory in any all-out test of strength with the Sino-Soviet bloc. . . . [We] wish you Godspeed in your mission."[13]

Kennedy paid little attention to their reassurance. He had convinced himself that the Joint Chiefs had failed him over the Bay of Pigs and given him bad advice over Laos. Besides, far from believing the United States possessed "decisive military superiority," he still could not admit he had been wrong about the missile gap. He believed that the U.S. and the U.S.S.R. had a rough parity in strategic weapons. The Chiefs were nonetheless right: the Soviets did not have even one nuclear missile or nuclear-armed bomber capable of striking the United States. Yet Kennedy ignored their memo.[14]

The President and the people around him, such as Sorensen and Salinger, expected the Vienna summit to be a lot like the first Nixon debate. The witty, articulate JFK was going to emerge as a clear winner on points over someone who was far less suave and nowhere near as attractive.[15]

Kennedy's one nagging doubt was that Khrushchev might misinterpret his willingness to compromise over Laos and his refusal to commit American forces at the Bay of Pigs. If so, he might see Berlin as the next place where Kennedy would yield to pressure. "Khrushchev must not misunderstand Laos and Cuba," he had told Arthur Krock.[16]

Shortly before Khrushchev arrived at the American embassy on the morning of June 3 for the first round of talks, Kennedy sent for Max

Jacobson. "This could go on for hours," he said. "I can't afford any complications with my back."

Dr. Feelgood was ready with his syringe. "You won't have that as an excuse."[17]

Kennedy had recently read and been profoundly impressed by Barbara Tuchman's *The Guns of August,* a meticulous reconstruction of the first month of World War I. The theme of Mrs. Tuchman's work was that European leaders had stumbled into war because they completely misunderstood one another. So much so that after the war ended, none of them seemed able to say what the war was about or why it was necessary.

The summit opened in the embassy's modest music room. Once the President and the Chairman of the Supreme Soviet, each accompanied by his advisers and interpreter, had crowded into the room, they found themselves facing each other only a few feet apart across a glass-topped coffee table. The first thing Kennedy wanted to say once the opening pleasantries were out of the way was that they shared a joint responsibility to avert a nuclear war.[18]

Khrushchev had a different priority. The Soviet Union was much poorer and, he was well aware, vulnerable to American missiles and bombers. Khrushchev was desperate to be taken seriously, and made volatile by an ineradicable inferiority complex; it wasn't easy much of the time to fathom what he truly felt and just what the intended audience for his bluster might be—his advisers? The Communist party hierarchy? Himself? The President? "The West and the United States must recognize one fact," he told Kennedy emphatically. "Communism exists and has won its right to develop."

He had no doubt, he insisted, that Communism would ultimately triumph over capitalism. The United States had been trying to extinguish Communism ever since the 1917 revolution, but "Once an idea is born, it cannot be chained or burned."

Once in full flow, Khrushchev could rant interminably. The man seethed with personal as well as political resentments. He harangued Kennedy at length about the allure of Communism, the evils of capitalism and the folly of Western attempts to stop it by force or threats of force. "Ideas should not be imposed by war," he said, as if this were his own discovery.

Kennedy instantly recognized that Khrushchev had just given him a chance to interrupt the flow. "Mao Tse-tung says power is at the end of a rifle."

Khrushchev feigned incredulity. "I do not believe Mao Tse-tung could have said this. He is a Marxist, and Marxists have always been against war."[19]

In August 1958 Khrushchev had traveled to Peking, where Mao had urged him to join with China in a nuclear war against the capitalist West. "What does it matter if three hundred million Chinese die?" said Mao rhetorically. A chastened Khrushchev returned to Moscow and informed the Soviet leadership that Mao was a madman and all transfers of nuclear technology to China had to stop immediately. But in Vienna he portrayed Mao as a champion of peace.[20]

After listening to another long rant on the glories of Communism, Kennedy once again talked about the risk of miscalculation. "My main ambition is to secure peace," he said.

Khrushchev responded dismissively. "Miscalculation is a very vague term, and it looks to me that what the United States wants is for the U.S.S.R. to sit like a schoolboy with his hands on the desk. . . . But the Soviet Union will defend its interests, even though the United States might regard some of its acts as 'miscalculation.'"

When the session broke up for lunch, Kennedy asked Llewellyn Thompson, "Is it always like this?"

"Par for the course, Mr. President." Thompson had spent many hours being harangued—often in the middle of the night—by Khrushchev. The difference was that Khrushchev could talk like this to any ambassador. But to berate the President of the richest and most powerful country in the world was discourteous and foolish. The best way to play a weak hand is confidently, but Khrushchev was playing his recklessly.[21]

Kennedy tried to ignore that, being the gracious, welcoming host at lunch. Khrushchev toasted the President's health and said he envied the President's youth and energy. But he could not resist boasting about Gagarin's flight and told Kennedy, "He sang songs while in orbit."

During the afternoon session, Khrushchev continued to argue that the United States was the great obstacle to the hopes of people all over the world. Look at Iran. "The Shah will certainly be overthrown. By supporting the Shah, the United States generates adverse feelings towards itself by the people of Iran." And then there was Cuba. "The President's decision to support a landing in Cuba only strengthened the revolutionary forces and Castro's own position. . . . Castro is not a Communist, but U.S. policy can make him one."[22]

Kennedy said Khrushchev was right about the Shah. Iran had to change, or there would be a revolution. As for Cuba, "It was a mistake." But, "Would you tolerate a regime friendly to the United States, with military bases, on your border in, say, Poland?"

"Of course not!" said Khrushchev.

"Well, that is the way we feel about Cuba."

Khrushchev nevertheless had plenty of ammunition left. The United States, the great champion of democracy, was propping up squalid reactionary regimes around the globe, something Kennedy not only knew but had denounced throughout his years in Congress. He sat abashed and tongue-tied as Khrushchev berated him. And when he protested, "I am *for* change," Khrushchev laughed in his face.

When this second discomfiting session ground to an end, Kennedy was exhausted and frustrated. "He treated me like a little boy," he raged that night. "Like a little boy." He had come to Vienna to make Khrushchev take him seriously, and failed.[23]

The President was driven to the Soviet embassy the next morning for a second day of talks. He was met by thousands of cheering Austrians. That seemed an auspicious beginning, but Khrushchev was as relentless as before. They agreed to settle the Laotian conflict peacefully, but when Kennedy turned the discussion to a ban on testing nuclear weapons, Khrushchev hunkered down.

A ban on testing would not reduce the number of nuclear weapons, he said. "I agree," Kennedy responded. "Nor will it reduce the production of such weapons. But a test ban will make the development of nuclear weapons by other countries less likely."

Khrushchev brushed that aside. Instead of saying *nyet* to nuclear testing, for years the Soviets had been demanding the impossible: a treaty on "general and complete disarmament" to be supervised by a reorganized United Nations. Khrushchev wanted the UN Charter to be rewritten so that it would have three chairmen—one each from the Soviet Union and the United States, and a neutral person acceptable to the two superpowers. Only then could there be a ban on nuclear tests.[24]

What Khrushchev really wanted to talk about that second day, however, was not a test ban but Berlin—"The bone in my throat," he angrily called it.[25]

Berlin had become a humiliation, proof to the civilized world of the failure of Communism both politically and economically. Every day several hundred East Germans with technical skills or professional qualifications boarded trams, buses and subways in East Berlin, crossed over to West Berlin, and stayed there. The repercussions were being felt not only across East Germany but across the whole of Eastern Europe. If the fragile East German economy collapsed, the other hated police states that sustained Soviet power would go down with it.

"The U.S.S.R. will sign a peace treaty unilaterally with East Germany," said Khrushchev, "and all rights of access to Berlin will expire."

Kennedy told him, "We are in Berlin not because of someone's sufferance. We fought our way there, although our casualties may not have been as high as yours." Beyond that, however, "U.S. national security is involved. If we were to accept the Soviet proposal, our commitments would be regarded as a mere scrap of paper. Western Europe is vital to our national security [and] if we leave West Berlin, Europe will be abandoned as well." He put it in personal terms, too. "I did not assume the office of President to preside over the isolation of my country."

Khrushchev was adamant. "I have to assure you that no force in the world will prevent the U.S.S.R. from signing a peace treaty with East Germany."

"Would this peace treaty block access to Berlin'?"

"Yes."

Each man restated his respective position for hours, before lunch, during lunch, after lunch. As the talks ended, Khrushchev told the President bluntly, "It is up to the United States to decide whether there will be war or peace. The Soviet Union will sign the peace treaty in December."

"Then, Mr. Chairman, there will be war."[26]

=

The mood in Washington that summer was grim and apprehensive, and Kennedy's mind turned to a subject he had been interested in for the past decade. At times he had been one of the very few members of Congress who even thought about civil defense.

Eisenhower had considered a shelter program but was informed that it would take at least ten years before remote towns such as Gettysburg would have their own nuclear bunkers. And ordering the population of a large city into the shelters would almost certainly trigger panic. Eisenhower promptly dropped the idea. After the Vienna summit, however, Kennedy couldn't help thinking about the millions of lives that might be saved if such problems could be overcome.

Hardly had the President arrived back in Washington before the leader of the East German regime, Walter Ulbricht, gave one of his rare press conferences, mainly to boast that a peace treaty with Moscow would be signed by December 31. Western access to Berlin would then come to a halt, he acknowledged, but Ulbricht tried to reassure Berliners by saying, "Nobody has any intention of building a wall."[27]

Just talking about a wall was enough to fuel desperation. Within a week, the number of people defecting from East Germany into West Berlin rose from around three hundred and fifty a day to more than a thousand. East Germany seemed likely to collapse before December 31.[28]

The President meanwhile asked Dean Acheson to produce a report on the Berlin problem, which Acheson promptly did. Like de Gaulle, he saw no point in negotiating over Berlin. The essential thing was to stand up to the Soviets, he advised the President.

He wanted Kennedy to declare a national emergency, send another eighty to a hundred thousand troops to Germany and launch a rapid increase in both nuclear and conventional forces. Berlin, he asserted, was not the real issue. It was merely a pretext for a direct Soviet challenge to American resolve.[29]

During a heated National Security Council meeting on June 29, Kennedy put a question to Acheson: "If we build up our forces, won't they build up theirs?" Acheson had to concede that was so but said he hoped there would be a way for the two sides to agree not to engage in an arms race.

Kennedy had unerringly put his finger directly on the basic flaw in Acheson's reasoning. If the two sides could agree on something as fundamental as the military threat, that assumed a lot of common ground between them already. And if there was that much common ground, surely they could reach a peaceful settlement over Berlin. Lighting on the weakness in Acheson's argument, Kennedy asked him to look into possible negotiating strategies.[30]

Laos . . . Cuba . . . now Berlin . . . and a clear pattern of crisis management was emerging. Kennedy had a bottomless appetite for competition and none for confrontation. He refused to allow his advisers to push him into any position where he might be right in principle but had no room left for maneuver. Young as he was, like the much older and more experienced Eisenhower, Kennedy insisted on maintaining a choice of options even as he picked up the gauntlet.

Nor did he ignore the pressures Khrushchev would have been under from *his* advisers. Kennedy was careful not to push Khrushchev into a position where the Russian felt trapped.

After several days of reflection, McNamara nevertheless endorsed Acheson's proposed military buildup. JFK, too, was attracted to the idea, for reasons that went beyond the immediate challenge over Berlin. A military buildup might help offset whatever impression of weakness Khrushchev had taken away from Vienna; it would reassure the NATO allies of American resolve; it would help correct some undeniable deficiencies in conventional weaponry; and it would stimulate the economy, something Kennedy was eager to do.

On July 25 he went on television to announce a military buildup—the third since he'd taken office. Draft calls would be more than doubled, a hundred and fifty thousand reservists would be called to active duty, obsolescent warships and B-47 strategic bombers would be taken out of mothballs and large stocks of conventional arms and ammunition would be purchased. He also wanted more than $200 million to begin a nuclear shelter program. "In the coming months," he declared solemnly, "I hope to let every citizen know what steps he can take without delay to protect his family in case of attack." It was a hair-raising experience for millions of Americans; war seemed frighteningly close that summer's night.[31]

Even so, within his speech, Kennedy had waved an olive branch in Khrushchev's direction. While he had justified the military buildup as a response to the Soviet challenge over Berlin, he pointedly said nothing about freedom of movement in Berlin for Berliners. As he put it to Bundy's deputy, Walt Rostow, "Khrushchev is losing East Germany. He cannot let that happen. If East Germany goes, so will Poland and all of Eastern Europe. He will have to do something to stop the flow of refugees—perhaps a wall. And we won't be able to prevent it. I can hold the Allies together to defend West Berlin, but I cannot act to keep East Berlin open."[32]

On August 4, ten days after the President's televised address, there was a meeting of Warsaw Pact leaders in Moscow. Ulbricht and Khrushchev agreed to physically divide Berlin; initially with barbed wire, then with a wall. The East Germans would be careful to make sure none of the barbed wire and not even a single brick touched West Berlin: the barrier would be raised entirely on the East German side.[33]

Khrushchev was certain Kennedy would not respond with force to the Wall. He felt he had gotten the measure of the man in Vienna. Dealing with him, Khrushchev had assured the Warsaw Pact leaders, was not like dealing with Eisenhower and Dulles. "They had more stability [but] Kennedy is too much of a lightweight."[34]

During the early hours of August 13, barbed-wire barricades went up across the city. Bus, tram and train services were halted. The number of crossing points between East and West was reduced from thirteen to just two. Nearly all movement by Germans came to a halt. "It's not a very nice solution," a resigned Kennedy told his staff, "but a wall is a hell of a lot better than a war."[35]

Warned by West Berlin's mayor, Willy Brandt, that morale among West Berliners was in danger of collapsing, Kennedy responded by dispatching a sixteen-hundred-man battle group down the autobahn from West Germany to West Berlin and sending a deeply reluctant, noticeably fearful Lyndon Johnson to the city. The Vice President was to be on hand to greet the troops when they arrived two days later.

The President also sent a retired general, Lucius D. Clay, with Johnson. West Berliners revered Clay as the man who had organized the Berlin Airlift in 1948 and defeated Stalin's attempts to starve and freeze them into submission. His return to Berlin in August 1961 dispelled many West Berliners' fears that they were about to be abandoned by their American protectors.[36]

Once Kennedy announced a major military buildup, Khrushchev felt forced to respond in kind, much as the President had anticipated. On August 9 he boasted that Soviet scientists could build a hundred-megaton hydrogen bomb—ten times bigger than anything exploded so far.[37]

While the Berlin crisis was unfolding that August, Elie Abel, a young journalist who had gotten to know Kennedy during the 1960 campaign, asked to see the President. They met upstairs, in JFK's bedroom, as a helicopter sat on the South Lawn, its rotor turning.

"What's on your mind?"

Abel said he was hoping to write a book on the first term. "Well, I haven't been in office long enough," Kennedy responded.

The time to start collecting material was now rather than after the first term became history, Abel explained. "I'm thinking of a 1964 book, but obviously it has to be completed over a period of years and I need your help."

Kennedy sat on the bed in a somber, introspective mood. "Why would anyone want to write about an administration that has nothing to show for itself but a string of disasters?"

Abel told him he was wrong; his administration was going to turn out to be a success. As Abel sought to shore up his confidence, Kennedy barked out an order to O'Donnell. "Tell him to turn that thing off. I'm not leaving yet." A minute or two later, the helicopter rotor stopped turning. Abel's assurances were what Kennedy wanted to hear; they told him something he needed to know—his presidency was still a work in progress. There was time yet to put it right. JFK needed someone to tell him that. To him, time had never been a friend: always a foe.[38]

CHAPTER 29

Commander in Chief

John Kennedy's mixed attitudes towards the military hadn't changed much since his days as a lieutenant (j.g.). He not only felt comfortable around military personnel, but many of those who were close to him had served as he had done in combat units during World War II. Torby Macdonald had won the Silver Star, William Walton had jumped into Normandy with the Eighty-second Airborne Division, Chuck Spalding had been a Navy fighter pilot and so on. At the same time, like many a junior officer, JFK had an innate and easily aroused contempt for brass hats.

Courage under fire seemed to impress him more readily than almost any other experience. Kennedy was fascinated by Douglas MacArthur and had memorized the proposed citation for the Medal of Honor that MacArthur was recommended to receive in World War I but unfairly did not get—"On a field where courage was the dominant feature, his courage excelled all." Early in his presidency, Kennedy visited the Waldorf Astoria for a long man-to-man talk with the eighty-one-year-old MacArthur.[1]

Eisenhower had allowed the annual Medal of Honor reception for all living recipients to lapse. Kennedy reinstated it. He also took a close interest in military uniforms, the design of medals, military bands, weapons demonstrations, the service academies and Army-Navy football games.

Captain John D. Bulkeley, the naval officer who had aroused John F. Kennedy's interest in PT boats and overlooked his physical problems to permit his command of one, had written an official history called "At Close Quarters: PT Boats in the United States Navy." The story it told was essentially a catalog of failures, and Bulkeley's manuscript had been languishing for years.

With JFK's election, the Navy suddenly saw reason to publish it and Kennedy provided the foreword. "Small though they were, the PT boats played a key role," he informed Bulkeley's readers. "They filled an important need in World War II in shallow waters, complementing the achievements of greater ships in greater seas."

As President, Kennedy was issued a unique dog tag, one he was immensely proud of. It was the standard issue aluminum model but inscribed, "Kennedy, John F., Commander in Chief." His blood group was "O" and religion "Roman Catholic."[2]

Generals and admirals nevertheless and almost by virtue of rank seemed to get under his skin. When Robert Donovan, a well-known journalist, came to talk to him about a book he was writing on the short, dramatic wartime exploits of *PT-109,* Kennedy told him what he remembered best about the Solomons campaign—"That whole story was fucked up. How do we ever win any wars anyway? You know the military always screws up everything."[3]

Kennedy's interest in war had run deep ever since he had walked through the London parks in August 1938 at the height of the Munich Crisis and seen Londoners preparing for war with antiaircraft guns among the trees. World War II had reinforced his fascination by giving it a personal dimension, not only through his own experiences but also the deaths of Joe Jr. and Billy Hartington.

Few politicians seemed to have war on their minds as much as he, or to be so attracted to its hazards. During his years in the House, JFK traveled to war zones from Israel to Vietnam. He spent many hours studying, writing and talking about the defense of Western Europe and spoke on war with all the conviction, if not the knowledge, of an expert.

In 1951, after talking to Eisenhower about NATO's strategy for holding back the Red Army, Kennedy convinced himself that, given enough troops, a conventional war in Europe was possible even if both sides possessed nuclear weapons. He did not get that idea from talking to Eisenhower, who had twenty atomic bombs and Truman's authority to use them if the Red Army launched a conventional attack. It was JFK's own idea, one that he carried into the White House a decade later.[4]

He brought, too, a sense that there was nothing more important to a President than thinking hard about war. "Domestic policy can only defeat us," he told his staff. "Foreign policy can kill us."[5]

During his 1952 campaign for the Senate, Kennedy had issued strident warnings about an impending "bomber gap" with the U.S.S.R. He had been alerted to a CIA estimate that turned out to be totally wrong. As a presidential candidate eight years later, he declaimed vehemently against the emerging "missile gap." He was relying on yet another CIA estimate that was riddled with dubious assumptions.[6]

The missile-gap controversy would not fade away, however. In the waning months of the Eisenhower administration, the Single Integrated Operational Plan (SIOP) was developed to integrate the Navy's Polaris submarines into a joint attack plan with the Strategic Air Command's force of strategic bombers and intercontinental ballistic missiles (ICBMs). On February 3, McNamara was briefed on it.

The SIOP targeted four nuclear weapons—one big bomb and three smaller bombs—on dozens of major objectives, such as Moscow and the Soviet missile complex at Plesetsk. It also called for placing hundreds of nuclear warheads on targets across China and Eastern Europe. It offered four options, but it was really designed for just one of them—"Plan 1-A." This was an annihilating first strike designed to obliterate the Soviet Union and devastate China. Up to 285 million people would die if Plan 1-A was ever implemented. Hundreds of millions more would be crippled or mutilated.[7]

Three days later, Pentagon correspondents had a meeting with McNamara, who wanted to talk about the DOD's budget. But what about the missile gap? they wanted to know. "There is no missile gap," said McNamara impatiently.[8]

On February 8, Kennedy told a press conference that McNamara hadn't really said there wasn't a missile gap. The Defense Department was still looking into the question, said the President. "It would be premature to reach a judgment as to whether there is a gap," he insisted, which skated over the fact that he had been claiming for more than a year that such a gap existed.[9]

He adjusted his appraisal, however, so that the Soviets were now on a par with the United States, and his meeting with Khrushchev in Vienna only convinced him he was right. On his return journey from Austria to Washington, Kennedy stopped over in London to meet with Harold Macmillan, the prime minister, and have dinner with the Queen.

The President told Macmillan, "The Russians have at least as powerful nuclear forces as the West. They have interior lines. They have a buoyant economy and soon will outmatch capitalist society in the race for material wealth. It follows they will make no concessions."[10]

Not surprisingly, then, the erection of the Berlin Wall seemed to him to signal even more dangerous developments to come. Khrushchev sounded as determined as ever to sign a peace treaty with the East Germans. Two weeks after the Wall went up, JFK sat in his rocking chair in the Oval Office in a somber mood, talking to Chalmers Roberts of *The Washington Post*. "We shall probably come very close to the edge," he told Roberts.[11]

To reduce the tension and, as he saw it, the risks of a fatal misunderstanding, Kennedy continued trying to find areas of agreement with the Soviets while insisting on access rights to Berlin. The State Department blandly called the President's approaches to Khrushchev exploratory talks, not negotiations. De Gaulle and Adenauer weren't convinced. To them, where Berlin was concerned, even seeking agreement on peripheral issues was tantamount to appeasing the Russians. That would only encourage Khrushchev to push harder, demand more and take risks with peace. While Kennedy was fretting over Berlin, his allies were fretting over him.[12]

A week after he told Chalmers Roberts that both sides might find themselves facing war over Berlin, Kennedy received an indirect message from Khrushchev that with the Wall doing its work, there might not be a peace treaty after all. Cyrus Sulzberger, the publisher of *The New York Times*, interviewed Khrushchev on September 5. The Chairman said he had a personal, off-the-record message for the President. It amounted to a signal that he was going to back off.[13]

Still worried that Berlin might yet drag the two sides into a nuclear war, Kennedy finally asked the military to brief him on the SIOP. Lemnitzer spent two hours explaining the general design of the plan and some of the specifics.

The President discovered that there was an implicit bias in favor of Plan I-A, and Lemnitzer strongly discouraged him from thinking he could take parts of the plan that he favored and discard the rest. "Any decision to execute only a portion of the entire plan would involve acceptance of certain grave risks. . . . There is no mechanism for a rapid reworking of the plan. . . ."[14]

Kennedy bristled at that. He disliked subordinates shutting off his options and thereby pushing him towards their preferred course of action. The SIOP, however, had never been tested, and never could be. Massive redundancy had been built into it because much of the plan probably would not work. Few ICBMs with nuclear warheads had ever been fired. Polaris submarines were hard to contact when under the sea. Strategic Air Command's B-52s might be the only reliable element in the entire plan.

The President was surprised to see that an attack on China was part of the SIOP. The Chinese had no nuclear weapons. "Why do we hit all those targets in China, General?"

"It's in the plan," replied Lemnitzer, as if it were a kind of targeting parameter that mere mortals had to accept.

Kennedy left the briefing angry and dismayed. "And we call ourselves the human race," he said to Dean Rusk, who had sat through the briefing with him.[15]

A few days later he accepted an invitation to address the United Nations. He would use his speech to indicate to Khrushchev that he was not seeking a Berlin confrontation, either. But just as important was what he had learned about the SIOP. He spoke mainly, and eloquently, on the peril of nuclear weapons. "Never have the nations of the world had so much to lose, or so much to gain," he concluded. "Together we shall save our planet, or together we shall perish in its flames."[16]

What the Germans—and presumably Khrushchev—paid more attention to was the absence of any reference to the Berlin Wall or to German unification. The West Germans were disappointed and the Soviets reassured.

A month later there was a tense confrontation at Checkpoint Charlie in which thirty American tanks and thirty Soviet tanks were almost muzzle-to-muzzle. Khrushchev defused the situation by ordering the Soviet tanks to pull back. With that, the threat of war over Berlin, which had haunted Kennedy for months, faded.

Nevertheless, the pressure was still being applied. At Vienna, Khrushchev had assured Kennedy that the Soviet Union would not be the first to breach the informal nuclear test moratorium that had been in place since 1959. On August 31 he announced that the Soviet Union was going to resume testing in the atmosphere.[17]

On September 21 the CIA produced an estimate of the Soviet missile arsenal and concluded that it might consist of only four ICBMs. These were monsters that took twenty hours to fill with liquid fuel, out in the open, in full sight of American satellites and wide open to attack—or misinterpretation.

At the time of JFK's inauguration there were three Polaris submarines in operation, and there would be three more by summer. That meant there would be two boats on station at all times, and sometimes three, and each boat carried 16 missiles with a range of 1,200 miles. There were few major cities in the Soviet Union out of their range. Kennedy ordered a further 23 Polaris submarines in the spring of 1961. Yet not even this was considered enough: he later raised the total Polaris force to 41 boats carrying 656 missiles.

Eisenhower had planned to have a force of 600 Minuteman ICBMs fully deployed by the fall of 1962. Kennedy asked for an extra 1,000 ICBMs. He and McNamara claimed this was the minimum figure they could get Congress and the military to accept, ignoring the fact that Eisenhower's much smaller force had been considered adequate. While professing horror at the huge number of nuclear weapons that the SIOP targeted on the Soviet Union, Kennedy increased the number of warheads available by more than 300 percent. As more warheads became available, SIOP planners inevitably looked for, and found, more targets.

Having finally accepted that there was no missile gap and that there was not going to be one, Kennedy wanted to tell Khrushchev he had seen through the Soviets' bluff. He was not going to do it directly, though. "When I get up and say those things, I sound too belligerent," he told Bundy. The choice fell on Roswell Gilpatric, McNamara's deputy.[18]

On October 21, with signals intelligence indicating that Khrushchev's "Big Bomb" was about to be detonated, Gilpatric addressed the National Business Council in Hot Springs, Arkansas. The President edited Gilpatric's speech line by line to make sure it struck the right tone—confident rather than saber-rattling, dramatic but not melodramatic.[19]

"This nation has a nuclear retaliatory force of such lethal power that an enemy move which brought it into play would be an act of self-destruction on his part," declared Gilpatric. "The destructive power which the United States could bring to bear even after a Soviet surprise attack would be as great as—perhaps greater than—the total undamaged force which the enemy can launch against the United States in a first strike. . . . The Soviets' bluster must be evaluated against the hard facts of United States nuclear superiority."[20]

Nine days later, on October 30, the Soviets triggered a fifty-eight-megaton hydrogen bomb, the biggest explosion in human history. The flash could be seen from six hundred miles away. Far from impressing people with Soviet might, the enormous amount of radioactive fallout terrified them. It was a propaganda disaster and had the paradoxical effect of only seeming to confirm that the Soviet Union really was an inferior power.

The President's public response to Khrushchev's Big Bomb was to assure his countrymen, "In terms of total military strength, the United States would not trade places with any nation on Earth and will take whatever steps are necessary to maintain our lead."[21]

Meanwhile, he was struggling to turn that overwhelming superiority into a national strategy. Truman had a basic national security policy; so did Ike. But when Bundy's deputy, Walt Whitman Rostow, produced a document that encapsulated the administration's thinking on national security issues, Kennedy wouldn't sign it. "It's a lot of words, isn't it?" he said dismissively. "Walt writes a lot of words."[22]

The point of having a statement on basic national security policy was to provide guidance to the huge federal bureaucracy and the armed services on just what the President wanted to achieve and how, in general terms, he proposed to achieve it. Such a statement would spell out the administration's attitude towards East-West trade, for example, or policy on the proliferation of nuclear weapons. Kennedy, though, feared the bureaucracy might use anything like this to tie him down and limit his room to maneuver.

What he did know was that he despised Eisenhower's strategy of massive retaliation, which had nothing to do with retaliation and everything to do with Plan 1-A. As Eisenhower had once bluntly expressed it, "SAC must not allow the enemy to strike the first blow." The word "retaliation" was designed to deflect public attention from the true national strategy of first strike if it ever appeared the Soviets were about to attack any country in NATO. Its premise was that if the Soviets knew they faced a choice between a nuclear war and no war, they would invariably opt for peace.[23]

Eisenhower's approach had guided the creation of the strategic nuclear triad of B-52 bombers, Polaris submarines and the Minuteman ICBM. It had also created a ring of bases around the Soviet Union that would enable SAC to carry out its mission within four hours of being ordered to attack. It was a strategy accepted without demur by the Joint Chiefs and by the governments of Britain, France and Germany as being the most realistic and effective available.

Kennedy found that impossible to accept. There was more emotion than logic behind his approach to nuclear weapons. He was temperamentally incapable of accepting a national strategy based on only two possibilities—nukes or surrender. Determined to have a range of options, he tried to create a third—"flexible response." The core idea was that a Soviet conventional attack against Western Europe would not necessarily trigger a first-strike nuclear attack on the Soviet Union.

The new approach was endorsed not only by Bundy and McNamara but also by retired Army Chief of Staff Maxwell D. Taylor. Following the Bay of Pigs, Kennedy had installed Taylor in the White House as his military adviser, thereby undercutting the Joint Chiefs.

Eisenhower used to meet with the Joint Chiefs every couple of weeks, and often there were no civilians present. He was the Commander in Chief talking with his military advisers, and without the Secretary of Defense or any of the service secretaries there, they felt free to say just what they thought. Kennedy, by contrast, treated them with disdain, as the appointment of Taylor demonstrated.[24]

No one in the professional military was sure just what flexible response was. The division had always been nuclear war and conventional war. Neither Kennedy, nor McNamara, nor Maxwell Taylor ever explained just what it was that distinguished flexible response from a conventional response. At NATO's Supreme Headquarters, the term "flexible response" was banned, in case it created confusion on planning staffs.[25]

The pursuit of flexible response was also placing severe strain on the alliance. NATO's European members took Kennedy's attempts to abandon Eisenhower's strategy as a loss of nerve in Washington; something that could only encourage the Soviets to push until they found where the new limits were.[26]

It had to be tacitly abandoned without admitting it. In Athens, in May 1962, McNamara tried to reassure NATO's senior European commanders that U.S. nuclear policy hadn't really changed from what it had been under Eisenhower. "The United States is prepared to respond immediately with nuclear weapons to the use of nuclear weapons against one or more members of the Alliance. The United States is also prepared to counter with nuclear weapons any Soviet conventional attack so strong it cannot be dealt with by conventional means." Then he came to what they really wanted to hear—"There is a high probability that in an ambiguous situation the West, not the East, would have to initiate the use of nuclear weapons." This meant the Soviets would not be allowed to prepare to strike without being struck first.[27]

Even as he worried about nuclear weapons and sought to improve the mechanisms that controlled them, Kennedy could be breathtakingly cavalier. One night in New York he eluded his Secret Service detail by leaving the Hotel Carlyle through the basement. There was a girl he had arranged to have sex with at a party in a town house nearby. In giving the Secret Service the slip, he'd also left on the sidewalk an Army lieutenant who was carrying "the Football," a black vinyl satchel handcuffed to his wrist that held the authorization codes to unleash the radioactive wraith roughly chained within the confines of the SIOP.[28]

Snowball

At five P.M. on the evening of March 13, the Democratic and Republican congressional leadership on Capitol Hill and more than a hundred diplomats from Latin America arrived at the East Room. Almost every diplomat had his wife or mistress on his arm. Jackie, chatting easily in Spanish, took them on a tour of the Red, Blue and Green rooms, bringing them back to the East Room at six o'clock. When the Marine band broke into "Ruffles and Flourishes," followed by "Hail to the Chief," a smiling, immaculate JFK entered and made his first foreign policy address as President.

Voice of America was broadcasting his speech across Latin America, instantaneously translated into Spanish and Portuguese as he spoke. "We meet together as firm and ancient friends," Kennedy told the gathering. "Our continents are bound together by a common history. . . . Our nations are the product of a common struggle, the revolt from colonial rule. And our people share a common heritage, the quest for the dignity and the freedom of man."

Yet there was still much to do. "Let me be the first to admit that we North Americans have not always grasped the significance of this common mission [and] many in your own countries have not fully understood the urgency of the need to lift people from poverty and ignorance and despair." This direct, undiplomatic rebuke was answered by an uneasy murmur among the small gilded chairs arranged in semicircles on either side of the dais.

The challenge was immense, Kennedy conceded, but America was ready to help. He was calling on all the nations of Latin America "to join in a new Alliance for Progress—*una Alianza para el Progreso*—a vast ten-year plan for the Americas."

Kennedy compared it to the Marshall Plan—American money and know-how would be deployed to lift up the economies and societies of America's friends and allies. The biggest contribution Latin American governments could make was greater democracy. "Political freedom must accompany material progress."

The diplomats applauded as enthusiastically, expressed their approval as volubly and beamed as hopefully as only rich cynics can do. Theirs was a performance, and Kennedy, no mean performer himself, probably sensed that. The diplomats were drawn from the tiny, privileged and often corrupt Spanish-descended cliques of Latin America. They were not going to give away their advantages in life to the impoverished majority of whatever country they represented. For now, though, all they had to do was smile, nod approvingly and applaud.[1]

Before becoming President, Kennedy had seemed interested in virtually every part of the globe except Latin America. What made the difference now was Castro and, not far behind, Khrushchev. Early in his presidency, Kennedy received a report from one of his advisers, Adolph A. Berle, describing Latin America as "an active Cold War theatre." The Soviets—and the Chinese—said Berle, were "stimulating and arming local political movements to the point where they can be converted into civil wars and used to seize and set up governments which will be hostile to the United States."[2]

The new President took Berle's apocalyptic visions seriously and pessimistically. Even here, in America's backyard, Khrushchev seemed to have the advantage. The Soviets would pour money into Cuba and make it a showcase for what Communism could do to transform an impoverished Third World country. "He's only got to worry about seven million Cubans," Kennedy complained to Walt Rostow, Bundy's deputy, "whereas I've got to be concerned with the future of two hundred million Latin Americans. He's bound to do better."[3]

Behind the glittering façade of the speech from the East Room on

March 13 was Kennedy's conviction that time was working against him in Latin America, as it was in so much of his life. Yet there was something to build on. Early in his presidency, Eisenhower had supported right-wing dictators to ward off the threat of Communist subversion in Latin America. Late in his presidency, however, in Cuba and elsewhere, many of the dictators were overthrown or forced to flee. Eisenhower had changed tack, launching new programs that presaged, in effect, Kennedy's Alliance for Progress.[4]

JFK secured $500 million from Congress to alleviate some of the worst poverty in Latin America and secured more money to tackle the effects of natural disasters. Yet any comparison with the Marshall Plan was misleading. In purely economic terms, the Alliance depended on its progress for private investment in Latin America. Kennedy knew he would never get Congress to put up even a tenth of the money that had gone to Western Europe after World War II.

Latin America was simply too corrupt for it to be otherwise. Almost from the start, the Alliance proved to be little more in practice than a new opportunity for Latin American elites to become ever richer. A reformed Inter-American Development Bank was suddenly willing to make loans, sometimes outright gifts, to dictators in exchange for easing back on repression. A few crumbs of comfort—a school here, a little less corruption there, a reduction in torture somewhere else—helped provide illusory suggestions of fundamental reform.[5]

Kennedy had no illusions about the difficulties he faced. When Adolfo López Mateos of Mexico told him "the Alliance for Progress is the best way to combat Communism," JFK said the necessary economic reforms would take too long for it to succeed: "I return again and again to the question, what do you think is the best way to deal with the obvious danger of an expansion of Communist influence in Latin America?" López Mateos said he would give the subject more thought.[6]

Kennedy's sympathies were nonetheless with the poor. He had nothing but contempt for the elites. The International Monetary Fund was willing to provide sizable loans but wanted to impose stringent conditions. Kennedy came close to telling the Argentine Minister for the Economy to take the money and ignore the conditions. "A too conservative and cautious and deflationary policy," said Kennedy, "would meet the interests and desires of the privileged groups and the bankers, but it would not serve the needs of the people."[7]

The Alliance for Progress was ultimately associated with repression, not liberation. While the emphasis John Kennedy publicly placed on it was always economic, social and political reform, he was also putting American money and expertise into counterinsurgency programs and the training of tens of thousands of paramilitary police. Imprisonment, state terrorism, torture and disappearances flourished across much of Latin America in the 1960s. There was no more democracy at the end of the Decade of Development than there had been at the beginning.[8]

One dictator who did not survive was one of the most cruel and corrupt, Rafael Trujillo of the Dominican Republic. Eisenhower had broken diplomatic relations with Trujillo in 1959, and shortly after he became President, Kennedy was briefed on a CIA plot to help Trujillo's enemies assassinate him.

He did not like the idea of assassination but did not explicitly rule it out. What seemed to trouble him more was whether it was worth the risk. "The United States should not initiate the overthrow of Trujillo before knowing what kind of government would succeed him," he told Allen Dulles at a National Security Council meeting on May 5, 1961.[9]

The plot continued to unfold. The CIA provided the weapons, and the State Department took them into the Dominican Republic in the diplomatic bag. They were handed over to a family that had a long-standing grudge against Trujillo. At the end of May, during his first evening in Paris, Kennedy received an urgent call from Rusk—"Trujillo is dead."

"Were we involved?"

"I don't think so," said Rusk. "There's some confusion."[10]

Following Trujillo's assassination, his son Ramfis seized power. The brutality, repression and corruption continued much as before. Kennedy's qualms about what might follow the removal of Rafael Trujillo proved to be justified.

Fletcher Knebel wrote an article on the prominent Americans, some of them friends of JFK, who had been on good terms with Rafael Trujillo. One of his instruments of torture included a black dwarf called "Snowball." The dwarf's specialty was biting off the testicles of the dictator's enemies. Several months after the article was published, Knebel interviewed Kennedy.

"Read your piece on the Dominican Republic," he said. "Hey, whatever happened to that dwarf?"[11]

Frustrated at the way the assassination had turned out, six months later, in November 1961, Kennedy had the Navy and Marines close in on the

Dominican Republic. Ramfis Trujillo was given a simple choice: get out or fight it out. He could see the invasion fleet from his bedroom window and started packing for exile in Paris.[12]

Meanwhile, Castro was becoming more secure and more popular with the Cuban people than he had been before the Bay of Pigs. Both the President and Bobby Kennedy were becoming obsessed with him. In the fall of 1961 JFK put Bobby in charge of "Operation Mongoose," a program to destabilize the Cuban government and, if all else failed, assassinate Castro. "Every President eventually gets an albatross," Kennedy lamented to newspaper publisher Gardner Cowles. "I've got Cuba." It was a metaphor more apt than he may have realized: by definition, once you've got an albatross, it stays with you until you die.[13]

=

John F. Kennedy came to the White House with a greater interest in the Third World than any President before or since. As a young congressman, he had visited countries that had just won their independence, and he invariably took the side of the native people. He believed that nationalism would ultimately prove stronger than Communism and felt the United States should simply accept that most new countries did not want to be dragged into the Cold War.

Unlike many in the Republican party, Kennedy did not consider neutralism immoral or a threat to American interests. Drafting a letter to Nasser one day, he remarked to a State Department official, "You know, we have to remember this guy has got his problems, too. He's got a public opinion. I understand there are some things he can't do."[14]

Ghana needed a major dam on the Volta River, but its leader, Kwame Nkrumah, was often in Moscow and continually blasting the United States. There was strong opposition in Congress—and from Bobby—to the dam, but Kennedy got the CIA to investigate Nkrumah. They concluded he wasn't a secret Communist. After that, Kennedy said the project would go ahead. "Nkrumah won't be there forever, but the dam will be." By the time the dam was finished five years later, so was Nkrumah.[15]

There was no powerful denunciation from the United States when Jawaharlal Nehru sent in the Indian Army to wrest Goa from the Portuguese, or when the Indonesian army seized West Irian from the Dutch. "I thoroughly disapprove," Kennedy told his friend David Ormsby-Gore, the British ambassador. "But let's face it, if at the end of the day Goa becomes Indian and West Irian becomes Indonesian, neither you in Britain nor we in America are going to suffer any irrevocable damage. . . . Let's not feel that the whole world is crumbling around us because we can't bring our influence to bear on this kind of issue."[16]

Kennedy intended to increase the amount of money going to Third World countries incrementally, year by year. To achieve that, he created the Agency for International Development, better known as AID. He was soon kicking himself—AID sounded too much like a charity. Eisenhower had presented all his foreign aid programs as a contribution to mutual security. "The Eisenhower people were right," Kennedy ruefully acknowledged. "The only way you can sell this on the Hill is as military security. It should have been the International Defense Fund or something like that." Instead of increasing year on year, economic assistance to the Third World—measured as a share of the U.S. gross national product—actually fell between 1960 and 1964.[17]

Eisenhower had persuaded Congress to pass Public Law 480, which made American agricultural surpluses available to poor countries at low cost or no cost. Kennedy cleverly repackaged—and expanded—PL 480 shipments as "Food for Peace." The great achievement of Food for Peace was getting Congress to sanction wheat sales to the Soviet Union. He would have liked to sell food to China, but that was politically impossible.

Kennedy's deepest desire for the Third World was to see it prosper, not to turn it into a battleground. He didn't think that money was the best way to provide help. Back in 1951, after making two long foreign trips, the young Congressman Kennedy had concluded that the U.S. could not save the world by throwing money at every problem. Rich as the country was, there was a limit to its resources. "A bottle of milk for every Hottentot is not only beyond our grasp," he told reporters, "it is far beyond our reach." Besides, what much of the world needed was less American money and more American technical skills. That was what foreign aid should focus on.[18]

He wasn't the only one who saw things that way. So did Hubert Humphrey. In 1960 Humphrey had introduced legislation that would have created a new kind of aid program based on American volunteers. He called it "the Peace Corps."[19]

Nothing came of his initiative, and it got hardly a mention in the primary campaigns. But late at night on October 15, 1960, when Kennedy flew into Ann Arbor, Michigan, he was expecting to meet a handful of student volunteers who had been working for his campaign. What he found instead was a throng of more than ten thousand students gathered to greet him. He grinned his lopsided grin. "I've come here to sleep, but I guess I should say something," he told his volunteers, then addressed the crowd.

"How many of you are willing to spend ten years in Africa or Latin America or Asia working for the United States and working for freedom?"[20]

As far as JFK was concerned, from this point on, the Peace Corps was *his* idea, and he intended to go ahead with it even though he knew he'd be criticized in Congress and the Republican press for being naive. Following his election, Kennedy organized a task force consisting of Sargent Shriver and Harris Wofford, a former Notre Dame law professor, to see whether a Peace Corps really was a practical idea. They soon discovered there was opposition from the State Department—but not from Dean Rusk, who thought it was a great idea.[21]

The more they worked on their task, the more enthusiastic Shriver and Wofford became. "Having studied at your request the problems of establishing a Peace Corps," Shriver informed the President, "I recommend its immediate establishment . . . we can be in business by Monday morning."[22]

There were critics in the Senate who had to be persuaded, beginning with J. William Fulbright, and there was overt opposition from House troglodytes such as Otto Passman of Louisiana, who hated foreigners and everything that involved them. Some senators and representatives nonetheless supported the Peace Corps because it looked like foreign aid on the cheap—that was the kind they liked best. Kennedy also had to appease right-wing members of Congress by requiring all Peace Corps volunteers to swear a loyalty oath.[23]

He tried to get his father's old friend Herbert Hoover to serve as honorary chairman of the Peace Corps, but at eighty-eight, Hoover felt he had to decline. Kennedy also asked Lem Billings to be director of the Peace Corps, but Billings promptly and firmly turned it down.[24]

Shriver and Wofford came up with a list of people who would be suitable to run it. Most were professors, but the administration had already exposed itself to scorn for having so many academics in high places. After Billings rejected the directorship, JFK offered it to Shriver, who didn't want it, either; he was happy in Chicago. In the end, though, Shriver felt he had to do whatever Jack wanted.[25]

Applications for the Peace Corps arrived by the truckload. Finding volunteers wasn't a problem; finding worthwhile projects to put them to work on was. Most ended up teaching English, since few volunteers possessed technical skills or qualifications in fields such as public health.

The Peace Corps brought a new kind of American missionary—someone who was not on a religious crusade. The emphasis was on youth, rather than experience, much like the White House these days.

Some countries weren't completely happy about taking Peace Corps volunteers. They had few skills to offer and little knowledge of the world. If they had a bad experience, wouldn't they complain to their congressman? And suppose this was a front organization for the hated CIA: wouldn't it be used to destabilize countries the Americans didn't like?

Despite their doubts, few governments felt they could afford to reject a project the President was so obviously involved with. Taking Peace Corps volunteers was not in itself a guarantee of American aid, but saying no might come close to guaranteeing it would never be offered.

Always interested in India and clearly proud of his creation, Kennedy sent a message to Nehru. "What do you think of the idea of our Peace Corps?" Nehru replied that he thought it had merit: there was a lot that privileged young Americans could learn from India's rural poor.[26]

On August 28, 1961, Kennedy invited the first batch of volunteers who were about to go overseas to come and meet him in the Rose Garden. The Peace Corps offered an outlet for the restlessness and idealism of the *On the Road* generation, eager to take on the world. And Nehru was right— the greatest beneficiaries of the Peace Corps were the volunteers, whose lives were immeasurably enriched. The Peace Corps was one of the enduring achievements of Kennedy's brief presidency, and its fundamental resource, a youthful eagerness to engage with life, was emblematic of him.

=

A week after Kennedy became President, Walt Rostow handed him a report on the situation in South Vietnam. Flipping rapidly through the pages, speed-reading at twelve hundred words a minute, Kennedy muttered, "This is going to be the worst one yet."[27]

Next day, January 28, the President had the report's author, Brigadier General Edward Lansdale, come to the Oval Office. Lansdale, an Air Force officer working for the CIA and credited with defeating Communist insurgents in the southern Philippines, had spent the past few years in Vietnam. He was also the hero, called "Colonel Hillandale," of *The Ugly American,* William Lederer and Eugene Burdick's bestselling novel set in Saigon, which Kennedy had read.

Lansdale's report said unequivocally that South Vietnam was losing the fight against Communist guerrillas. Its leader, Ngo Dinh Diem, was a staunch anti-Communist but had done nothing to rally his countrymen behind him. Unless something happened soon, South Vietnam would go under.[28]

Three weeks later McNamara more or less confirmed Lansdale's dismal prognostication. "We have too little ability to deal with guerrilla forces, insurrection and subversion," he told the President.[29]

As the Vietnam debate within the administration unfolded, Kennedy found himself under unremitting pressure from the Joint Chiefs, Robert McNamara, McGeorge Bundy, Walt Rostow and Dean Rusk to make ever-greater commitments to the government of South Vietnam. Nearly every recommendation he received urged, explicitly or implicitly, the introduction of American combat troops, which would turn a small war into a big one.

Throughout the spring and summer of 1961, Kennedy rejected this hawkish advice and looked for less dangerous and dramatic ways of shoring up South Vietnam. Meanwhile, he sanctioned an increase in Diem's army from 150,000 men to 170,000 and told Lyndon Johnson to visit Southeast Asia. Johnson's mission was to assure Diem and the other leaders in the region of American resolve. Johnson did not want to go. "Mr. President, I don't want to embarrass you by getting my head blown off in Saigon."

Kennedy mocked his fears. "Don't worry, Lyndon, if anything happens to you, Sam Rayburn and I will give you the biggest funeral that Austin, Texas, ever saw."[30]

Johnson hand-carried a letter to Diem in which the President said that if the increase to 170,000 men did not prove to be enough, the United States would be willing to pay for even more troops. Not surprisingly, Diem wasted little time in writing back to say that what he really needed was another 100,000 troops, as well as the extra 20,000.[31]

As disenchanted with the Joint Chiefs as they were with him, Kennedy appointed the former Army Chief of Staff Maxwell D. Taylor to a new post, the President's "Military Representative," and installed him in the

White House. He could hardly have made a worse appointment. Taylor advised him to seize northern Laos, even though it had a ninety-mile border with China; to occupy much of the valley of the Mekong in southern Laos; to wage a guerrilla war from Laos into North Vietnam; and to launch an air and naval offensive against the North Vietnamese.[32]

Kennedy was not about to take Taylor's advice. "I'd like nothing better than to get out of Laos," he told Bundy.[33]

He had to do something, however, to tackle the guerrilla problem. The Army had built up a small elite unit, the Special Forces, which consisted of three hundred and fifty men, many of them combat veterans, and all were able to speak at least one East European language, such as Czech or Bulgarian. They were to be infiltrated behind enemy lines in case of war in Europe to organize and lead guerrillas who would wreak havoc at the enemy's rear.

The President seized on the Special Forces and brandished them like a spear. He wanted their numbers increased to two thousand; their training to be altered to fighting against guerrillas and not as guerrillas; and for them to be deployed to Southeast Asia, no matter how well they spoke Polish or German. Impressed by the unique headgear of such units as the British Army's Parachute Regiment (red berets) and the French Foreign Legion (kepis), he decreed that the Special Forces would henceforth wear green berets, and their existence, until then barely known, was widely publicized.[34]

In his address to the United Nations on September 25, Kennedy focused on Berlin and the threat of nuclear war. He also wanted to say something about Southeast Asia. "South Vietnam is under attack, sometimes by a single assassin, sometimes by a band of guerrillas, recently by full battalions." If such wars were permitted to succeed, "the gates will be wide open." Nowhere in the world would be safe.[35]

McNamara and the Joint Chiefs swiftly followed up with a memo that said a force of 23,000 combat troops—mainly American, but with a strong component provided by America's allies in Southeast Asia—was needed urgently to save South Vietnam. If that didn't work, the United States might eventually have to send in 150,000 soldiers. Having lunch with Arthur Krock on October 11, Kennedy told his father's old friend that he wasn't going to approve the Chiefs' recommendation.[36]

Instead, he'd send Taylor and Rostow to look at the situation on the ground. "I still think United States troops should not be involved on the

Asian mainland," said Kennedy. "Anyway, the United States can't interfere in civil disturbances created by guerrillas, and it's hard to prove that isn't largely what's happening in Vietnam."[37]

Departing as hawks in late October, Taylor and Rostow came back as greater hawks ten days later. The United States had to send eight thousand combat troops to fight alongside Diem's army, Taylor told the President, and a bombing campaign should be launched against North Vietnam immediately. Otherwise, "I do not believe our program to save South Vietnam will succeed."[38]

At a National Security Council meeting to discuss the Taylor-Rostow report, Kennedy continued to agonize over what to do. "I could make rather a strong case against intervening in an area ten thousand miles away against sixteen thousand guerrillas with a native army of two hundred thousand, where millions have been spent for years without success."[39]

In the end, though, he felt he had to do something. "There's a limit to the number of defeats I can defend in a twelve-month period," he told John Kenneth Galbraith, whom he'd appointed ambassador to India. "I've had the Bay of Pigs. I've pulled out of Laos. I can't accept a third."[40]

He sent combat troops but called them advisers. The Geneva Accords, which had brought the withdrawal of France from Indochina in 1954, had placed a limit of 685 on the number of foreign military advisers that could be assigned to aid the government of South Vietnam. At the end of November 1961 Kennedy metaphorically threw the Geneva Accords aside. He increased the U.S. Military Assistance and Advisory Group in Saigon to 2,100 men. Before the year was out, they were engaged in combat and taking casualties.[41]

There were so many foreign policy crises that first year that one day, as it drew to a close, Bundy and Rostow walked into the Oval Office and Kennedy, glancing up, sighed. "What's gone wrong now?" he said. "What's fallen away from us now?"[42]

The JFK Style

N ot even being President changed Kennedy's behavior towards women. He brazenly put his hand up their skirts, propositioned them within minutes of meeting and groped their breasts and buttocks even as he danced with them. Being President made conquest easier than ever. If he met a good-looking young woman at a White House event, he was likely to murmur, "My car will come to collect you at midnight," flash a smile and move on.[1]

There was also a string of regular girlfriends, including up to four young women who worked in the White House, one of whom was Jackie's press secretary, Pam Turnure. Another was the former Radcliffe student working on the NSC. The other two were close friends who dressed like Jackie, had hairstyles like Jackie's, made themselves up much like Jackie, and who from time to time gladly joined in presidential troilism with Jack.[2]

He seems to have made a play for nearly every attractive woman who came anywhere near him, such as Ben Bradlee's sister-in-law, Mary Meyer. At first she resisted. In October 1961 Mary was at the White House with her sister, Toni Bradlee, when Kennedy asked her, "Mary, do I have any chance with you?"

"I'm afraid not," she said. "I like people who are more aesthetic, more feminine."

"I could try to be more feminine."[3]

Eventually, he prevailed. The slightly self-mocking charm that won him the friendship of numerous men matriculated effortlessly into seduction when he met an attractive woman. The affair with Mary Meyer began in December 1961.[4]

There was a pattern to White House trysts by this time. Kenny O'Donnell or Dave Powers escorted her into the White House. The Secret Service sealed off the private quarters. JFK and Mary would eat dinner together, have sex and get dressed, and then he took her back downstairs in a small elevator that was just off the South Portico, gave her a kiss and bid her farewell. That first night he smiled sardonically as the elevator doors opened and told her, "Now you're in the hands of the Secret Service. Look virginal."

This affair lasted eighteen months, during which Kennedy told Mary Meyer that sometimes he felt isolated from reality. As President, he complained, no one would tell him what they really thought about how well he was doing. He also confessed he had two ambitions—"I want to be a great President and I don't want to end up like my father."[5]

Joe Kennedy, felled by a massive stroke in December 1961, was now wheelchair-bound. This man who had expressed himself emphatically all his adult life still did so, but could utter only two words, a moaning, winding "Nooooooo!" and an angry "Shit!" His mind was still sharp, though, and he could scrawl what he could not speak on a slate with a piece of chalk. At first, Kennedy had feared his father was going to die. Before long, as he contemplated his physically paralyzed and mentally oppressed father, death seemed the better fate.[6]

On July 16, 1962, Kennedy and Mary had dinner in the White House with Philip Graham, publisher of *The Washington Post,* and his wife, Katharine. After the Grahams departed, JFK and Mary Meyer had sex in the Lincoln bedroom.

She said she had something else for him to try and opened a small silver box. It held six joints. He'd never smoked marijuana before and puffed on a joint as if it were a regular cigarette. He was disappointed. "It's not like cocaine," said JFK. He didn't feel anything. She coached him on how to smoke dope, and after a while, he began giggling.[7]

The numerous girlfriends included, famously, Judith Campbell, to whom Peter Lawford and Frank Sinatra had introduced Kennedy in Las

Vegas shortly before his election. It was the kind of affair that he could not have realistically expected to keep secret from the FBI, which had taken an interest in his love life for nearly twenty years.

On March 21, 1962, J. Edgar Hoover received a memo that said, "Information has been developed that Judith E. Campbell, a free-lance artist, has associated with prominent underworld figures Sam Giancana of Chicago and Johnny Roselli of Los Angeles." The memo went on to say that Campbell had been phoning Evelyn Lincoln. This amounted to having the President's telephone number, and the most recent phone call listed was on February 14, Saint Valentine's Day.

A note was attached to the memo—"The Director may wish to bear this information in mind in connection with his forthcoming appointment with the President." Next day, Hoover showed the memo to JFK and Bobby. The affair with Campbell ended right there.[8]

Kennedy's fascination with movie stars made it essential that he bed some; so, too, did the fact that his father boasted of having numerous affairs with the screen goddesses of the 1920s and 1930s. JFK's own tally included Gene Tierney, Arlene Dahl and Jayne Mansfield.[9]

In April 1962 he added Marilyn Monroe to his collection when he visited Bing Crosby's house in Palm Springs. The singer wasn't there, but the swimming pool was filled with naked starlets excited at the prospect of sex with the President. He disappointed them all, letting his retinue trawl the pool for partners. Peter Lawford had arranged something special for Jack that weekend: Marilyn Monroe.[10]

A month later she flew to New York to sing at a Democratic party fundraiser at Madison Square Garden that marked Kennedy's forty-fifth birthday. For the occasion, she spent $6,000 on a dress (around $30,000 in current values) made of gauze and rhinestones. The dress fit so tightly that Marilyn had to be sewn, naked, into it. Close up, her nipples could be seen; so could her pudenda. This dress was less a garment than the setting for a gem, with herself as a gift.

JFK sat in his box, smoking a small cigar, his feet on a rail. The show's producer, Richard Adler, told him that Marilyn was having trouble remembering her lines and should probably be dropped from the show. He disagreed. "Oh, I think she'll be very good," said Kennedy.

She was nervous and nearly an hour behind schedule when she finally appeared to sing "Happy Birthday," and Kennedy was impressed, but not by her singing. "What an ass!" he exclaimed. *"What an ass!"*[11]

In October that same year, he invited Marlene Dietrich to dine at the White House one Saturday evening. When she arrived, she was taken up to the family quarters and Kennedy, after a minimum of conversation, told her, "We haven't got much time," and started undressing. She was startled. At sixty-one, Dietrich did not expect to be propositioned by a President, but gamely obliged. As they dressed, he asked, "Did you ever sleep with my father? He always claimed you did." She assured him she hadn't, something he clearly wanted to hear.[12]

He still made love like an adolescent. The quickie was the only kind of intercourse he knew. A showgirl who claimed she'd had sex with JFK told people he was in such a hurry that she caught him sneaking a glance at his watch while she ground away on top.[13]

Sex for him was not the release of emotion but escape from emotion; not a finding of the self but a release from the self. He was pursuing, too, the typical and slightly pathetic journey down roué road, with increasingly extreme encounters needed to maintain the excitement. When Jayne Mansfield was nearly eight months pregnant, he persuaded her to fellate him while he stroked her huge, distended belly. At other times he required masks, games and chemical stimulants, and on occasion even these failed, leaving him stranded on the shoulder, temporarily flaccid and embarrassed.[14]

In the presence of an attractive woman, Kennedy could be little more than a prisoner of erotogenesis. That owed something to the competition with Dad but possibly even more to the drugs swilling around in his body. He was also a man, not just John F. Kennedy and his father's son. His sexual urges were hardly unique to him. Given his opportunities, countless men would have been equal studs.[15]

In the end, knowing that Kennedy had casual sex with hundreds of women tells us nothing much. Context is what matters, and while he had one foot deep in the sleazy side of life, the other was planted firmly on the uplands of achievement. And over time, JFK's Don Juanism had become something more than racking up a huge score, something else. It was an exploration not only of his own inner life but a penetration of the world around him.

In 1963 Kennedy told a former Georgetown neighbor, Jane Eustice Wheeler, "I have never forgotten a girl I went to bed with." He probably believed that, because he wanted to believe it. He was intent not only on having as many and as wide a variety of experiences as he could cram into a short life but to carry all of those experiences close to his consciousness right to the end. There was little JFK could afford—or wanted—ever to forget.[16]

The woman who bore the price of his promiscuity was Jackie. John Davis, her cousin, saw the effect it had on her, calling it "Jacqueline's festering wound, one which remained for a lifetime." Although she worried that he might give her a venereal disease, there is no evidence that he ever contracted VD, and her four pregnancies attested to his fertility. So, too, could at least three other women he made pregnant, all of whom were persuaded to have abortions.[17]

Jack and Jackie were the most glamorous couple of their time, yet the romance of Jack and Jackie was about them, not between them. Irresistibly fascinating, both were emotional cripples. The kind of relationship they wanted was simply beyond them. They hardly ever dined alone, did not share the same bed or even the same bedroom and spent far more time apart than together.[18]

Jackie spent so much time away from the White House that there was a radio broadcaster who, until the White House asked him to stop, was concluding his show, "Good night, Mrs. Kennedy . . . wherever you are!"[19]

The one kind of love Kennedy was capable of was familial: he adored his children, was a dutiful son and a loyal brother. He was one of those men caught between the biological imperatives of human evolution and the human imperatives of social evolution: to spread his seed and to find true love. The first demand, the easy one, was what he succeeded at, like his father. But also like his father, JFK was unable to commit himself completely to any woman, including Jackie. Towards the end of his life, an old family friend asked him if he had ever been in love. He thought about it for a moment, then replied, "No. Very interested a few times. But never in love."[20]

Not surprisingly, there was often an undercurrent of tension in his relationship with Jackie. Kennedy's legislative aide Langdon Marvin had dated Jackie before JFK ever met her, and he had dumped her. She seemed too calculating and devious. After that, Marvin called her "Jacqueline Borgia." JFK put it to use, too, calling her Jacqueline Borgia to her face when he was displeased with her.[21]

He could also be dismissive towards her. Kennedy had a habit of striding out, his rapid walk leaving Jackie far behind. "It doesn't look good," Pierre Salinger advised him.

"Tell Jackie she'll just have to walk faster," Kennedy replied.[22]

In some respects, her indifference to politics was welcome. As Bobby once remarked, "She's not the kind of wife who, when he comes home at night, is going to say, 'What's new in Laos?' "[23]

Nevertheless, they had too little in common ever to be truly close. Their tastes were not simply different: they were almost antagonistic. He loved Westerns, preferably starring John Wayne, or historic epics such as *Spartacus,* which he thought was magnificent. But when Jackie arranged for *Jules et Jim* to be shown in the White House movie theater, he became restless and fidgety and left long before the *fin.*[24]

She loved French chansons and could listen for hours to Charles Trenet or Edith Piaf. JFK could not stand them. His favorite song was "Danny Boy," and Jackie mockingly told people that his favorite tune was "Hail to the Chief."

An enthusiastic horsewoman, she insisted on taking him to the 1961 Washington horse show. He hated it almost from the first. Protesting loudly, "Let me out of here!," he departed after half an hour, leaving her to watch the rest of it alone, except for her Secret Service bodyguard.[25]

Similarly, he loved being at the family compound in Hyannis, and she detested it. "Get me out of here!" she begged the family chauffeur, Frank Saunders, one day.

"Where do you want to go?"

"Anyplace. Anyplace," she told him. "Just out, out!"[26]

The loneliness Kennedy admitted to might have been mitigated had there not been an unbridgeable distance between him and Jackie. The ordinary yet invaluable love between a husband and wife that makes life worthwhile for countless millions never existed between them. While there was affection at times on both sides, he did not seem to miss her when she was away. Nor did she seem to miss him.

Hurt by his lack of love, she accepted her lot for the promise he bore. She told Henry Brandon, a British journalist who became part of the Kennedy circle, that there were three artistic immortals she wished she had known: Oscar Wilde, Charles Baudelaire and Sergey Diaghilev. What they had in common was that they led dissolute private lives, were homosexuals, defied the conventions of their time and left behind personal legends.[27]

The strongest bond between Jack and Jackie was the children, Caroline and John-John. Kennedy was a deeply emotional man. The cool, detached persona he had cultivated was mostly façade. Under pressure, his hands shook; easily moved, he wept freely.[28]

Just looking into the eyes of a puppy could bring a melting expression to JFK's features. Allergic to dogs but craving their company, he ordered that Caroline's Welsh terrier, Charlie, be out on the lawn to greet him whenever he returned to the White House from a weekend away. He needed a dog barking with excitement and licking his hand to feel he'd truly come home.[29]

Kennedy was immensely tactile with his children, pulling their clothes gently aside so he could run his hand over the silky skin of the lower back, as if to convince himself they were real while conveying to them, through his touch, something of the love he felt. He also filled his wallet with pictures of his children and, like any bourgeois paterfamilias, whipped them out to show to staff, friends and strangers alike, saying, "Aren't they great?"[30]

Not only did the children provide a bond with Jackie, but Kennedy knew, too, what a political asset she was and admired the brilliance with which she pulled off her role as First Lady. She ruled the East Wing, keeping it quiet and private, while he presided over a West Wing that was filled with political busyness and masculine laughter.

Stylish rather than refined, Jackie served huge helpings of caviar out of a solid gold bucket and there were ashtrays everywhere. She smoked up to forty cigarettes a day and was so high-strung she could not sleep without an eye mask and ear plugs. She exercised zealously to remain slim but didn't want anyone to know it. Whatever she did had to appear to be effortless, not sweaty.[31]

Jackie oversaw the refurbishment of the White House, filling it with the right kind of period furniture and having it redecorated in the best English country-house style. She also raised nearly half a million dollars towards the cost by writing a handsome, bestselling White House guidebook.

Not all her innovations worked. She installed a French chef, René Verdon, in the kitchen and had White House menus printed in French. That drew so much criticism in the press that Jackie backed down and had the menus printed once more in English.[32]

Roosevelt, Truman and Eisenhower had served alcohol only when they were entertaining friends or other politicians. On formal occasions such as state dinners, there was nothing but a lightly spiked fruit punch; otherwise, no alcohol. JFK and Jackie changed that: there was wine on the table and hard liquor for anyone who wanted it.

Her tastes—in music, literature, art and food—were more sophisticated than her husband's. JFK's preferences at the table were petit bourgeois and adolescent. Everything had to be creamy or sugary, preferably both. His diet revolved around ice cream, clam chowder and white coffee syrupy from the three spoonfuls of sugar he dumped into it. The only red meat he ate was steak, broiled medium rare.

In some ways he never got over his time at Harvard. He created around him something of a college-dorm atmosphere and indulged in the casual profanity of the locker room as if to show what a guy's guy he really was. He liked to surround himself with former college athletes such as Torby Macdonald and Kenny O'Donnell. He prized toughness in others and liked to think of himself as tough. "What I need over here to make this government run is ten or twelve sons of bitches," he told an old friend from Massachusetts, John Sharon. "One of the reasons that Dillon and McNamara are so effective is they are tough bastards. Too many of the rest of them are just soft."[33]

Around Kennedy was a wide circle of male friends, augmented by "characters" such as Patsy Mulkern and Muggsy O'Leary. All his life he was drawn to people who were singular—those who were eccentric, original in some way or simply stylish. He also seemed to like old people, unlike most younger men.

Since college he had used other people to understand and express different aspects of his complex personality and polyvalent life. Hence the wide—almost wildly varied—circle of friends. Yet all of JFK's close male friends were people who had one thing in common: they did not compete with him or challenge him. He got ample competition within his family and from other politicians.

His friends, regardless of their degree of closeness, were followers rather than leaders, people who did not mind being used, at least not by him. They pimped for Jack, kept his secrets and lied readily on his behalf. Rather than dispelling his loneliness, such slavishness probably added to it. The best friendships are among equals, but once in the White House he began referring to himself in the third person, as "Kennedy." Not much equality there.[34]

Not particularly introspective, he nonetheless knew what was driving him. At the dinner held for French writer and adventurer André Malraux on May 11, 1962, Kennedy remarked, "I suppose all of us wish to participate in all the experiences of life." That was true of him, but he knew too little of how most people lived to realize that it was not true of them. His was the appetite for life of the condemned man, rather than the free one.[35]

JFK was guided, too, by his lifelong fascination with Byron. His political thought reflected a central tenet of the Romantic movement in which Byron was the brightest star: that good and evil grow from the same stem. The Romantics also believed that life is really a performance, as Byron's was and Kennedy's became. And he knew what every performer knows—you can go only as far as your audience allows.

Under him, the presidency became a production. John F. Kennedy was the first celebrity President, which changed the office itself. The politician who is also a celebrity—a Reagan, a Clinton—somehow transcends politics and has an appeal that goes beyond party and reaches wider than political ideology. Politicians are boring. Celebrities are interesting.

He began by overhauling the rituals of the presidency, making them more regal and spectacular. Following the Vienna summit with Khrushchev in June 1961, Kennedy stopped over in London for two days and was invited to dinner at Buckingham Palace. As he and his chief of protocol, Angier Biddle Duke, disembarked from their limousine in the inner courtyard, JFK told Duke, "Let's study how they do it."

Within weeks of his return, he introduced the Buckingham Palace style of formal entertainments to the White House. Truman and Eisenhower had met other heads of state at the airport and hosted fairly informal state dinners with people mingling in small groups, the men dressed in business suits, their wives dressed as if they were going to the country-club golf awards dinner. Kennedy had important visitors brought to him from the airport and met them at the White House.

The Queen's practice was to have a drink with her guests in an upstairs room, with a few members of her family and senior Cabinet officers. Her principal male guests wore white ties, tails, and diamond-encrusted orders of something or other, with bright sashes to match. Their wives were expensively dressed by world-famous couturiers and glittered with million-dollar jewelry. The Queen led her guests down to the state dining room, where the rest of the company was assembled. The royal party entered to a fanfare of trumpets.

JFK had the presidential study on the second floor remodeled as a drawing room where he and Jackie could have a drink with their distinguished visitors before taking them down to dinner. Trumpets blared as they approached the state dining room, then the Marine Band struck up "Hail to the Chief." It was monarchical and formal and the nation loved it.[36]

As President, Kennedy felt obliged to transcend his limited middle-brow tastes without pretending for a moment that he was an aesthete. The music he preferred was sentimental Irish ballads and Broadway show tunes. He read widely, and quickly, but not deeply. Although he had a genuine love of poetry, JFK's taste in verse was for the inspirational rather than the profound.

While other Presidents explored the boundaries of what it was to be an American, Kennedy was going to endure in the imagination because he seemed embarked on a more dangerous exploration—the meaning of life for a man. And as he did so, he became a new kind of time traveler: out of his speeded-up life, he emerged as a totemic figure of the speeded-up future.

He had few serious conversations because they took too much time. Talking to him, as he fired one question after another, was like putting your brain through a car wash. His taste in art was restricted to Edward Hopper and the more sentimental Impressionists, such as Renoir. He was capable only of grasping the obvious in art; the emotions that informed the artist's vision eluded him.

Kennedy was comfortable in the company of intellectuals without being one or wanting to be one. He took no serious interest in abstract thought; but early on he had grasped the fundamental belief behind all philosophy, that the world is ultimately ruled by ideas. In this he lived at the opposite pole from his father, who saw the world revolving entirely around self-interest and material forces.

Without ever wanting to be a man of high culture, Kennedy had cultivated a strong sense of style and had a good eye for design. More important, though, was the powerful sense of history that shaped his remaking of the presidency.

JFK recognized the historic importance of artists and thinkers. He knew that the greatest treasures of any nation are the works of genius that only gifted individuals create. And it was because he felt history pressing on him so strongly that he had to acknowledge them personally and as President. He owed that to both himself and his country.

To their astonishment and delight, Nobel Prize winners, famous authors, the incomparable cellist Pablo Casals, and great men scorned, such as Linus Pauling and J. Robert Oppenheimer, were invited to dine at the White House. Pauling, holder of two Nobel Prizes (for chemistry and for peace) had been harassed and threatened by vigilantes in 1944 for denouncing the wartime internment of the West Coast Japanese. He accepted Kennedy's invitation to dinner but spent the afternoon picketing the White House with a group of Ban the Bomb protesters.

In 1954 Oppenheimer's security clearance had been unjustly revoked and his reputation ruined by two men, Lewis Strauss and Edward Teller, who were jealous of his historic accomplishment in building the first atomic bomb. Kennedy had the courage and decency to try making amends to Oppenheimer for a historic injustice.

Gestures such as this made many Americans proud. All Presidents represent in some way the zeitgeist of their time, but he seemed to be receiving memos from his. Somehow his inner life formed a seamless bond with the inner life of 1960s culture. To an impossible degree for any other politician—as opposed to an artist or writer—he *was* the culture—sex, drugs, rock 'n' roll, the celebrity life, the movie-star magnetism—and the culture was him.

That is why, in some recent opinion polls, John F. Kennedy is rated as the greatest President ever, above George Washington and Thomas Jefferson, Abraham Lincoln and Franklin D. Roosevelt. In the course of three years he redefined the United States. And in redefining it he did what individuals do in redefining themselves—he changed it forever. Cool yet idealistic, sexy and daring, living a life that was all riffs all the time, placing himself at the center of whatever was new and exciting—that wasn't just how he saw himself. That was the way millions of Americans wanted to see their country and how they wanted other countries to see them. He was the President of the buzz, then and forever.

As we now know, Kennedy was living out nearly every male fantasy imaginable. The result was a life that, in its deliberate crafting, was almost a work of performance art—powerful imaginative forces given realization in public.

Every day brought excitement and despair. Only a deeply romantic person could live with that. Kennedy surpassed even that immortal creation Walter Mitty, for Mitty's fantasies skipped the despair, which is an adult taste.

Being emotionally damaged only adds to his appeal. All the deep people, all those worth studying, turn out to be damaged in some way. JFK carried behind that million-dollar smile a fractal inner life, all broken up, with sharp edges, uneven planes and stabbing points.

To those who try to separate a President's character from a President's conduct, he had his own reply. *Profiles in Courage* emphasizes the connection between what a man is and what a man does.

Yet his own life was hedged about with secrets and lies. *Profiles in Courage* declares emphatically, "Courage, conscience and integrity give meaning to life itself." No doubt he meant it. Kennedy was not a charlatan but a paradox—the liar in love with the truth.

Much of the time, he seemed to be operating within a morality we all know: the ambiguous morality of dreams. JFK knew more than he could tell; understood more than he could express—that was true of everything that mattered: his health, his marriage, his family, his emotions.

The most important lies were always those that involved his health. One way or another, he could not manage without the aid of psychotropic substances. Many a morning he woke up so stiff, and in such pain, that his personal physician, Dr. Janet Travell, had to give him a shot of procaine before he could get out of bed. Max Jacobson, Dr. Feelgood, was coming to the White House every two weeks to give the President a shot of amphetamines. His most important appointments were usually scheduled for late afternoon, following his hour-long nap. And he was still taking cortisone to compensate for his missing adrenals.[37]

The side effects of the cortisone were beginning to show in the shape of full cheeks and a small upper-back hump, both caused by fat deposits. Kennedy was horrified, protesting vainly, "That's not me. That's not my face!"[38]

He suffered from low blood pressure and sky-high cholesterol. He could not sit still for more than half an hour and had to get up and walk around for a few minutes, even when he was having dinner or watching a movie. Although he hated being seen in public on crutches, he often had to use them just to move around in the White House, at Hyannis and Palm Beach. During his presidency, Kennedy's back was deteriorating so inexorably that long before he finished a second term, he, like Franklin Roosevelt, would have been in a wheelchair.[39]

Even so, he managed to create a vigorous image that much of the country fell in love with. The image was conveyed not only by the permanent tan and youthful air but by that famous mop. No President had ever had hair like his. An exuberant growth, radiating vitality, it fascinated millions. During the inauguration it seemed to be waving its approval of the rhetorical high points of Kennedy's speech. On other occasions, his right hand flying up to bring that dancing hair back under control was part of a body language that, like the stabbing forefinger, declared JFK was here, taking charge, overflowing with nervous energy and irresistible bravura.

His was a privileged life that no sensible person would want. There was no time or space to be truly happy or idle or committed to others; no time or energy for anything but the pursuit of a goal ordained by Dad. He was rarely alone and couldn't stand solitude except when hurt or depressed. Here, too, was a young man who was playing one of the trickiest hands the Fates have dealt anyone. He did not simply play this hand well; he played it with a strange kind of talent, eventually making it his true destiny.

He took his father's banal dynastic goal—the dull dream of millionaire egotists down the ages—absorbed it, achieved it and ultimately transformed it into something that took his shape, not his father's. Dynasties always peter out. A legend might live forever.

The unifying element in the various personae that Kennedy had developed—frustrated jock, perennial stud, political operator, writer manqué, drug addict and hipster, high-minded leader, dutiful son, cultural impresario, political idealist, lousy husband, doting father, ambitious President— was the intensity of the life being lived. From an early age he had known something that few rich men's sons ever learn this side of serious illness: there is no wealth but life. Convinced he would die young, there was the same intensity to his existence as of a life lived in wartime, with himself permanently at the front.

Over Thanksgiving at Hyannis in November 1961, Kennedy spent two days working on the budget that would go to Congress in January, but he broke away from work to have Thanksgiving dinner with family and friends. Afterwards, everyone got up and sang something while Patricia played the piano. JFK was the last to sing. He began to sing "September Song" in the most melancholy, deeply felt style anyone there had ever heard. He reached the final verse:

> And the days dwindle down
> To a precious few—
> September . . . November . . .
> And these few precious days
> I'll spend with you.

Every man in the room was choked up; every woman there was weeping.[40]

Doomed, then, to a race against death, he was living with his enemy every moment of every day. The last thing he needed was a reminder, but

Caroline had a pet canary called Robin that she found dead in its cage one morning.

Needing to share her loss, she walked into the Oval Office, deeply upset, carrying Robin in her hands. Going over to her father as he sat at his desk reading, she held up her hands and opened them. The feathered, lifeless creature filled JFK's gaze. He shrieked, "Get it away! Get it away!" Robin was later buried in the Rose Garden.[41]

CHAPTER 32

Domestic Tranquillity

J ackie was slightly amused at the almost gleeful pleasure that Jack took in being President. He was like a teenager who can't believe his luck. "They ought to make you President for life!" she told him.

"No," he responded seriously. "Eight years in this job would be enough for anyone."[1]

There were days when JFK would have liked nothing more than a guarantee that he would have eight years. He was discovering what all Presidents discover, that much of his power is contingent and some is illusory. The opportunities to do bad things are infinite, while the opportunities for good are limited.

Whenever liberal Democrats pressed him to take the initiative on liberal programs, Kennedy was likely to tell them, "Well, you know, I've got to be reelected." He did not have a mandate to do anything much, and that troubled him constantly.[2]

He had pledged during his campaign to "get America moving again," and at the very least that was a promise to end the jobless recovery that followed the 1958 recession and get unemployment down. But Kennedy soon grew impatient with advisers like Walter Heller, the chairman of the Council of Economic Advisers, and his ultraliberal Secretary of Labor,

Arthur Goldberg, who kept telling him to spend more as a way of reducing unemployment to around 4 percent.

The government was running a large deficit when he became President, and even as a Congressman, Kennedy had deplored deficit spending. "I know what they [Heller and Goldberg] want—a deficit of $7 billion," he grumbled to Gore Vidal in the fall of 1961. "Well, they should be happy. Berlin is going to cost us $3.5 billion and that will just do the trick, all the pump priming they want." He knew, too, that Congress would put billions into the space program: more pump priming.[3]

None of it made much difference. Unemployment hit a postwar peak in February 1961 when it touched 6.8 percent. After that it fell to around 6 percent and remained stuck there well into 1963. Average unemployment under JFK was higher than it had been during the last three years of the Eisenhower administration.[4]

During Kennedy's first two years in office, the New Frontier's explicitly anti-recession measures consisted of a modest increase in the minimum wage, a public works bill that cost less than $1 billion, some extra money for distressed areas such as West Virginia and a training program for the unemployed, the Manpower Development and Training Act. It was hardly stirring stuff, and stirring stuff was what Kennedy was all about.

The biggest antipoverty program of his administration turned out to be the Alliance for Progress. He did nothing to tackle poverty at home, apart from trying to reduce unemployment.[5]

In March 1963 Kennedy read a review in *The New Yorker* of *The Other America,* a book by a young Catholic intellectual, Michael Harrington. According to Harrington, tens of millions of Americans were living in dire poverty. Kennedy found it hard to believe Harrington's figures were accurate and asked Walter Heller to look into them. Two months later, JFK received a report from Heller that said not only were the figures right, but the number of people living in poverty was growing, not shrinking, under the Kennedy administration. He began thinking about a domestic antipoverty program, but that, too, would have to wait for a second term.[6]

To Kennedy's alarm, the government was meanwhile developing a fractious relationship with big business. His old friend Red Fay, whose father was a big contractor in San Francisco, had advised him to bring some businessmen into the administration, but Kennedy wasn't interested. "Red, all businessmen are basically Republicans. And if they're not, their wives will soon make them Republicans."[7]

To some degree, his attitude towards businessmen was colored by his father's contempt for the men in gray flannel suits. Joe Kennedy was less a businessman than a buccaneer in the marketplace. JFK could not help admiring buccaneers as kindred free spirits. He would not accept—probably because some facts are detestable, and this was one of them—that the dull, shallow organization men possessed powers he couldn't touch.

Worried about inflation, the administration managed to pressure the unions into moderating their wage claims in the spring of 1962. The President assumed the big employers, led by the steel companies, would reciprocate. But on April 10, 1962, Roger M. Blough, chairman of U.S. Steel, came to the Oval Office and handed Kennedy a mimeographed copy of a statement that was about to be released.

The press release said U.S. Steel was raising its prices by $6 a ton, an increase of 3.5 percent, and ten other steel companies would do the same. Kennedy gritted his teeth, seething. "I think you have made a terrible mistake," he told Blough. The President treated the steel increase like a national emergency, holding meetings late into the night, summoning advisers back to Washington from all over the country. "That son of a bitch has kicked us in the nuts," said Kennedy. "The bastard."[8]

Arthur Goldberg advised him he couldn't win a slugging match with U.S. Steel. "Mr. President, this industry cannot be tamed. They rule this country, and even Mr. Truman couldn't take them on."[9]

Nevertheless, Kennedy publicly denounced the steel companies and demanded they rescind the price increase. As he aroused public opinion against steel company bosses, Bethlehem Steel broke ranks and announced it would hold its prices steady. Blough had little choice but to do the same. The price hike was canceled.

Striving to appear magnanimous in victory, Kennedy went to the Yale graduation ceremony in June 1963 to deliver a speech that was designed to placate big business. Awarded an honorary doctorate, he wryly observed, "It could be said that now I have the best of both worlds, a Harvard education and a Yale degree."

The core of his speech was a defense of government, which he insisted was not opposed to business. Nor was the present deficit a threat to the economy.

Towards the end of his speech, Kennedy mused aloud about the great domestic struggles of the past—"The National Bank, nullification or union, freedom or slavery, gold or silver." But a modern President confronted a mundane domestic agenda. "The central issues of our time are more subtle and less simple. They relate not to basic philosophy or ideology but to ways and means of reaching common goals," he observed wistfully.[10]

His attempt to reassure the business community was a failure. Cartoonists mocked it; political commentators made fun of it; and businessmen shrugged it off. Worse, the stock market slumped a few days later, falling as sharply as it had done in October 1929, and the President got the blame. Kennedy was deeply depressed.[11]

The clash with steel, which he had seized on as a chance to appear before the nation as the people's champion, was turning into a drawn-out defeat. U.S. Steel scrapped its existing plans to increase investment in the United States. All new plants would be built abroad.[12]

Bruised by this experience, Kennedy ignored a succession of small but steady increases in the price of steel that by early 1963 gave the steel companies exactly what they had sought. Even the President's belated appeasement didn't do much good. Business remained hostile to the administration. Kennedy later realized that Goldberg was right—Big Steel couldn't be tamed by presidential power—bitterly remarking to Sorensen, "My father always told me that steel men were sons of bitches, but I never realized till now how right he was."[13]

He was afraid, too, that he was losing the battle for public opinion. Agitated at the coverage that a new team of television journalists—Chet Huntley and David Brinkley—gave to the steel crisis, he asked Tom Wicker of *The New York Times,* "Are they trying to load the news against me?"

"No, sir," said Wicker. "They are very fair-minded reporters."

"It's bad enough for me with the newspapers," Kennedy said ruefully. "If I can't get a fair shake on television, I'm fucked."[14]

During the fall of 1962 he campaigned all over the country, appealing to the nation to vote for Democratic candidates in the mid-term election and raising millions of dollars to help them. It was a rehearsal, as well, for his campaign in 1964, but the results were disappointing. The Democrats picked up four seats in the Senate and lost four in the House.

There was no mid-term swing to the Republicans. Yet neither was there a gain for the White House in terms of getting a Congress more responsive to the President's program. The result only confirmed the electoral stalemate of 1960. The one satisfaction Kennedy could take from the election was that his old Senate seat was back in the family.

When he'd been elected President in 1960, he got the governor of Massachusetts to put his former Harvard roommate and football-playing pal Benjamin Smith into the seat for two years. Teddy Kennedy would turn thirty in 1962, making him just old enough to run for the Senate that year, and he was eager to have Jack's old seat. More important, Joe Kennedy made it clear with his slate and chalk that he wanted Teddy in the Senate, cementing the dynasty.

JFK, however, was slightly irritated. "The House of Representatives was good enough for me. I don't see why Teddy has to come in as a senator," he told his friend Charles Bartlett.[15]

He was worried, too, because Teddy's challenger in the Democratic primary was Edward McCormack, the nephew of John McCormack, who had become Speaker of the House of Representatives following Sam Rayburn's death in the late fall of 1961. Kennedy despised McCormack. "You can't believe anything he tells you," he told Arthur Krock.[16]

Even so, McCormack could make life very hard for JFK on Capitol Hill, if he chose. Kennedy sent for Tip O'Neill. "I'm getting along well with McCormack, and I don't want this Senate race to come between us," he told O'Neill. "Besides, with me in the White House and Bobby in the Cabinet, I don't want to create a backlash by putting a third Kennedy in office. But you know my father. He's determined that my old seat belongs to Teddy, and that's all there is to it."[17]

Shortly before the primary, the news broke that Teddy had been expelled from Harvard after he got somebody else to take a Spanish exam for him. He had atoned by asking to be drafted and spent two years in the Army as a military policeman, after which Harvard allowed him to resume his studies.

When the press began running the story, Kennedy reacted with a mixture of scorn and irritation. "It's out, and now he's got to fight it. It won't go over with the WASPs," he told Ben Bradlee. "They take a very dim view of looking over your shoulder at someone's exam paper. They go in more for stealing from stockholders and banks."[18]

JFK spent hours talking to journalists about how the story ought to be covered, trying to make sure the press did not wreck Teddy's chances. "Gee, we haven't spent as much fucking time on anything since Cuba," he remarked to his staff shortly before the primary.[19]

Teddy trounced McCormack by a two-to-one margin and easily defeated George Cabot Lodge—son of Henry Cabot Lodge—in the November election. His campaign slogan was the same as Jack's had been back in the 1952 campaign: "He Can Do More for Massachusetts."

The fact remained that, even with his brother in the Senate, Kennedy would have to deal with a Senate in 1963 that was immovably conservative. And instead of trying to create political alliances across party lines, as Eisenhower had done, Kennedy had a habit of referring to congressional Republicans publicly as "The people who always say No." His intense partisanship was a self-imposed handicap, a reflection no doubt of his fiercely competitive spirit. The Republicans were the opposing team, and the opposing team was there to be beaten.[20]

The result was a succession of legislative failures, including an attempt to enact Medicare, which would have provided health care to those over sixty-five. The most important symbolic defeat, though, was his proposal to create a Department of Housing and Urban Affairs. This was intended to be one of the major achievements of Kennedy's first term, and he announced in advance that Robert C. Weaver, who was black and an expert on housing, would run it.

Thrusting Weaver on them before they had even created the new department infuriated members of the committees that dealt with housing and urban affairs. It sounded like "take it or leave it," and they didn't have any trouble choosing which way to go. "I played it too cute," Kennedy admitted. "It was so obvious it made them mad."[21]

He had breakfast every Tuesday morning with the leadership of the House and Senate, but it didn't seem to make much difference, especially in the Senate. When the new Congress convened in January 1963, most of the legislation Kennedy had sent to the Hill in 1961 and 1962 was bogged down. There was a stillness to Capitol Hill that year such as no one had seen since the 1920s; less movement, not more.[22]

=

There were too few black people in Massachusetts for civil rights to count for much in the phenomenal rise of John F. Kennedy from freshman congressman to President in only fourteen years. Yet he had joined the NAACP in 1948, and whatever black votes there were to be had, he wanted them. Besides that, like all Irish Bostonians, he'd heard about the evils of discrimination since he was in diapers. For all his father's wealth and a privileged upbringing, Kennedy never had any trouble identifying with the oppressed.

Early in his presidency he learned that a former heavyweight champion, the engaging and modest Jersey Joe Walcott, had tried to get a low-level job with the Defense Department. Walcott had never made much money in the ring and was struggling to survive on welfare. The Defense Department refused to hire him because he had a conviction for illegal gambling. Kennedy told his friend Rip Horton, whom he'd made Assistant Secretary of Defense, to get the department to waive the rules. "These poor people had nowhere to go in the past. They either had to turn to gambling connections or in too many cases turned to Communism." Jersey Joe deserved a break.[23]

At about the same time, JFK was tempted to submit a civil rights bill to Congress, one that was limited to improving voting rights. What worried him was that it would have to go through a subcommittee of the Judiciary Committee, and the subcommittee was so stacked with Northern liberals, from both parties, that any legislation it reported out would be too strongly worded to become law.[24]

The Senate Majority Leader, Mike Mansfield, was discouraging, too. Any bill that was offered now, he told Kennedy, would be filibustered to death in the Senate, whatever happened in the House. Kennedy gave up on the legislation without even trying.[25]

The only way forward, he and Bobby agreed, was to get blacks registered to vote. Both Kennedys were convinced that once the number of black voters reached a kind of critical mass, white politicians would start courting the black vote, and political resistance to civil rights would crumble away. That was how the Irish and Italians had overcome discrimination in Massachusetts; it was how black people would ultimately achieve power in the South.

Kennedy also tried to outlaw discrimination throughout the federal government by issuing executive orders. He tackled discrimination in places under federal regulation, such as airports in southern states and new public facilities financed in whole or in part with federal money. He also insisted that government departments, such as State, hire more blacks and promote them. And the administration scored a great symbolic victory in forcing the Washington Redskins, the last all-white team in the NFL, to hire some black players or lose the right to play at D.C. Stadium.[26]

Under Eisenhower, the Department of Labor had become the biggest employer of black people in the government. One in six of the department's workers was nonwhite. Kennedy's Secretary of Labor, the very liberal Arthur Goldberg, built on that, and Labor became the standard by which other government departments were judged. The Kennedy administration more or less recognized that if a black middle class was to be created, government at all levels would have to take the lead. It was not going to happen otherwise.[27]

Despite Kennedy's personal sympathy with African Americans, he was well aware that Franklin D. Roosevelt had never lost a southern state in four elections. Harry Truman, however, had infuriated the South over civil rights and lost five southern states in 1948. With 1964 always on his mind, Kennedy's model on civil rights was FDR's—encouraging equality but not taking any chances—rather than Truman's more interventionist and outspoken stance.

Kennedy fretted over the ultra-liberals in his own party and twice begged the outspoken Hubert Humphrey to stop giving impassioned speeches on the need for government action. Humphrey said that was impossible. Having argued for racial equality all his adult life, he could hardly be expected to shut up now.[28]

Kennedy tried to placate the South both in what he did and in what he chose not to do. During his campaign, he had declared he would end discrimination in public housing "with the stroke of a pen." After he became President, JFK kept finding excuses for not doing what he'd promised, and the White House was flooded with pens from outraged black activists.

When it came to judicial appointments, Clark Clifford advised Kennedy to appoint only the very best people to the bench. "Doing that would set the tone for the whole administration." The President said, "I agree." In practice, though, every federal judge he appointed in the South was an avowed segregationist.[29]

Between his election and inauguration, the Supreme Court had outlawed segregation on those railroads, buses and terminals that were involved in interstate commerce. In May 1961 seven blacks and six whites calling themselves "Freedom Riders" announced they would put the new ruling to the test. Kennedy was appalled. He sent for Harris Wofford, his assistant on civil rights. "Tell them to call it off!"

"I don't think anybody's going to stop them right now," said Wofford. He was right. The ride went ahead, ending in a mini-riot and bus burning in Anniston, Alabama.[30]

There were more Freedom Rides, sit-ins and street protests as the pent-up force of the civil rights movement erupted across the South. Kennedy stayed aloof as long as he could, but in September 1962 a black Air Force veteran, James Meredith, prepared to enroll at the University of Mississippi, even if doing so cost him his life. Armed with a court order that required the university to enroll him, on September 25 Meredith was driven to the Ole Miss campus at Oxford by the chief U.S. marshal and a high-ranking official from the Justice Department.

During the crisis over integrating the Little Rock schools in September 1957, Senator John Kennedy had denounced Eisenhower's decision to use troops to impose public order and enforce a court ruling. President Kennedy intended to do things differently: integration without rifles and fixed bayonets. Three hundred border patrolmen and Federal Prison Service officers were hurriedly deputized as U.S. marshals and sent to Mississippi to supplement the handful of regular marshals available for duty.

The marshals, in plastic helmets painted a peaceable white, moved into Oxford. They carried batons and tear gas and handguns. Just in case Kennedy's less forceful approach didn't work, a battalion of tough, head-cracking airborne military police was moved to Memphis, eighty miles north of Oxford.

By nightfall, Meredith was trapped on the campus and still had not been able to register. The governor of Mississippi, Ross Barnett, ordered the two hundred highway patrolmen who were holding a growing mob at bay to return to their barracks. Throwing Molotov cocktails and brandishing iron bars, the mob swarmed around the administration building. The marshals opened up with volleys of tear gas.

Just then Kennedy went on television to announce that the situation in Mississippi was tense but under control: he had not had to send in soldiers, he declared with evident satisfaction. While he was making his broadcast, a Justice Department official reported to Bobby, "It's getting like the Alamo down here."[31]

With the riot in Oxford growing beyond the marshals' ability to contain it, gunfire broke out. One of Bobby's assistants called the White House from a pay phone on campus and requested permission for the marshals to use their weapons in self-defense. "No!" barked Kennedy into the telephone. They could fire only in defense of James Meredith, not in defense of themselves. But Kennedy ordered the MP battalion in Memphis deployed to Oxford immediately.[32]

A little after midnight, reports came in that two people had died, one of them a British reporter. The President called the Secretary of the Army, Cyrus Vance. "Where's the Army? Why aren't they moving?" Then he called the Army commander in Memphis, General Creighton Abrams. "People are dying in Oxford. This is the worst thing I've seen in forty-five years. I want the MP battalion to enter the area immediately!"[33]

The siege continued until four o'clock the next morning. Just as the hard-pressed and weary marshals appeared on the verge of being overrun, the soldiers arrived. Six marshals had been seriously injured. Meredith registered later that day.[34]

Even as he sought to hold on to the South, Kennedy was hoping to placate the civil rights movement. His approach to the most difficult problems of his presidency was usually to give something to one side and something to the other, while retaining something for himself—room to maneuver. In a gesture unprecedented in American history, Kennedy invited four hundred prominent black figures and their wives to a reception at the White House on Lincoln's birthday, February 12.

To his horror, he learned that one of his civil rights advisers had included Sammy Davis, Jr., on the guest list, along with Davis's blond, blue-eyed Swedish wife, the actress Mai Britt. Kennedy was supposed to be photographed with his guests. The thought of being photographed with an interracial couple horrified him, but Jackie thought they should be treated like everyone else. The reception began without the President and First Lady as Jack and Jackie remained in the family quarters, arguing heatedly over her concept of courtesy and his concept of political suicide. They eventually appeared at the reception, but Jackie stayed only a few minutes before departing in tears.[35]

At the end of the month, the President finally overcame his doubts and submitted a civil rights bill limited to protecting voting rights. Yet even something as unambitious as this was going to get a rocky passage. On April 3, Martin Luther King, Jr., and a Birmingham pastor named Fred L. Shuttlesworth launched a wave of street demonstrations to push for an end to segregation at workplaces and lunch counters in Birmingham, Alabama.[36]

The police rounded up the protestors, and the courts imposed fines, probation or short jail terms. After three weeks the protest was on the verge of fizzling out when King and Shuttlesworth came up with a new tactic: child protesters—thousands of them. The police set their attack dogs on black children; the firemen turned on powerful hoses that sent children skidding across the street on their backs and smashing into cars and trees. "It makes me sick," said Kennedy as he looked at photographs from Birmingham, but even now he worried about how white southerners would vote in 1964. If things don't improve soon in Alabama, he gloomily told the chairman of the Democratic National Committee, "I can kiss the South goodbye."[37]

As King and Shuttlesworth brought the Birmingham protest to a close, two black students were about to enroll at the University of Alabama. The governor, George Wallace, was vowing to block them "at the schoolhouse door."

On May 17 the President made a one-day tour of northern Alabama, ostensibly to celebrate the Tennessee Valley Authority's thirtieth anniversary. His real reasons for going were to placate southern opinion, calm the atmosphere after the recent Birmingham riots and try to talk Wallace out of fomenting bloodshed at the University of Alabama when the two black students registered.

The crowds that greeted the President were enthusiastic but small, and he invited Wallace to join him aboard his helicopter on a fifty-five-minute flight from Muscle Shoals to Huntsville. Kennedy said he didn't understand why Birmingham businessmen wouldn't hire black workers. "They have Negroes serving their tables at home."

"I have no objection to businessmen hiring who they want. What I do object to is government telling a businessman what he should or should not do," said Wallace. Anyway, the riots hadn't been caused by local black people but by "fakers" like Martin Luther King, Jr., and Fred Shuttlesworth. They weren't seriously interested in poor black people, declared Wallace. "What they want is to see who can go to bed with the most nigger women, and white women, too. And they ride around town in big Cadillacs smoking expensive cigars."[38]

Kennedy returned to Washington convinced there wasn't anything left but federal intervention. "There is no other remedy," he told his staff. "They can't demonstrate. They can't get a solution. I think we can't duck this one."[39]

On June 11, with a showdown looming in Tuscaloosa, the home of the university, Kennedy federalized the Alabama National Guard. Then he asked two leading Republicans, Senator Everett Dirksen and Representative Charles Halleck, to meet with him and LBJ in the Cabinet Room.

Kennedy sounded them out on how far he could go with a civil rights bill without risking it being filibustered to death or killed in committee.

Even as JFK tried to win the support of the Republican leadership, Wallace was agreeing to back down. He had never intended to stand in the schoolhouse door.[40]

Kennedy decided to make a television address that night. A speech was hastily put together, but it was full of gaps where Kennedy would have to improvise on air. It wasn't a fluent or smooth performance, but it was a gripping and historic one.

He began by talking about the poor educational opportunities for a black person, low income and a life expectancy seven years shorter than a white person's. "This is not a sectional issue," he observed. "Nor is this a partisan issue. . . ." His voice rose and he became slightly shrill as he declared, "We are confronted primarily by a moral issue. It is as old as the Scriptures and is as clear as the American Constitution. . . . We face, therefore, a moral crisis as a country and as a people. . . ." He was going to ask Congress to act on new legislation.[41]

The bill he had submitted to Congress in February was drastically revised and resubmitted in June 1963. The new civil rights act not only sought to defend and extend voting rights but also tackled head-on the most provocative issue, public accommodations. It aimed to translate the Supreme Court's December 1960 decision into legislation that outlawed discrimination in hotels and motels, restaurants, bars, lunch counters, theaters, stores and almost anywhere else that people gathered. Kennedy's new bill would not end all forms of discrimination, but it would allow millions of black people to participate at last in ordinary, mainstream American life.

Mansfield told Kennedy that the new bill probably could not make it out of committee; the public accommodations section was too much. "You've got to get it done," the President responded. "It's the heart of the matter. These people are entitled to that consideration."

"Well," said Mansfield, not disguising his pessimism, "I'll do my best, Mr. President."[42]

What had happened to Kennedy in May 1963 was not a conversion but a development, one almost waiting to happen. He had learned the truth about noblesse oblige. Someone blessed by good fortune begins by pushing a cause, only to find after a while that the cause is pushing him. He liked to call himself an "idealist without illusions," yet behind the detached attitudes was a well of emotion. Jack Kennedy, that nonpareil of urbanity and hedonism, yearned for moral crusades. The Cold War was one. This was the other.

CHAPTER 33

ExComm

Most mornings in the White House started much the same for JFK. He got up around seven-thirty, had a bath to ease his back, and then speed-read his way through a thick folder of intelligence material that Bundy's staff had assembled from the secret cables that came in overnight. Then, in his bathrobe and slippers, he read *The New York Times* and *The Washington Post* while gulping down his unvarying breakfast of coffee, orange juice, eggs, bacon and toast.

After that, Kennedy dressed with the help of his valet, George Taylor, and by nine o'clock he was ready for Caroline and John-John to come and receive a morning kiss. He descended to the Oval Office, a child on each side, a tiny hand in each of his, the loving father lucky enough to work from home.

The morning of October 16, 1962, there was a knock on his bedroom door as he was having breakfast, and Bundy entered, carrying a folder with some photographs in it. "Mr. President," said Bundy, spreading the photographs out on the bed, "there is now hard photographic evidence, which you will see, that the Russians have offensive missiles in Cuba."

Kennedy looked at the photographs closely. It was difficult to make out just what it was they showed, apart from some crude-looking structures surrounded by dense tropical vegetation. But he knew that what Bundy was telling him was true. "We are probably going to have to bomb them," said Kennedy.

Three hours later Art Lundahl, the CIA's leading expert on aerial photography, briefed the President, Cabinet members and key members of the White House staff such as Sorensen and O'Donnell on what the U-2 had found. The Soviets were installing medium-range ballistic missiles (MRBMs) that could reach as far as Washington and were preparing to install intermediate-range ballistic missiles (IRBMs) that, with a range of up to twenty-two hundred miles, would cover 90 percent of the continental United States.[1]

"What is the advantage?" Kennedy wondered aloud. "Must be some major reason for the Russians to set this up. Must be that they're not satisfied with their ICBMs"—their intercontinental ballistic missiles, which had a range of five thousand miles.[2]

The President had just guessed the principal reason for the missiles in Cuba. When the Joint Chiefs had assured him "our power is supreme" shortly before Kennedy met Khrushchev in Vienna in June 1961, they were not boasting or bluffing.

The position had not changed since then. In October 1962 the U.S. possessed roughly 5,000 nuclear warheads that could be used against the Soviet Union. The CIA estimated the Soviets had around 300 strategic weapons—of which 20 were SS-6 intercontinental ballistic missiles— 155 long-range bombers and a small force of submarines that among them carried no more than 20 MRBMs and surfaced to fire them.

Ostensibly, the U.S. held a 17–1 advantage in nuclear weaponry. In reality, Soviet strategic weapons were so primitive, so unreliable and so vulnerable that the American advantage was closer to 100–1. And as Kennedy had discovered in September 1961, the Joint Chiefs intended to use this overwhelming strategic advantage to destroy the U.S.S.R. in a preemptive strike if the Soviets appeared ready to attack American forces in Europe or anywhere else. The U.S. would strike before being struck. There would be no nuclear Pearl Harbor.[3]

In the winter of 1961, as Khrushchev brooded on the Soviet Union's strategic inferiority, the precarious fate of Cuba and the challenge of getting the Allies out of Berlin, he saw a chance for a stunning masterstroke. Putting ballistic missiles into Cuba would equalize the strategic balance, protect the Castro regime and perhaps allow him at last to force the Americans to yield on Berlin.[4]

All of the missiles would be in place by the end of November 1962, when Khrushchev was due to address the UN. He was going to demand a final resolution of the Berlin problem before flying from New York to Havana, where he and Castro would sign a defense pact. That was when he would announce the presence in Cuba of the IRBMs. The Americans would no longer be able to play their trump card, strategic superiority.

The governing factor over the decisions that were made during the Cuban missile crisis reflected the fundamental attitude towards nuclear weapons of John F. Kennedy and the men he consulted. His own reaction when he was briefed on the Single Integrated Operational Plan (SIOP) had been one of sheer horror and revulsion. Kennedy admired toughness but abhorred war. In the fall of 1960, at about the time he was briefed on American missile strength, he told Gore Vidal, "I'm almost a peace-at-any-price man."

Not surprisingly, his reaction on the first day of the crisis was to deny the military importance of what Khrushchev had done. "What difference does it make? They've got enough to blow us up now anyway." This wasn't true, but he preferred to believe it, probably because if he accepted the truth about American nuclear superiority, he would find it virtually impossible to avoid authorizing an invasion of Cuba, which was what the Joint Chiefs wanted.

Yet Kennedy was convinced that any attack on Cuba was likely to push the Soviets into seizing Berlin. If that happened, he could easily find himself forced to authorize the dreaded and terrifying preemptive strike called for in the SIOP.[5]

The Joint Chiefs had no doubt that the missiles in Cuba posed a direct threat to national survival. Dozens of medium-range missiles in Cuba were going to be more accurate and reliable and would pose a more serious threat than the handful of vulnerable Soviet ICBMs five thousand miles away. There was also the fact that the United States had created a ring of SAC bases far from its territory to contain Soviet adventurism. Khrushchev had now penetrated that ring and established himself well inside America's forward defenses.

Once the IRBMs became operational, every SAC base in the world—including SAC headquarters in Nebraska—would come within range of Soviet missiles. A Soviet first strike would destroy at least 85 percent of American nuclear weapons, possibly more.[6]

After lunch and a nap on October 16, the President met with more than a hundred newspaper editors for an off-the-record briefing at the State

Department. He ended by quoting from memory a short poem written by the Spanish bullfighter Domingo Ortega and translated by Robert Graves:

> Bullfight critics ranked in rows
> Crowd the enormous plaza full;
> But only one is there who knows,
> And he's the one who fights the bull.[7]

During the next two days, McNamara passed on urgent advice from the Joint Chiefs to mount a seven-day aerial offensive against the missile sites, followed by an invasion. On the first day of the crisis, Robert Kennedy had wanted to hit back at the people who had done this to his brother and even favored manufacturing an incident to justify an invasion. On the second day, he opposed any attack. He called it "a Pearl Harbor in reverse" and emotively told other presidential advisers, "My brother is not going to be the Tojo of the sixties."[8]

During that second day, Kennedy moved the focus of discussion firmly away from military action and towards something less risky, a naval blockade. On the third day, October 18, he was scheduled to receive the Soviet foreign minister, Andrei Gromyko. Kennedy reminded Gromyko that he had made two public statements in September saying the United States would not tolerate Soviet offensive weapons in Cuba.

Gromyko blandly assured him there were no such weapons in Cuba. There were photographs proving the opposite in Kennedy's desk as they talked, and the President had to fight off the temptation to pull them out and shove them under Gromyko's nose.[9]

Khrushchev was certain he would prevail. A short time before the missiles went into Cuba, he told one of his speechwriters, Fedor Burlatsky, that although President Kennedy was intelligent, he was also weak. "He will crumble when tested." The cable that Khrushchev received from Gromyko reporting on his Oval Office meeting with Kennedy seemed like a confirmation. Gromyko said the missiles in Cuba had caught Kennedy so completely by surprise he would be unable to respond.[10]

Close to midnight, as Gromyko's cable was making its way to Moscow, the President and his advisers were holding yet another meeting. They had finally decided what to do: the Navy would blockade Cuba. At present, there were at least twenty ships moving from Soviet ports towards Cuba, seven of them with holds big enough to carry IRBMs.

A naval blockade would not get the missiles out of Cuba and would make it harder to mount an effective air attack later, when the missile sites were more advanced and better defended. But Kennedy was trying to buy time. He needed Khrushchev to reflect carefully on ways of ending this crisis and was determined not to push his adversary into an impulsive act to redeem a reckless venture.

Until now Kennedy had kept the Joint Chiefs at arm's length, dealing with them through McNamara and the new chairman of the JCS, Maxwell Taylor. Deeply impressed by Taylor's 1960 book, *The Uncertain Trumpet,* Kennedy had brought the former Army chief of staff back to active duty in May 1961 as his military adviser. That move had undercut the Joint Chiefs, whom the President blamed for the Bay of Pigs fiasco. On October 1, 1962, he had installed Taylor as chairman of the Joint Chiefs of Staff. With Taylor riding herd on the Chiefs throughout the missile crisis, the President controlled the military hierarchy by divide and rule.

On Friday, October 19, when Kennedy finally met with the Chiefs face-to-face, they found that they were not there to offer him advice; they were there so he could tell them what he had decided to do—institute a blockade. They tried to talk him into invading Cuba and assured him the Soviets would not seize Berlin in retaliation. Kennedy told them they were wrong, then headed for Chicago.

So far he had managed to keep the crisis secret, and because he was scheduled to talk to the Democrats of Cook County, Illinois, that was what he would do. The next morning, however, he hurried back to Washington. The latest photographs showed work on the missile sites accelerating. And while Kennedy was away, the preeminent political commentator of the time, Walter Lippmann, had told an editor at *The Washington Post,* "We are on the brink of war." Hours after returning to the White House, Salinger heard of it and told the President. "This town is a sieve!" Kennedy fulminated. Salinger told him he had only one more day, possibly two, before the story broke.[11]

Jack called Jackie at their new house in the Virginia countryside and told her to come back to Washington at once and bring the children. "We are very, very close to war," he told her.[12]

During discussions in the Cabinet Room that Saturday afternoon, Adlai Stevenson urged Kennedy to offer Khrushchev something for removing the missiles. Maybe the U.S. should give up its base at Guantánamo Bay in southeastern Cuba, which it had held since the Spanish-American War. Or maybe it could trade American missiles in Turkey for the Soviet missiles. John McCone ridiculed the idea of rewarding Khrushchev for doing something he should have avoided, but Kennedy reacted circumspectly.[13]

On Sunday the President had his friend David Ormsby-Gore, the British ambassador, come to the White House for lunch, then told him about the missiles in Cuba. There were only two possible responses, said Kennedy. One was an air campaign starting Monday morning to destroy the missile sites. The second option was a naval blockade.

Ormsby-Gore told him, "Very few people outside the United States would consider the provocation serious enough to merit an American attack. Besides, action like that might provide a smoke screen behind which the Russians might move against Berlin. Some form of blockade is probably the right answer."

Kennedy said he had decided on a blockade but conceded, "If we *are* going to invade, we'll never have a better opportunity."[14]

Maybe the best way to settle this crisis, he told Ormsby-Gore, was not piecemeal but as part of a wider agreement, one that covered Berlin, nuclear disarmament, the missiles in Cuba and the SAC bases around the borders of the Soviet Union. That would mean pulling its Jupiter IRBMs out of Italy and Turkey, but he had no problem with that—"They're more or less worthless."[15]

The next morning, October 22, Kennedy presided over yet another meeting on the missile crisis. From this day on, he would call the group of roughly twenty people who participated in these meetings the Executive Committee of the National Security Council, or ExComm.[16]

During this ExComm meeting, Kennedy told Paul Nitze, one of the foremost experts on nuclear strategy, to look into the possibility of withdrawing the Jupiters.[17]

Although Kennedy had given little thought to these weapons until now, Khrushchev took them personally. He had a habit of greeting visitors to his Black Sea dacha by handing them a pair of binoculars and telling them to look towards the south. "What do you see?" he asked. They said they saw nothing much, only sea and sky. Then he'd take the binoculars back and raise them to his eyes and bellow, "I see American missiles in Turkey aimed at *my dacha*!"[18]

On Monday evening the President finally addressed the nation and the world. His televised presentation was forceful rather than belligerent. "This secret, swift and extraordinary buildup of Communist missiles is a deliberately provocative and unjustified change in the status quo which cannot be accepted by this country," he declared. Inevitably, perhaps, he compared the present crisis to Munich and the lesson it had taught— "aggressive conduct, if allowed to go unchallenged and unchecked, ultimately leads to war."

Because a naval blockade was a traditional casus belli, Rusk advised him to use a more imprecise term, such as "quarantine," instead. So Kennedy announced he was imposing "a strict quarantine on all offensive military equipment under shipment to Cuba."[19]

The next morning, Tuesday, October 23, after days of arm-twisting and diplomatic blandishments, the Organization of American States resolved unanimously that the missiles in Cuba were in violation of the Rio Treaty of 1947. The treaty allowed OAS members to act jointly in defense of peace in the Americas. Kennedy claimed the resolution provided the authority he needed to impose a quarantine. This slighted the fact that the Soviet Union was not a party to the treaty and under international law had no duty to respect the wishes of the OAS.[20]

At the crisis meeting in the Cabinet Room on Tuesday morning, the President decided that if the Soviets shot down a U-2, there would be immediate retaliation against the Soviet SAM sites in Cuba.[21]

Late that afternoon Kennedy, Bobby and Bundy were glued to the television set in the Oval Office as Stevenson prepared to make a presentation to the UN Security Council. With the help of photo interpreters, he was going to show large-scale prints of photographs that revealed missiles, storage bays and missile launchers.

Before Stevenson had a chance to show even one picture, the Soviet ambassador to the UN, Valerian Zorin, ridiculed the presentation. It was all fake, snorted Zorin, all fabrications straight from the laboratories of the CIA.

"All right, sir," said Stevenson, "do you deny that the Soviet Union has placed and is placing medium- and intermediate-range missiles and sites in Cuba. Yes or no?"

Zorin protested. "I am not in an American courtroom!"

"You are in the court of world opinion right now!"

Zorin blustered for a while, concluding weakly, "In due course, sir, you will have your reply."

Stevenson responded vigorously, "I am prepared to wait for my answer until hell freezes over."

"Terrific!" said Kennedy, beaming broadly. "I didn't know Adlai had it in him."[22]

McNamara had urged strenuously that the quarantine line be placed eight hundred miles from Havana, out of range of the Soviet bombers in Cuba. That evening, however, Kennedy asked Ormsby-Gore what he thought, and he advised putting the line only five hundred miles out. It was risky, Ormsby-Gore conceded, but it would give Khrushchev a few more hours to back down.[23]

That evening Kennedy signed a proclamation that the quarantine would go into effect at nine A.M. eastern time on Wednesday. Having signed the proclamation, and with the showdown little more than twelve hours away, he remarked to Bobby, "It looks really mean, doesn't it? But on the other hand, there wasn't any other choice . . . I don't think there was a choice."

Bobby agreed. "Well, there isn't any choice. I mean, you would have been, you would have been impeached."

"Well," said Kennedy, seeming to take some comfort from his brother's idea, "I think I would have been impeached."[24]

On Wednesday morning eight Soviet ships approached the line, escorted by four Soviet submarines. A U.S. Navy destroyer and a hunter-killer submarine were following each Soviet boat. The alert status of American military forces was moved to Defense Condition 2. The only level above this was Defense Condition 1—and that was war.

When the meeting began, John McCone, director of the CIA, gave the intelligence picture, and McNamara said the Soviet submarine nearest the line was such a threat to American ships that it had to be forced to the surface, where it would be harmless. Kennedy was aghast as McNamara explained how the Navy would bombard the Soviet submarine with small depth charges. They were so accurate they would bounce off the hull, and carrying such a small amount of explosive they would serve as a warning signal to the boat's captain to surface, without much risk of sinking the vessel. Or so the Navy believed.[25]

JFK stared across the gleaming table at Bobby, putting his hand over his mouth in horror, then opening and clenching his fist in silent frustration as the blood drained from his face. For a minute or two, the President seemed to be somewhere else, become someone else.[26]

As the group around the table discussed which ships to stop first, McCone brought a message based on intercepted and decoded Soviet-signals intelligence that said the Soviet vessels approaching the line had suddenly stopped dead in the water or were turning around. Rusk leaned across to Bundy. "We are eyeball to eyeball," said Rusk, "and I think the other fellow just blinked."[27]

Throughout the missile crisis, Kennedy pulled not only his family but also his friends around him. He had Ormsby-Gore come to dinner twice, and his friend Charles Bartlett dined at the White House three times before it was over. When Bartlett arrived that Wednesday evening, he asked Kennedy, "Shouldn't we be celebrating?"

"No. It's too early for that." There were still more than a dozen ships steaming towards Cuba and the quarantine line.

In the early hours of Thursday morning, the President was awakened and given a long cable from Khrushchev. The heart of it was a passage that read, "The Soviet government cannot give instructions to the captains of Soviet vessels bound for Cuba to observe the instructions of American naval forces," because what the Americans were doing was illegal under international law. Khrushchev was right. It *was* illegal. Kennedy called Bartlett. "I just got a cable from our friend, and he says those ships are coming through. They're coming through tomorrow."[28]

At breakfast Thursday morning, Kennedy scanned *The Washington Post,* in which a column by Walter Lippmann said Cuba was comparable to Turkey—"the only place where there are strategic weapons right on the frontier of the Soviet Union." Pulling American missiles out of Turkey was the best way to get Soviet missiles out of Cuba.[29]

Kennedy's reaction was "Shit!"

If anyone was going to offer to trade the Jupiters for Soviet missiles in Cuba, it had to be him, not Lippmann, and it had to be done secretly. If he pulled IRBMs out of a NATO country under Soviet pressure, it would look like he was prepared to sacrifice an ally to defend Chicago or Boston. NATO might not survive.[30]

That day there was no challenge to the quarantine by Soviet ships, but work on the IRBM sites now proceeded day and night, and there were elaborate efforts at camouflage. The medium-range missiles would be operational within a few days; the IRBMs within a few weeks.

This crisis had given John Kennedy an understanding of nuclear weapons that he had shied away from heretofore. "Even if the quarantine's a hundred percent effective, it's only a first step," he reminded the ExComm the morning of October 26. "My priority is to get the missiles out."[31]

The military was planning for a seven-day air campaign starting no later than Tuesday, October 30, against the missile sites, the SAM sites and Cuban air bases. This would be followed by an invasion of a hundred and fifty thousand soldiers and marines, something Kennedy profoundly wanted to avoid. Talking to Pierre Salinger in the Rose Garden the afternoon of Friday, October 26, JFK said, "You know, if we don't succeed in bringing this crisis to an end, hundreds of millions of people are going to be killed."[32]

Late that evening, as he prepared to go to bed, the President received a long, rambling communication from Khrushchev. Towards the end of it, the Soviet leader offered a deal: "We, for our part, will declare that our ships bound for Cuba will not carry any kind of armaments. You would declare that the United States will not invade Cuba with its forces. . . . Then the necessity for the presence of our military specialists in Cuba would disappear."[33]

In the morning Khrushchev sent a letter that had a less reasonable tone and made additional demands, including getting the Jupiters out of Turkey. During Saturday afternoon, as Kennedy and the ExComm debated how to deal with Khrushchev's starkly different letters, came news that two low-level reconnaissance aircraft had returned riddled with shrapnel and a U-2 had been shot down.

The Cubans had opened fire on the plane with their 20-millimeter light flak guns. The Soviet general in command of Cuban air defenses had ordered his SAM batteries to fire, too, "in a basic spirit of solidarity." The general's order violated his instructions, although no one in Washington knew that at the time.[34]

Kennedy agonized over the dead U-2 pilot, Major Rudolph Anderson. This was a Commander in Chief whose big brother, Joe Jr., had died flying a perilous mission. During his own military service, JFK had lost two members of his *PT-109* crew in action and been haunted by their deaths long afterwards. Anderson's loss was no abstract event to him. He grieved deeply for brave men killed in the service of their country. Worried about the fate of the pilot of the next U-2 that flew over Cuba, he ordered a temporary halt to the flights. And he stayed his hand, ignoring his own stated policy of immediate retaliation against the SAM sites if a U-2 was downed, giving Khrushchev yet another chance to think about where this crisis was headed.

That evening of October 27 the President called together the exhausted White House staff. He thanked them for their efforts to help resolve the crisis, then told them, "Go home and see your wives and children. Tonight we decide whether to make war or not." Then he went to an ExComm meeting and authorized the call-up of Air Force reserve units to support an invasion.[35]

He chose to ignore Khrushchev's tough-worded letter of October 27 and replied instead to the more reasonable message that preceded it. If what Khrushchev was offering was a commitment to remove his missiles in exchange for a pledge that the United States would not invade Cuba, said Kennedy's reply, he would accept that.[36]

Even now, Kennedy was prepared to give Khrushchev what he had demanded in his second, hard-line letter. He told Bobby to go see the Soviet ambassador, Anatoly Dobrynin, with this message: "The U.S. will pull its missiles out of Turkey and Italy, but we need four to five months." There was a second essential condition—the deal had to remain secret.[37]

Kennedy had a fallback position. If even this concession failed, he would ask the Secretary General of the United Nations, U Thant, to make a public appeal for a trade: Jupiters out of Turkey, Soviet missiles out of Cuba. By giving the UN something he could not publicly give Khrushchev, he might yet resolve the crisis without destroying NATO.[38]

Moscow time was nine hours ahead of eastern time, and as Kennedy slept, Khrushchev was coming to a decision: he would pull the missiles out. In downing a U-2 and killing its pilot, the Soviets had made a potentially suicidal mistake—they had drawn first blood.

Khrushchev had been careful not to give the Americans any pretext to launch a preemptive nuclear attack on the Soviet Union. No attempt had been made to fuel the ICBMs at Plesetsk and Soviet forces were not brought to a high state of readiness. But the destruction of the U-2 showed he could no longer trust his senior field commanders to obey orders. The crisis seemed about to spin out of control. Announcing his decision, Khrushchev told the members of the Soviet Presidium, "In order to save the world, we must retreat."[39]

On the Sunday afternoon that the missile crisis ended, Kennedy suddenly thought of Abraham Lincoln. In the hour of his greatest triumph, Lincoln had gone to Ford's Theatre and been murdered. Death was never far from JFK's thoughts, and whatever happened after this, he could never have a greater moment or a more certain place in History.

"This is the night I should go to the theater," he mused aloud to Bobby, revealing obliquely to his brother something he could never have admitted to anyone outright.[40]

Throughout the missile crisis, John Kennedy had held in his hands the power of a god and the responsibility of a man. If he stumbled, he might bring about the destruction of half—possibly all—of humanity. This was where life lived as a challenge to death had brought him, not away from oblivion but straight towards it, his family, his country and his species crowded at his back, needing him to find a way out. This was a life lived intensely, taken as far as it could go.

CHAPTER 34

Aftermath

Two days after the missile crisis ended, Kennedy had his routine weekly meeting with the congressional leadership. "We've won a great victory," he told them. "There is no more threat from Russia. The threat in the years ahead will be China."[1]

He had also learned something else from the crisis, something he did not share with anyone but McNamara and Bundy. The problem with the Soviet Union was not its military power but its comparative weakness. Inferiority had made its leadership reckless. Kennedy was going to change that by eroding America's military lead and helping the Soviets improve their strategic weapons. Both JFK and McNamara believed that a superpower relationship dominated by what McNamara later called "Mutual Assured Destruction" would be less dangerous and more manageable.

In early December, Kennedy had the Pentagon's general counsel, John T. McNaughton, address the annual International Arms Control Symposium at the University of Michigan. In little more than an hour McNaughton revealed top-secret information on how the United States controlled its nuclear weapons. "It is of course hoped—and I wish to emphasize this—that the Soviet Union will see the logic behind these policies and take comparable steps," said McNaughton. And just to make sure the Soviets did not overlook McNaughton's speech, in the days that followed, American diplomats in Moscow asked their Soviet counterparts what they thought of it.[2]

The President soon received the answer. Since 1958 committees of technical experts from the U.S., Britain and the Soviet Union had been haggling in Geneva over how to limit nuclear testing. The stumbling block was Soviet refusal to countenance on-site inspections, which Khrushchev invariably denounced as "espionage." On December 19 Khrushchev wrote to JFK and said there might be a way to get around the inspection issue, by using seismic detection equipment. The tone of Khrushchev's letter was also striking. Gone was the usual bluster. In its place was a more amenable tone.[3]

JFK had promised during his campaign to create a disarmament agency, but once in office, he scoffed at Stevenson or Humphrey when they tried to get him to take disarmament seriously. "Disarmament," he'd say, "that's a propaganda thing, isn't it?" Even so, he was worried about the effects of atmospheric testing. In April 1961 Kennedy told one of his favored journalists, Chalmers Roberts, that he wasn't convinced Eisenhower had really wanted a test ban. "But I do." At about the same time, he was telling Under Secretary of State Chester Bowles why he felt so strongly about it. "I know it may sound a little corny," Kennedy said, "but our world doesn't matter very much. Caroline's world does matter, and I'm prepared to take every conceivable step to bring about a nuclear agreement with the Russians."[4]

When he addressed the UN for the first time as President, on September 25, 1961, his speech was mainly a plea for nuclear disarmament. The next day Kennedy signed the legislation that created the Arms Control and Disarmament Agency.

Yet only three weeks after this, the Soviets set off a fifty-eight-megaton blast, ending a testing moratorium that had held for nearly three years. The United States reacted by pushing ahead with dozens of smaller nuclear blasts, both underground and in the atmosphere in 1962. The point of so much testing, said Kennedy, was not to match the Soviets bomb for bomb but "to maintain arms superiority."[5]

The already faltering drive for arms control came to a halt, and there seemed little prospect of it being revived. Then came the missile crisis. Macmillan urged Kennedy to see the resolution of the crisis as a chance for a fresh start in East-West relations, beginning with arms control. Kennedy agreed and began looking for allies.

Normally he would have shunned an ultra-liberal organization like the National Committee for a Sane Nuclear Policy, which was founded by a left-wing journalist, Norman Cousins. But in the spring of 1963 he used Cousins as an informal intermediary with Khrushchev. This was typical of the JFK approach: he had officials working on the disarmament problem, and people who had no role in government working on the same problem, but separately.[6]

Meanwhile, the committee in Geneva was revisiting a treaty that had been tabled a year earlier by American and British negotiators. The Soviets had scorned it then, but what had once been unacceptable was suddenly negotiable.[7]

Another, more concrete consequence of the crisis was an agreement reached on June 5, 1963, to set up a Washington-Moscow "hot line." He and Khrushchev would each have a teletype connecting instantly and directly with the other. This was the first U.S.-Soviet arms control agreement of the nuclear age.

Five days later JFK delivered the commencement address at American University, barely a mile from the White House. "Let us re-examine our attitude toward the Soviet Union," he urged his gowned and excited young audience. The Russians had achieved much in space and suffered greatly in defeating Hitler.

"In the final analysis our most basic common link is that we all inhabit this small planet," said the President. "We all breathe the same air. We all cherish our children. And we are all mortal." He declared an end to American nuclear testing and invited the Soviets to do the same.

Throughout his speech, Kennedy returned repeatedly to the theme of peace, but he qualified it—"By peace I do not mean a Pax Americana enforced on the world by weapons," a statement aimed directly at someone not there, Nikita Khrushchev.[8]

The next day he told Averell Harriman to go to Geneva, "get an agreement [on nuclear testing] and come home." The other thing he wanted Harriman to do in Geneva was find out as much as he could from the Russians about China's nuclear program. How close were they to building the Bomb?[9]

By the middle of July the main provisions of a test-ban treaty had been negotiated; all that remained were the fine details. The treaty would ban testing in the atmosphere, outer space and under the sea. The Soviets would not have to accept on-site inspections; seismic monitoring equipment would suffice.

With the treaty about to be initialed by the three present nuclear powers, Kennedy asked the Joint Chiefs to come to the Oval Office on July 23 and spell out their views on the test ban. All were opposed to it but the Commandant of the Marine Corps, General David M. Shoup. A ban on atmospheric tests would make it virtually impossible to develop an anti-ballistic missile, the Chiefs said, because it could only work if it had a nuclear warhead.

JFK urged them to try looking at the issue from a political as well as a military perspective. What he did not tell them was that he had already decided to freeze the ABM program.[10]

When the Senate debate began on September 9, public opinion was split almost evenly over the bill, and congressional mail was running strongly against it. For once, though, Kennedy involved himself deeply and daily in getting a bill passed. He knew Dean Acheson would be opposed to the treaty and persuaded him not to lobby against it on Capitol Hill. The key player, however, was Everett McKinley Dirksen of Illinois, the Republican leader in the Senate, and Dirksen denounced the treaty on the Senate floor. Bobby Baker, the most astute Democratic head counter in the Senate, called the President and told him that Dirksen had just killed the treaty.

Kennedy replied calmly, "Maybe not."[11]

In 1962 Robert Kennedy had discovered that Eisenhower's White House Chief of Staff, Sherman Adams, had solicited large cash gifts for himself from rich Republicans. Bobby wanted to indict Adams for tax evasion. Mamie Eisenhower told Ike she was afraid Adams would commit suicide if indicted. Eisenhower felt it was unseemly as a former President to beg personal favors of his successor. Instead, he sent Dirksen to ask JFK not to prosecute Adams. Dirksen told Kennedy that he and Ike would be in his debt, and Adams was not indicted.

After taking Baker's call, Kennedy called for Dirksen and told him, "Ev, I want you to reverse yourself. I also want Ike's public endorsement of the treaty before the Senate votes. We'll call it square on that other matter." On September 23 the Senate passed the bill 80–19. The President signed it on October 7.[12]

He acknowledged that the test ban was not going to end all testing or block the proliferation of nuclear weapons. The Chinese were not going to stop their drive to acquire nuclear weapons; nor would the French. Even so, he said, "A journey of a thousand miles has to begin with a single step."

Kennedy nevertheless remained worried about the Chinese. Mao Tse-tung had boasted that he wasn't afraid of a nuclear war. Hundreds of millions of Chinese would die, but "So what?" said Mao. "War is war. The years will pass and we'll get people fucking so they'll produce more babies than ever before."[13]

JFK was so concerned that Mao wasn't bluffing that he weighed the possibilities of a preemptive attack. "You know, it wouldn't be too hard if we could somehow get an anonymous airplane to go over there and take out the Chinese facilities," he told William C. Foster, the head of the Arms Control and Disarmament Agency, one day. "They've only got a couple. And maybe we could do it, or the Soviet Union could do it, rather than face the threat of Chinese nuclear weapons."[14]

The ratification of the test-ban treaty elated Kennedy. He considered it—and rightly—the most important achievement of his presidency so far. It also made it possible at long last to do what no President had done since FDR—visit the Soviet Union. That would have to wait until after the 1964 election, he told David Ormsby-Gore, "But I am determined to go."[15]

=

NATO had emerged from the missile crisis unscathed. Every NATO government had supported Kennedy throughout. American prestige in NATO countries soared after Khrushchev's capitulation.

Even so, as France became prosperous and shed its colonies, it began seeking a new role in the world, out of the American shadow. In 1963 de Gaulle vetoed British entry into the Common Market, pushed ahead with the development of an independent French nuclear force, pulled out of the military command structure of NATO and told NATO to get its headquarters off French soil.

With France making life difficult for the U.S. and NATO, Kennedy decided to visit Europe in the summer of 1963. Unwelcome in France, he would visit the other major European countries—Britain, Germany and Italy—and a nation that wasn't part of NATO or ever likely to join it, Ireland.

Kenny O'Donnell told him that was ridiculous. He already had every Irish-American vote. "People will say it's just a pleasure trip."

"That's exactly what I want," said JFK. "A pleasure trip to Ireland!"[16]

He departed June 22 and arrived in Bonn, the capital of West Germany, the next morning, on his way to Berlin. He visited the Wall twice, and was deeply troubled each time. He noticed women waving handkerchiefs at him from windows on the East German side. "Isn't that dangerous?" he asked the commander of the Berlin garrison, Lieutenant General James Polke.

"It is, Mr. President."

He smiled at them, and did not wave.[17]

Outside the city hall a large platform had been erected, and more than two million people—out of a population of little more than three million—jammed the streets and sidewalks to acclaim him as he was driven towards it from the hated Wall. Here was what they wanted, needed and deserved: a brave young American President had come to them as the smiling, charming embodiment of his nation's resolve that their oasis of liberty in a wasteland of tyranny was going to survive.

Emotions were running so high as Kennedy spoke that he had a troubling feeling that the crowd was responding too eagerly. There was something slightly hysterical in the atmosphere, and if he had said, "I want you all to cross into East Germany and pull down that Wall," the crowd immediately would have rushed into East Berlin and attacked it.[18]

The response to his famously defiant observation, "*Ich bin ein Berliner*," was so rapturous that he, too, got carried away. "There are some who say that Communism is the wave of the future," Kennedy declared. "Let them come to Berlin." Then he ad-libbed, "And there are some who say in Europe and elsewhere that we can work with the Communists. Let them come to Berlin!" Later he kicked himself for saying that when he was still trying to get agreement on the test ban.

The excitement of the crowd had energized him; while they needed something from him, he needed something, too. Of all the drugs that JFK consumed, nothing thrilled him as much as an ecstatic crowd, and this had been a phenomenal day. As he prepared to depart, he told the German chancellor, Konrad Adenauer, that he was going to advise whoever succeeded him as President on what to do when everything seemed to be going badly: "Go to Germany."[19]

From Berlin, he flew to Ireland and visited the docks at New Ross, where his great-grandfather Patrick J. Kennedy had sailed for Boston in 1848. The crowds that greeted him were not as big as those in Germany, but they held a special meaning for a man whose record collection ran heavily to Irish songs and Irish tenors. JFK told one cheering Irish crowd, "This is not the land of my birth, but it is the land for which I hold the greatest affection."[20]

He drank tea with his cousins and had dinner with the Irish President,

Eamon De Valera. During the state dinner that De Valera gave in his honor, JFK said something about leaving from Shannon Airport in the morning, and De Valera's wife responded by reciting a poem. Kennedy reacted as he always did to poetry that enthralled him, reaching for his place card to write it down.

> 'Tis the Shannon's brightly glancing stream,
> Brightly gleaming, silent in the morning beam,
> Oh, the sight entrancing,
> Thus returns from travels long,
> Years of exile, years of pain,
> To see old Shannon's face again.

Next day he said farewell to the crowd at Shannon Airport by referring to the poem—"Well, I am going to come back and see old Shannon's face again." And he later described his Irish trip to his friend Jim Reed: "The happiest two days of my life."[21]

From Ireland, he flew to England to visit Kick's grave at Chatsworth, the home of the Devonshires. He somberly placed some Irish roses he'd brought from Shannon on his sister's resting place.[22]

Kennedy also wanted to see Harold Macmillan, the prime minister, whom he had talked to on the phone throughout the missile crisis. Despite the wide gulf in their ages, he felt a deep affection for Macmillan, whom he did not regard as he did other national leaders such as Adenauer or Nehru. "I feel at home with Macmillan because I can share my loneliness with him," said Kennedy. "The others are all foreigners to me."[23]

From England, he flew back to the Continent to meet with the president of Italy and have a private audience with the new Pope, Paul VI. Meeting the Pope, he pointedly refrained from kissing the papal ring or appearing in any way deferential. The Pope reciprocated by announcing after their audience that he was praying for America's black people.[24]

Jacqueline Kennedy was pregnant for the fourth time, and the baby was expected in September. She had rented a small house on Squaw Island for the summer, within sight of Hyannis but removed from the frenzied Kennedy compound. JFK had the Air Force set up an emergency maternity unit at Otis Air Force Base, just in case the baby arrived prematurely. Jackie, who was hoping for another girl, planned to call her Susan.[25]

Evelyn Lincoln came into the Oval Office shortly before noon on August 7 and told the President, "Mrs. Kennedy is on her way to Otis." An hour later Kennedy was airborne, heading for Boston. The baby—a boy—was not only five weeks premature but also fighting for his life. JFK spent much of the flight praying and counting his rosary beads. Most of his adult life he had looked sardonically on the Church's tenets and customs. But at moments like this, he sought the consolations of his faith as keenly as ever his mother had done.[26]

The baby had trouble breathing and was rushed to the Boston Children's Hospital in an incubator. Baptized Patrick, the baby died at four in the morning on August 9, after surviving less than forty-eight hours.[27]

Kennedy was awakened and, numb with grief, walked down the corridor and held one tiny lifeless hand, weeping inconsolably. Afterwards, he said bitterly to Dave Powers, "It is against the laws of nature for parents to bury their children."[28]

For the next two days, JFK was too grief-stricken to face anyone, including Jackie. He did what he always did when he was deeply upset—he withdrew into himself. Wounded and unreachable, he spent those two days and nights virtually alone, even eating by himself, something he normally loathed.

Jackie arranged a monthlong trip to Europe with her sister, Lee Radziwill, to come to terms with her loss. Like Joe and Rose, Jack and Jackie were still unable after ten years of marriage, to comfort each other in the depths of a shared despair. That called for a kind of emotional maturity that neither possessed.[29]

═

By the fall of 1963 Kennedy's thoughts constantly and inevitably focused on the 1964 presidential election. Both his greatest successes—the missile crisis and the test-ban treaty—were in foreign affairs. Presidents get elected, and re-elected, on their domestic agenda.

The economy was growing strongly, yet unemployment remained high. JFK had managed to push through a tax investment credit that would aid business and, he hoped, create jobs, but it would take time. And he had lost his Manpower Development and Training Bill—another attempt to reduce unemployment—earlier in the year.

The Civil Rights Act he had sent to Congress in June faced an uncertain future in the House Rules Committee, which would have to decide whether the bill would even make it to the floor for a vote. And the legislation still had not been introduced into the Senate, where southern Democrats would decide its fate.

The White House had hoped that the August 28 March on Washington and Martin Luther King's electrifying "I Have a Dream" speech would so galvanize public opinion that Congress would have to act on the President's civil rights legislation. But by the time Congress reconvened in October, whatever momentum the march and the speech had generated was rapidly fading.[30]

On Monday, November 18, Kennedy had a meeting with Democratic leaders in the House. "The train is off the track," he said. "We can't get anything through Congress. What's going on here? How can we straighten things out?"[31]

On the day of his inauguration, Kennedy had been dismayed as he rode down Pennsylvania Avenue at just how seedy and depressing the area between Capitol Hill and the White House looked. He had set up a committee to redesign it. By November 1963 the committee had finally produced a design.

"I'd like to see that," he told his artist friend Bill Walton, a member of the committee. Kennedy invited the congressional leadership to come to the White House, where the plan would be presented to him, over coffee, following his two-day visit to Texas.[32]

CHAPTER 35

It Flies Forever

The war in Vietnam—part civil conflict, part independence struggle and part Communist insurgency—rumbled angrily in the background of Kennedy's presidency. In 1961 JFK had shifted responsibility for managing the American role in the war from the State Department over to the Pentagon or, more precisely, to McNamara, whom Kennedy considered unimpeachably tough and preternaturally smart. After that, the President more or less ignored Vietnam, focusing his attention on it only when the Saigon government of Ngo Dinh Diem was so spectacularly incompetent or brutal that it generated headlines on the front page of *The New York Times*.

Then, in May 1963, Ngo Dinh Thuc, the Catholic archbishop of the northern city of Hue, used the Civil Guard to crack down on local Buddhists who were demanding equality with Catholics. Eight Buddhists were killed, and others were wounded. Under American pressure, Diem reluctantly agreed to seek a compromise with the Buddhists, but his brother, Ngo Dinh Nhu, and his sister-in-law, Madame Nhu, objected fiercely to any concessions.

Ngo Dinh Nhu was not only Diem's brother but the head of South Vietnam's feared and hated paramilitary police. As for Madame Nhu, she used her influence over her husband and brother-in-law to such nefarious effect that she might as well have been a follower of Ho Chi Minh, the Communist leader of North Vietnam.

With South Vietnam bitterly divided between its Buddhist majority and its westernized, Catholic elite, Kennedy decided to appoint a new ambassador. The present ambassador, Frederick Nolting, was blind to the shortcomings of Diem, Nhu and the Madame. Henry Cabot Lodge, who had distinguished himself as an Army officer in World War II and had the additional advantage of speaking fluent French, replaced Nolting.[1]

Kennedy met with Lodge on August 15 to give him his instructions. The aim of the United States was to defeat the Communist threat in South Vietnam, said JFK. "Anything that helps that policy, we are in favor of, and anything that hinders it, we are opposed to."[2]

Before Lodge could take up his new appointment, Nhu's paramilitary police went on a rampage through Buddhist pagodas—the equivalent of Catholic cathedrals—beating up monks, looting religious treasures and molesting Buddhist nuns. Nhu wanted to beat the Buddhists into submission before the new ambassador could arrive. Buddhist monks retaliated by burning themselves to death in the streets, tragedies that Madame Nhu ridiculed on American television as "barbecues."[3]

On August 20 Buddhists mounted anti-Diem protests in the three largest cities of South Vietnam. Diem overreacted by imposing martial law. Lodge, arriving two days later, found that Diem would not even talk about the crisis. Diem could not control South Vietnam, and the United States could not control Diem.[4]

Several of Kennedy's closest advisers on Vietnam, including Lodge, were now ready to write off Diem as a wasting asset and believed that Diem's generals were just as unhappy with him as they were. On August 24 Kennedy approved a telegram to officials in Saigon that said, "If in spite of all your efforts, Diem remains obdurate, then we must face the possibility that Diem himself cannot be preserved."[5]

McNamara and Taylor argued vehemently against any coup, but once Diem's generals learned that the Americans would sanction a coup, they began putting one together. "We are launched on a course from which there is no respectable turning back: the overthrow of Diem," Lodge informed the President.[6]

Kennedy always resented anything that made him feel his subordinates were boxing him in. Before heading to Hyannis Port for the Labor Day weekend, he replied to Lodge's cable: "I must reserve a contingent right to change course and reverse previous instructions."[7]

On September 2, sitting on the lawn furniture outside his house in the Kennedy compound, he was interviewed by Walter Cronkite for CBS's first half-hour broadcast of the evening news. Cronkite asked him about civil rights, the test-ban treaty, unemployment and the 1964 election before turning eventually to Vietnam.

In typically elliptical fashion, Kennedy began to prepare public opinion for the impending coup. Cronkite asked him whether the Saigon government could still win the support of the people of South Vietnam. "With changes in policy—and perhaps in personnel—I think it can," Kennedy replied.[8]

To get what he hoped would be a definitive picture of how the war was going, Kennedy sent McNamara and Taylor to South Vietnam in late September. They returned to inform him that the war would be won by the end of 1965. In fact, it was going so well right now that he could bring home a thousand American military advisers at the end of 1963.

This merdivorous assessment reflected less a desire to get at the truth than a need to generate public support for a war that Americans were at last becoming interested in. In fact, although the military situation in the northern provinces of South Vietnam was stable, in the Mekong Delta— where half the population lived—the Viet Cong was growing stronger politically and becoming militarily bolder.[9]

Kennedy did not want Vietnam to become an issue in the 1964 election. Ideally, it would fade into the background, and bringing some troops home would help create a picture of a war under control. So might the impending coup, provided it wasn't botched, leaving Diem in place, the South Vietnamese army split and the United States exposed. Nor did JFK want to see Diem, Nhu or Madame Nhu harmed. He wanted them out, but out alive.

The coup took place on November 1. Initial reports were sketchy and confused. It was Saturday morning, November 2, and Kennedy was meeting with Rusk, McNamara, Taylor and Bobby in the Oval Office when he was handed the latest cable from Lodge. It said the fate of Diem and Nhu was unknown, but they might well be dead—"murdered or suicides." Kennedy, distraught, hurriedly left the room. Upstairs in the family quarters, he burst into tears.[10]

He did not believe that fellow Catholics such as Diem and Nhu would commit suicide. They had obviously been murdered. "Why have they killed such a well-meaning individual?" he asked Red Fay. "He wasn't a schemer or vicious. He really only wanted to do well by his people." Kennedy fell silent for a moment while he regained his composure. "That bitch," he said. "That bitch with all her greed for power . . . *she* killed him."[11]

≡

He had inherited Castro and Cuba, and after three years, Castro was still there and Cuba was firmly within the Soviet orbit. Kennedy needed to get the Cuban problem resolved in some way before November 1964, otherwise he would be vulnerable to accusations that the missile crisis proved he lacked the guts to go in and remove both the missiles and Castro.

After the Bay of Pigs, Castro had tried to open a dialogue with Kennedy. Dick Goodwin, the presidential assistant for Latin America, had met with Che Guevara in Punta del Este, Uruguay, in the fall of 1961. Che gave Goodwin two gifts for the President—a box of Havana cigars and the offer of a rapprochement with Castro. Kennedy never smoked anything but Havanas thereafter, but he spurned the rapprochement.[12]

There was one thing, however, that continued to trouble him—the eleven hundred survivors of Brigade 2506, the men who had tried to invade Cuba. "I was thinking about those poor guys in prison down in Cuba," he told O'Donnell one day shortly after the Bay of Pigs. "I'm willing to make any kind of deal to get them out of there."[13]

It was not until after the missile crisis that he finally got his chance. The administration had scored a Cuban triumph, and the Castro regime was being hurt badly by American sanctions. Since the Bay of Pigs fiasco, Bobby had been overseeing Operation Mongoose, the attempt to undermine Castro and, if possible, assassinate him. In November 1962 Mongoose was put on hold, and Bobby's energies were turned to getting the Brigade 2506 survivors released. The cost turned out to be $3 million in cash plus $50 million in tractors, medical supplies and baby food.[14]

On December 26, 1962, Kennedy greeted the returned survivors in a ceremony at the Orange Bowl. Jackie wowed them with a short speech of welcome in Spanish. Then JFK rose to speak. The liberated survivors started chanting, "*Guerra! Guerra!*"

He intended to calm them by delivering an unemotional speech of thanks, but the brigade commander presented him with the battle-scarred

Brigade 2506 flag, which a prisoner had saved throughout twenty months of captivity, ingeniously finding places to hide it despite frequent searches. Kennedy was so moved that he responded passionately: "I can assure you that this flag will be returned to this brigade in a free Havana!"[15]

Mongoose was revived fitfully in the spring of 1963, but Kennedy had really lost interest in it. His mind was turning towards an accommodation with Cuba now that all the missiles and the Soviet bombers capable of carrying nuclear weapons were out and the brigade survivors freed. If he could find a way to get rid of his albatross, he intended to do it. On November 18 he invited a French journalist, Jean Daniel, to the Oval Office. Daniel was about to travel to Cuba. Kennedy had a message that he wanted Daniel to pass on to Castro: the United States was ready to talk about recognizing Castro's regime.[16]

=

It is seven o'clock on the morning of November 22, 1963, when the tapping of his valet, George Taylor, on his door wakes John F. Kennedy from sleep in his bedroom on the eighth floor of the Texas Hotel in Fort Worth. He does not want to be here, in Texas, and the old dread is weighing on his mind—a man, a rifle, a vantage point.

Yet JFK feels he has little choice. His back is more painful than ever. The small back brace he has worn for years is no longer enough. These days he wears a semi-rigid corset that covers him from his waist to his armpits. Besides his agonizing back, his travel schedule this fall has left him exhausted. But the 1964 election is now less than a year away, and he has always believed long campaigns are more likely to succeed than short ones. This trip is, in effect, the beginning of Kennedy's reelection campaign.[17]

Success is far from certain. Unemployment remains stubbornly high, the President has few legislative successes to point to and the test-ban treaty remains controversial. Texas will be a crucial state, as it was in 1960, but a right-wing conservative, John Tower, won the special election to fill the Senate seat that Johnson held before being elected Vice President. Polls show the state is now split fifty-fifty between Democrats and Republicans.[18]

This trip will not only start the campaign but will give JFK a chance to try out his ace draw—Jackie. She despises politicians and hates campaigning, and when he asked her during the summer if she would come with him to Texas, she refused. But then Patrick died, and after she left the hospital, she headed for Europe.

The press noticed her prolonged absence from Jack and the children during her monthlong Mediterranean vacation. Journalists also observed that her recuperation from losing the baby seemed to consist of sunning herself in a bikini aboard some of the world's most luxurious private yachts by day and dining with Gianni Agnelli, the charismatic and aristocratic boss of Fiat, each night. Rumors and gossip circulated that she was having an affair with Agnelli, and possibly one with Aristotle Onassis, too.[19]

When she returned from her vacation, Jack asked her once again to come with him to Texas, and this time she agreed. This trip gives both of them a chance to put on a show of togetherness that might stop all the salacious speculation about their marriage.

After dressing, gulping down a cup of coffee and taking a bite out of a bun, Kennedy descends to the hotel lobby, where Lyndon Johnson, Democratic Senator Ralph Yarborough, Governor John Connally and various congressmen meet him. The group walks outside and mounts a crude platform that has been erected overnight on the back of a flatbed truck. It is a little after seven-thirty and a light rain is falling, but the crowd—which comprises more than two thousand trade union members—fills the Fort Worth parking lot and is exuberant despite the puddles and the rain.

JFK recycles a quip he used during the trip to Paris, telling the crowd, "I am the man who accompanied Mrs. Kennedy to Texas."

Someone shouts out, "Where's Jackie?"

JFK smiles and points up at her window. "Mrs. Kennedy is organizing herself. It takes her a little longer, but, of course, she looks better than we do when she does it." After talking for ten minutes, he winds up by telling the crowd, "We are going forward!" then walks back into the hotel for breakfast with the Fort Worth Chamber of Commerce.[20]

This trip is not only the kickoff for his 1964 campaign but also a chance to raise money. He has already raised large sums on his way here, in San Antonio and Houston. And Jackie was a huge hit in both places.[21]

During the Chamber of Commerce breakfast, Kennedy is presented with a cowboy hat, but he laughingly declines to put it on. That isn't his style; never has been.[22]

Back upstairs, O'Donnell grimly gives him that day's *Dallas Morning News*. It contains a full-page, black-bordered ad that poses twelve questions to which it demands answers: Why is Kennedy allowing American food to be sold to Communists who are killing American soldiers in South Vietnam? What is the truth about his secret pact with the Communist party of the United States? Why does he allow his brother to persecute "loyal Americans"? And so on. He turns to Jackie. "Oh, you know, we're heading into nut country today."[23]

Adlai Stevenson had visited Dallas on October 24 to commemorate UN Day. An angry crowd of right-wing zealots jostled him and spat on him, and someone hit him over the head with a piece of wood attached to an anti-Stevenson poster. Kennedy cannot resist voicing the thought that won't go away. "If someone wants to shoot me from a window with a rifle, nobody can stop it."[24]

It is a short drive from the hotel to the airport to board Air Force One for a thirteen-minute flight over to Love Field, in Dallas, where the President will ride through the city and raise even more money at a hundred-dollar-a-plate lunch in the Trade Mart. At Love Field, Dearie Cabell, the wife of Mayor Earle Cabell, presents Jackie with a large bouquet of red roses.

Jack and Jackie then work their way along a storm fence lined with well-wishers, shaking hands, smiling, being gracious, campaigning. John Connally and his wife, Nellie, wait by the presidential Lincoln while Jack and Jackie work the crowd. This isn't Connally's kind of campaigning. Kennedy is one of the few politicians who campaigns like this and more or less invented it.

Jackie looks like a movie star in her stylish pink suit and pillbox hat, carrying her red roses. As she turns away from the fence to walk towards the Lincoln, Chalmers Roberts of *Newsweek* asks her how she likes campaigning. Jackie beams at him. "It's wonderful, it's wonderful."[25]

Before they left Fort Worth, the Secret Service asked how JFK wanted the Lincoln prepared. There are three possible configurations—a black vinyl-coated metal top; a canvas convertible top; and a clear plastic bubble top that offers protection against the rain. "I want the bubble top," said Jackie.

"No," said Jack. "If you're going out to see the people, the people ought to be able to see you."[26]

It was cloudy and wet in Fort Worth, but in Dallas, the sun is shining and the weather is warm, with men in short sleeves and young women in light summer dresses. This is Jack's kind of day and Jack's kind of car.

The only automobiles he has ever owned have been convertibles, and this is a unique Lincoln Continental. Three and a half feet longer than the standard Continental, it includes two jump seats. The feature he likes best is the rear seat, which rises ten and a half inches at the flip of a switch, and there is a footrest to make him more comfortable. With the rear seat elevated, he does not have to stand to be seen by a crowd.

As the Lincoln pulls away from the airport, Jackie puts on her sunglasses. Jack tells her to take them off. "When you're riding in a car like this, in a parade, if you have your dark glasses on, you might as well have stayed at home."[27]

Kenny O'Donnell has worked out the route from Love Field to the Dallas Trade Mart. The Secret Service felt it was too insecure to move the President slowly through a crowd downtown in a city where Stevenson had recently been physically attacked, but O'Donnell would not budge. The route would not be changed. Jack has to be seen by as many people as possible on this trip.[28]

On Jackie's side of the car, she has raised the window halfway to keep her hat from blowing off or being snatched off; like British royalty, she wears white gloves to wave to the crowd. Up to two hundred fifty thousand people have turned out to greet Jack and Jackie; far more than anyone— the Kennedy advance men, the Johnson staff, the Dallas police—has anticipated. And Jackie is the reason why. There are probably twice as many people here than would have turned out for Jack alone.

The crowd is not just huge; it surges in behind the motorcycle escort and at times brings the Lincoln almost to a halt. Jack smiles and waves languidly as the car inches its way along the middle lane, the only one that remains passable. There are a few anti-Kennedy posters and some catcalls, but the crowd in the canyon of Main Street, where skyscrapers block out the sun, applauds warmly and shouts cheerfully. The Connallys, in the jump seats, sit facing the Kennedys. Nellie Connally leans forward, beaming. "The Dallas people sure love you today, Mr. President."

The luncheon at the Trade Mart is scheduled to begin at one o'clock, and the presidential motorcade is right on schedule when the Lincoln turns left off Main Street at 12:24 onto Houston Street. The presidential and national flags on the front bumper refurl themselves as the car swings into a sweeping, 120-degree turn.

The blue Lincoln once again dazzles in brilliant sunshine, and away from the shadowy canyon of downtown, the crowd seems to have vanished. There are now only a handful of people standing around.

As the Lincoln completes the turn onto Houston Street, it travels only a couple of blocks before it makes another turn, to the right, onto Elm Street, which borders Dealey Plaza, home of *The Dallas Morning News.* Its speed drops to 11 mph as it passes in front of the Texas Schoolbook Depository. Gazing down from a sixth-floor window, cradling a cheap, Italian-made 6.5-millimeter Mannlicher-Carcano rifle in his arms, stands Lee Harvey Oswald, a former marine, dishonorably discharged. He raises the rifle and squints through the sniperscope. Oswald is acting alone, for reasons all his own.[29]

Jack Kennedy thinks he is lucky. He has been given the chance to be President at a time when the stakes for his country were high. No one could be a great President without great challenges. He was certain of that. "What would Lincoln have been with no Civil War?" he asked Gore Vidal one day. The secret of presidential greatness was to match the man with the hour.[30]

With the sun in her face, Jackie puts her sunglasses on again. Jack tells her, "Take them off, Jackie." Smiling, he raises his hand and waves at a five-year-old boy. The back of his head fills the sniperscope. The bullet flies.

Jack has been here before. It is almost twenty years since he stood on the deck of an LST with a marine beside him, rifle raised, shooting at a man in the water, a downed Japanese pilot, barely fifty yards distant. He had seen the bullet strike the pilot in the top of the head, seen the head explode, seen the man die.

Oswald's bullet strikes Kennedy in the back of the neck, passes through his windpipe and emerges at the front of his throat, clipping the knot of his tie. It is a survivable wound, but he cannot know that as he calls out, "My God! I'm hit!"

The bullet travels on and strikes John Connally, who screams, "No, no, no, no, no! They're going to kill us both."[31]

Oswald fires again. The bullet flies, misses, strikes the road and ricochets towards the triple underpass that the Lincoln is heading for to reach the Trade Mart. The Secret Service agent driving the car, William Greer, guns the big four-hundred-horsepower engine.

In the store of poetry he has accumulated in his memory over the years is Jack Kennedy's favorite verse from Tennyson's "Ulysses":

> How dull it is to pause, to make an end,
> To rust unburnished, not to shine in use!

As though to breathe were life! Life piled on life
Were all too little . . .[32]

The gunfire has startled the flock of pigeons that gather every day in Dealey Plaza. They fill the sky, fluttering their wings in fear, alarmed and squawking.

Oswald fires again. He is doing this for Cuba. The bullet flies

Notes

AHC	American Heritage Center, University of Wyoming
BU	Boston University
CU	Columbia University
COHP	Columbia Oral History Project, Columbia University
DDEL	Dwight D. Eisenhower Library
FDRL	Franklin D. Roosevelt Library
FRUS	*Foreign Relations of the United States*
HSTL	Harry S Truman Library
JFKL	John F. Kennedy Library
JFKPP	John F. Kennedy Personal Papers
JPKP	Joseph P. Kennedy Papers
LC	Library of Congress
NHP/MHS	Nigel Hamilton Papers, Massachusetts Historical Society
OH	Oral History
PRO	Public Records Office
PU	Princeton University
RFKP	Robert F. Kennedy Papers
SHO	Senate Historical Office
SU	Stanford University

CHAPTER 1. QUESTION MARK

1. Boston newspapers, May 29–31, 1917.
2. *Boston Herald,* May 29, 1917.
3. *Boston Post,* June 2, 1917.
4. Rose Kennedy, *Times to Remember* (New York: 1974), 75–76.
5. Charles Higham, *Rose* (New York: 1995), 57–58.
6. Doris Kearns Goodwin, *The Fitzgeralds and the Kennedys* (New York: 1987), 226–31.

7. Joseph F. Dineen, *The Kennedy Family* (Boston: 1960), 5.
8. Richard J. Whalen, *The Founding Father* (New York: 1964), 20–21.
9. Joseph P. Kennedy student file, Harvard University Archives.
10. "Joe Kennedy Has Never Liked Any Job He's Tackled," *The American Magazine,* May 1928.
11. Whalen, *The Founding Father,* 4.
12. Goodwin, *The Fitzgeralds and the Kennedys,* 212–16.
13. In *Times to Remember,* 16, Rose loyally elevated her father to five feet seven, but that would have made him an inch taller than the average man of his generation. He was, as contemporaneous accounts indicate, a short man.
14. John Henry Cutler, *"Honey Fitz"* (Indianapolis: 1962), 40–42.
15. Higham, *Rose,* 7–8.
16. Dineen, *The Kennedy Family,* 8.
17. Rose Kennedy, *Times to Remember,* 38.
18. Ibid., 21; Goodwin, *The Fitzgeralds and the Kennedys,* 105.
19. Cutler, *"Honey Fitz,"* 78–80; George Kibbe Turner, "The Mayor of Boston," *Colliers,* Nov. 16, 1907.
20. Rose Kennedy, *Times to Remember,* 28.
21. Higham, *Rose,* 19–20.
22. Francis Russell, *The Great Interlude* (New York: 1964), 176; Cutler, *"Honey Fitz,"* 18.
23. Barbara Gibson and Ted Schwarz, *Rose Kennedy and Her Family* (Secaucus, N.J.: 1995), 35. Mrs. Gibson was Rose's nurse-companion in later life.
24. *The Republic* (Boston), June 13, 1914.
25. Higham, *Rose,* 52.
26. Goodwin, *The Fitzgeralds and the Kennedys,* 247.
27. *Boston Post,* July 26, 1915.
28. Transcript of National Park Service interview with Rose Kennedy, JFKL. Also see Higham, *Rose,* 53; Rose Kennedy, *Times to Remember,* 70–71.

CHAPTER 2. CHILDISH THINGS

1. Doris Kearns Goodwin, *The Fitzgeralds and the Kennedys* (New York: 1987), 272.
2. Geoffrey Perret, *A Country Made by War* (New York: 1989), 312.
3. Richard J. Whalen, *The Founding Father* (New York: 1964), 49.
4. Goodwin, *The Fitzgeralds and the Kennedys,* 281; James W. Davis, Jr., and Kenneth M. Dolbeare, *Little Groups of Neighbors: The Selective Service System* (Chicago: 1968), 19, 81.
5. Nigel Hamilton, *JFK: Reckless Youth* (New York: 1992), 40.
6. John Henry Cutler, *"Honey Fitz"* (Indianapolis: 1962), 244.
7. L. Emmett Holt, *The Care and Feeding of Children: A Catechism for the Use of Mothers and Children's Nurses,* 7th rev. ed. (New York and London: 1914),

211. Holt's book sold in the millions and went through dozens of editions between its original publication in 1894 and the last revision, in 1941.

8. Charles Spalding OH, JFKL.

9. Charles Higham, *Rose* (New York: 1995), 78.

10. Cutler, *"Honey Fitz,"* 219–28.

11. Goodwin, *The Fitzgeralds and the Kennedys,* 307.

12. Higham, *Rose,* 79.

13. Rose Kennedy, *Times to Remember* (New York: 1974), 80.

14. Gene Schoor, *Young John Kennedy* (New York: 1963), 18–19.

15. Rose Kennedy, *Times to Remember,* 214.

16. Geraldine Hannon, "Reminiscences of the Kennedys," JFKPP, JFKL.

17. Geoffrey Perret, *America in the Twenties* (New York: 1982), 29–50.

18. Whalen, *The Founding Father,* 51–55.

19. Leo Damore, *The Cape Cod Years of John Fitzgerald Kennedy* (Englewood Cliffs, N.J.: 1967), 19; Ralph Martin, *Seeds of Destruction* (New York: 1995), 66.

20. C. David Heymann, *RFK: A Candid Biography of Robert F. Kennedy* (New York: 1998), 9–10.

21. *New York Times,* June 30, 1938.

22. Perret, *America in the Twenties,* 169–78; Heymann, *RFK,* 9–10.

23. Gloria Swanson, *Swanson on Swanson* (New York: 1980), 356–62; Ronald Kessler, *The Sins of the Father* (New York: 1996), 62–63, 78; Axel Madsen, *Gloria & Joe* (New York: 1988), is devoted entirely to this affair. Unfortunately, the author does not provide a named source or a verifiable documentary source for any of the book's sensational claims.

24. *New York Times,* January 1, 1929. For an excellent recent account of financial booms over the past five hundred years, see Edward Chancellor, *Devil Take the Hindmost* (New York: 1999).

25. Willard K. Rice OH, JFKL. Rice was the football coach.

26. Hamilton, *JFK: Reckless Youth,* 52–58.

27. Schoor, *Young John Kennedy,* 20.

28. Rose Kennedy, *Times to Remember,* 89.

29. Barbara Gibson and Ted Schwarz, *Rose Kennedy and Her Family* (Secaucus, N.J.: 1995), 10. Mrs. Gibson read Rose Kennedy's diary for these years.

30. Transcript of Rose Kennedy interview for CBS, JFKL. The irony in all this was that, as the Human Genome Project has shown, the genes that promote intelligence descend through the mother's line, not the father's. They come, that is, largely from the maternal grandparents.

31. Letter, Charlotte Canfield to JFK, July 1953, JFKL. She was his nurse when he was six years old.

32. Eunice Shriver interview, Blair Papers, AHC.

33. Clement Norton OH, JFKL.

34. Letter, JFK to Joseph P. Kennedy, n.d. but circa 1927, JFKPP, JFKL.

35. Gertrude H. Frazer, "The Governess's Tale," *Cape Cod Life,* Feb. 1990; Hank Searls, *The Lost Prince* (New York: 1969), 40.

36. *Good Housekeeping,* Sept. 1985; JFK school reports, JFKPP, JFKL.

37. Frazer, "The Governess's Tale."

38. Rose Kennedy, *Times to Remember,* 158.

39. Jacqueline Kennedy interview notes, Theodore White Papers, JFKL.

40. Letter, JFK to Joseph P. Kennedy, n.d. but 1930, JFKPP, JFKL.

CHAPTER 3. GROWING PAINS

1. Seymour St. John, unpublished memoir, "JFK: 50th Reunion of 1,000 Days at School," NHP/MHS.

2. Nigel Hamilton, *JFK: Reckless Youth* (New York: 1992), 90.

3. *The Brief,* 1934 edition, published by Choate School.

4. Charles Higham, *Rose* (New York: 1995), 136.

5. Ralph G. Martin, *Seeds of Destruction* (New York: 1995), 33.

6. Ibid., 38.

7. Joanne Barboza OH, JFKL.

8. Rose Kennedy, *Times to Remember* (New York: 1974), 98.

9. Martin, *Seeds of Destruction,* 24.

10. Gloria Emerson, "How Rose Kennedy Survived," *McCall's,* Aug. 1975.

11. Doris Kearns Goodwin, *The Fitzgeralds and the Kennedys* (New York: 1987), 455.

12. *Life,* July 17, 1970; *Providence Sunday Journal,* March 7, 1971.

13. Higham, *Rose,* 33.

14. Rose Kennedy, CBS interview transcript, JFKL.

15. Lester David and Irene David, *JFK* (New York: 1988), 26; Ralph Horton interview, Blair Papers, AHC.

16. Letter, JFK to Joseph P. and Rose Kennedy, Feb. 19, 1933, JPKP, JFKL.

17. Letter, JFK to Rose Kennedy, n.d., JPKP, JFKL.

18. Letter, JFK to Joseph P. Kennedy, Jan. 26, 1932, JPKP, JFKL.

19. Letter, Joseph P. Kennedy, Jr., to Joseph P. Kennedy, Feb. 15, 1931, JPKP, JFKL.

20. Harold L. Tinker OH, JFKL; *Vineyard Gazette,* May 15, 1987. Tinker recalled this episode as centering on the Frost poem, inspired by Santayana, "Happiness Makes Up in Height for What It Lacks in Length." But Frost's poem was not published until September 1938.

21. JFK, "Justice" essay, JFKPP, JFKL.

22. K. LeMoyne Billings OH, JFKL.

23. Kaye Halle OH, JFKL. She visited him briefly with Joe Kennedy one evening, under the impression that he had been hospitalized with a football injury.

24. Peter Collier and David Horowitz, *The Kennedys* (New York: 1984), 65; Joan Blair and Clay Blair, Jr., *The Search for JFK* (New York: 1976), 33–35.

25. Erik Erikson's reputation was such that after JFK's assassination, Jacqueline Kennedy called the psychologist for advice on ensuring that Caroline and John Jr. did not suffer permanent psychological damage from the loss of their father: Edward Klein, *Just Jackie* (New York: 1998), 27.

26. Letter, JFK to Lem Billings, June 27, 1934, Billings Papers, JFKL. In later life, Billings boasted that he had fellated John Kennedy from Choate to the White House: see Lawrence J. Quirk, *The Kennedys in Hollywood* (Dallas: 1996), 133–37. There is not a shred of evidence to support this claim. In fact, the documentary record points in the opposite direction. First, there is this firm rejection of Billings's toilet-paper mash note. Second, in March 1942 Jack again wrote to rebuke Billings after he informed Jack that he had recently met up with a classmate from Choate. "After you hear someone call you a fairy and discuss it for two solid hours, and argue whether or not you went down on Worthington Johnson, you don't write a letter saying you think that fellow is a great guy." Gore Vidal, *Palimpsest* (New York: 1995), 380.

27. Report from J. J. Maher to George St. John, n.d. but 1935; Choate School archives; Ralph Horton interview, Blair Papers, AHC; JFK to Joseph P. Kennedy, n.d. but probably October 1934, JFKPP, JFKL.

28. Letter, Joseph P. Kennedy to JFK, April 29, 1935, JPKP, JFKL.

29. David and David, *JFK,* 25.

30. Shea and Ralph Horton OH, JFKL.

31. *Vineyard Gazette,* May 15, 1987.

32. Shea and Ralph Horton OH.

33. Goodwin, *The Fitzgeralds and the Kennedys,* 488.

34. Letter, JFK to Billings, n.d. but October 1935, NHP/MHS. When Maher died in 1957, the *Choate News* asked JFK to write a few paragraphs on his old housemaster. Kennedy declined, saying he had not had much contact with Maher. Letter, Paul S. Cowan to JFK, n.d. but 1957; JFK to Paul S. Cowan, April 4, 1957, JFKL.

CHAPTER 4. LIFE FORCES

1. Edward M. Kennedy, ed., *The Fruitful Bough* (privately published: 1965), 221–24.

2. James Grant, *Bernard M. Baruch* (New York: 1997), 251; Richard J. Whalen, *The Founding Father* (New York: 1964), 63–66.

3. Geoffrey Perret, *America in the Twenties* (New York: 1982), 286.

4. Ronald Kessler, *The Sins of the Father* (New York: 1996), 92.

5. *Boston Globe,* September 25, 1932.

6. Arthur Krock interview, COHP; Arthur M. Schlesinger, Jr., *The Coming of the New Deal* (Boston: 1958), 307–10; Michael R. Beschloss, *Kennedy and Roosevelt* (New York: 1980), 7–13.

7. Rose Kennedy, *Times to Remember* (New York: 1974), 198; *Boston Post,* July 1, 1934.

8. Beschloss, *Kennedy and Roosevelt,* 88; Donald A. Ritchie, *James M. Landis: Dean of the Regulators* (Cambridge, Mass.: 1980), 60.

9. See Joel Seligman, *The Transformation of Wall Street* (Boston: 1982), 103–23.

10. See SEC resignation correspondence of 1935 in JPKP, JFKL.

11. Kessler, *The Sins of the Father,* 90–91.

12. Jordan A. Schwarz, *The Speculator* (Chapel Hill, N.C.: 1981), 171–72. Among Baruch's lovers was Clare Boothe, who tried hard to persuade him to marry her: Sylvia Jukes Morris, *Rage for Fame* (New York: 1997), 220 passim.

13. Lester David and Irene David, *JFK* (New York: 1969), 36.

14. Ralph G. Martin, *Seeds of Destruction* (New York: 1995), 37.

15. Robert Conquest, *The Great Terror: Stalin's Purge of the Thirties* (New York: 1968), 469–70.

16. *The New Yorker,* May 1, 1961.

17. This prolonged struggle is related, directly and indirectly, in numerous letters from JFK to Lem Billings in NHP/MHS.

18. Letter, JFK to Billings, Jan. 27, 1936, NHP/MHS.

19. Peter Collier and David Horowitz, *The Kennedys* (New York: 1984), 66–67; Martin, *Seeds of Destruction,* 51.

20. Letter, JFK to Billings, Feb. 28, 1936, NHP/MHS.

21. Arthur Krock interview, Blair Papers, AHC; Letter, JFK to Billings, May 9, 1936, NHP/MHS.

22. Letter, JFK to Billings, May 25, 1936, NHP/MHS.

23. *Boston Herald,* Aug. 20–21, 1938.

24. Letter, JFK to Billings, n.d. but May 1936, NHP/MHS.

25. James Rousmanière OH, Herbert Parmet Collection, COHP.

26. *Harvard Red Book,* 1940.

27. Edward Gallagher interview, Blair Papers, AHC.

28. Letter, JFK to Billings, Oct. 16, 1936, NHP/MHS.

29. Paul B. Fay, Jr., OH, JFKL.

30. Harold S. Ulen OH, JFKL.

31. Letter, Joseph P. Kennedy to JFK, April 26, 1935, JPKP, JFKL.

32. Letter, JFK to Billings, Jan. 13, 1937, NHP/MHS.

CHAPTER 5. ON THE ROAD

1. This chapter is based mainly on the journals that Jack Kennedy and Lem Billings kept during their trip, as well as Billings's recollections in *The New Yorker,* May 1, 1961. See also David Michaelis, *The Best of Friends* (New York: 1983), 153–58. These various accounts complement one another. For example, Jack Kennedy does not even hint at his back problem, but Billings describes it. Some important details are missing, such as just where and on which day Kennedy bought a back support, but it seems possible to work out roughly the week when that occurred. It is my surmise that pushing the car off the beach caused the original back problem, although the convertible top might have been to blame: it was difficult even for two young men to get it up

and down. What is certain is that Jack's back troubles began during this trip. He himself informed a Navy doctor of that fact five years later. The usual accounts of Jack Kennedy's bad back originating in a football game—elevating it to a manly kind of wound—are false. The striking asymmetry of his body is described by Dr. Janet Travell in her oral history at the Kennedy Library.

CHAPTER 6. WHEN WORLDS COLLIDE

1. *Time,* July 22, 1935.
2. Rose Kennedy, *Times to Remember* (New York: 1974), 221–22.
3. Michael R. Beschloss, *Kennedy and Roosevelt* (New York: 1980), 157.
4. The most influential military expert in the country was probably Sir Maurice Hankey, a retired Army officer, Secretary to the War Cabinet from 1916 to 1918 and Secretary to the Cabinet from 1918 to 1938. "The Cabinet are overrating the imminence of the German peril," he advised the prime minister in August 1935. "The peril is there all right, but it will take much more than 5 years to develop in the military and air sense." The Air Staff took a similar view. Martin Gilbert, *Winston S. Churchill* VI (London: 1986), 559.
5. Ernest K. Lindley, "Will Kennedy Run for President?," *Newsweek,* May 21, 1938; Arthur Krock, *Memoirs: Sixty Years on the Firing Line* (New York: 1968), 334.
6. A. Scott Berg, *Lindbergh* (New York: 1998), 374.
7. State Department, *FRUS 1938* I (Washington, D.C.: 1955), 73. Lindbergh's estimate of German aircraft production for 1938 was three times greater than the reality.
8. Williamson Murray, *Luftwaffe* (Baltimore: 1985), 19–20; Edward L. Homze, *Arming the Luftwaffe: The Reich Air Ministry and the German Aircraft Industry, 1919–1939* (Lincoln, Neb.: 1976), Chapter XI. Also see David Irving, *Göring* (New York: 1989), 226–29.
9. Public Records Office, 800/309, Part IV; PRO Cab 23/95, Cab 39 (38), Cabinet Meeting, September 17, 1938; PRO Cab 53/41, COS 773, COS Subcommittee memo, September 29, 1938, "The Czechoslovak Crisis."
10. Paul Stehlin, *Temoignage pour l'Histoire* (Paris: 1964), 86–91.
11. R.A.C. Parker, *Chamberlain and Appeasement* (New York: 1993), 156–74.
12. Letter, FDR to John Boettiger, n.d. but Feb. 1941, FDRL.
13. Warren F. Kimball, ed., *Churchill & Roosevelt: The Complete Correspondence* I (Princeton: 1984), 7–9, 23–81.

CHAPTER 7. THE END OF EVERYTHING

1. Letter, JFK to Billings, Feb. 10, 1938, Billings Papers, JFKL.
2. Letter, JFK to Billings, Feb. 20, 1938, Billings Papers, JFKL.
3. George Thomas interview, JFKL; John F. Kennedy, ed., *As We Remember Joe* (privately printed: 1945), 31.

4. Hank Searls, *The Lost Prince* (New York: 1969), 80–81.
5. Ralph Blumenthal, *The Stork Club: America's Most Famous Nightspot and the Lost World of Café Society* (Boston: 2000), 22.
6. Nigel Hamilton, *JFK: Reckless Youth* (New York: 1992), 210. The only source cited is an interview in 1989 with Holton Wood, another member of the Harvard JV football team. During World War II, JFK repeatedly discussed how he had developed back problems and never alluded to this alleged incident.
7. *Time,* Oct. 6, 1958.
8. *Harvard Crimson* yearbook, 1938; William C. Foster OH, JFKL; Tazewell Shepard, Jr., *John F. Kennedy: Man of the Sea* (New York: 1965), 27–28.
9. Recording of JFK radio interview, June 1940, Audiovisual M69-3, JFKL.
10. Chester Hanford interview, JFKL. Hanford was the dean of Harvard College and taught JFK Government 9A that fall.
11. Hamilton, *JFK: Reckless Youth,* 250–52.
12. Letter, JFK to Billings, Feb. 1, 1939, Billings Papers, JFKL.
13. Letter, JFK to Billings, April 16, 1940, Billings Papers, JFKL.
14. *Daily Mirror,* March 4, 1939.
15. Letter, JFK to Billings, n.d. but March 1939, JFKL.
16. J. F. Powers's classic novel, *Morte D'Urban* (Garden City, N.Y.: 1962), offers an amusing but mordant glimpse into this aspect of American Catholicism.
17. Letter, JFK to Billings, March 23, 1939, Billings Papers, JFKL.
18. Letter, JFK to Billings, n.d. but May 1939, Billings Papers, JFKL.
19. Ibid.
20. Ibid.
21. Irena Wiley, *Around the Globe in Twenty Years* (New York: 1962), 94; *Boston Globe,* June 22, 1962.
22. *Chelsea* (Mass.) *Record,* Jan. 30, 1952.
23. Rose Kennedy, CBS interview transcript, JFKL.
24. Letter, JFK to Joseph P. Kennedy, n.d. but 1939, JFKPP, JFKL.
25. Letter, JFK to Billings, March 23, 1939, Billings Papers, JFKL.
26. Ralph G. Martin, *Seeds of Destruction* (New York: 1995), 76–77.
27. Torbert Macdonald interview, Blair Papers, AHC.
28. Lawrence Lader, "Jack Kennedy at Harvard," *Parade,* June 11, 1961.
29. Ralph F. De Bedts, *Ambassador Joseph Kennedy 1938–1940* (New York: 1985), 147.
30. Martin Gilbert, *Winston S. Churchill* V (London: 1983), 1111.
31. Joseph Alsop and Robert Kintner, *American White Paper* (New York: 1940), 68.
32. *Evening News* (London), Sept. 7, 1939; *Daily Telegraph* (London), Sept. 8, 1939; *Evening News* (Buffalo), September 8, 1939.
33. *Harvard Crimson,* October 9, 1939.
34. Lader, "Jack Kennedy at Harvard."
35. Martin Gilbert, *Winston S. Churchill* VI (London: 1986), 550–59, 569–75.
36. Letter, JFK to Billings, April 6, 1939, Billings Papers, JFKL.
37. See chapter 8.

38. Letter, Vernon S. Dick to William P. Herbst, Jr., March 20, 1953, JFKPP, JFKL.
39. For an opposite view, see Hamilton, *JFK: Reckless Youth,* 808–9. Hamilton claims that JFK suffered from "gonococcal urethritis," but this diagnosis does not appear in any of the medical records he cites. He has inferred a gonococcal infection from the fact that both the symptoms of NSU and its treatment are virtually identical with those of gonorrhea.
40. Letter, Joseph P. Kennedy, Jr., to Joseph P. Kennedy, n.d. but 1940, Robert Coughlan Papers, BU.
41. JFK's reaction to the camera, when being photographed in a group, is reminiscent of Budd Schulberg's 1949 novel, *What Makes Sammy Run?* It begins with Sammy's face appearing twice in a photograph of his eighth-grade class. Sammy was photographed on the left, then as the camera panned to the right, he raced around the back of his classmates to appear once again on the right. Sammy, like JFK, was determined to be noticed.

CHAPTER 8. JACK INTERMEZZO

1. Letter, JFK to Joseph P. Kennedy, n.d. but 1940, JFKPP, JFKL.
2. Letter, JFK to Henry James, n.d. but evidently January 1941; Guernsey's Catalog, *Documents and Artifacts Relating to the Life and Career of John F. Kennedy* (New York: 1998).
3. Letter, JFK to Joseph P. Kennedy, n.d. but 1940, JFKPP, JFKL.
4. "Mimeographed Draft Comments by Harvey Klemmer," JFKPP, JFKL; Henry Luce OH, JFKL; Letter, JFK to Henry Luce, July 9, 1940, Luce Papers, LC.
5. Recording in Rochester, Minnesota, June/July 1940, Audiovisual MR-69-3, JFKL.
6. Letter, FDR to JFK, August 27, 1940, FDRL.
7. James Leutze, ed., *The London Journal of General Raymond E. Lee, 1940–1941* (Boston: 1971), 28.
8. See R. A. C. Parker, *Chamberlain and Appeasement* (New York: 1993), 276–79; Sebastian Ritchie, *Industry and Air Power: The Expansion of British Aircraft Production, 1935–1941* (London: 1997), Chapters 3 and 4; and Erik Lund, "The Industrial History of Strategy: Reevaluating the Wartime Record of the British Aviation Industry in Comparative Perspective, 1919–1945," *Journal of Military History* (January 1998). Lund claims that the British had the most organized and efficient aviation industry of the war.
9. Derek Wood and Derek Dempster, *The Narrow Margin* (London: 1961), 46–59; Robert Wright, *Dowding and the Battle of Britain* (London: 1969), 66–79.
10. See David Irving, *The Rise and Fall of the Luftwaffe* (Boston: 1973). This biography of Erhard Milch describes the chaotic buildup of the German aviation industry in the 1930s. The complete confidence of the British and the French that they would ultimately defeat Germany is amply documented in Ernest R. May, *Strange Victory* (New York: 2000).

11. Among the letters he received was a seven-page tribute from the highly esteemed military commentator and theorist Sir Basil Liddell Hart, who praised *Why England Slept* for "the outstanding way it combines insight with balanced judgment." Liddell Hart, however, was a soldier and bound to find fault with a strategy that had meant rearming the Royal Air Force and the Royal Navy during the 1930s, to the detriment of the British Army, which had just been thrown out of France at Dunkirk. Letter, B. H. Liddell Hart to JFK, Oct. 24, 1940, JFKL.

12. John F. Kennedy, *Why England Slept* (New York: 1940), 155.

13. John Hellmann, *The Kennedy Obsession* (New York: 1997), 23; see also Nancy Gager Clinch, *The Kennedy Neurosis* (New York: 1973), 108–10.

14. Eleanor Harris, "The Senator Is in a Hurry," *McCall's*, Aug. 1957.

15. Harry Muheim, "Rich, Young and Happy," *Esquire*, Aug. 1966.

16. Naval medical records, JFKPP, JFKL.

17. Muheim, "Rich, Young and Happy."

18. *Stanford Daily*, Oct. 15, 1940.

19. Paul B. Fay, Jr., OH, JFKL.

20. *Stanford Daily*, Oct. 30, 1940.

21. Letter, JFK to Billings, Nov. 14, 1940, NHP/MHS.

22. Letter, JFK to Cammen Newberry, n.d. but Oct.–Nov. 1940, JFKPP, JFKL.

23. John Buchan, *Pilgrim's Way* (Boston: 1940), 61.

24. Nigel Hamilton, *JFK: Reckless Youth* (New York: 1992), 545.

25. Letter, Joseph P. Kennedy to JFK, Sept. 10, 1940, JFKPP, JFKL.

26. Joseph E. Persico, *Edward R. Murrow* (New York: 1988), 163–71.

27. Michael R. Beschloss, *Kennedy and Roosevelt* (New York: 1980), 211.

28. Doris Kearns Goodwin, *The Fitzgeralds and the Kennedys* (New York: 1987), 614–17.

29. Letter, Joseph P. Kennedy to Clare Luce, Oct. 1, 1941, Clare Luce Papers, LC.

30. Herbert Hoover Diary, November 22, 1940, Herbert Hoover Papers, Hoover Institution, SU.

31. Letters, JFK to Joseph P. Kennedy, Dec. 5 and 6, 1940, JFKPP, JFKL.

32. Letter, J. J. Astor to Brendan Bracken, Feb. 19, 1941, NHP/MHS.

33. Letter, Clare Luce to Joseph P. Kennedy, Feb. 8, 1941, Clare Luce Papers, LC.

34. Letter, James Parton to Nigel Hamilton, Nov. 19, 1992, NHP/MHS.

35. Charles Higham, *Rose* (New York: 1995), 236.

36. Rose Kennedy, *Times to Remember* (New York: 1974), 284.

37. Letter, Alan G. Kirk to Joseph P. Kennedy, Aug. 8, 1941, Alan G. Kirk Papers, Naval Historical Center.

38. Joan Blair and Clay Blair, Jr., *The Search for JFK* (New York: 1976), 113; naval medical records, JFKPP, JFKL.

CHAPTER 9. LOVE AND WAR

1. Joan Blair and Clay Blair, Jr., *The Search for JFK* (New York: 1976), 121.

2. Ronald Kessler, *The Sins of the Father* (New York: 1996), 259.

3. John White interview, Blair Papers, AHC.
4. Arvad Records, 1941, Director's Confidential Files, FBI Archives.
5. Washington *Times-Herald,* Nov. 27, 1941.
6. Frank C. Waldrop, "JFK and the Nazi Spy," *Washington Magazine,* April 1975.
7. Nigel Hamilton, *JFK: Reckless Youth* (New York: 1992), 426–27.
8. Arvad Records, 1942, op. cit.
9. Robert Donovan interview, JFKL.
10. Waldrop, "JFK and the Nazi Spy."
11. Arthur Krock interview, Blair Papers, AHC. Jack Kennedy never considered premature ejaculation a problem. Angie Dickinson was said to have described sex with him as "The most wonderful fifteen seconds of my life." Even so, he was probably typical of most men of his time. Alfred Kinsey's *Sexual Behavior in the Human Male,* published in 1948, approvingly termed the swift delivery of the genetic package as "both normal and natural."
12. Letter, JFK to William Coleman, n.d. but evidently Nov.–Dec. 1941, JFKPP, JFKL.
13. Letter, JFK to Billings, March 11, 1942, NHP/MHS.
14. Frederick W. Rosen interview, Blair Papers, AHC.
15. Letter, JFK to Billings, Feb. 12, 1942, NHP/MHS.
16. Laurence Leamer, *The Kennedy Women* (New York: 1994), 336–37.
17. Letter, JFK to Kathleen Kennedy, March 10, 1942, JFKPP, JFKL.
18. Navy medical records, JFKPP, JFKL.
19. Doris Kearns Goodwin, *The Fitzgeralds and the Kennedys* (New York: 1987), 635.
20. Sylvia Jukes Morris, *Rage for Fame* (New York: 1997), 436, 445.
21. William B. Breuer, *Sea Wolf* (Novato, Cal.: 1989), 108.
22. Letter, JFK to Clare Luce, n.d. but Sept. 1942, Clare Luce Papers, LC.
23. George H. R. Ross interview, Blair Papers, AHC.
24. Anthony B. Akers OH, JFKL.
25. Letter, JFK to Paul B. Fay, Jr., Feb. 21, 1944, JFKL.
26. Goodwin, *The Fitzgeralds and the Kennedys,* 648.
27. Arthur M. Schlesinger, Jr., *Robert Kennedy and His Times* (Boston: 1978), 51.

CHAPTER 10. ". . . AND BRAVE"

1. Letter, Ted Guthrie to JFK, Oct. 3, 1961, JFKL. Guthrie was a sailor aboard *LST-449.*
2. Kit C. Carter and Robert Mueller, *Combat Chronology, 1941–1945* (Washington, D.C.: 1991), 117.
3. Wesley F. Craven and James L. Cate, eds., *The Army Air Forces in World War II* IV (Chicago: 1948–58), 213.
4. Samuel Eliot Morison, *History of United States Naval Operations in World War II* VII: *New Georgia and the Admiralties* (Boston: 1947–62), 110–12.
5. Tazewell Shepard, Jr., *John F. Kennedy: Man of the Sea* (New York: 1965), 32.

Shepard was JFK's naval aide and talked to him often and at length about his naval experiences.

6. Letter, JFK to Billings, May 6, 1943, NHP/MHS; Letter, JFK to Joseph P. and Rose Kennedy, May 19, 1943, JPKP, JFKL.

7. Letter, Guthrie to JFK, op. cit.

8. Letter, JFK to Joseph P. and Rose Kennedy, May 14, 1943, JFKL.

9. Letter, JFK to Kathleen Kennedy, n.d. but June/July 1943, JFKPP, JFKL.

10. Johnny Iles interview, Blair Papers, AHC.

11. Joan Blair and Clay Blair, Jr., *The Search for JFK* (New York: 1976), 172.

12. John M. Searles and John Iles interviews, Blair Papers, AHC.

13. *Daily Evening Item* (Lynn, Mass.), Nov. 22, 1988.

14. Letter, JFK to Billings, May 6, 1943, Billings Papers, JFKL; Nigel Hamilton, *JFK: Reckless Youth* (New York: 1992), 537.

15. John Miller, *Cartwheel: The Reduction of Rabaul* (Washington, D.C.: 1959), Chapter VI; Geoffrey Perret, *There's a War to Be Won* (New York: 1991), 244–47.

16. Clay Blair, *Silent Victory* (Philadelphia: 1975), 144–51.

17. Robert J. Donovan, *PT-109* (New York: 1961), 87–88.

18. Blair and Blair, *The Search for JFK,* 207.

19. Naval medical records, JFKPP, JFKL.

20. Warfield's report, National Archives; Samuel Eliot Morison, *History of United States Naval Operations in World War II* VI: *Breaking the Bismarcks Barrier 22 July 1942–1 May 1944* (Boston: 1947–62), 210–13.

21. Hamilton, *JFK: Reckless Youth,* 557.

22. Donovan, *PT-109,* 129.

23. John Hersey, "Survival," *New Yorker,* June 17, 1944.

24. Memo, "Sinking of *PT-109* and Subsequent Rescue of Survivors," B. R. White and J. C. McClure to Commander, Motor Torpedo Boat Flotilla One, Aug. 12, 1943, JFKPP, JFKL.

25. Blair and Blair, *The Search for JFK,* 241–42.

26. Paul S. Dull, *A Battle History of the Imperial Japanese Navy, 1941–1945* (Annapolis, Md.: 1978), 119–24.

27. Hamilton, *JFK: Reckless Youth,* 585.

28. George Ross interview, CBS, Audiovisual Archives, JFKL.

29. Blair and Blair, *The Search for JFK,* 246–54.

30. Memo, "Sinking of *PT-109* and Subsequent Rescue of Survivors," op. cit.

31. Nebuchadnezzar Biuku and Aaron Eroni interviews, Miscellaneous Manuscripts, JFKL.

32. Donovan, *PT-109,* 184–85.

33. Walter Lord, *Lonely Vigil* (New York: 1977), 273.

CHAPTER 11. FULL CIRCLE

1. "What JFK Told a PT Boat Buddy," *New York Post,* Jan. 13, 1976.

2. Nigel Hamilton, *JFK: Reckless Youth* (New York: 1992), 606.

3. *Daily Evening Item* (Lynn, Mass.), Nov. 22, 1988.

4. Letter, JFK to Joseph P. and Rose Kennedy, Aug. 10, 1943, JPKP, JFKL.

5. Nebuchadnezzar Biuku and Aaron Eroni interviews, Miscellaneous Manuscripts, JFKL; Letter, JFK to Clare Luce, n.d. but September 1943, Clare Luce Papers, LC.

6. Clark G. Reynolds, *The Fast Carriers* (New York: 1968), Chapter 4.

7. Joan Blair and Clay Blair, Jr., *The Search for JFK* (New York: 1976), 278.

8. Hamilton, *JFK: Reckless Youth*, 625.

9. Richard Tregaskis, *Guadalcanal Diary* (Redhill: 1943), 83.

10. Letter, JFK to Inga Arvad, Sept. 26, 1943, NHP/MHS.

11. John Miller, *Cartwheel: The Reduction of Rabaul* (Washington: D.C.: 1959), 25–48.

12. Letter, JFK to Joseph P. Kennedy, Oct. 30, 1943, JPKP, JFKL.

13. Paul B. Fay, Jr., interview, CBS, Audiovisual Archives, JFKL.

14. "Report on Fitness of Officer," Jan. 6, 1944, JFKPP, JFKL; Hamilton, *JFK: Reckless Youth*, 630–31.

15. Letter, Sarah M. Jordan to Frederick L. Conklin, July 14, 1944, JFKPP, JFKL; Hamilton, *JFK: Reckless Youth*, 640–41.

16. *Boston Globe*, Feb. 13, 1944.

17. Blair and Blair, *The Search for JFK*, 321; Hamilton, *JFK: Reckless Youth*, 641, 652–53; John Hersey, "Survival," *New Yorker*, June 17, 1944.

18. Blair and Blair, *The Search for JFK*, 325.

19. Francis X. Morrissey OH, JFKL.

20. There is a folder of Navy Department correspondence concerning the award of JFK's medal and his postwar attempt to have it upgraded in JFKPP, JFKL.

21. "Report of Medical Survey," Dec. 6, 1944, Bureau of Medicine and Surgery, JFKPP, JFKL. The doctors at the Lahey Clinic diagnosed this illness as chronic colitis, but they quickly realized their diagnosis was wrong. JFK never received medication for any version of chronic colitis, nor did he undergo surgery for it.

22. Joseph Timilty interview, Blair Papers, AHC.

23. Geoffrey Perret, *Winged Victory* (New York: 1993), 283–96; *Boston Globe*, May 8, 1944.

24. Letter, Joseph P. Kennedy, Jr., to JFK, Aug. 10, 1944, JFKPP, JFKL.

25. Hank Searls, *The Lost Prince* (New York: 1969), 145 passim. See also Jack Olsen, *Aphrodite: Desperate Mission* (New York: 1970), 219 passim; and David Irving, *The Mare's Nest* (London: 1964).

26. In a denouement chillingly reminiscent of the famous short story "The Monkey's Paw," Joe Jr. did win the Navy Cross he wanted so badly, but posthumously.

27. Rose Kennedy, *Times to Remember* (New York: 1974), 301; Edward M. Kennedy, ed., *The Fruitful Bough* (private printing: 1965), 201.

28. Doris Kearns Goodwin, *The Fitzgeralds and the Kennedys* (New York: 1987), 698.

29. John F. Kennedy, ed., *As We Remember Joe* (privately printed: 1945), 8.

30. Eleanor Harris, "The Senator Is in a Hurry," *McCall's,* Aug. 1957. Joe Kennedy boasted to Harris that he had forced Jack to run. See also Blair and Blair, *The Search for JFK,* 357–60; Hamilton, *JFK: Reckless Youth,* 672–73.

CHAPTER 12. I'M JACK KENNEDY

1. Letter, Walter S. MacRae to JFK, May 20, 1957, JFKL. MacRae was at the Castle Hot Springs hotel and remembered vividly how ill JFK was when he checked in.
2. Letter, Rose to "Dear Children," Feb. 1, 1945, JPKP, JFKL. In her letter she incorporates a letter from Jack at Castle Hot Springs.
3. John F. Kennedy, "Let's Try an Experiment in Peace," Feb. 1945, JFKPP, JFKL.
4. Joan Blair and Clay Blair, Jr., *The Search for JFK* (New York: 1976), 367. Patrick Lannan claimed that he persuaded a naive Jack Kennedy to take an interest in labor questions, but this statement is hardly credible, given the fact that domestic news in 1944 and 1945 was dominated by stories of labor unrest. In early 1945 up to fifty strikes broke out each day. See Geoffrey Perret, *Days of Sadness, Years of Triumph* (New York: 1973), 403–4.
5. Inga Arvad, "Truth" (unpublished memoir), in NHP/MHS; Robert Rhodes James, *Bob Boothby: A Portrait* (London: 1991), 331–32; BBC program, "The Peer, the Rent Boy and the Krays," May 14, 1997.
6. Robert Stack with Mark Evans, *Straight Shooting* (New York: 1980), 72.
7. Charles Spalding interview, Blair Papers, AHC.
8. Blair and Blair, *In Search of JFK,* 371–472.
9. Letters, Edward Weeks to JFK, May 16, 1945, and JFK to Weeks, n.d. but May/June 1945, NHP/MHS.
10. New York *Journal-American,* May 8, 23, 1945.
11. Charles Spalding OH, JFKL; Nigel Hamilton, *JFK: Reckless Youth* (New York: 1992), 689.
12. Chicago *Herald-American,* May 29, 1945.
13. Deidre Henderson, ed., *Prelude to Leadership: The European Diary of John F. Kennedy, Summer 1945* (Washington, D.C.: 1996): JFK diary entries, July 2–3, 1945.
14. New York *Journal-American,* July 7, 1945.
15. Ibid., July 29, 1945; JFK diary entries, July 24–25, 1945. Along with the dated entries are extended ruminations on De Valera's personality and on the partition of Ireland.
16. JFK diary entry, July 31, 1945.
17. JFK diary entry, Aug. 1, 1945.
18. JFK diary entry, Aug. 2, 1945; Hamilton, *JFK: Reckless Youth,* 719–20.
19. Naval medical records, U.S. Naval Dispensary, August 3, 5, 1945, JFKPP, JFKL.
20. JFK diary entry, Aug. 7, 1945, James V. Forrestal Papers, Mudd Library, PU.

21. Francis X. Morrissey OH, JFKL.
22. Thomas Broderick OH, JFKL.
23. Jack Beatty, *The Rascal King* (Reading, Mass.: 1992), 456–57; Ralph G. Martin, *Seeds of Destruction* (New York: 1995), 133.
24. John Lynch OH, JFKL.
25. John Henry Cutler, *"Honey Fitz,"* (Indianapolis: 1962), 308–9.
26. Samuel Bornstein OH, JFKL; Tip O'Neill with William Novak, *Man of the House* (New York: 1987), 76.
27. John M. Hynes OH, JFKL. Hynes was mayor of Boston three times and concluded that Neville had no chance if only because of the number of returning veterans, who were clamoring for change.
28. Cutler, *"Honey Fitz,"* 308.
29. Broderick OH, JFKL.
30. John Droney OH, JFKL.
31. Anthony Galluccio interview, Blair Papers, AHC.
32. Patrick J. Mulkern OH, JFKL.
33. Unpublished memoir, David F. Powers Papers, JFKL.
34. Rose Kennedy, *Times to Remember* (New York: 1974), 189.
35. Broderick OH, JFKL.
36. Peter Cloherty and Francis X. Morrissey OH, JFKL.
37. Anthony Galluccio OH, Paul B. Fay, Jr., OH, JFKL.
38. Mary S. Colbert OH, JFKL; see also Hamilton, *JFK: Restless Youth,* 737–38.
39. Martin, *Seeds of Destruction,* 142; Cutler, *"Honey Fitz,"* 308.
40. Rose Kennedy, *Times to Remember,* 196–97; Charles Higham, *Rose* (New York: 1995), 269.
41. Frank O'Connor interview, JFKL.
42. Blair and Blair, *In Search of JFK,* 476.
43. Broderick interview, JFKL; *Boston Herald,* June 20, 1946.

CHAPTER 13. GOLDEN BOY

1. Mary McNeely OH, JFKL.
2. William Sutton OH, JFKL.
3. Mary Davis interview, Blair Papers, AHC.
4. *Boston Herald,* April 17, 1947.
5. Richard M. Nixon, *RN: The Memoirs of Richard Nixon* (New York: 1978), 42–43; *McKeesport Daily News,* April 22, 1947.
6. Ernest G. Warren OH, JFKL; *Boston American,* July 31, 1947.
7. *Boston Globe,* March 14, 1947.
8. *Milwaukee Journal,* March 20, 1947.
9. "Investigation of Harold Christoffel," House Report 1508, Eighth Congress, Second Session.
10. *Boston Post,* April 23, 1947.
11. William Sutton interview, Blair Papers, AHC.

12. Hersh Freed and Samuel Bornstein OH JFKL; *Boston Herald* and *Boston Post,* June 16, 1947.
13. *New York Post,* Jan. 22, 1961.
14. *Washington Star,* July 29, 1947.
15. Gore Vidal, *Palimpsest* (New York: 1995), 415; Christopher Ogden, *Life of the Party* (Boston: 1994), 196.
16. Letter, JFK to James MacGregor Burns, Aug. 25, 1959, JFKPP, JFKL; Joan Blair and Clay Blair, Jr., *The Search for JFK* (New York: 1976), 558–59.
17. Sargent Shriver interview, Blair Papers, AHC.
18. Arthur Krock OH, COHP; Frank Waldrop interview, Blair Papers, AHC; *Boston Herald,* October 25, 1947.
19. Barbara Ward Jackson interview, JFKL.
20. Grace Burke OH, Francis X. Morrissey OH, JFKL.
21. Paul B. Fay, Jr., OH, JFKL.
22. Letters, Philip Kelly to JFK, Dec. 13, 1951; JFK to Kelly, Dec. 19, 1951, JFKPP, JFKL; Earl Latham, ed., *J. F. Kennedy and Presidential Power* (Lexington, Mass.: 1972), 266.
23. John Galvin interview, Blair Papers, AHC.

CHAPTER 14. THE REPRESENTATIVE

1. William Sutton interview, Blair Papers, AHC.
2. *New Bedford Standard Times,* Jan. 7, 1950.
3. George Smathers OH, JFKL.
4. Charles Bartlett OH, JFKL.
5. Eleanor Harris, "The Senator Is in a Hurry," *McCall's,* Aug. 1957; Clement Norton OH, JFKL.
6. The others above him were Jimmy Stewart, Howard Hughes, the Speaker of the House, Joe Martin, and Clark Gable. *Boston Herald,* March 1, 1948.
7. Alice Stockdale Proudfoot interview, Blair Papers, AHC. Her husband, Grant Stockdale, told her that Jack had mentioned a one-night stand with Clare Luce. Stockdale and JFK were close friends. As President, Kennedy gave Stockdale a post that many around him coveted—ambassador to Ireland. Ten days after Kennedy's assassination, Stockdale committed suicide.
8. *National Enquirer,* May 26, 1974; "Those Wild Kennedy Boys," *National Star,* September 28, 1974; Gene Tierney with Mickey Herskowitz, *Self-Portrait* (New York: 1979), 141–47; Mary Pitcairn Davis interview, Blair Papers, AHC.
9. *Boston Globe,* May 24, 1964.
10. Washington *Times-Herald,* Feb. 18, 1947.
11. Mary Davis OH, JFKL; *National Star,* Sept. 28, 1974.
12. *Boston Post,* Sept. 1, 1947.
13. *New York Times,* May 11, 1947; *Boston Globe,* May 19, 1947.
14. *New York Times,* May 11, 1947.
15. *Boston Post,* May 27, 1947.

16. *Boston Herald,* June 18, 1948.

17. *Boston Post,* March 31 and April 21, 1950.

18. Letter, Sam Rayburn to JFK, Feb. 22, 1947, JFKL.

19. Susan M. Hartmann, *Truman and the 80th Congress* (Columbia, Mo.: 1971), 139–40; *Salem News,* Nov. 20, 1951.

20. *Boston Globe,* March 13, 1949.

21. Drew Pearson and Robert Allen, "Merry Go Round," *Washington Star,* July 14, 1949.

22. *Boston Post,* March 8, 1950.

23. Drew Pearson, *Diaries, 1949–1959* (New York: 1974), 30.

24. *Boston Herald,* March 26, 1949.

25. *Boston Post,* Jan. 30, 1950.

26. *Boston Globe,* Jan. 28, 1950; *Congressional Digest,* Dec. 1952.

27. *Boston Globe,* March 19, 1949.

28. *Boston Globe,* Aug. 20, 1951.

29. Letter, JFK to editors of *Look,* March 3, 1952, JFKPP, JFKL.

30. *Boston Post,* Oct. 31, 1948.

31. *Taunton* (Mass.) *Gazette,* Sept. 20, 1948.

32. *Worcester* (Mass.) *Gazette,* Aug. 6, 1948.

33. *Boston Post,* Oct. 31, 1948.

34. Letters, JFK to Harry S. Truman, Sept. 12, 1949, HSTL; Bernard Baruch to JFK, Oct. 10, 1949, JFKL; *Boston Globe,* Oct. 9, 1949.

35. *Boston Post,* Jan. 13, 1950.

36. *Berkshire* (Mass.) *Evening Eagle,* June 5, 1950.

37. John P. Mallan, "Massachusetts: Liberal and Corrupt," *New Republic,* Oct. 13, 1952.

38. Lynne McTaggart, *Kathleen Kennedy* (Garden City, N.Y.: 1983), 228–39.

39. William Sutton interview, Blair Papers, AHC; Dinah Bridge OH, JFKL.

40. Peter Collier and David Horowitz, *The Kennedys* (New York: 1984), 171.

CHAPTER 15. GLOBE-TROTTER

1. Torbert Macdonald interview, Blair Papers, AHC.

2. JFK diary entry, n.d. but Jan. 1951, JFKPP, JFKL.

3. Ibid.

4. *Malden News,* Feb. 27, 1951. On their trip, Macdonald filed reports for the *Malden News.*

5. David K. Bruce diary, Bruce Papers, Virginia Historical Society; Ibid., February 1951.

6. JFK diary entry, n.d. but Feb. 1951, JFKPP, JFKL.

7. *Malden News,* March 13, 1951.

8. JFK diary entry, n.d. but Feb. 1951, JFKPP, JFKL.

9. *Malden News,* March 14, 1951.

10. *Uxbridge Times,* March 22, 1951.

11. *Boston Globe,* Feb. 7, 1951.
12. *Boston Herald,* Feb. 7, 1951.
13. "Statement Before Senate Foreign Relations Committee, Feb. 22, 1951," JFKL; *Boston Globe,* Feb. 23, 1951.
14. Ibid.
15. Geoffrey Perret, *Old Soldiers Never Die* (New York: 1996), 567–68.
16. *Boston Globe* and *Boston Post,* April 12, 1951.
17. Letter, JFK to General Douglas MacArthur, May 10, 1951, MacArthur Memorial and Archives, Norfolk, Virginia.
18. *Boston Post,* May 31, 1951.
19. Ibid., May 30, 1951.
20. Letter, Mary Davis to Edward H. White, May 21, 1951, JFKL.
21. Mary Davis OH, JFKL.
22. Letter, Walter B. Hoover to JFK, July 5, 1951, JFKL.
23. JFK travel diary, 1951, JFKPP, JFKL; *Boston Globe,* Dec. 2, 1951.
24. JFK travel diary, 1951, JFKPP, JFKL; Robert F. Kennedy travel diary, 1951, RFKP, JFKL.
25. JFK travel diary, 1951, JFKPP, JFKL.
26. *Boston Post,* Oct. 19, 1951, carried a special report by JFK on his visit to Pakistan.
27. Robert F. Kennedy travel diary, 1951, RKFP, JFKL; Arthur M. Schlesinger, Jr., *Robert Kennedy and His Times* (Boston: 1978), 98–99.
28. Henry Brandon, *Special Relationships* (New York: 1988), 190.
29. *Lynn* (Massachusetts) *Item,* Dec. 3, 1951.
30. JFK travel diary, 1951, JFKPP, JFKL.
31. Noel Barber, *The War of the Running Dogs* (London: 1971), 123–35.
32. Edward Klein, *All Too Human* (New York: 1996), 89.
33. Edmund Gullion OH, JFKL; David Halberstam, *The Best and the Brightest* (New York: 1972), 94; Selig S. Harrison, "Kennedy as President," *New Republic,* June 27, 1960.
34. Robert F. Kennedy travel diary, 1951, RFKP, JFKL.
35. Letter, JFK to Joseph P. Kennedy, n.d. but October 1951, JPKP, JFKL.
36. JFK travel diary, 1951, JFKPP, JFKL.
37. Robert F. Kennedy travel diary, 1951, RFKP, JFKL.
38. Joan Simpson Meyers, ed., *John F. Kennedy: As We Remember Him* (New York: 1965), 73.
39. Transcript from WOR broadcast, December 1951, JFKL.
40. *Boston Globe,* Dec. 2, 1951.
41. *Boston Herald,* Dec. 3, 1951.
42. *Boston Globe,* Nov. 20, 1951.

CHAPTER 16. LADIES—I NEED YOU

1. Writings File, David F. Powers Papers, JFKL.
2. Eleanor Harris, "The Senator Is in a Hurry," *McCall's,* Aug. 1957.

3. Mark Dalton, Joseph F. Leahy, Mary S. Colbert OH, JFKL.
4. Letter, Van Ness Bates to T. J. Reardon, Jr., May 11, 1959, JFKL.
5. David F. Powers interview, Blair Papers, AHC.
6. Thomas P. "Tip" O'Neill OH, and Dan Fenn OH, JFKL.
7. Joseph DeGugliemo OH, JFKL.
8. Joseph P. Healey interview, Blair Papers, AHC; Francis X. Morrissey OH, JFKL.
9. *Medford Mercury,* Feb. 11, 1952; *Washington Post,* April 12, 1952.
10. *Baltimore Sun,* Dec. 27, 1948; *Boston Herald,* Jan. 3, 1949.
11. William Sutton interview, Blair Papers, AHC.
12. *Life,* Feb. 7, 1944.
13. *New York Herald Tribune,* Feb. 6, 1952; Langdon P. Marvin interview, Blair Papers, AHC.
14. John B. White interview, NHP/MHS.
15. Writings File, David F. Powers Papers, JFKL.
16. O'Neill OH, JFKL.
17. "Political Beginnings" memo, n.d., David F. Powers Papers, JFKL.
18. Writings File, David F. Powers Papers, JFKL; Morrissey OH, JFKL.
19. Joseph Curnane OH, JFKL.
20. *Boston Chronicle,* Jan. 20, 1952.
21. Tip O'Neill with William Novak, *Man of the House* (New York: 1987), 119.
22. Ralph G. Martin and Ed Plaut, *Front Runner, Dark Horse* (Garden City, N.Y.: 1960), 171–73.
23. Herbert Tucker OH, JFKL.
24. DeGugliemo OH, JFKL.
25. Laura Bergquist, "What Women Really Meant to JFK," *Redbook,* Nov. 1973.
26. *Chicago Tribune,* Sept. 17, 1952.
27. Memo, Wickliffe W. Crider and John Elliott to JPK, Feb. 26, 1952, JPKP, JFKL.
28. Letter, Alfred M. Lilienthal to JFK, March 13, 1952, JFKL.
29. John B. Hynes interview, BU.
30. *Boston Herald,* Oct. 8, 1952.
31. Letter, Walter B. French to JFK, April 9, 1952, JPKP, JFKL; *Boston Herald,* April 9, 1952.
32. Cabell Phillips, "Case History of a Senate Race," *The New York Times Magazine,* October 25, 1952.
33. Rose Kennedy, *Times to Remember* (New York: 1974), 298–99; Martin and Plaut, *Front Runner, Dark Horse,* 161.
34. Sargent Shriver interview, Blair Papers, AHC.
35. Joseph Timilty interview, Blair Papers, AHC; John B. Hynes interview, BU; George Douglas et al., "Stalking the Ghost of the Post," *Boston Magazine,* Dec. 1973; Martin and Plaut, *Front Runner, Dark Horse,* 181; Writings File, David F. Powers Papers, JFKL.
36. Letters, Joseph P. Kennedy to B. A. Brinkley, March 24, 1952; B. A. Brinkley

to Joseph P. Kennedy, June 12, 1952; James M. Landis to Joseph P. Kennedy, June 26, 1952, JPKP, JFKL.

37. Joseph P. Healey interview, Blair Papers, AHC.

CHAPTER 17. ALLIANCE FOR PROGRESS

1. John H. Davis, *Jacqueline Bouvier: An Intimate Memoir* (New York: 1996), 162.
2. Benjamin Smith interview, Blair Papers, AHC.
3. Paul B. Fay OH, JFKL; *Washington Post,* Dec. 16, 1977; Seymour M. Hersh, *The Dark Side of Camelot* (Boston: 1997), 112–20; Edward McLaughlin, Blair Papers, AHC. The *Blauvelt Family Genealogy,* privately published in 1956, claimed that JFK had married Durie Malcolm of Palm Beach. This work is riddled with factual errors. The FBI investigated the purported JFK marriage and found nothing. Durie Malcolm herself denied she had ever done anything but date John Kennedy: *Time,* Dec. 2, 1962.
4. Edward Klein, *All Too Human* (New York: 1996), 36; Jeffrey Potter, *Men, Money & Magic* (New York: 1976), 292.
5. Gore Vidal, *Palimpsest* (New York: 1995), 309; Klein, *All Too Human,* 19.
6. Charles Bartlett OH, JFKL; *New York Times,* Jan. 21, 1952.
7. Davis, *Jacqueline Bouvier,* 159.
8. *Time,* Dec. 2, 1956.
9. Vidal, *Palimpsest,* 372.
10. John H. Davis, *The Bouviers* (New York: 1969), 128–29; Doris Kearns Goodwin, *The Fitzgeralds and the Kennedys* (New York: 1987), 769–70.
11. Donald Spoto, *Jacqueline Bouvier Kennedy Onassis* (New York: 2000), 85.
12. Eleanor Harris, "The Senator Is in a Hurry," *McCall's,* Aug. 1957.
13. Davis, *Jacqueline Bouvier,* 162.
14. Harris, "The Senator Is in a Hurry"; Spoto, *Jacqueline Bouvier Kennedy Onassis,* 89, 99.
15. Laurence Leamer, *The Kennedy Women* (New York: 1994), 430–31.
16. Frank Saunders with James Southwood, *Torn Lace Curtain* (New York: 1982), 7; Klein, *All Too Human,* 127.
17. JFK, Doodles Folder, 1955, JFKPP, JFKL.
18. Letter, JFK to Jacqueline Bouvier, Feb. 11, 1953, JFKPP, JFKL.
19. C. David Heymann, *A Woman Named Jackie* (Secaucus, N.J.: 1989), 162–63.
20. *Manchester Union-Leader,* Oct. 5, 1973; *North Shore Weekender,* Oct. 17, 1985.
21. Kennedy Files, Laura Bergquist Papers, BU.
22. Spoto, *Jacqueline Bouvier Kennedy Onassis,* 98.
23. Letter, JFK to Paul B. "Red" Fay, June 10, 1953, Paul B. Fay, Jr., Papers, SU.
24. John Droney OH, JFKL.
25. Writings File, David F. Powers Papers, JFKL.
26. Gunilla von Post with Carl Johnes, *Love, Jack* (New York: 1997), 29, 32.

27. Letter, JFK to J. V. Bouvier III, Nov. 26, 1956, JFKL; Davis, *The Bouviers,* 167.
28. Harris, "The Senator Is in a Hurry."
29. Paul B. Fay, Jr., OH, JFKL.
30. Elmer Bartels interview, Blair Papers, AHC.
31. Charles Bartlett, Blair Papers, AHC; Vidal, *Palimpsest,* 309; Leamer, *The Kennedy Women,* 451.
32. Carl Sferrazza Anthony, *As We Remember Her* (New York: 1997), 88; Writings File, David F. Powers Papers, JFKL.
33. Leamer, *The Kennedy Women,* 433; Robin Douglas-Home, "Jacqueline: Behind the Myth," *McCall's,* 1975.
34. Vidal, *Palimpsest,* 312.
35. Unpublished manuscript, Evelyn Lincoln Papers, JFKL.
36. Davis, *Jacqueline Bouvier,* 168.
37. Leamer, *The Kennedy Women,* 438.
38. Harris, "The Senator Is in a Hurry."
39. Vidal, *Palimpsest,* 106; Anthony, *As We Remember Her,* 88.
40. Kennedy Files, Laura Bergquist Papers, BU.

CHAPTER 18. JOE AND ROSE

1. There are more than a hundred letters like this in the Joseph P. Kennedy Papers, JFKL.
2. Ronald Kessler, *The Sins of the Father* (New York: 1996), 281.
3. Paul B. Fay mss., Fay Papers, SU.
4. Ibid.; Dinah Bridge OH, JFKL.
5. Barbara Gibson and Ted Schwarz, *Rose Kennedy and Her Family* (Secaucus, N.J.: 1995), 76.
6. Ralph G. Martin, *A Hero for Our Time* (New York: 1983), 55.
7. Edward Gallagher OH, JFKL.
8. Sargent Shriver interview, Blair Papers, AHC.
9. Ibid.; Kessler, *The Sins of the Father,* 274; Richard J. Whalen, *The Founding Father* (New York: 1964), 379–80.
10. Kessler, *The Sins of the Father,* 327–28.
11. Letter, Joseph P. Kennedy to Patricia Kennedy Lawford, March 7, 1955, JPKP, JFKL.
12. *Time,* Dec. 2, 1957.
13. Letter, Timothy A. McInerny to Joseph P. Kennedy, Feb. 18, 1952, JFKL.
14. *Boston Herald,* Oct. 24, 1947; *Boston Post,* Oct. 26, 1947.
15. John Droney OH, JFKL.
16. Kennedy Files, Laura Bergquist Papers, BU.
17. Bridge OH, JFKL.
18. Rose Kennedy, *Times to Remember* (New York: 1974), 262.
19. *Time,* May 31, 1963.

20. *New York Herald Tribune,* Dec. 14, 1952.
21. Charles Higham, *Rose* (New York: 1995), 267, 286.
22. Nigel Hamilton, *JFK: Reckless Youth* (New York: 1992), 411–12.
23. Doris Kearns Goodwin, *The Fitzgeralds and the Kennedys* (New York: 1987), 640.
24. Gibson and Schwarz, *Rose Kennedy and Her Family,* 63.
25. Letter, Joseph P. Kennedy to JFK, Jan. 23, 1957, JFKPP, JFKL.

CHAPTER 19. PATIENT PROFILE

1. William F. Buckley, Jr., and L. Brent Bozell, *McCarthy and His Enemies* (Chicago: 1954), 45. Bozell, who worked for McCarthy, wrote most of this speech.
2. New Bedford *Standard Times,* Sept. 4, 1948.
3. Tristram Coffin, "John Kennedy: Young Man in a Hurry," *The Progressive,* Dec. 1959.
4. Transcript, *Meet the Press,* Feb. 14, 1954, JFKL.
5. Elmer Bartels interview, Blair Papers, AHC.
6. Eleanor Harris, "The Senator Is in a Hurry," *McCall's,* Aug. 1957.
7. Edward Klein, *All Too Human* (New York: 1996), 185.
8. Letter, Ted Reardon to JFK, Sept. 29, 1954, JFKPP, JFKL.
9. Charles Spalding OH, JFKL.
10. Arthur Krock Memos, Krock Papers, PU; Donald Spoto, *Jacqueline Bouvier Kennedy Onassis* (New York: 2000), 109; J. Randy Taraborrelli, *Jackie, Ethel, Joan* (New York: 2000), 67.
11. James A. Nicholas et al., "Management of Adrenocortical Insufficiency During Surgery," *Archives of Surgery,* Vol. 71, 1955.
12. Taraborrelli, *Jackie, Ethel, Joan,* 68–69.
13. Ralph G. Martin, *A Hero for Our Time* (New York: 1983), 89; Klein, *All Too Human,* 189, offers a slightly different version of this famous episode, in which Jack wakes up and groggily asks Grace Kelly, "Is that really you?"
14. In a discarded opening chapter for *Profiles in Courage,* JFK had these men appear in a dream, urging him to choose principle over expediency. See "Chapter 1—The Meaning of Courage," Manuscripts Folder, JFKPP, JFKL.
15. Letter, Theodore Sorensen to JFK, Jan. 14, 1955, Sorensen Papers, JFKL.
16. Ronald Kessler, *The Sins of the Father* (New York: 1996), 348–49; Spoto, *Jacqueline Bouvier Kennedy Onassis,* 111.
17. Letters, Theodore Sorensen to JFK, Jan. 25 and 31, 1955, Sorensen Papers, JFKL.
18. Charles Bartlett OH, JFKL.
19. Spalding OH, JFKL.
20. There are four of these tapes in the Audiovisual Department at JFKL. In three of them, he speaks in the weary monotone typical of someone enfeebled by poor health.
21. Letter, Cass Canfield to JFK, Feb. 15, 1955, JFKPP, JFKL.

22. Letter, Evan Thomas to JFK, Feb. 16, 1955, JFKPP, JFKL.
23. Christopher Matthews, *Kennedy & Nixon* (New York: 1996), 102.
24. Janet Travell OH, JFKL.
25. Letter, Evan Thomas to JFK, Aug. 4, 1955, JFKL; Evan Thomas OH, COHP.
26. Letter, Theodore Sorensen to JFK, Feb. 4, 1955, Sorensen Papers, JFKL.
27. Letter, JFK to Ernest Hemingway, July 26, 1955, JFKPP, JFKL.
28. Letter, Evan Thomas to JFK, Nov. 28, 1956, Evan Thomas Papers, CU; Kessler, *The Sins of the Father,* 112–13.
29. Arthur Krock OH, COHP.

CHAPTER 20. LOSING

1. Margaret Coit file, NHP/MHS; Kennedy Files, Laura Bergquist Papers, BU. New Bedford *Standard-Times,* May 22, 1955. Both Coit and Bergquist noticed JFK's hair turning gray before he resorted to coloring it.
2. Rowland Evans OH, JFKL.
3. Letter, JFK to LBJ, Dec. 12, 1952, JFKL; Bobby Baker with Larry L. King, *Wheeling and Dealing* (New York: 1978), 64–65.
4. Joseph Alsop OH, JFKL.
5. "Memorandum on Committee Status of Senator John F. Kennedy," Jan. 1956, Sorensen Papers, JFKL.
6. Letters, Dave Powers to JFK, Jan. 24, 1956, and Francis X. Morrissey to JFK, Feb. 9, 1956, JFKL.
7. Memo, Ted Sorensen to JFK, "The Catholic Vote in 1952 and 1956," n.d., Sorensen Papers, JFKL; Fletcher Knebel OH, Joseph DeGugliemo OH, JFKL; Ralph G. Martin and Ed Plaut, *Front Runner, Dark Horse* (Garden City, N.Y.: 1960), 27–28.
8. Herbert S. Parmet, *Jack: The Struggles of John F. Kennedy* (New York: 1980), 359.
9. Thomas Winship OH, JFKL.
10. John Lynch OH, BU; Writings File, David F. Powers Papers, JFKL; James MacGregor Burns, *John Kennedy: A Political Profile* (New York: 1960), 176–80; Lawrence F. O'Brien, *No Final Victories* (Garden City, N.Y.: 1974), 47–49.
11. James Spada, *Peter Lawford* (New York: 1991), 209–12.
12. Dore Schary and Clinton Anderson OH, JFKL.
13. Tip O'Neill with William Novak, *Man of the House* (New York: 1987), 82.
14. Letter, Ted Sorensen to Ken Hechler, Aug. 1, 1956, Theodore Sorensen Papers, JFKL.
15. *Boston Daily Record,* July 12, 1956.
16. John Bartlow Martin, *Adlai Stevenson and the World* (Garden City, N.Y.: 1977), 348.
17. Robert Dallek, *Lone Star Rising* (New York: 1991), 491.
18. Letter, Arthur Krock to Joseph P. Kennedy, July 11, 1956, Krock Papers, PU.
19. Maurice Donahue OH, JFKL.

20. Martin and Plaut, *Front Runner, Dark Horse,* 51.
21. Ibid., 75; John E. Fogarty OH, JFKL.
22. Winship OH, JFKL; *Chicago Tribune,* Aug. 17, 1956.
23. Newton Minow interview, John Bartlow Martin Papers, LC; Joseph Bruce Gorman, *Kefauver: A Political Biography* (New York: 1971), 252.
24. Arthur M. Schlesinger, Jr., *Robert Kennedy and His Times* (Boston: 1978), 142.
25. Theodore C. Sorensen, *Kennedy* (New York: 1965), 100.
26. Kennedy Files, Laura Bergquist Papers, BU; Benjamin Jacobson OH, JFKL.
27. Gore Vidal, *Palimpsest* (New York: 1995), 510.
28. Tempest Storm with Bill Boyd, *Tempest Storm: The Lady Is a Vamp* (Atlanta: 1987), 158.
29. Charles F. Spalding interview, NHP/MHS.
30. J. Randy Taraborrelli, *Jackie, Ethel, Joan* (New York: 2000), 74. Taraborrelli was told this by Lem Billings.
31. Schlesinger, *Robert Kennedy and His Times,* 143.
32. Letter, Rose Kennedy to Patricia Kennedy Lawford, Aug. 26, 1956, JPKP, JFKL.
33. George Smathers OH, SHO; Edward Klein, *All Too Human* (New York: 1996), 215.
34. Laurence Leamer, *The Kennedy Women* (New York: 1994), 462–63.
35. Spalding interview, NHP/MHS.

CHAPTER 21. RUNNING, ALWAYS RUNNING

1. Peter Collier and David Horowitz, *The Kennedys* (New York: 1984), 209.
2. Letters, Evan Thomas to JFK, Sept. 4, Oct. 30, 1956, JFKL.
3. Clark Clifford with Richard Holbrooke, *Counsel to the President* (New York: 1991), 306–9; Drew Pearson, *Diaries, 1949–59* (New York: 1974), 420.
4. Joseph P. Clark OH, JFKL.
5. Letter, JFK to Herbert Lehman, July 29, 1953, Lehman Papers, CU.
6. Joseph Bruce Gorman, *Kefauver: A Political Biography* (New York: 1971), 256–57.
7. Harris Wofford, *Of Kennedys and Kings* (New York: 1980), 46.
8. Letters, JFK to Samuel H. Beer, Aug. 3, 1957; Roy Wilkins to Peter Arlos, May 16, 1958; Roy Wilkins to JFK, May 29, 1958, JFKL.
9. Arthur A. Sloane, *Hoffa* (Cambridge, Mass.: 1991), 122.
10. Andrew Biemiller OH, JFKL; David L. Stebenne, *Arthur J. Goldberg: New Deal Liberal* (New York: 1996), 174–75.
11. Stewart E. McClure OH, SHO; Ken Gormley, *Archibald Cox: Conscience of a Nation* (Reading, Mass.: 1997), 99–105.
12. Kai Bird, *The Color of Truth* (New York: 1998), 151.
13. Walt Whitman Rostow OH, JFKL.
14. Silvio O. Conte OH, JFKL.
15. Lawrence F. O'Brien, *No Final Victories* (Garden City, N.Y.: 1974), 54–55; Helen Lempart OH, JFKL.

16. Letters, Elmo Roper to JFK, Feb. 1, 1960, and JFK to Elmo Roper, Feb. 11, 1960, University of Connecticut. JFK strenuously denied in 1960 that he had made such remarks, but Roper and Burke had taken notes of this conversation.

17. *Los Angeles Times,* Aug. 16, 1954.

18. "Facing Facts in Algeria," JFKL; *Washington Post,* July 9, 1957.

19. Geoffrey Perret, *Eisenhower* (New York: 1999), 563–64.

20. *Congressional Record,* Eighty-fifth Congress, First Session, 17569–70.

21. Carl Sferazza Anthony, *As We Remember Her* (New York: 1997), 90; Edward Klein, *All Too Human* (New York: 1996), 11–12.

22. J. William Fulbright OH, JFKL.

23. K. LeMoyne Billings OH, NHP/MHS.

24. Anthony, *As We Remember Her,* 92; Kennedy Files, Laura Bergquist Papers, BU.

25. Gore Vidal, *Palimpsest* (New York: 1995), 335–36.

26. Paul B. Fay, Jr., OH, JFKL.

27. William Douglas-Home OH, JFKL.

28. Robin Cross, *JFK: A Hidden Life* (Boston: 1992), 83; Fay OH, JFKL.

29. Robert Lacey, *Grace* (New York: 1994), 203–4.

30. George Smathers OH, SHO.

31. Transcript of meeting with Nieman Fellows, Feb. 2, 1959, JFKL.

32. Writings File, David F. Powers Papers, JFKL.

33. William Goolrick, "Jack Kennedy Takes Two Tough Tests," *Life,* April 27, 1959.

34. Klein, *All Too Human,* 257.

35. *New York Times,* Oct. 23, 1959.

36. Letter, Ted Sorensen to J. M. Burns, Oct. 27, 1959, Theodore Sorensen Papers, JFKL.

37. James MacGregor Burns, *John Kennedy: A Political Profile* (New York: 1960), 276–81.

38. Jacqueline Kennedy to J. M. Burns, Oct. 8, 1959, NHP/MHS.

39. *New York Times,* Dec. 8, 1958.

40. Fletcher Knebel, "A Catholic in 1960," *Look,* March 3, 1959.

41. *Harper's,* Dec. 1959.

42. Charles Bartlett OH, JFKL.

43. Paul B. Fay, Jr., mss., Paul B. Fay, Jr., Papers, SU.

44. Paul B. Fay, Jr., *The Pleasure of His Company* (New York: 1966), 9.

45. Benjamin C. Bradlee, *Conversations with Kennedy* (New York: 1975), 36.

46. Evelyn Lincoln, *My Twelve Years with John F. Kennedy* (New York: 1965), 128–29.

CHAPTER 22. JACK BE NIMBLE

1. *Saturday Evening Post,* June 13, 1953; letters, Arthur Schlesinger, Jr., to JFK, June 25, 1953, and JFK to Schlesinger, July 10, 1953, JFKL.

2. Rowland Evans OH, JFKL.

3. Letters, JFK to Chester Bowles, Jan. 29, 1960, and Bowles to JFK, Feb. 15, 1960, JFKL.

4. George Smathers OH, SHO.

5. Charles Bartlett OH, JFKL; Evelyn Lincoln, *My Twelve Years with John F. Kennedy* (New York: 1965), 125.

6. Myer Feldman OH, JFKL.

7. Andrew Biemiller OH, JFKL.

8. Walt Whitman Rostow OH, JFKL.

9. Paul Corbin OH, NHP/MHS.

10. Fletcher Knebel OH, JFKL.

11. Benjamin C. Bradlee, *Conversations with Kennedy* (New York: 1975), 17.

12. Walter Cronkite, *A Reporter's Life* (New York: 1996), 185–86.

13. Hubert Humphrey OH, JFKL.

14. Bradlee, *Conversations with Kennedy,* 26.

15. Rostow OH, JFKL.

16. Evans OH, JFKL.

17. Dan B. Fleming, Jr., *Kennedy vs. Humphrey: West Virginia, 1960* (Jefferson, N.C.: 1992), 80, 122, 130. Fleming's book is the most authoritative examination of mob involvement in the West Virginia primary.

18. Helen Lempart OH, JFKL.

19. Feldman OH, JFKL.

20. William O. Douglas, *Go East, Young Man* (New York: 1974), 101.

21. Fleming, *Kennedy vs. Humphrey: West Virginia, 1960,* 151; Kennedy Files, Laura Bergquist Papers, BU.

22. Bartlett OH, JFKL.

23. Feldman OH JFKL.

24. Homer H. Hickam, Jr., *Rocket Boys* (New York: 1998), 335–36. Hickam later worked on the moon program, and his memoir of growing up in West Virginia was filmed as *October Sky.*

25. William Lawrence OH, JFKL.

26. Benjamin C. Bradlee, *A Good Life* (New York: 1995), 208.

27. Theodore C. Sorensen, *Kennedy* (New York: 1965), 167.

28. J. Leonard Reinsch OH, JFKL.

29. Letter, Arthur Schlesinger, Jr., to Adlai E. Stevenson, May 16, 1960, Stevenson Papers, PU.

30. Newton Minow OH, JFKL.

31. Ted Sorensen OH, JFKL.

32. Adlai E. Stevenson III interview, John Bartlow Martin Papers, LC; George W. Ball, *The Past Has Another Pattern* (New York: 1982), 68.

33. Paul B. Fay, Jr., mss., Paul B. Fay, Jr., Papers, SU.

34. Reinsch OH, JFKL.

35. Bradlee, *Conversations with Kennedy,* 19–20.

36. Sorensen and Feldman OH, JFKL; Newton Minow interview, John Bartlow Martin Papers, LC.

37. Letter, Arthur Schlesinger, Jr., to Adlai E. Stevenson, May 16, 1960, Stevenson Papers, PU.

38. Letter, Lawrence A. Kubic to Arthur Schlesinger, Jr., July 16, 1965, Arthur Schlesinger Papers, JFKL. One characteristic of Addison's is that it involves only the adrenal cortex, not the whole gland, and that was the form it took in Kennedy's case.

39. James Reston, Jr., *The Lone Star* (New York: 1989), 189–92.

40. Bradlee, *Conversations with Kennedy,* 31; see also David Bell OH, JFKL.

41. John Bartlow Martin, *Adlai Stevenson and the World* (Garden City, N.Y.: 1977), 524–26; Adam Cohen and Elizabeth Taylor, *American Pharaoh: Mayor Richard J. Daley* (Boston: 2000), 258–59.

42. Bobby Baker, *Wheeling and Dealing* (New York: 1978), 118–19; Robert Dallek, *Lone Star Rising* (New York: 1991), 573.

43. Theodore White, *The Making of the President 1960* (New York: 1961), 203.

44. Evans OH, JFKL; Clark Clifford OH, NHP/MHS.

45. Memo for Record, Sept. 22, 1960, Arthur Krock Papers, PU.

46. Thomas P. "Tip" O'Neill OH, JFKL; Dallek, *Lone Star Rising,* 575–78.

47. Reinsch OH, JFKL.

CHAPTER 23. TOO CLOSE TO CALL

1. David McCullough, *Truman* (New York: 1992), 974; Kenneth P. O'Donnell and David F. Powers, *Johnny, We Hardly Knew Ye* (Boston: 1972), 232.

2. Memo, Eleanor Roosevelt to Ruth Field, n.d. but Aug. 1960, Eleanor Roosevelt Papers, FDR Library. See also Gore Vidal, *Palimpsest* (New York: 1995), 347–48.

3. Letter, JFK to Lord Beaverbrook, Sept. 6, 1960, House of Lords Library.

4. Letter, Paul Hoffman to Arthur Krock, March 9, 1960, Arthur Krock Papers, PU.

5. Charles F. Spalding interview, NHP/MHS.

6. O'Donnell and Powers, *Johnny, We Hardly Knew Ye,* 239–41; Theodore White, *The Making of the President 1960* (New York: 1961), 310–13. White says he implied a threat to resign, yet Kennedy's statements invariably stressed that he would stand against his own church if necessary. A candidate who promised to resign under pressure—improper pressure, at that—would never be elected.

7. J. Leonard Reinsch OH, JFKL; Pierre Salinger, *P.S., A Memoir* (New York: 1995), 83–84.

8. Charles F. Spalding interview, NHP/MHS; C. David Heymann, *A Woman Named Jackie* (Secaucus, N.J.: 1989), 222–23.

9. Edward Klein, *All Too Human* (New York: 1996), 256.

10. Reinsch OH, JFKL.

11. Benjamin C. Bradlee, *Conversations with Kennedy* (New York: 1975), 32n.

12. Tip O'Neill with William Novak, *Man of the House,* (New York: 1987), 96.

13. Marietta Tree and Henry Brandon OH, JFKL.
14. Ken Gormley, *Archibald Cox: Conscience of a Nation* (Reading, Mass.: 1997), 129–31.
15. Kennedy Files, Laura Bergquist Papers, BU.
16. Bradlee, *Conversations with Kennedy,* 20.
17. William Lawrence OH, JFKL.
18. Rowland Evans OH, JFKL.
19. Taylor Branch, *Parting the Waters* (New York: 1988), 357–59.
20. Anthony Shriver et al., "Kennedy's Call to King," JFKL.
21. George H. Gallup, *The Gallup Poll, 1935–1971* III (New York: 1972), 262–69.
22. Laura Bergquist OH, JFKL.
23. James G. Blight et al., *Cuba on the Brink* (New York: 1993), 130.
24. John Fischer, "Easy Chair," *Harper's,* Dec. 9, 1959; Peter Grose, *Gentleman Spy: The Life of Allen Dulles* (Amherst: 1996), 507.
25. Earle Wheeler OH, JFKL.
26. Transcripts, *Meet the Press,* July 10, 1960, and Oct. 16, 1960, JFKL.
27. Karen Schwarz, *What You Can Do for Your Country* (New York: 1991), 27–28.
28. Brent Ashabranner, *A Moment in History* (Garden City, N.Y.: 1971), 14.
29. Fletcher Knebel OH, JFKL.
30. "Candidate JFK: Scribbles from the Trail," *Washington Post,* May 28, 1987.
31. Bradlee, *Conversations with Kennedy,* 33; Adam Cohen and Elizabeth Taylor, *American Pharaoh: Mayor Richard J. Daley* (Boston: 2000), 263–79. There was widespread ballot fraud in Chicago. Whether it was greater than the fraud elsewhere in the state, from which Nixon benefited, is uncertain. See also Myer Feldman OH, JFKL.
32. White, *The Making of the President 1960,* 29–30.
33. Evelyn Lincoln, *My Twelve Years with John F. Kennedy* (New York: 1965), 187.
34. Writings File, David F. Powers Papers, JFKL.

CHAPTER 24. LEARNING CURVE

1. Maud Shaw, *White House Nannie* (New York: 1966), 69–71.
2. Mary McGrory, *New York Post,* Jan. 22, 1961. McGrory, a veteran political journalist from Boston, was at the Hyannis Armory.
3. Theodore C. Sorensen, *Kennedy* (New York: 1965), 218–23; Arthur M. Schlesinger, Jr., *A Thousand Days* (Boston: 1965), 118–19.
4. Henry Brandon OH, JFKL.
5. Benjamin C. Bradlee, *Conversations with Kennedy* (New York: 1975), 33–34; Ralph G. Martin, *Seeds of Destruction* (New York: 1995), 99.
6. John Sharon OH, JFKL.
7. Dwight D. Eisenhower, "Account of My December 6th Meeting with President-elect Kennedy" and "Memorandum for Record," Dec. 6, 1960, both in Anne

Whitman File, DDEL; John Sharon and George Ball, "Briefing Memoranda for Meeting with President Eisenhower, December 6, 1960," JFKL.

8. Francis X. Morrissey OH, JFKL; Writings File, David F. Powers Papers, JFKL.

9. Clark Clifford OH, JFKL.

10. Myer Feldman OH, JFKL.

11. Robert F. Kennedy OH, JFKL.

12. Kai Bird, *The Color of Truth* (New York: 1998), 152.

13. Dean Rusk, *As I Saw It* (New York: 1990), 202–5; Deborah Shapley, *Promise and Power: The Life and Times of Robert McNamara* (Boston: 1993), 79.

14. Thomas J. Shoenbaum, *Waging Peace and War: Dean Rusk in the Truman, Kennedy, and Johnson Years* (New York: 1988), 16–22; John Bartlow Martin, *Adlai Stevenson and the World* (Garden City, N.Y.: 1977), 561–62.

15. *Time,* Dec. 2, 1960.

16. Robert S. McNamara OH, JFKL; Shapley, *Promise and Power,* 83–86.

17. Feldman OH, JFKL.

18. Tristram Coffin, "John Kennedy: Young Man in a Hurry," *The Progressive,* Dec. 1959.

19. Memo, John Sharon to Adlai Stevenson, Nov. 16, 1960, Stevenson Papers, PU.

20. Harris Wofford, *Of Kennedys and Kings* (New York: 1980), 67.

21. Edward Klein, *All Too Human* (New York: 1996), 11–12.

22. Langdon P. Marvin interview, Blair Papers, AHC.

23. George Smathers in Gerald S. and Deborah H. Strober, *Let Us Begin Anew* (New York: 1993), 111.

24. William Lawrence OH, JFKL.

25. Bradlee, *Conversations with Kennedy,* 38.

26. Andrew J. Goodpaster, Memo for Record, Jan. 25, 1961, Transition File, DDEL.

27. Ibid; JFK Memo for Record, Jan. 19, 1961, JFKL; Clark Clifford memo to JFK, Jan. 24, 1961, JFKL; Robert McNamara memo to JFK, Jan. 24, 1961, JFKL; "Topics Suggested by Senator Kennedy for Meeting," Jan. 19, 1961, Anne Whitman File, DDEL.

28. Walter Cronkite, *A Reporter's Life* (New York: 1996), 188.

CHAPTER 25. FIRE AND ICE

1. Dorothye G. Scott OH, SHO; Tip O'Neill with William Novak, *Man of the House* (New York: 1987), 101–3.

2. Barbara Gibson and Ted Schwarz, *Rose Kennedy and Her Family* (Secaucus, N.J.: 1995), 218–19.

3. Gore Vidal, *Palimpsest* (New York: 1995), 352.

4. John Christie, "Parade Car," *Automotive History Review,* Spring 1999.

5. Robert F. Kennedy OH, JFKL; Geoffrey Perret, *Eisenhower* (New York: 1999), 344.

6. J. Randy Taraborrelli, *Jackie, Ethel, Joan* (New York: 2000), 26; Lawrance Thompson and R. H. Winnick, *Robert Frost* (New York: 1976), vol. 3, 277.

7. J. Leonard Reinsch OH, JFKL.

8. Jack Raymond memo (n.d.) to Arthur Krock, Krock Papers, PU.

9. Vidal, *Palimpsest,* 354–55.

10. Gore Vidal presciently observed in the London *Sunday Telegraph* on April 9, 1961, "Despite his youth, Kennedy may very well not survive. A matter, one suspects, of no great concern to him."

11. Michael R. Beschloss, ed., *Taking Charge* (New York: 1997), 12. The LBJ version of this episode is wildly—and typically—exaggerated. He has Jack Kennedy picking up the deer and strapping it to the fender of a car. Due to his back problems, Kennedy could not even pick up his children.

12. Alice Proudfoot interview, Blair Papers, AHC; Vidal, *Palimpsest,* 364; Tom Wicker, *JFK and LBJ* (New York: 1968), 39; Paul B. Fay, Jr., *The Pleasure of His Company* (New York: 1966), 113–14.

13. C. David Heymann, *A Woman Named Jackie* (Secaucus, N.J.: 1989), 257; Arthur M. Schlesinger, Jr., *A Thousand Days* (Boston: 1965), 4.

14. Fred Dutton OH, JFKL.

15. Walter Cronkite, *A Reporter's Life* (New York: 1996), 225.

16. Harris Wofford, *Of Kennedys and Kings* (New York: 1980), 99.

17. Jane Eustice Wheeler interview, Blair Papers, AHC; Heymann, *A Woman Named Jackie,* 260.

18. Heymann, *A Woman Named Jackie,* 261.

19. Joseph W. Alsop, *I've Seen the Best of It* (New York: 1992), 434–35.

20. JFK is often purported to have had sex with various people that night at Alsop's house. None of these stories appears to be true. Author interview with Paul B. Fay, Jr.; Edwin M. Yoder, Jr., "Naughty News to Me," *Washington Post,* Aug. 14, 1999.

CHAPTER 26. STANDARD OPERATING PROCEDURE

1. Dean Acheson OH, JFKL.

2. Myer Feldman OH, JFKL; Clark Clifford OH, NHP/MHS.

3. Archibald Cox in Gerald S. and Deborah H. Strober, *Let Us Begin Anew* (New York: 1993), 148. See also Najeeb Halaby OH, JFKL.

4. Robert Amory and Eugene Rostow OH, JFKL.

5. Amory OH, JFKL.

6. Paul B. Fay, Jr., OH, and Arleigh Burke OH, JFKL.

7. Frank Saunders with James Southwood, *Torn Lace Curtain* (New York: 1978), 58.

8. Ralph Horton OH, JFKL.

9. Charles Bartlett OH, JFKL.

10. Helen O'Donnell, *A Common Good* (New York: 1998), 295.

11. John Sharon OH, JFKL.

12. Clifford OH and Paul Corbin OH, NHP/MHS; Seymour M. Hersh, *The Dark Side of Camelot* (Boston: 1997), 442–45.
13. Tom Killefer interview, Blair Papers, AHC.
14. Strober, *Let Us Begin Anew,* 141.
15. Ibid., 60.
16. Bobby Baker with Larry L. King, *Wheeling and Dealing* (New York: 1978), 143.
17. Francis R. Valeo OH, SHO.
18. Baker, *Wheeling and Dealing,* 141; Strober, *Let Us Begin Anew,* 145.
19. Ronald L. Heinemann, *Harry Byrd of Virginia* (Charlottesville, Va.: 1996), 383–85.
20. *Public Papers of the Presidents: John F. Kennedy, 1961* (Washington, D.C.: 1962), 143; Tom Wicker, *JFK and LBJ* (New York: 1968), 128–45.
21. Baker, *Wheeling and Dealing,* 146; Charles S. Caldwell OH, SHO.
22. Sharon OH, JFKL; Robert Dallek, *Flawed Giant* (New York: 1998), 12–16; O'Donnell, *A Common Good,* 271.
23. Baker, *Wheeling and Dealing,* 117.
24. Wicker, *JFK and LBJ,* 31; George Smathers OH, SHO.
25. Bartlett OH, JFKL.
26. Paul B. Fay, Jr., OH, JFKL; Gore Vidal, *Palimpsest* (New York: 1995), 364.
27. Edward Klein, *All Too Human* (New York: 1996), 271.
28. Najeeb Halaby OH, JFKL.
29. Vidal, *Palimpsest,* 362; Fay, Jr., OH, JFKL.
30. Pierre Salinger, *P.S., A Memoir* (New York: 1995), 95.
31. James Reston, *Deadline* (New York: 1991), 289.
32. Feldman OH, JFKL.
33. Robert Pierpoint OH, JFKL.
34. Memo for Record, Oct. 11, 1961, Arthur Krock Papers, PU.

CHAPTER 27. HANDS-ON

1. Sergei Khrushchev, *Khrushchev on Khrushchev* (Boston: 1990), 181–82; Chester Bowles OH, JFKL.
2. *Time,* Feb. 10, 1961.
3. John Lewis Gaddis, *We Now Know* (New York: 1997), 205–7.
4. John Fisher interview with JFK in *Harper's,* Dec. 9, 1959; Kai Bird, *The Color of Truth* (New York: 1998), 186; Richard Reeves, *President Kennedy* (New York: 1993), 41, 52; William O. Douglas OH, JFKL.
5. Seymour M. Hersh, *The Dark Side of Camelot* (Boston: 1997), 111.
6. Bird, *The Color of Truth,* 189.
7. Benjamin C. Bradlee, *A Good Life* (New York: 1995), 218.
8. Robert Amory OH, JFKL.
9. David Kaiser, *American Tragedy* (Cambridge, Mass.: 2000), 43.
10. Walt Whitman Rostow OH, JFKL.

11. "Memorandum of Conversation," March 24, 1961, Department of State, *FRUS, 1961–1963* V (Washington, D.C.: 1996), 110–14; Michael R. Beschloss, *The Crisis Years: Kennedy and Khrushchev, 1960–1963* (New York: 1991), 87; David Halberstam, *The Best and the Brightest* (New York: 1972), 90.

12. Arleigh Burke OH, JFKL.

13. Rostow OH, JFKL; Memo for Record, May 5, 1961, Arthur Krock Papers, PU.

14. Chester Bowles OH, JFKL; Theodore Sorensen interview, John Bartlow Martin Papers, LC.

15. Fletcher Knebel OH, JFKL.

16. Peter Grose, *Gentleman Spy: The Life of Allen Dulles* (Amherst: 1996), 512–13.

17. Bird, *The Color of Truth,* 194.

18. "Memorandum from General Lemnitzer to Secretary of Defense," Feb. 3, 1961, Department of State, *FRUS, 1961–1963* X (Washington, D.C.: 1997), 69.

19. George Smathers OH, JFKL; Ralph G. Martin, *Seeds of Destruction* (New York: 1995), 327; Hersh, *The Dark Side of Camelot,* 200–1; Grose, *Gentleman Spy,* 516–17.

20. Robert Amory OH, JFKL; Grose, *Gentleman Spy,* 560.

21. Richard M. Bissell, *Reflections of a Cold Warrior* (New Haven: 1996), 172–7.

22. "Memorandum from Joint Chiefs of Staff to Secretary of Defense," March 10, 1961, *FRUS 1961–1963,* X, 135.

23. Ibid., 159.

24. Bowles OH, JFKL.

25. "Memorandum of Conversation," April 4, 1961, *FRUS 1961–1963,* X, 185–86; J. William Fulbright OH, JFKL.

26. Richard N. Goodwin, *Remembering America* (Boston: 1988), 177.

27. Gus Russo, *Live by the Sword* (Latham, Md.: 1998), 17.

28. *Public Papers of the Presidents: John F. Kennedy, 1961* (Washington, D.C.: 1962), 304–6.

29. Bissell, *Reflections of a Cold Warrior,* 183–86.

30. Fred Dutton OH, JFKL.

31. Barry M. Goldwater, *Goldwater* (New York: 1988), 135–36. Kennedy later acquired a taste for Cuban cigars. They were provided by the Soviet embassy, which brought them into the United States by diplomatic pouch. See also Richard Goodwin, "Cigars and Che and JFK," *Cigar Aficionado,* Fall 1996.

32. Kennedy Files, Laura Bergquist Papers, BU.

33. Earle Wheeler OH, JFKL.

34. E. B. Potter, *Admiral Arleigh Burke* (New York: 1990), 437–38.

35. Lester David and Irene David, *Bobby Kennedy* (New York: 1986), 157.

CHAPTER 28. HOLDING FAST

1. Richard Reeves, *President Kennedy* (New York: 1993), 136.
2. *Public Papers of the Presidents: John F. Kennedy, 1961* (Washington, D.C.: 1964), 401.
3. Reeves, *President Kennedy*, 139.
4. *PPP: John F. Kennedy, 1961*, 404.
5. Chalmers M. Roberts, *First Rough Draft* (New York: 1973), 198.
6. *Time*, June 9, 1961.
7. Evan Thomas, *Robert Kennedy* (New York: 2000), 191.
8. Henry Brandon, *Special Relationships* (New York: 1988), 193.
9. Department of State, *FRUS, 1961–1963*, X (Washington, D.C.: 1997), 221–22.
10. Geoffrey Perret, *Eisenhower* (New York: 1999), 573–76.
11. Reeves, *President Kennedy*, 149.
12. Jean Lacouture, *De Gaulle* (New York: 1992), 370–72; *FRUS 1961–1963*, XIII (Washington, D.C.: 1998), 667.
13. This memorandum is reproduced in Lyman Lemnitzer OH, JFKL. The Joint Chiefs of Staff also conveyed the same message to Congress when Lemnitzer secretly testified before the House Military Affairs Committee: *New York Times,* May 18, 1961.
14. Jerrold L. Schecter and Peter S. Deriabin, *The Spy Who Saved the World* (New York: 1992), 101–8.
15. Reeves, *President Kennedy,* 158.
16. Arthur Krock, *Memoirs: Sixty Years on the Firing Line* (New York: 1968), 345.
17. Max Jacobson memoir, NHP/MHS.
18. Llewellyn Thompson, Jr., OH, JFKL.
19. *FRUS, 1961–1963*, V, 174–76.
20. Strobe Talbott, ed., *Khrushchev Remembers: The Last Testament* (Boston: 1974), 255.
21. Arthur M. Schlesinger, Jr., *A Thousand Days* (Boston: 1965), 365; *FRUS, 1958–1960*, X, 547–555.
22. *FRUS, 1961–1963*, V, 184.
23. Reeves, *President Kennedy,* 166.
24. *FRUS, 1961–1963*, XIV, 211–14.
25. Michael R. Beschloss, *The Crisis Years: Kennedy and Khrushchev, 1960–1963* (New York: 1991), 223.
26. Reeves, *President Kennedy,* 171. Khrushchev later conceded that he had made a tactical mistake: "What I said might have sounded like a threat." Talbott, ed., *Khrushchev Remembers,* 503.
27. Hope Harrison, "Ulbricht and the Concrete Rose," Cold War International History Project *Bulletin,* No. 3 (Fall 1993).
28. Norman Gelb, *The Berlin Wall* (New York: 1988), 99–100.
29. *FRUS, 1961–1963*, XIV, 138–59; Douglas Brinkley, *Dean Acheson: The Cold War Years* (New Haven: 1992), 140–46.

30. *FRUS, 1961–1963*, XIV, 161, 245–259.
31. *PPP: John F. Kennedy, 1961*, 533–39.
32. W. W. Rostow, *The Diffusion of Power* (New York: 1972), 232.
33. David E. Murphy et al., *Battleground Berlin: CIA vs. KGB in the Cold War* (New Haven: 1997), 373.
34. Cold War International History Project *Bulletin*, No. 3 (Fall 1993), 60.
35. Kenneth P. O'Donnell and David F. Powers, *Johnny, We Hardly Knew Ye* (Boston: 1972), 350.
36. Jean Edward Smith, *Lucius D. Clay* (New York: 1990), 638–46; John C. Ausland, *Kennedy, Khrushchev, and the Berlin-Cuba Crisis 1961–1964* (Oslo: 1996), 31–33.
37. *New York Times*, Sept. 1, 1961.
38. Elie Abel OH, JFKL.

CHAPTER 29. COMMANDER IN CHIEF

1. Tapes and transcripts, Audiovisual Archives, JFKL.
2. Richard Cardinal Cushing OH, JFKL.
3. Herbert S. Parmet, *Jack: The Struggles of John F. Kennedy* (New York: 1980), 111–12.
4. Letter, JFK to the Editor, *Newburyport News*, April 11, 1951, JFKPP, JFKL; see also John Fischer, "Easy Chair," *Harper's*, Dec. 9, 1959.
5. Arthur M. Schlesinger, Jr., *A Thousand Days* (Boston: 1965), 426.
6. John Prados, *The Soviet Estimate* (New York: 1982), 111–25.
7. The original SIOP was later published in *International Security Review*, Summer 1987.
8. Memo, Jack Raymond to Arthur Krock, n.d. but February 1961, Krock Papers; *Public Papers of the Presidents: John F. Kennedy, 1961* (Washington, D.C.: 1962), 68.
9. *PPP: John F. Kennedy, 1961* (Washington, D.C.: 1962), 68.
10. Alistair Horne, *Macmillan*, vol. II (London: 1989), 303.
11. Chalmers M. Roberts, *First Rough Draft* (New York: 1973), 201.
12. Frank A. Mayer, *Adenauer and Kennedy* (New York: 1996), 44 passim.
13. C. L. Sulzberger, *The Last of the Giants* (New York: 1970), 801–2.
14. "Briefing on SIOP-62," Sept. 13, 1961, National Security Files, JFKL.
15. Richard Reeves, *President Kennedy* (New York: 1993), 230.
16. *New York Times*, Sept. 26, 1961.
17. *FRUS, 1961–1963*, V (Washington, D.C.: 1993), 178–81.
18. Hugh Sidey, *John F. Kennedy, President* (New York: 1963), 282.
19. Reeves, *President Kennedy*, 246; John Lewis Gaddis, *We Now Know* (New York: 1997), 256–57.
20. U.S. Arms Control and Disarmament Agency, *Documents on Disarmament, 1961* (Washington, D.C.: 1962), 542–50.
21. *PPP: John F. Kennedy, 1961*, 447.

22. Meena Bose, *Shaping and Signaling Presidential Policy* (College Station, Tex: 1998), 56.

23. Geoffrey Perret, *Eisenhower* (New York: 1999), 459.

24. David Shoup OH, JFKL.

25. Lyman L. Lemnitzer OH, JFKL; L. James Binder, *Lemnitzer* (Washington, D.C.: 1997), 243, 322.

26. *Wall Street Journal*, Nov. 9, 1961; Mayer, *Adenauer and Kennedy,* 72.

27. Transcript, "Remarks by Secretary McNamara," May 5, 1962, National Security Files, JFKL.

28. C. David Heymann, *A Woman Named Jackie* (Secaucus, N.J.: 1989), 291.

CHAPTER 30. SNOWBALL

1. Richard N. Goodwin, *Remembering America* (Boston: 1988), 145–50. Goodwin wrote the speech and was going to become a key figure in the Alliance project.

2. Report, "Summary of Recommendations of Task Force on Latin America," Jan. 9, 1961, Adolph A. Berle Papers, FDRL.

3. W. W. Rostow, *The Diffusion of Power* (New York: 1972), 216.

4. Stephen G. Rabe, *Eisenhower and Latin America* (Chapel Hill, N.C.: 1988), 102–10.

5. Adolph A. Berle OH, JFKL; U.S. House of Representatives, *New Directions for the 1970s: Toward a Strategy of Inter-American Development, Hearings, Ninety-first Congress, First Session* (Washington, D.C.: 1969), 665 passim.

6. *FRUS, 1961–1963,* XII (Washington, D.C.: 1997), 313–14.

7. Ibid., 398–99.

8. Stephen G. Rabe, *The Most Dangerous Area in the World: John F. Kennedy Confronts Communist Revolution in Latin America* (Chapel Hill, N.C.: 1999), 173 passim; Jerome Levinson and Juan de Onis, *The Alliance That Lost Its Way* (Chicago: 1970), 8–16.

9. *FRUS, 1961–1963,* XII, 638–39.

10. Bernard Diedrich, *Death of the Goat* (Boston: 1978), 107–10; Richard Reeves, *President Kennedy* (New York: 1993), 149–50.

11. Fletcher Knebel OH, JFKL.

12. Diedrich, *Death of the Goat,* 191–96.

13. *FRUS, 1961–1963,* X, 666–67; Laura Bergquist Knebel OH, JFKL.

14. John S. Badeau OH, JFKL.

15. Walt Whitman Rostow OH and Chester Bowles OH, JFKL.

16. Lord Harlech (William David Ormsby-Gore) OH, JFKL.

17. Robert Amory OH and Marietta Tree OH, JFKL.

18. *Boston American*, Nov. 19, 1951.

19. Hubert H. Humphrey, *The Education of a Public Man* (Garden City, N.Y.: 1976), 229–30; Carl Solberg, *Hubert Humphrey* (New York: 1984), 216.

20. Karen Schwarz, *What You Can Do for Your Country* (New York: 1991), 27–28.
21. Paul B. Fay, Jr., OH, JFKL.
22. Gerard T. Rice, *The Bold Experiment* (Notre Dame, Ind.: 1985), 44, 47; Harris Wofford, *Of Kennedys and Kings* (New York: 1980), 98.
23. Rice, *The Bold Experiment*, 87–88.
24. Telegrams, JFK to Herbert Hoover, March 2, 1961; Hoover to JFK, March 4, 1961, Hoover Library; K. LeMoyne Billings OH, NHP/MHS.
25. Sargent Shriver in Gerald S. and Deborah H. Strober, *Let Us Begin Anew* (New York: 1993), 137.
26. Reeves, *President Kennedy*, 69.
27. Rostow, *The Diffusion of Power*, 264.
28. Department of Defense, *U.S.-Vietnamese Relations, 1945–1967*, XI (Washington, D.C.: 1971), 1–13. This is the DOD's edition of the *Pentagon Papers*.
29. *FRUS, 1961–1963*, VIII, 17.
30. Reeves, *President Kennedy*, 119.
31. *FRUS, 1961–1963*, I, 137–38.
32. Ibid., 94.
33. David Kaiser, *American Tragedy* (Cambridge, Mass.: 2000), 88; Kai Bird, *The Color of Truth* (New York: 1998), 201–2.
34. Shelby L. Stanton, *The Green Berets at War* (Novato, Cal.: 1989), 11–23.
35. *New York Times,* Sept. 26, 1961.
36. Memo, Joint Chiefs of Staff to Maxwell D. Taylor, Oct. 9, 1961, National Security Files, JFKL.
37. Memo for Record, Oct. 11, 1961, Arthur Krock Papers, PU.
38. DOD, *U.S.-Vietnamese Relations*, XI, 342.
39. *FRUS, 1961–1963*, I, 243.
40. Wofford, *Of Kennedys and Kings*, 379.
41. DOD, *U.S.-Vietnamese Relations*, II, 453–54.
42. Rostow OH, JFKL.

CHAPTER 31. THE JFK STYLE

1. John B. White interview, NHP/MHS.
2. Ronald Kessler, *Inside the White House* (New York: 1996), 35.
3. Herbert Parmet interview with William Attwood, Sept. 11, 1980, in NHP/MHS. Attwood dated Mary Meyer back in 1935, when he was a student at Choate. That was when JFK first met her.
4. *National Enquirer,* Feb. 2, 1976. The source of the story was James Truitt, a former vice president at the *Washington Post* and confidant of Mary Meyer.
5. Unpublished draft, "JFK's Secret Romance," by Joan Blair and Clay Blair, Jr., Blair Papers, AHC. The Secret Service had similarly aided FDR in his affairs: see Jeffrey Potter, *Men, Money & Magic: The Story of Dorothy Schiff* (New York: 1976), 90.
6. Joseph Timilty interview, Blair Papers, AHC.

7. Nina Burleigh, *A Very Private Woman* (New York: 1998), 186–94; *Washington Post,* Feb. 23, 1976.

8. Memo, March 20, 1962, Director's Official and Confidential File No. 96, FBI Archives.

9. Wesley O. Hagood, *Presidential Sex* (Secaucus, N.J.: 1995), 135 passim; Lawrence J. Quirk, *The Kennedys in Hollywood* (Dallas: 1996), 145 passim.

10. Paul B. Fay, Jr., interview, Blair Papers, AHC; Barbara Leaming, *Marilyn Monroe* (New York: 1998), 403–4.

11. Hagood, *Presidential Sex,* 170; James Spada, *Peter Lawford* (New York: 1991), 303–5; Donald H. Woolf, *The Last Days of Marilyn Monroe* (New York: 1998), 408–12.

12. *The New Yorker,* Aug. 7, 2000; C. David Heymann, *A Woman Named Jackie* (Secaucus, N.J.: 1989), 287.

13. Fred Sparks, "Those Wild Kennedy Boys," *The Star,* Sept. 28, 1974.

14. Raymond Strait, *The Tragic Secret Life of Jayne Mansfield* (Chicago: 1974); Hagood, *Presidential Sex,* 164; Quirk, *The Kennedys in Hollywood,* 264–65; Mariella Novotny, unpublished memoir, Blair Papers, AHC. Strait was Mansfield's assistant and confidant throughout her years in Hollywood.

15. The first great biographer, James Boswell, was but one of them. "I went to St James's Church and heard service and a good sermon on 'By what means shall a young man learn to order his ways.' What a curious, inconsistent thing is the mind of man! In the midst of divine service I was laying plans for having women, and yet I had the most sincere feelings of religion." Boswell felt that, throughout his life, "the foul fiend of the genitals" was hounding him. See Peter Martin, *A Life of James Boswell* (New Haven: 2000).

16. Jane Eustice Wheeler interview, Blair Papers, AHC.

17. J. Randy Taraborrelli, *Jackie, Ethel, Joan* (New York: 2000), 49.

18. George Smathers OH, SHO; Benjamin C. Bradlee, *A Good Life* (New York: 1995), 222; Traphes Bryant, *Dog Days at the White House* (New York: 1975), 62.

19. Kennedy Files, Laura Bergquist Papers, BU.

20. Nigel Hamilton, *JFK: Reckless Youth* (New York: 1992), 714.

21. Langdon Marvin interview, Blair Papers, AHC.

22. Kennedy Files, Laura Bergquist Papers, BU.

23. Fletcher Knebel OH, JFKL.

24. William Walton interview, Blair Papers, AHC.

25. Kennedy Files, Laura Bergquist Papers, BU.

26. Frank Saunders with James Southwood, *Torn Lace Curtain* (New York: 1982), 67.

27. Henry Brandon, *Special Relationships* (New York: 1988), 195.

28. Paul B. Fay, Jr., OH, JFKL.

29. Bryant, *Dog Days at the White House,* 58–59.

30. Stanley Tretick OH, JFKL.

31. Joseph W. Alsop, *I've Seen the Best of It* (New York: 1992), 437–38; Bryant, *Dog Days at the White House,* 59.

32. Letitia Baldridge, *In the Kennedy Style* (New York: 1998), 32.
33. John Sharon OH, JFKL.
34. Memo for Record, May 22, 1962, Arthur Krock Papers, PU.
35. Baldridge, *In the Kennedy Style,* 106.
36. Angier Biddle Duke OH, JFKL; Baldridge, *In the Kennedy Style,* 123.
37. George Smathers OH, SHO; White House gate logs, JFKL; Max Jacobson memoir, NHP/MHS; *New York Post,* Jan. 22, 1961.
38. Michael M. Baden with Judith Adler Hennessee, *Unnatural Death: Confessions of a Medical Examiner* (New York: 1989), 15.
39. George Tames OH, SHO; Pamela Turnure OH, JFKL; Ralph G. Martin, *Seeds of Destruction* (New York: 1995), 231; Richard Reeves, *President Kennedy* (New York: 1993), 242–44.
40. Paul B. Fay, Jr., OH, JFKL.
41. Charles Spalding OH, JFKL; Bryant, *Dog Days at the White House,* 29.

CHAPTER 32. DOMESTIC TRANQUILLITY

1. Edward Klein, *All Too Human* (New York: 1996), 187.
2. William O. Douglas OH, JFKL.
3. Gore Vidal, *Palimpsest* (New York: 1995), 359; J. William Fulbright OH, JFKL.
4. Increased spending on space and defense eventually brought unemployment down to Kennedy's goal of 4 percent, but not until 1965. Herb Gebelein, "Economic Policy in Practice: Perspective on the 1960s," in Paul Harper and Joann P. Krieg, eds., *John F. Kennedy: The Promise Revisited* (New York: 1988). See also David L. Stebenne, *Arthur J. Goldberg* (New York: 1996), 241.
5. Daniel P. Moynihan OH, NHP/MHS.
6. *New Yorker,* Jan. 19, 1963; Michael Harrington, *The Other America* (New York: 1962).
7. Paul B. Fay, Jr., mss., Paul B. Fay, Jr., Papers, SU.
8. "Memo of Conversation," April 10, 1962, Walter Heller Papers, JFKL; Ken Gormley, *Archibald Cox: Conscience of a Nation* (Reading, Mass.: 1997), 161–62; Helen Lempart OH, JFKL.
9. Stebenne, *Arthur J. Goldberg,* 296.
10. *Public Papers of the Presidents: John F. Kennedy, 1962* (Washington, D.C.: 1963), 234.
11. Lord Harlech (William David Ormsby-Gore) OH, JFKL.
12. Paul A. Tiffany, *The Decline of American Steel* (New York: 1988), 180–82.
13. James N. Giglio, *The Presidency of John F. Kennedy* (Lawrence, Kan.: 1991), 132–34.
14. Tom Wicker OH, JFKL.
15. Charles Bartlett OH, JFKL.
16. Memo for Record, Oct. 11, 1961, Arthur Krock Papers, PU.
17. Tip O'Neill with William Novak, *Man of the House* (New York: 1987), 173.

18. Benjamin C. Bradlee, *A Good Life* (New York: 1995), 241.
19. Thomas Winship OH, JFKL.
20. Wicker OH, JFKL.
21. Tom Wicker, *Kennedy Without Tears* (New York: 1964), 54–55; Joseph Clark OH, JFKL.
22. Francis R. Valeo, *Mike Mansfield, Majority Leader* (Armonk, N.Y.: 1999), 59–60.
23. Ralph Horton OH, JFKL.
24. Richard Bolling, *House Out of Order* (New York: 1965), 100.
25. Valeo, *Mike Mansfield,* 106–12; Mike Mansfield OH, JFKL.
26. Najeeb Halaby OH, JFKL; Thomas G. Smith, "Civil Rights on the Gridiron: The Kennedy Administration and the Desegregation of the Washington Redskins," *Journal of Sport History,* Summer 1987.
27. Stebenne, *Arthur J. Goldberg,* 245.
28. George Smathers OH, JFKL.
29. Clark Clifford OH, NHP/MHS.
30. Arthur M. Schlesinger, Jr., *Robert Kennedy and His Times* (Boston: 1978), 307–8.
31. Walter Lord, *The Past That Would Not Die* (New York: 1965), 196 passim; Taylor Branch, *Parting the Waters* (New York: 1988), 666.
32. Presidential tape recording, Sept. 25, 1962, JFKL.
33. Schlesinger, Jr., *Robert Kennedy and His Times,* 354.
34. James Meredith, *Three Years in Mississippi* (Bloomington, Ind.: 1966), 212–13.
35. Richard Reeves, *President Kennedy* (New York: 1993), 464.
36. Branch, *Parting the Waters,* 796–99.
37. Reeves, *President Kennedy,* 488; David Lawrence OH, JFKL.
38. Memo, "Conversation Between President Kennedy and Governor Wallace," May 17, 1963, JFKL.
39. Presidential tape recording, May 20, 1963, JFKL.
40. Dan T. Carter, *The Politics of Rage* (New York: 1995), 135–48; Stephen Lester, *George Wallace: American Populist* (Reading, Mass.: 1994), 233–39.
41. *Washington Post,* June 12, 1963; Hugh Sidey, *John F. Kennedy, President* (New York: 1963), 401; *PPP: John F. Kennedy, 1963,* 469.
42. Mansfield OH, JFKL.

CHAPTER 33. EXCOMM

1. Dino A. Brugioni, *Eyeball to Eyeball* (New York: 1991), Chapter 7.
2. Ernest R. May and Philip D. Zelikow, *The Kennedy Tapes: Inside the White House During the Cuban Missile Crisis* (Cambridge, Mass.: 1997), 59. See also Sheldon M. Stern, "Too Good to Be True?," *Presidential Studies Quarterly,* Sept. 2000, and "What JFK Really Said," *Atlantic Monthly,* May 2000.
3. Eisenhower's stated policy of "massive retaliation" was intended to obscure the fact that the real plan was a preemptive strike. Geoffrey Perret, *Eisen-*

hower (New York: 1999), 459–60; Raymond L. Garthoff, *Reflections on the Cuban Missile Crisis* (Washington, D.C.: 1987), 21–24: James G. Blight et al., *Cuba on the Brink* (New York: 1993), 136–37; Anatoli I. Gribkov and William Y. Smith, *Operation ANADYR* (Chicago: 1994), 9–12. Soviet ICBMs were not designed to place a warhead on a distant target but to place a man in orbit. They stood in the open, exposed to preemptive attack, and took up to twenty hours to fill with highly volatile liquid fuel; their poorly designed warheads were blown far off target by strong winds on reentry. See Andrew Cockburn, *The Threat: Inside the Soviet Military Machine* (New York: 1984), 192 passim.

Soviet long-range bombers would have gone into combat without fighter escort because their fighters had no in-flight refueling capability. Distant early-warning radar could track the bombers long before they reached American airspace. They would be intercepted over Alaska, Canada and the North Atlantic by American fighters equipped with Falcon air-to-air missiles armed with nuclear warheads. Any bombers that survived then had to penetrate American airspace, which was defended by surface-to-air missiles and more than a thousand fighters. The chances of even one bomber reaching its target were virtually zero. Similarly, the few Soviet submarines carrying ballistic missiles had to surface to fire them. The missiles had a range of only a few hundred miles and could not be fired quickly. The first-generation missile boats were noisy and easy to track on sonar, which made them highly vulnerable. See Sherry Sontag et al., *Blind Man's Bluff: The Untold Story of American Submarine Espionage* (New York: 1998), 57–64; John Piña Craven, *The Silent War* (New York: 2001), 193, 202–5.

4. Blight et al., *Cuba on the Brink,* 345–47; Yuri Pavlov, *The Soviet-Cuban Alliance, 1959–1991* (Coral Gables, Fla.: 1996), 38–40.

5. May and Zelikow, *The Kennedy Tapes: Inside the White House During the Cuban Missile Crisis,* 91–92.

6. Raymond L. Garthoff, "The Meaning of Missiles," *Washington Quarterly,* Autumn 1982.

7. Chalmers M. Roberts, *First Rough Draft* (New York: 1973), 204.

8. Evan Thomas, *Robert Kennedy* (New York: 2000), 215.

9. Robert Lovett OH, JFKL.

10. Henry Brandon, *Special Relationships* (New York: 1988), 178. Andrei Gromyko, *Memoirs* (New York: 1989), 176–78; Anatoly Dobrynin, *In Confidence: Moscow's Ambassador to America's Six Cold War Presidents (1962–1986)* (New York: 1995), 78.

11. Pierre Salinger, *P.S., A Memoir* (New York: 1995), 116.

12. Kenneth P. O'Donnell and David F. Powers, *Johnny, We Hardly Knew Ye* (Boston: 1972), 372.

13. Richard Reeves, *President Kennedy* (New York: 1993), 389.

14. L. V. Scott, *Macmillan, Kennedy, and the Cuban Missile Crisis* (New York: 1999), 43.

15. Ibid., 162.

16. Exactly what gave him this idea isn't certain, but when JFK was at Stanford, the student government was directed by the executive committee, or "ExComm," of the Stanford Students' Association.

17. May and Zelikow, *The Kennedy Tapes: Inside the White House During the Cuban Missile Crisis,* 212.

18. Department of State, *FRUS, 1958–1960,* X (Washington, D.C.: 1996), 363; John Lewis Gaddis, *We Now Know* (New York: 1997), 264.

19. *Public Papers of the Presidents: John F. Kennedy, 1962* (Washington, D.C.: 1963), 806–8.

20. *FRUS, 1961–1963,* XI, 116–17.

21. May and Zelikow, *The Kennedy Tapes: Inside the White House During the Cuban Missile Crisis,* 299.

22. John Bartlow Martin, *Adlai Stevenson and the World* (Garden City, N.Y.: 1977), 733–34; O'Donnell and Powers, *Johnny, We Hardly Knew Ye,* 387.

23. Lord Harlech (William David Ormsby-Gore) OH, JFKL.

24. May and Zelikow, *The Kennedy Tapes: Inside the White House During the Cuban Missile Crisis,* 342; Robert F. Kennedy, *Thirteen Days* (New York: 1969), 67.

25. May and Zelikow, *The Kennedy Tapes: Inside the White House During the Cuban Missile Crisis,* 355.

26. Robert F. Kennedy, *Thirteen Days,* 69–70.

27. May and Zelikow, *The Kennedy Tapes: Inside the White House During the Cuban Missile Crisis,* 358.

28. Charles Bartlett OH, JFKL.

29. *Washington Post,* Oct. 25, 1962.

30. Reeves, *President Kennedy,* 405.

31. May and Zelikow, *The Kennedy Tapes: Inside the White House During the Cuban Missile Crisis,* 455, 461.

32. Salinger, *P.S., A Memoir,* 119.

33. *FRUS, 1961–1963,* XI, 240.

34. Blight et al., *Cuba on the Brink,* 108.

35. *FRUS, 1961–1963,* XI, 271–72; Salinger, *P.S., A Memoir,* 119.

36. *FRUS, 1961–1963,* XI, 268–69.

37. Cable, Anatoly Dobrynin to Soviet Foreign Ministry, Oct. 27, 1962, in Cold War International History Project *Bulletin* 5, Spring 1995.

38. Blight et al., *Cuba on the Brink,* 83–84.

39. Aleksandr Fursenko and Timothy Naftali, *One Hell of a Gamble* (New York: 1997), 281–82.

40. Robert F. Kennedy, *Thirteen Days,* 110.

CHAPTER 34. AFTERMATH

1. Glenn T. Seaborg, *Kennedy, Khrushchev and the Test Ban* (Berkeley, Cal.: 1981), 181–83; Michael R. Beschloss, *The Crisis Years: Kennedy and Khrushchev, 1960–1963* (New York: 1991), 542–45.

2. "Shh! Let's Tell the Russians," *Newsweek,* May 5, 1969; Patrick Glynn, *Closing Pandora's Box* (New York: 1992), 201–2.

3. U.S. Arms Control and Disarmament Agency, *Documents on Disarmament, 1962,* II (Washington, D.C.: 1970), 1239–42.

4. Harlan Cleveland OH and Chester Bowles OH, JFKL; Chalmers M. Roberts, *First Rough Draft* (New York: 1973), 215.

5. *New York Times,* Oct. 18, 1961.

6. Norman Cousins, *The Improbable Triumvirate* (New York: 1972), 111 passim.

7. William C. Foster OH, JFKL.

8. *Public Papers of the Presidents: John F. Kennedy, 1963* (Washington, D.C.: 1964).

9. Rudy Abramson, *Spanning the Century* (New York: 1992), 596.

10. David Shoup OH, JFKL; Glynn, *Closing Pandora's Box,* 203. After Kennedy's death, McNamara went even further, encouraging the Soviets to put their ICBMs in deep, hardened silos and placing a freeze on anti-submarine warfare research as a way to ensure the survival of the Soviets' Polaris-type boats.

11. Douglas Brinkley, *Dean Acheson: The Cold War Years* (New Haven: 1992), 197.

12. Bobby Baker with Larry L. King, *Wheeling and Dealing* (New York: 1978), 98–99; Francis Valeo OH, SHO.

13. Strobe Talbott, ed., *Khrushchev Remembers: The Last Testament* (Boston: 1974), 255.

14. William C. Foster OH, JFKL.

15. Lord Harlech (William David Ormsby-Gore) OH, JFKL.

16. Helen O'Donnell, *A Common Good* (New York: 1998), 296.

17. Peter Wyden, *Wall* (New York: 1989), 568–69.

18. Lord Harlech OH, JFKL.

19. *Time,* July 5, 1963.

20. Frank Saunders with James Southwood, *Torn Lace Curtain* (New York: 1982), 210.

21. Writings File, David F. Powers Papers, JFKL; James Reed OH, JFKL.

22. Rose Kennedy, *Times to Remember* (New York: 1974), 406.

23. Henry Brandon, *Special Relationships* (New York: 1988), 160.

24. *Time,* July 12, 1963.

25. Saunders with James Southwood, *Torn Lace Curtain,* 213; Tip O'Neill with William Novak, *Man of the House* (New York: 1987), 157.

26. Edward Klein, *All Too Human* (New York: 1996), 331–32; Writings File, David F. Powers Papers, JFKL.

27. Roy Heffernan OH, JFKL. He was the chief surgeon at the Boston Children's Hospital.

28. Klein, *All Too Human,* 333.
29. Kennedy Files, Laura Bergquist Papers, BU.
30. Francis Valeo, *Mike Mansfield, Majority Leader* (Armonk, N.Y.: 1999), 100–101.
31. O'Neill, *Man of the House,* 176.
32. Daniel P. Moynihan OH, NHP/MHS.

CHAPTER 35. IT FLIES FOREVER

1. Department of State, *FRUS 1961–1963,* III (Washington, D.C.: 1991), 169; Michael Forrestal OH, JFKL.
2. *New York Times,* Aug. 16, 1962.
3. *FRUS, 1961–1963,* III, 244–45.
4. Henry Cabot Lodge, *The Storm Has Many Eyes* (New York: 1973), 207.
5. *FRUS, 1961–1963,* III, 281.
6. *FRUS, 1961–1963,* IV, 12; David Kaiser, *American Tragedy* (Cambridge, Mass.: 2000), 239.
7. *FRUS, 1961–1963,* IV, 16.
8. Transcript of CBS Evening News broadcast, Sept. 2, 1963, JFKL.
9. *FRUS, 1961–1963,* IV, 169 passim; Kaiser, *American Tragedy,* 261–62.
10. *FRUS, 1961–1963,* IV, 526–27; Charles Spalding interview, NHP/MHS.
11. Paul B. Fay, Jr., OH, JFKL.
12. Richard N. Goodwin, *Remembering America* (Boston: 1988), 199–202.
13. Kenneth P. O'Donnell and Dave F. Powers, *Johnny, We Hardly Knew Ye* (Boston: 1972), 317.
14. Jean Edward Smith, *Lucius D. Clay* (New York: 1990), 674–75; Evan Thomas, *Robert Kennedy* (New York: 2000), 235–37.
15. Donald F. Barnes OH, JFKL; *Public Papers of the Presidents: John F. Kennedy, 1962* (Washington, D.C.: 1963), 911.
16. James G. Blight et al., *Cuba on the Brink* (New York: 1993), 236–40; Robert E. Quirk, *Fidel Castro* (New York: 1993), 480–83; Pierre Salinger, *P.S., A Memoir* (New York: 1995), 215.
17. Seymour M. Hersh, *The Dark Side of Camelot* (Boston: 1997), 12.
18. Charles S. Caldwell OH, SHO.
19. C. David Heymann, *A Woman Named Jackie* (Secaucus, N.J.: 1989), 388–93; Edward Klein, *All Too Human* (New York: 1996), 315–16, 341; Wesley O. Hagood, *Presidential Sex* (Secaucus, N.J.: 1995), 148.
20. William Manchester, *The Death of a President* (New York: 1967), 114–16.
21. Caldwell OH, SHO; Chalmers M. Roberts OH, JFKL; Klein, *All Too Human,* 10–11.
22. Tom Wicker, *Kennedy Without Tears* (New York: 1964), 46.
23. Manchester, *The Death of a President,* 121.
24. Klein, *All Too Human,* 343.
25. Roberts OH, JFKL.
26. Klein, *All Too Human,* 344; Pam Turnure/Nancy Tuckerman OH, JFKL.

27. Klein, *All Too Human,* 344; Jacqueline Kennedy interview, Theodore White Papers, JFKL.

28. Helen O'Donnell, *A Common Good* (New York: 1998), 332.

29. See Gerald Posner, *Case Closed* (New York: 1994), and Gus Russo, *Live by the Sword* (Latham, Md.: 1998).

30. Gore Vidal, *Palimpsest* (New York: 1995), 578.

31. Manchester, *The Death of a President,* 157.

32. Rose Kennedy, *Times to Remember* (New York: 1974), 415.

Index

GEOFFREY PERRET is the award-winning author of *Old Soldiers Never Die: The Life of Douglas MacArthur, Ulysses S. Grant: Soldier and President* and, most recently, *Eisenhower*. Mr. Perret was educated at Harvard and the University of California at Berkeley and served in the U.S. Army for three years.

He has been a consultant on documentaries shown on C-SPAN, PBS, ABC and the History Channel. Mr. Perret has also been a contributor to *Talk, American Heritage* and *Military History Quarterly*. *Jack* is his eleventh book.

ABOUT THE TYPE

This book was set in Times Roman, designed by Stanley Morrison specifically for *The Times* of London. The typeface was introduced in the newspaper in 1932. Times Roman had its greatest success in the United States as a book and commercial typeface, rather than one used in newspapers.